Luminos is the Open Access monograph publishing program
from UC Press. Luminos provides a framework for preserving
and reinvigorating monograph publishing for the future and
increases the reach and visibility of important scholarly work. Titles
published in the UC Press Luminos model are published with the
same high standards for selection, peer review, production, and
marketing as those in our traditional program. www.luminosoa.org

# Islamic Shangri-La

# Islamic Shangri-La

*Inter-Asian Relations and Lhasa's Muslim Communities,
1600 to 1960*

David G. Atwill

UNIVERSITY OF CALIFORNIA PRESS

University of California Press, one of the most distinguished university presses in the United States, enriches lives around the world by advancing scholarship in the humanities, social sciences, and natural sciences. Its activities are supported by the UC Press Foundation and by philanthropic contributions from individuals and institutions. For more information, visit www.ucpress.edu.

University of California Press
Oakland, California



Library of Congress Cataloging-in-Publication Data

Names: Atwill, David G., author.
Title: Islamic Shangri-La : inter-Asian relations and Lhasa's Muslim
    communities, 1600 to 1960 / By David G. Atwill.
Description: Oakland, California : University of California Press, [2018] |
    Includes bibliographical references and index. | Atwill, David G. 2018
    This work is licensed under a Creative Commons [CC-BY-NC-ND] license.
    To view a copy of hte license, visit http://creativecommons.org/licenses |
    Description based on print version record and CIP data provided by
    publisher; resource not viewed.
Identifiers: LCCN 2018020188 (print) | LCCN 2018024303 (ebook) ISBN
    9780520971332 (Ebook) | ISBN 9780520299733 (pbk. : alk. paper)
Subjects: LCSH: Muslims—China—Lhasa—History. |
    Muslims—China—Tibet
    Autonomous Region—History.
Classification: LCC DS731.M87 (ebook) | LCC DS731.M87
    A89 2018 (print) | DDC 3005.6/97095150903—dc23
LC record available at https://lccn.loc.gov/2018020188

27  26  25  24  23  22  21  20  19  18
10  9  8  7  6  5  4  3  2  1

*For Christophe, from whom I have learned so much*

# CONTENTS

# ILLUSTRATIONS

## FIGURES



## MAPS

ACKNOWLEDGMENTS

The debts I have incurred in researching and writing this book are many. But if I could thank only one entity it would be the Mellon Foundation. For without the Mellon Foundation's generous New Directions Fellowship I would not have dreamed of beginning this project. It allowed me to study Tibetan, travel to libraries and carry out interviews on three continents, and work my way through the maze of false starts and dead ends that constituted the convoluted route to completing this book. The American Institute of Indian Studies provided a grant that allowed me to spend half a year in Delhi, Kalimpong, and Darjeeling carrying out interviews and archival research. A senior fellowship from the Association for Nepal and Himalayan Studies allowed me to make one last visit to Kalimpong and Darjeeling as I finished writing. I appreciated the opportunity to speak (and work through many of my ideas) at Oxford University, University of Puget Sound, University of California, Berkeley, University of Rochester, Cornell University, and Whitman College. The feedback, questions, and enthusiasm for my project at these colleges and universities were a crucial part of the process.

Parts of chapter 5 originally appeared as "Boundaries of Belonging: Sino-Indian Relations and the 1960 Tibetan Muslim Incident," in *Journal of Asian Studies* 75, no. 3 (August 2016). I thank Cambridge University Press for permission to reprint parts of it here. Large portions of chapter 2 originally appeared as "A Tibetan by Any Other Name: The Case of Muslim Tibetans and Ambiguous Ethno-religious Identities," in *Cahiers d'Extrême Asie* 23 (2014).

The individuals serving as department head at the beginning and end of this project, Sally McMurray and Michael Kulikowski, demonstrate the profound ways that administrative leadership can affect our scholarly trajectory, even as they carry out what is otherwise a largely thankless task. Sally first nominated and encouraged me to apply for the New Directions Fellowship, and Michael deftly juggled being both a close friend and my supervisor as he cajoled, motivated, and provided countless words of encouragement when I needed them most. The line between friend and colleague is often a thin one in academia, but Tolga Esmer, Tijana Kristic, Kate Merkel-Hess, Kathy Salzer, Greg Smits, Lior Sternfeld, Kate Baldanza, Nina Safran, Jon Brockopp, Ronnie Hsia, and Sophie De Schrijver provided much-needed intellectual and emotional support as both friends and colleagues. Mark Elliott, Ken Pomeranz, and Minnie Sinha expended countless hours serving as sounding boards for my ideas and selflessly writing numerous letters in support of the project.

The Holmes-Foster friends Rob Nairn and Heidi von Bernewitz; Steve and Eleanor Schiff; Ron and Mary Lou Markle; Nick, Carolyn, and Nika Kello; and, more recently, Nicolai Volland, Chang Tan, and Jackie made for many wonderful evenings that provided salve for the soul in ways that often went unremarked but consistently reminded me how lucky I was to have such kind and intelligent neighbors. Annie Copeland, Christina Clair, Buck Wild, Nina Jablonski, and George Chaplin enriched many meals and always welcomed after-dinner discussions. Finally, to Denise Solomon, Jim Dillard, and Ellen Stroud, long live First Fridays (and second Thursdays and third Wednesdays).

Many of the earliest ideas for this project were gently coaxed to life by the wonderful leadership of Stéphane Gros (Center for Himalayan Studies, CRNS) and the broad group of scholars he assembled under the *Territories, Communities and Exchanges in the Sino-Tibetan Kham Borderlands (China)* program funded by the European Research Council. The gracious welcome I received (and continue to receive) from Paddy Booz, Katia Buffetrille, Rémi Chaix, Chen Bo, Fabienne Jagou, and Jinba Tenzin gave me the confidence to build on my early studies of Kham.

While serving as a fellow in the Public Intellectual Program (PIP) sponsored by the National Committee on China–United States Relations, I presented portions of this project and was challenged to explain how such a small group of "marginal" people mattered. The discussions that stemmed from my participation in PIP were among the most helpful and stimulating of the entire project. Special thanks to Jan Berris, who made it all happen, but also to Maura Cunningham, John Delury, Allison Friedman, Sheena Greitens, Karrie Koesel, Gao Qin, and all the other PIP IV fellows.

In China, I benefited from instruction and guidance from Tse Wang Lhamo, Lin Chaomin, Li Donghong, Zhang Zhongyun, and Tsomu Yudru. I appreciate the ongoing support of the faculty and staff at Yunnan University, Minzu University, and other institutions that will remain unnamed. Long Ruihua, Yang Yulong, and Yang Weili facilitated my many research trips with a degree of love that makes China my true second home.

In New Delhi, Anjana Kapoor and her husband, Pradeep, made me feel like I was a member of their family while I carried out research for three months. The staff of the Nehru Memorial Museum and Library hosted my stay and made my research both productive and comfortable. The many individuals in the Indian National Archives transformed what could have been an exercise in frustration into one of my most productive archival stints of the entire process.

In Kalimpong, the entire Tibetan Muslim community welcomed me with an enthusiasm that gave me the inspiration to write this book. In particular, Amanullah Chisti during countless visits over several years shared both his memories and many documents relating to the Tibetan Muslim history, which greatly enriched the account that follows.

In Kathmandu, Abdul Rehman Khallo graciously took time out of his day during numerous visits to share much of his vast knowledge about the Tibetan Muslim diaspora. He repeatedly answered questions, extended names and contacts for numerous others, and always expressed unconditional support of my efforts even when the process of finishing this book took far longer than expected.

If any single individual deserves praise from the beginning to the end of this project it would be Arye Chakravartty, without whom I would not have ventured to half the places I went, been able to speak with a quarter as many people, or enjoyed a fraction as many evenings drinking Gorkha Beer. Rachel MacKnight was a positive force to get the book across the finish line. More recently, Steven Xu, Chen Bin, Wang Xiaoyue, Michael Hicks, and Ugyan Choedup assisted my research and engaged in fruitful discussions that were invaluable to shaping the final manuscript. Helping my mental health, Ben Whitesell, Lynn Hepfer, Alesha Gavlock, Cody Miller, and Erin Eckley were always there with a laugh.

Reed Malcolm, executive editor at the University of California Press, has been from my very first contact with him the paradigm of efficiency (and patience). Cris Livecchi took my crude explanations of what I wanted in my maps and made them real. Ben Pease under an even stiffer deadline worked magic to create the Lhasa map. With a deft touch and near-magical talent, Sheila Berg copyedited the manuscript.

As anyone who is taking the time to read these acknowledgments knows, it is those closest to you who share both the highs and the lows of academic research. John Atwill and Laura Hull read many drafts and bolstered my confidence while also pointing out inevitable infelicities. Margaret Ershler and Sally Rodgers always listened intently and asked about my progress. My son and daughter, Peter and Kate, always accepted my extended absences, the summers and years abroad with me following my research, and, at the end, gleefully telling me to just finish the f**king thing. But it has been Yurong, always my favorite Lolo, who has borne the bulk of listening to my latest "discovery," or anxiety, with grace and an unerring sense of how to reply. Whether or not you can see it, you are all written into this book.

But it is to Christophe Portaire, my closest friend, who I dedicate this book. We met by chance as desk mates in Lycée Louis Bartou more than three decades ago in the southwest of France, yet somehow he still invites me into his home and always has a fine bottle awaiting my next visit. Together with his amazing family (Marie, Simon, Luanna, and Emma), he has always been there with a smile and *des gros bisous* whenever I can make my way back to his home. This dedication is but a small token of my deep appreciation of his friendship.

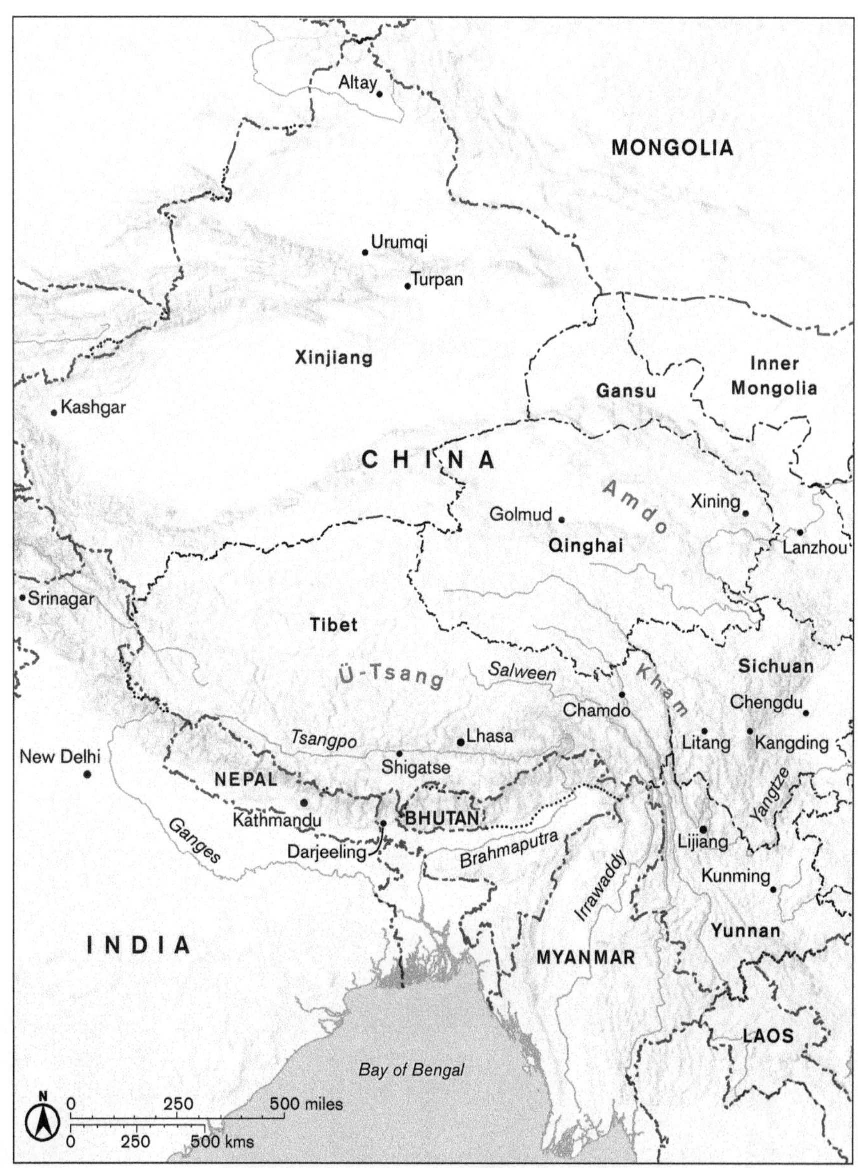


MAP 1. Tibet in Asia with current international boundaries

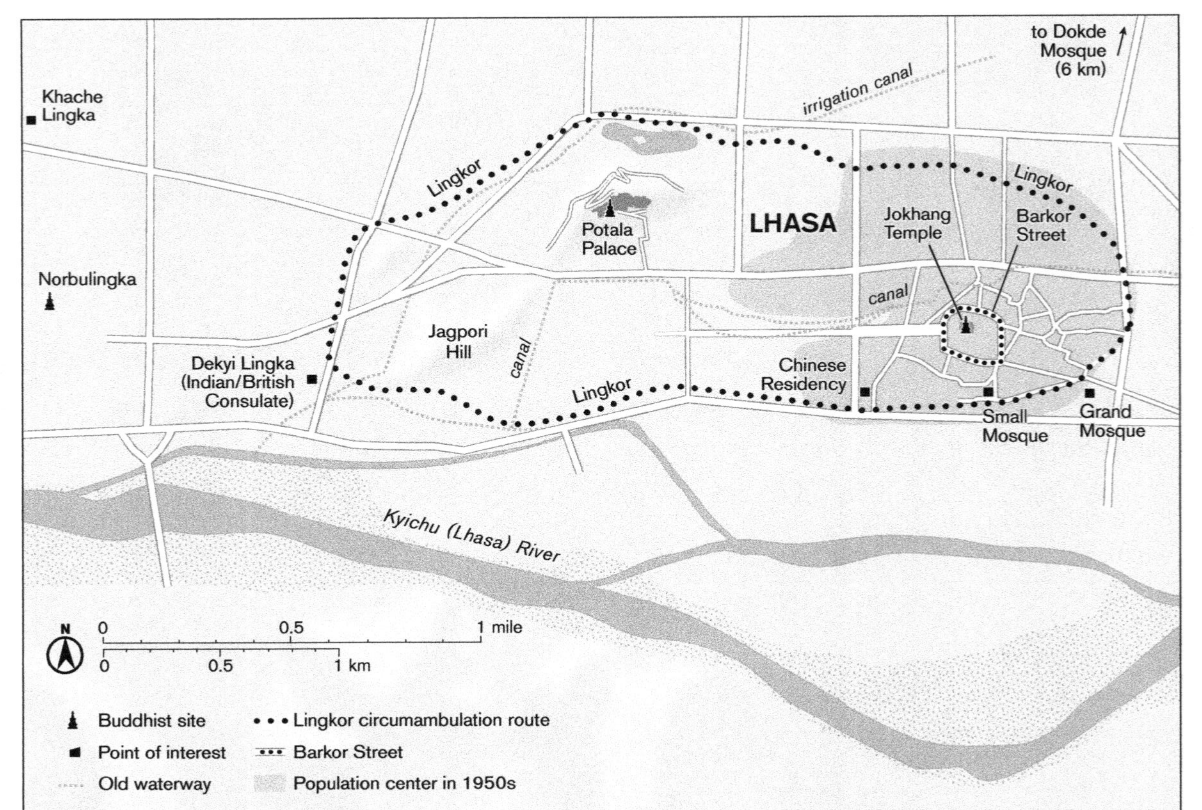


MAP 2. Lhasa, ca. 1950

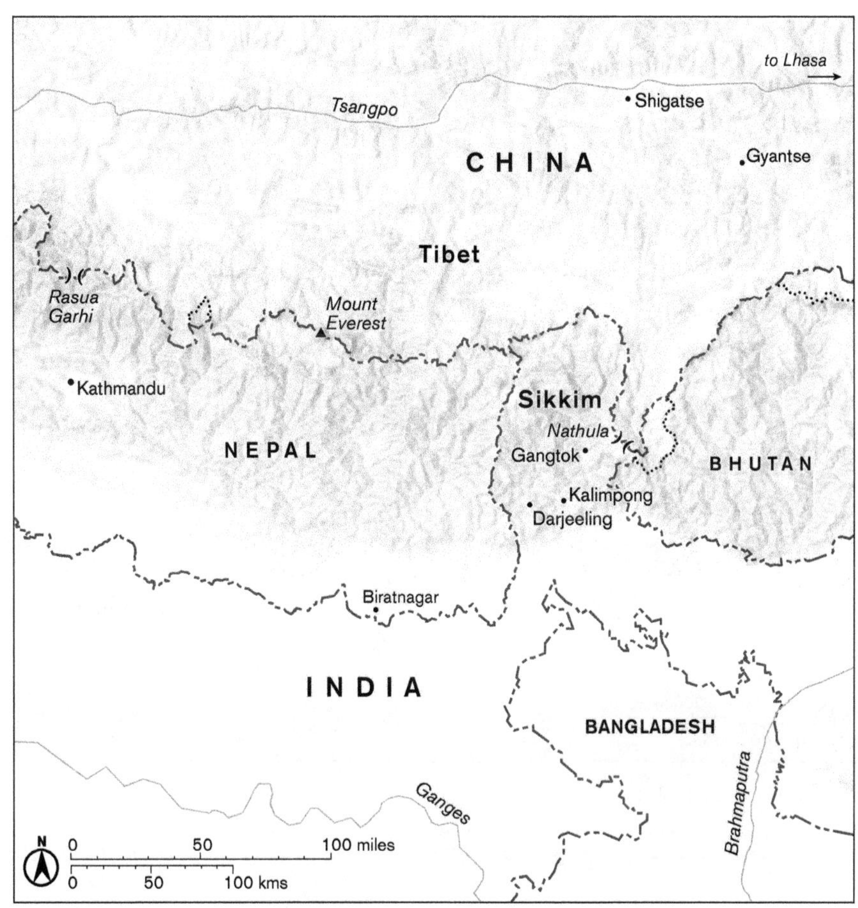


MAP 3. Nepal, Sikkim, Bhutan, and Tibet

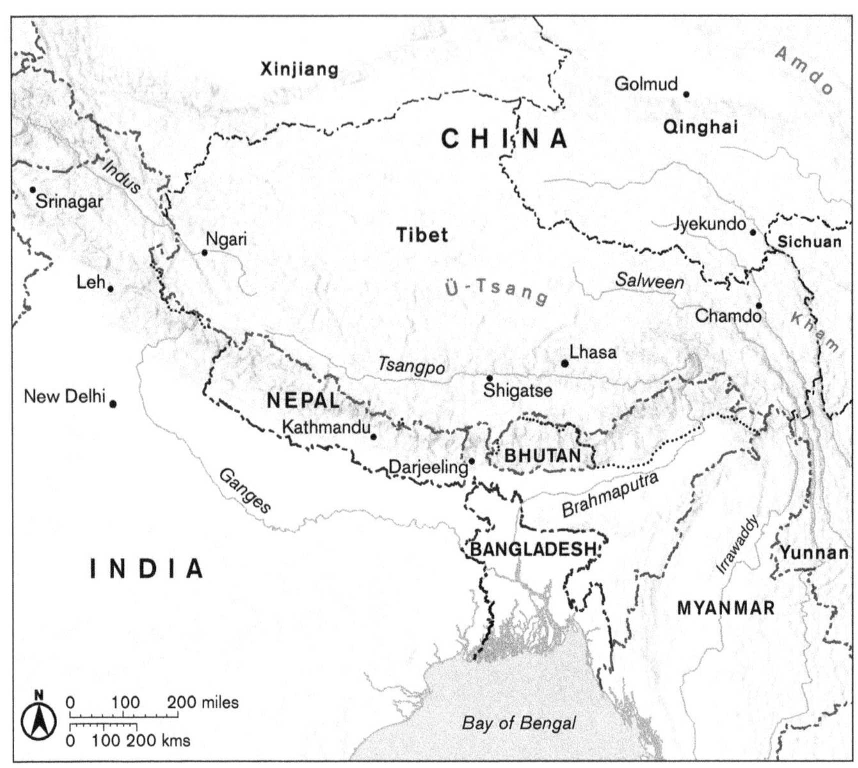


MAP 4. Himalayan Tibet

1

————

# Boundaries of Belonging

In October 1936, the British Resident Frederick Chapman, or "Freddie" as he was known by his close associates, received an invitation to a game of soccer from a team calling themselves Lhasa United. The British Diplomatic Mission in Lhasa, unable to resist such a summons, hastily cobbled together a team of four British officials, four of their Sikkimese clerks, and a few of their Tibetan servants. The Mission Marmots, as the British called themselves, quickly came together as a team ready for all challengers.[1] When the British team arrived at the field, two miles past the Nörbulingka Summer Palace, they found a large crowd and a carefully marked out pitch as well as their opponents. Decked in "garish harlequin-coloured silk shirts with the initials 'L.U.' sewn onto their pockets," Lhasa United were, as one British official later observed, "a remarkable looking team, and certainly needed to be 'United!' There was a tough-looking Nepali soldier, a Chinese tailor, three bearded Ladakhis wearing red fezzes—the most hirsute being the goal-keeper, a Sikkimese."[2] The final score was 1–0 in favor of the British. That fall, a total of four teams organized themselves to play the occasional match. While British officials would later insist they remained undefeated, others remembered the results differently.[3] In addition to Lhasa United and the Mission Marmots, a team of young Tibetan officials and clerks known as the Kudraks (Tib. *sku drag*), or the Aristocrats, joined the competition sporting silk uniforms adorned with a snow lion. The fourth and final team was composed wholly of Lhasa Muslims, referred to by the British simply as the "Lhasa Mohammedans."

The four teams neatly reproduced Lhasa's main social divisions, and the matches quickly turned into elaborate social affairs with several matches occurring in quick succession that fall. The impromptu matches were brought to an abrupt end late

1

The Lhasa United soccer team, composed of Tibetan Sikkimese, Ladhaki, and Nepalese players, whose league opponents were such teams as the Mission Marmots, the Aristocrats, and the Lhasa Muslims. October 20, 1936. Source: Pitt Rivers Museum, University of Oxford.

one October evening when the wooden goalposts were pilfered–perhaps to be used as firewood. The missing goalposts aside, plummeting temperatures had made it too uncomfortable to play, so it was decided to wait until spring to find replacement goalposts and recommence the matches.

The following year the matches grew in popularity, attracting an ever greater number of spectators. Curious onlookers flowed out to the field near Tsidrunglingka Park (Tib. *rtse drung gling ka*) by the river in the southeast part of Lhasa to watch the foreign games. The season wore on until one day, just as a match was about to get under way, a rabbit ran onto the field. As this is deemed one of twenty-one ill omens (Tib. *ltas ngan*), several onlookers gasped and attempted to postpone the match. They were dismissed as being overly superstitious, however, and the game got under way with no immediate ominous consequences. In the second half, just as the Kudraks took a 2–1 lead over the Marmots, a fierce hailstorm abruptly materialized. Great gusts of wind shredded the spectators' large umbrellas. Hail pelted the area with pellets so large that nearby crops were seriously damaged.

Many officials, already disquieted by the growing popularity and influence of foreign pastimes, took this opportunity to bring the entire matter before the government. The next day, the Tibetan Assembly (Tib. *tshogs 'du*) formally deliberated the issue. While advocates of the game argued its social and health benefits, its critics called it sacrilegious and expressed concern that such games disturbed the local gods. One official heatedly declared, "It was like they were kicking the head of Buddha around the field." After several hours of debate, the regent's secretariat (Tib. *shöga*) declared soccer improper, ordered that no further matches be permitted, and directed that the involved players be fined several *sang* of gold.[4]

The impromptu soccer league presents an enthralling snapshot of the rarely scrutinized divisions within twentieth-century Lhasa society: the Kudraks, young lay Tibetan officials, demonstrating a keen interest in a foreign sport introduced by the British to the Lhasa valley; and the Lhasa United team, composed of unambiguously "foreign residents" but "united" and familiar enough to be welcomed into the league. Yet it is the final team, the Lhasa Mohammedans, that is perhaps the most beguiling. Considered neither foreign residents, like the Ladakhi Muslims, nor nominal British subjects, like the Sikkimese, the Lhasa Mohammedan team was composed of Tibetan subjects who were almost certainly not foreign.[5] The creation of the soccer league offers a valuable corrective to the frequency with which one encounters descriptions of Tibet as singularly Buddhist, isolated, and impervious to external influences. The organic manner in which the Lhasa Muslims and Ladakhi Muslims played on separate teams—one foreign and one Tibetan—also raises the question of how a Tibetan Muslim community thrived in a land so often portrayed as monolithically Buddhist.

Situated on a high mountain plateau bounded by steep peaks, Tibet is undeniably remote. Despite this remoteness, Tibet has been, through a diverse set of commercial, artistic, and cultural interactions, consistently and profoundly interconnected with the rest of Asia.[6] Although the impression of Tibet as a "closed country" from the nineteenth century on lingers in the popular imagination of Tibet, Armenian and Russian merchants in the sixteenth century regularly crisscrossed Tibet to Lhasa, Shigatse, and Siling (Ch. *Xining*), as did half a dozen or so European missionaries by the seventeenth century. Nor should we limit our definition of "foreigners" simply to non-Asians. More familiar to Tibetans but nonetheless undeniably foreign were the far larger numbers of trans-Himalayan peoples of Kashmir, Sikkim, Bhutan, and Nepal who contributed to shaping Tibetan society, as traders, religious scholars, architects, and myriad other specialists. Tibetan leaders welcomed foreigners and their skills. Mongolians aided militarily; Nepalese, artistically; and Kashmiris, commercially. Foreigners in Tibet were embraced, accepted, and appreciated, not reviled, vilified, or segregated.[7]

The Tibetan Muslim community, called Khache (Tib. *khaché*), reflects a paradox of indigeneity. It comprises a people who indisputably originated outside of Tibet but who swiftly embraced Tibetan culture, excelled linguistically, artistically, and commercially as Tibetans, who settled in central Tibet and, from the seventeenth century on, were accepted as Tibetan. It is a community that has its origins in the disparate cultural traditions of South, Central, and East Asia, yet remains undeniably Tibetan; that was renowned among the Tibetan elite for its mastery of the elaborate honorific-laden Tibetan language, yet consistently classified as non-Tibetan in foreign descriptions of Tibet. And finally, it is a community that strikes at the heart of most popular definitions of Tibetans as exclusively Buddhist.

Foreign travelers' accounts also usefully augment Tibetan documents by highlighting the ethnic and racial diversity of daily life in Tibet. The French missionary Évariste Huc's *Travels in Tartary, Thibet and China, 1844–1846* is perhaps the preeminent example of this genre. His account provides a dazzling portrait of mid-nineteenth-century Lhasa capturing the unique cosmopolitanism that typified the quotidian life of Tibet's capital.

> In the town [of Lhasa] itself, the nature of the population has an altogether different character; with shouting, a hustle and bustle, and pushing and shoving, with each person intent on pursuing their next purchase or sale with an ardent zeal. Commerce and sacred devotion tempting a steady stream of foreigners, rendering this city as a gathering point of all the peoples of Asia; the streets are constantly crowded with pilgrims, traders, so that one observes an endless variety of facial features, attire and languages. For the large part this immense multitude is transitory, renewing itself on a daily basis. The permanent population of Lhasa consists of Tibetans, Newaris [Nepalis], Khache [Muslims] and Chinese.[8]

Huc's description of Lhasa's vibrant street life is striking in its meticulous attention to the city's ethnocultural diversity. Despite having arrived with almost no prior knowledge of Tibet and only a modicum of Tibetan, his sharp eye and his attentiveness to the city's rhythms and flows made his account of Tibetan life among the best records we have of daily life in Lhasa and central Tibet.[9] He is also one of only a handful of foreigners who, prior to the twentieth century, both resided in Lhasa for an extended period and wrote about it. It is thus significant that Huc devotes considerable attention to the Khache and returns to them consistently as a reference point in descriptions of other groups and social activities.

Even though Huc's description of Lhasa and Chapman's account of the soccer matches were written nearly a century apart, they both demonstrate that far from insulated, Tibet had vigorous and active interactions with an array of polities and peoples from across Asia. As the anthropologist Enseng Ho has suggested in his reflections on Asia's inter-Asian dimensions, the "inter-Asian world was suffused with such spatially broad and patterned engagements between mobile societies to a degree that we have forgotten and no longer know."[10]

From a Tibetan perspective, the Khache's conspicuous presence is not nearly as surprising. Geoffrey Samuel's landmark study of Tibetan culture, society, and religion, *Civilized Shamans*, advances just such a conclusion. His analysis is at its core a multithemed soliloquy positing a single point–that "premodern Tibet contained a greater variety of social and political formations than is often appreciated."[11] Reflecting this ethnic and regional diversity, the Khache communities exist in virtually all areas of Tibet: as far west as Srinagar in Kashmir, as far east as Dartsedo (Ch. *Kangding*) in Kham, as far north as Labrang Monastery in Amdo, and as far south as the Himalayan hill towns of Kalimpong and Darjeeling in northern India.[12] Similar to Samuel's work, a central goal of this study is to pioneer a thick transregional history of the Tibetan Muslims written against the grain of state-based national histories of Asia's past. While other histories of Asia have artfully demonstrated the distorting nature of such brittle nationalisms, by adopting a Himalayan-centered vantage point, this history of the Tibetan Muslims, and specifically the Lhasa Muslims, seeks to make visible what remained invisible under the more standard localist, nationalist, or global frames of analysis.[13] When the Khache do appear in histories of Asia, they tend to be tinged by the preconceptions of the center. While such descriptions may have made them more intelligible to the distant imperial or national audiences thousands of miles away, they rarely corresponded to local Tibetan realities. In the essentialized orientalist narratives written by most Westerners, the Khache appear as non-Tibetan foreigners; when seen through the idiosyncratic religioethnic lens of the Chinese state they appear as Muslim Chinese Hui; or when viewed through an irredentist Indian nationalist perspective they are cast as members of the Kashmiri diaspora. In these accounts Khache appear as foreign, separate, and mutually unrecognizable rather than as indigenous, integrated, and familiar. So while a history of Tibetan Muslims on the surface appears insignificant and peripheral, it is precisely their centrality to Tibet's inter-Asian positioning that makes them an ideal subject. More than an isolated case study of a remote group, the history of the Tibetan Muslims allows startling new insights into the events of Asia's past.[14] It is my hope that this study of the Tibetan Muslims will join the numerous studies that already highlight Tibet's diverse Mongolian, Bon, Newari, and Sherpa communities to further dispel the false notion of Tibet as a monolithic Buddhist society that remains so prominent in many mainstream accounts of Asia.[15]

## BEING TIBETAN WHILE MUSLIM

A central obstacle to understanding the widespread presence of the Khache across Tibet has been the lack of clarity in previous studies between Tibetan Muslim permanent residents and Muslim sojourner communities within Tibet. As early as the eighth century, Islamic historians and geographers recorded numerous Muslim travelers, caravaneers, and merchants, even a mosque.[16] While there is virtually no sustained documentary evidence—in Tibetan, Chinese, or any other language— that traces the presence of the Muslim community prior to 1900, the fragmentary details that do survive suggest that until the late sixteenth century few Muslims resided in Tibet permanently.

Some evidence for this can be inferred from the fact that in Tibetan documents Muslims were typically designated by a variety of more or less pejorative terms. In religious texts such as the *Kālacakra Tantra,* Tibetans referred to Muslims as outsiders (Tib. *kla klo*), from the Sanskrit term *mlecchas,* or as nonbelievers (Tib. *mustegs pa*). Less literary Tibetan texts employed the term "foreigner" (Tib. *phe rang*), analogous to the Persian term *farangi.* Informally, the most common term was simply "white hats" (Tib. *mgo dkar*).[17] All these terms emphasized on some level the Muslims' externality to Tibetan society and remained in use among educated Tibetans well into the twentieth century.[18]

By the fifteenth century, the Kashmiri were the first long-term Muslim residents in central Tibet. The Nepalese chronicle *Vamshavalis* notes that the first Kashmiri settlers in the Kathmandu valley were Muslim Kashmiris traveling between Kashmir and Lhasa.[19] They were known as Khache, a term soon adopted by Tibetans to refer to any Tibetanized Muslim who resided within Tibet. Over time, this term widened even further semantically to include other Muslims who traced their origins to China and Central Asia.[20]

The confusion over the Khache typically falls into two categories. First, outsiders tended to adopt external, non-native terminologies that treated the Khache as foreign. Matters were further confused when foreign observers used such terms more or less interchangeably, sometimes calling the entire community "Ladakhi," at other times "Kashmiri," and, in Chinese, glossing any Muslim in Tibet as "Hui"—a blunder that few Tibetans would make.[21] Representative of just such a proclivity, the Indian government in 1959 in negotiating with the People's Republic of China could not even settle on a single term for the Khache, sometimes referring to "Ladakhi and Kashmiri Moslems," then just simply "Kashmiri Moslems," and later "Kajis."[22] The Chinese for their part tended to simply call them Hui, a highly ambiguous term that, depending on the context, could mean Chinese Muslim, any Muslim, or members of the state-defined nationality (Ch. *minzu*).

Second, attempting to gloss the Khache unequivocally as Tibetan Muslim is hindered by the fact that there exists no single Tibetan word in the premodern era that is equivalent to the modern word *böpa* (Tib. *bod pa*) used in Tibetan to refer to "Tibetan." To confuse the picture even further, in Tibetan a considerable amount of slippage existed between the religious and ethnic registers. In this way, in Tibetan, Khache could, and sometimes did, simply mean someone who practiced Islam. In other contexts, Khache acquired a more ethnic (or ethnoreligious) connotation, referring to those Muslims who had lived in central Tibet for generations, were native speakers of Tibetan, and, in many cases, had intermarried with local Tibetans. Finally, there remained a presumption among many non-Tibetans that, even in the mid-twentieth century, the Khache were some sort of perpetual non-native.

## TO BE TIBETAN MUSLIM

It is often assumed that to be Tibetan is to be Buddhist and, axiomatically, that to be Muslim precludes one from being Tibetan. Yet from a Tibetan perspective, particularly in central Tibet, a Tibetan Muslim's non-Buddhist religious beliefs did not preclude him from being considered active and full participants in local Tibetan society.[23] Nor were Tibetan Muslims a small or insignificant part of that society. By 1950, about 10 percent of Lhasa's roughly 30,000 lay inhabitants were Muslim.[24] Lhasa alone had four mosques and two Muslim cemeteries, and by the early twentieth century mosques were present in every large central Tibetan city, including Shigatse, Gyantse, and Tsetang.[25] During the Great Prayer Festival (Tib. *smon lam*) held at the start of the lunar new year, Khache were exempted from the strict rules governing the eating of meat imposed by the Buddhist monks who ruled Lhasa during the holiday. Similarly, Tibetan residents were tolerant of the early morning calls to prayer during the Muslim holy month of Ramadan.[26]

Despite the characterization of the Khache as perpetual non-natives in many foreign accounts of Lhasa, Tibetan Muslims lived as Tibetans among Tibetans by the early seventeenth century. Most historical records point to the earliest permanent Khache community as being established no later than the reign of the Fifth Dalai Lama (1617–82), when Tibet emerged as a major political force in Asia. The noted Tibet scholar José Cabezón suggests a strong linkage between the appearance of this Muslim community and the Fifth Dalai Lama's "invitation of the [non-Tibetan] peoples" as "part of a larger policy of encouraging ethnic, cultural and economic diversity in Tibet."[27] Given the Fifth Dalai Lama's leading role in establishing the Ganden Podrang, the political administration of central Tibet, and his interest in attracting a diverse array of artistic, intellectual, and religious influences to Tibet, it is not surprising that his rise to power marks the first period in which we see sustained evidence of a permanent Khache community. The vibrancy and political stability of the Fifth Dalai Lama's reign enabled the Khache to habituate themselves to Tibet and its culture in ways that transformed them from a simple immigrant community to one deeply integrated in Tibetan society.[28]

Khache can be found in almost every segment of Tibetan life. They were acknowledged as among the most literate and multilingual lay segment of the society. Tibetans, including the Fourteenth Dalai Lama, often praise the Khache for their linguistic abilities, particularly their mastering of the elaborate Lhasa dialect (Tib. *zhe sa*). They were also renowned for their multilingualism, with many Tibetan Muslims speaking Chinese, Hindi, Urdu, and Arabic, fostered by their prominent role in Tibet's trade with their Himalayan neighbors. What many regard as the most important secular Tibetan literary work ever written, the *Khache Phalu's Advice on the Art of Living* (Tib. *Kha che pha lu'i 'jig rten las 'bras rtsis lugs kyi bslab bya*), was penned by a Tibetan Muslim.[29] As a result of these skills, Khache served as advisers to a succession of Dalai Lamas and operated as key brokers promoting Tibet's inter-Asian ties.

By the twentieth century, central questions about the Khache's precise history, their position in Tibetan society, and their transnational identity remained obscured, ambiguous, and largely undocumented in Chinese, Indian, and Western sources as a result of external political claims on Tibet. The extended post-independence/post-liberation diplomatic tension between China and India usefully illustrates what Akhil Gupta has noted are the limits of modern concepts of citizenship to define those people who occupy "diversely spatialized, partially overlapping or non-overlapping collectivities."[30] A history of the Tibetan Muslims highlights these early twentieth-century concerns while starkly demarcating the limits of the nonaligned, anti-imperialist, and pro-Asian solidarity movements of the 1950s. These movements defined the euphoric post-independence/post-liberation period of India and China. The nature of Khache integration into Tibetan society also speaks to the large inter-Asian diasporic communities and to the strong financial and political ties these communities had to their ancestral countries of origin, primarily India and China.

As discussed in greater detail in later chapters, the traditional political, cultural, and commercial Himalayan relationships between Tibet and the neighboring states of Nepal, Bhutan, and Sikkim remained far more resilient than initially understood in Beijing and Delhi, which by the early 1950s began to see Asia in a distinctly postcolonial, Cold War manner. Yet political unrest across the Himalayas played out in unexpected and nonlinear ways that suggest the Khache were not alone in their experience. The trepidation surrounding the People's Republic of China's occupation of Tibet and ongoing ambiguity surrounding China's ultimate goals in the Himalaya region created uncertainty that was manifested in a variety of ways from Kalimpong to Kathmandu and most visibly in Lhasa. Tracing these Himalayan connections, which continued to function years after the arrival of the People's Liberation Army in Lhasa, disrupts the supposedly stable, continuous, and overarching control often attributed to China's occupation of Tibet in 1950. The complex interrelationships, circulation, and transregional mobility so common in this area force us to look below the standard narratives of Indian and Chinese actions and throw into sharper relief the messy cosmopolitan interconnections that typified society across the Tibetan and Himalayan worlds well into the 1950s.

## KASHMIRI INDIAN OR TIBETAN CHINESE

The meaning and power of such historical events are enhanced when seen through the eyes of individuals who lived them. With the Dalai Lama's flight to India and the subsequent 1959 March Uprising against Chinese control, the entire Tibetan Muslim community's status was irrevocably altered. Fearful of retribution, several Tibetan Muslim leaders, including one named Habibullah Naik, demanded that by virtue of their historical ties to Kashmir they be treated as foreign residents (like the Nepalese, Bhutanese, and other foreign residents of Lhasa who were also scrambling to be allowed to migrate back to their home countries in the wake of the 1959 March Uprising). The local Chinese authorities, deeply unnerved by any signs of dissent, arrested over a dozen Tibetan Muslim leaders, including Habibullah Naik, charging them with inciting the Khache to "claim a foreign nationality."[31]

The Khache's claims were not unusual for the period. Similar to many diasporic communities across Asia in the post-colonial period, the Khache asserted that their Kashmiri ancestry gave them the right to classify themselves as Indian citizens. They rallied as a community and began to assiduously avoid any actions that would identify them as Chinese. The difficulty arose in the very basic contradiction that most Khache had up until that point adamantly asserted themselves to be Tibetan. The Chinese state, playing its own game of self-deception, namely, that Tibet had always remained Chinese, saw the Khache's declaration of being Tibetan as tantamount to declaring oneself a citizen of the People's Republic of China.

Outside of Tibet, the Khache's situation was poorly understood. The *New York Times* in 1960 ran an article chronicling their plight with the headline "India's Traders held by Chinese." In the retaliatory Cold War logic of the period, many assumed the Khache were Indian nationals simply caught out by the abruptly shifting political winds. As the article was quick to point out, however, the "Indian traders" were not unequivocally Indian citizens. Described by the Indian government as "Kashmiri Muslims," the group arrested by the Chinese was part of a community that had resided in Tibet for generations and by their own admission had "never carried [Indian] travel documents and identification certificates," yet now "wanted to register themselves as Indian nationals."[32]

The *New York Times'* terminological ambiguity is unsurprising. By virtually every measure, Habibullah Naik was Tibetan. Born in Lhasa at the turn of the twentieth century, he grew up living above his store in central Lhasa where his family had resided for generations. He spoke the pure Lhasa dialect of Tibetan, dressed in Tibetan clothing, and revered the Dalai Lama as the leader of Tibet. He and the other Khache, prior to 1950, had long been considered Tibetan subjects by the Tibetan government. Tibetan Buddhist pilgrims circumambulating the sacred inner pilgrimage circuit streamed past the front gates of the mosque where he prayed daily. His relatives had, over the generations, intermarried with Tibetans, blurring any lingering divisions—physical, ancestral, or imagined—between his Buddhist and Muslim neighbors.[33] Until the Dalai Lama's decision to flee to India in 1959, Habibullah Naik was undeniably Tibetan and was treated as such by the Tibetan government and his Tibetan neighbors. In order to verify their Kashmiri ancestry, the Tibetan Muslim leaders were informed by the Chinese authorities that all claims of foreign citizenship would require "fresh documentary proof."[34] When the Chinese government's stern cautions went unheeded, they deemed Naik and other Khaches' efforts to declare themselves foreign as seditious activities and imprisoned them. The Tibetan Muslim community as a whole faced daily harassment, middle-of-the-night interrogations, and starvation-level rations.

As Naik and his fellow Khaches had discovered, the ability of Himalayan states like Tibet, Nepal, Bhutan, and Sikkim to defy the hardening boundaries of post-liberation and postcolonial Asia was quickly coming to an end. Under both international pressure from India and domestic pressure to resolve the diplomatic crisis, the Chinese government abruptly acquiesced. All Tibetan Muslims who "voluntarily stat[ed] that they wanted to change their nationality from Chinese to Indian" would be allowed to resettle in India.[35] By late 1960, nearly one thousand Khache demonstrated adequate proof of their Kashmiri, and thus "Indian," ancestry and were issued exit permits.

The Chinese did not extend this amnesty to individuals, like Naik, who had committed offenses against the state.[36] However, on March 29, 1961, with no explanation, the Chinese made a single exception and released Naik. Alone of those arrested, he was escorted by Chinese officials from his Lhasa prison cell to a truck waiting outside the prison and transported to the southern Tibetan border town of Dromo (Ch. *Yadong*). There he joined one of the last convoys of Nepalese, Khaches, and other Tibetans, who by virtue of their foreign ancestry were issued Chinese exit visas and allowed to leave Tibet after the violent crackdown on 1959 March Uprising. Habibullah Naik would never again step foot in Tibet. He and the other Khaches crossed into India, acquired Indian citizenship, and began their new lives.

The emigration of Habibullah Naik and several thousand other Khaches offers a little-known coda to the history of the Khache in central Tibet. On the surface, the Khaches' return to India and Kashmir is founded on the false premise that the Khache had retained their distinct and separate Kashmiri identity across several centuries and thus returning to their country of origin. But under closer examination, the 1960 Khache Incident is only the most recent example of the Khache challenging the ostensibly hard boundaries of imperial / national identity and subjecthood / citizenship. A history of the Khache experience in central Tibet underscores how the ethnic, religious, and political categories of modern Asian nationhood conceal significant dimensions of Asia's past and the significant relationships between numerous Himalayan states and Tibet up to the present.

Habibullah Naik's assertion that he should be allowed to declare himself a citizen of India emerged out of a much larger constellation of events, modalities, and peoples than just the proximate issues surrounding the 1959 March Uprising in Lhasa. The Khaches' demands for Indian citizenship strike at the heart of how postcolonial regimes erected new boundaries of national citizenship at variance with those inherited from the earlier, imperial regimes. Numerous diasporic communities were confronted with a choice between allegiance to their ancestral home or citizenship in a newly formed nation-state that had emerged out of the former colonial state where their families had lived for generations.

Nor was this a question only for small populations like the Khache, Nepalese, or Bhutanese who discovered themselves at odds with the Chinese government in Tibet. As the sociologist Itty Abraham has pointed out, "Within Asia, the presence of Indians and Chinese outside their traditional homelands had been a part of the local social and cultural and economic landscape for long enough that their nationality was quite ambiguous."[37] The difference for the Khache was the fact that simmering tension between these "foreign" communities and the "local" populations was not the primary factor in their decisions. Instead, the decision of many Tibetan Muslim individuals to declare themselves Indian was a direct result of the Chinese government's questioning of the community's political loyalties in the wake of India offering the Dalai Lama asylum in 1959. In this light, the question of the Khaches' national identity, or loyalty, offers an alternative understanding of inter-Asian relations. The Khaches' predicament demonstrates the experience of many Asians when questions of ancestry and citizenship were imperfect solutions to the question of national identity in a Himalayan context.

To appreciate the complexities of the Khache past we need, on the one hand, to pay attention to the processes that reterritorialized, relabeled, and renationalized the Khache as "Kashmiri Muslims." On the other hand, we must examine the manner by which the Khache had, in time, space, and memory, become incontrovertibly Tibetan. The history and memory of the Khaches' past have interacted in unusual ways with mainstream Tibetan and Asian historiography, making it a particularly elusive narrative to reconstruct.

## ARRESTED HISTORIES?

Even the briefest introduction to the Khache demonstrates that to grasp their complex position is to grapple with multiple overlapping misconceptions. Just as "Kashmiri" was an imperfect term to refer to the Khache living in Tibet, across Asia questions were being asked about the status of the resident "Indian" or "Chinese" populations who had resided outside their country of origin, in many cases for generations.

The seemingly innocuous labels for such communities hid highly fraught undercurrents and prejudices. The depth of emotion that such terms elicited in the postcolonial era caught many unaware. For as Anna Lowenhaupt Tsing reminds us:

> Words in motion surprise us. Their far-flung antics interrupt conventional intellectual history, with its assumption of stable genealogies of thought. They are spread too far for the boundaries of national history; they ricochet too widely to follow strictly colonial geographies. Words in motion urge us to consider multiple linguistic and cultural legacies in dialogue.[38]

The power of the Tibetan Muslims to serve as an analytical lens lies in its ability to capture in unexpected ways the changing relationship of space and identity that accompanied the decolonialization and reterritorialization of Asia across the nineteenth and twentieth centuries. In this light, the evolution of the Khache identity is emblematic of a much broader dilemma occurring across postcolonial Asia over hardening conceptualizations of "nation" and "citizen."

If the Khaches' transnational and inter-Asian positioning masked their Tibetan identity, Carole McGranahan's concept of arrested histories provides a constructive way to delineate how their position in Tibet's history remains intact but inaccessible. The Khaches' historical position in Tibet parallels that of the Tibetan people more generally, in that it "is more complicated than a sweeping under the rug of inconvenient past and politics; it is a delay or postponement of histories for the present only."[39] Not abandoned or erased, the Khache have always remained in plain sight, yet never quite in focus. They have been screened off within the official chronicling of the past since they do not fit comfortably in the historical narrative of Tibet.

It is in this awkward space—never entirely ignored but never fully integrated—that the Khache have persisted in the historical narrative for over three centuries. Virtually every Western visitor who passed through Tibet, from the earliest Jesuits to Heinrich Harrer, Lhasa's most famous foreign resident, noted in some manner the presence of the Khache.[40] Chinese sources follow a similar pattern, recording the size and number of mosques in Lhasa, describing Khache routes, and enumerating the Khache communities across Tibet.[41] To grasp the complex nature of the Tibetan Muslim community, one must first address the means by which the Khache so successfully integrated themselves into Tibetan society. How they retained the hybrid influences of Tibet's external neighbors—South Asia, Central Asia, and China—as well as Tibet's complex internal intricacies is part of this history. While the Tibetan Muslim communities across the eastern Tibetan regions of Amdo and Kham shared many qualities with those described below, above all else, this study seeks to provide an alternative history of Himalayan Asia that is positioned in and around the experiences of the Lhasa Khache.

While this work is the first book-length study of the Lhasa Khache, it is not a history of Islam in Tibet. Rather it engages the cosmopolitan nature of the Khache by attempting to situate them within Tibet and its relationship across the Himalayan world. Although it explores many new sources, its value lies less in the unearthing of new manuscripts or detailing hitherto unexplored religious networks than in considering the latent intersectional identity of the Khache as a means to offer a new approach to Tibet's past and look with fresh eyes upon a place and era we believed we already knew quite well.

# Confronting the Unexpected

On November 30, 1943, two American pilots, Robert Crozier and Harold "Mac" McCallum, eased their C-87 plane into the air carrying a load of ammunition, fuel, and supplies from an American air base in northeastern India to the southwestern Chinese city of Kunming. The U.S. Air Force had deployed these modified B-24 bombers along a 530-mile corridor since April 1942 after Japanese troops had overrun the Burma Road, the Allies' last significant land route supplying the Nationalist Chinese forces based in western China.[1] With President Franklin D. Roosevelt's call to transport ten thousand tons of cargo a month from India into China, hundreds of aircraft were plying this route, maintaining a desperately needed air link, known as "the Hump," in the battle against Japanese forces occupying much of eastern China.

Both pilots were experienced, and this had been a routine trip into Kunming. After a brief respite to unload, refuel, and allow the crew to eat a hasty meal, they returned to the plane, only to be told they needed to first offload supplies in Yunnanyi, a town some 150 miles due west of Kunming. Flying at night and slightly north of their usual route to India, the Americans encountered completely different conditions from those on the flight up.

The greatest obstacle to flying the Hump came from the constantly changing weather conditions, monsoon rains in the summer and blizzards in the winter. The flight crew had few navigation tools at their disposal other than a method known as dead reckoning, whereby the navigator, knowing his point of departure and compass heading, would calculate time, air speed, and approximate distance traveled. By 1943, several radio beacons had been placed along the route to guide pilots,

Tibetan Muslim Sanaullah (third from right) next to Harold McCallum (fourth from right) posing with the American flight crew in traditional Tibetan hats and coats at the British Consulate in Lhasa, December 1943. Sanaullah would die the following year from pneumonia. Credit: Reproduced with permission from Richard Starks and Miriam Murcutt, *Lost in Tibet: The Untold Story of Five American Airmen, a Doomed Plane, and the Will to Survive*, 2004, and from the family of William Perram.

and finally they could communicate with the control towers at the bases in both India and China for updates on their positions.

As they took off from Yunnanyi, the crew encountered heavy turbulence, and frigid temperatures caused the plane to begin icing up. The pilots, looking for better conditions, took the plane up to 24,000 feet. Unable to get a reading from any of the radio beacons for several hours and running low on fuel, the pilots' anxiety grew. For reasons still unclear, when the pilots called in and asked for a compass heading to their base in Jorhat, the control tower miscalculated and told them to continue to fly along its westerly heading. Unbeknownst to the flight crew, their plane had encountered 100-mile-an-hour headwinds, causing them to fly several hundred miles north of their intended flight path. Still believing they were headed southwest toward India, they decided to drop down from their cruising altitude, expecting to break through the cloud cover and locate their air base visually. With the plane's altimeter reading 17,500 feet as they broke through the clouds, instead of another 10,000 feet of air below them, McCallum exclaimed, "Damit, that's not a cloud it's a mountain."[2]

Now nearly out of fuel, in the middle of the night, and with few other options, the crew decided to bail out and parachute to safety. Having all survived the much shorter than anticipated jump, the crew found themselves scattered across the side of a steep river ravine, with temperatures well below freezing.[3] As the *New York Times* recounted, "When their feet touched earth they were in 'Shangri-La'—the forbidden land of Tibet of the novel 'Lost Horizon'—and they were starting one of the strangest adventures ever to befall United States Fliers."[4] Initially unable to find their entire crew, McCallum, Crozier, and the radio operator followed a small trail for some distance, when they encountered a 6-foot-tall Tibetan. Approaching the American air crew, he called out, "As salaam alaikum" (May peace be upon you). McCallum, having taken a few language and culture classes while in India, offered the appropriate reply: "Alaikum as salaam" (And with you).[5] After this exchange, McCallum and the Tibetan began to converse in broken Hindi. Asked where they were, India or Tibet, the man replied, "Tibbat" in Hindi, confirming to the Americans that they had landed not in India but in Tibet.

The story of McCallum and his crew flying wildly off course, being forced to bail out of their airplane, and being rescued from Tibet has been retold numerous times. Yet little emphasis has been given to the fact that the first greeting the crew received was the Islamic salutation, "May peace be upon you," and not the traditional Tibetan greeting, "Tashi delek" (lit., "Good wishes").[6] The incongruity of such a greeting between an American pilot and Tibetan trader perhaps explains why the *New York Times, Collier's Magazine,* and *Reader's Digest* omitted the detail in their telling of the story. That absence reflects a much larger erasure of Tibetan Muslims, or Khache, from almost all accounts of Tibet.

As the American crew would later piece together, their plane had crashed several miles outside of the Tibetan town of Tsetang, roughly 100 miles southeast of Lhasa. Sanaullah, the man who befriended the American flight crew, was a prominent member of Tsetang's vibrant Tibetan Muslim community. His ability to communicate in Hindi with McCallum was a result of his frequent trips as a trans-Himalayan trader to Kalimpong and Calcutta. It was not until after the crash of the C-49 and in the aftermath of the 1959 March Uprising that the complex realities of the Tibetan Muslims' role in Tibet came onto the international stage.

The account of the American pilots on one level is a standard white intermediary tale similar to many firsthand British travelers' accounts, as well as the best-sellers *Seven Years in Tibet* by Heinrich Harrer and *Out of This World: Across the Himalayas to Forbidden Tibet* by Lowell Thomas. The danger of such an approach lies in the implication that we can only understand Tibet when the tale is told through the eyes of a white, often male, protagonist. It is included here for an entirely different reason.

Crozier and McCallum's crash neatly exhibits that even when outsiders unexpectedly find themselves in central Tibet, the first person they encounter could be a Tibetan Muslim. Yet there is also a deeper significance. Sanaullah's ability to recognize a white foreigner, attempt to speak to him in Hindi, and also have the wherewithal to make contact with the central Tibetan government all underscore the Khaches' sense of place within a Himalayan world. The fact that Sanaullah was able to interact with Tibetan, British, and Chinese officials in Lhasa with no complications and that his Khache status was not flagged on some level to the Americans (indeed, in most accounts his status as a Khache, aside from the opening salutation to McCallum, is rarely mentioned) alert us to the seamless integration of the Khache in Tibetan society.

The American crew members were hardly the first outsiders to encounter and rely on the Khache to navigate their way in and out of Tibetan society. Due to their multilingualism, commercial expertise, and social ease within Tibet, Khaches had since the sixteenth century served as guides for outsiders in Tibet, including the earliest Italian and Portuguese missionaries in the seventeenth century.[7] The depth of missionary reliance on Khache assistance was so pervasive that, in the words of the French ethnographer Marc Gaborieau, Western missionaries came to see Tibet "through Muslim eyes."[8] The ways the Tibetan Muslims both facilitated and influenced early Western accounts is rarely engaged since the presence and role of Tibetan Muslims remains a rarely examined topic. Nor is the presence of Tibetan Muslims any less surprising for first-time visitors to Tibet today when they encounter the centuries-old Grand Mosque just steps away from central Lhasa. What follows below and in the next chapters is an attempt to provide a better understanding and delineate the central place of Tibetan Muslims in Tibetan society.

## LHASA'S MUSLIM LANDSCAPE

Despite its cosmopolitan nature, Lhasa, awash in white, with eaves, doors, and windows framed in red and gold borders, remained a relatively small town until the mid-twentieth century. Lhasa's lay population hovered between 25,000 and 30,000 permanent residents.[9] Its location—distant from military threats and protected by a high mountain plateau—precluded the need for city walls.[10] Instead, Lhasa was organized both physically and spiritually by a set of concentric pilgrimage circuits, or *koras,* emanating outward from the center of Lhasa. At the spiritual center of the city was the Nangkor, or inner kora (Tib. *nang skor*), that pilgrims traced around the Jokhang temple's main chapel. The Barkor (Tib. *bar skor*), or outer kora, encircled the numerous sacred temples and shrines clustered around the Jokhang at the heart of Lhasa. The district bound by the circuit, also called the Barkor, served as the town's central market area where for centuries merchants sold their wares. The third and outermost kora, the Lingkor (Tib. *gling skor*), ringed the entire town (prior to its post-1980s growth). Nearly 5 miles long, it cut in close to the eastern edge of Lhasa before looping out westward around the Potala Palace and other sacred sites.[11]

If the description of Lhasa concluded here, it would suffice as a concise and quite standard summary of its sacred geography. Such a description, though typical, omits the presence of a Muslim community. The omission is surprising in that their existence is difficult to ignore. The Tibetan capital has been home to four mosques for well over a century and Tibetan Muslims have been prominent there for well over three centuries.[12] Positioned in and around Lhasa, the mosques not only were highly visible, but played an integral role in Lhasa's social life (see map 2).

Lhasa's first mosque, typically referred to by Tibetans as the Khache Lingka (Tib. *kha che gling kha*), traditionally dated to 1650, is situated in the Garden of the Far-Reaching Arrow (Tib. *rgyang mda' khan*) several miles west of Lhasa, just north of the Dalai Lama's Summer Palace (Tib. *nor bu gling kha*).[13] This small compound was a prominent feature in Lhasa's religious and social sphere. As the Khache community grew, a second, larger mosque was erected just opposite the original mosque to accommodate the larger number of Khaches during religious holidays.[14]

The most prominent mosque in Lhasa is the Grand Mosque. Built no later than the beginning of the eighteenth century, it is situated at the southeastern edge of the city in the Wapaling neighborhood (Tib. *wa pa gling*).[15] Over the centuries, the Grand Mosque has been known by several names. Today in Lhasa, the most common designation is Grand Mosque (Tib. *lha khang chen*) or simply the Chinese Mosque (Tib. *rgya kha che lha khang*).[16] Less frequently, particularly prior to 1959, it adopted the name of the neighborhood in which it was located, the Wapaling Mosque (Tib. *wa pa gling kha che lha khang*).[17]

Located several miles across the valley north of Lhasa, the Dokdé Mosque (Tib. *dog sde lha khang*) lay adjacent to the Muslim cemetery.[18] It is the least well-documented of the four mosques. The Jesuit missionary Ippolito Desideri, in the early eighteenth century, remarked that the Wapaling Khache previously "had a small field close to Lhasa for burying their dead," but the Tibetan government "forced [the Wapaling Khache] to vacate [their cemetery] and relocate it farther out in the uninhabited countryside."[19] The Dokdé valley, more isolated and less likely to draw attention to the Muslim custom of burying bodies, also became home to a small mosque that was attached to the cemetery. Some date this mosque to 1716, the year of Desideri's arrival in Lhasa, which might explain his unusually detailed mention of the Tibetan government's request to have the Muslims build a cemetery away from the city.[20]

In the early twentieth century, the fourth and final mosque was built in the Barkor neighborhood just within the southern edge of Lhasa's sacred Lingkor pilgrimage circuit. The mosque is most commonly referred to today in Tibetan as simply the Small Mosque (Tib. *lha khang chung*) but was also colloquially known to many Lhasa residents as the Barkor or Rapsel Alley Mosque (Tib. *rap sel lha khang*). While its exact date of construction remains debated, it likely was built in the early years of the twentieth century.[21]

Aside from Lhasa, numerous other cities contained smaller though not insignificant Khache populations. Shigatse, in many ways the only city rivaling Lhasa in terms of religious, political, and military prestige, by the early twentieth century was home to well over a hundred Khache households.[22] Although some suggest the Shigatse mosque was originally constructed in 1443 (with some even suggesting as early as 1343), it seems more likely that it was built around the same time as the early Lhasa mosques and certainly no later than the late seventeenth century.[23]

Outside the larger urban centers of Shigatse and Lhasa, the Khache communities tended to be composed of a handful of families. The one exception to this appears to be the Tibetan Muslims in Tsetang, the former pre-Buddhist Tibetan capital southeast of Lhasa near where the American crew crashed. Home to several dozen Khache households, the Tsetang Tibetan Muslim community remained highly active into the 1950s.[24] Permanent Khache communities, almost all having a mosque, existed across central Tibet, including Gyantse, Kuti, Lhatse, and Drigung.[25]

As the widespread presence of mosques suggest, Khache communities were common, integrated, and accepted elements of Tibetan society. Their communities also buttress claims of Tibet as multicentered, multiethnic, and multilingual. Given the complexity of Tibet's political, ethnic, and linguistic makeup, it is prudent to begin by addressing exactly what we mean when we use the terms "Tibet" and "Tibetan."

## THE POWER OF DISAMBIGUATION

Most scholars of Tibet distinguish between "political Tibet," the area historically controlled by the Dalai Lama's government centered in Lhasa, and "ethnographic Tibet," the broader stateless areas that fell outside the Dalai Lama's control. By definition, political Tibet tends to be Lhasa-centric, although as Hugh Richardson, Gillian Tan, and others have suggested, Tibet "operated on a far more diverse political basis than simple allegiance to the rule of Lhasa."[26] Acknowledging the dangers of examining political Tibet to the exclusion of ethnographic Tibet, or of conflating the two, this study uses the term "Tibet" broadly while attempting to indicate specific regions when needed. It does not employ "Tibet" at any point to narrowly mean the People's Republic of China's Tibetan Autonomous Region, which was only formally established in 1965.

To the nonspecialist, emphasizing the fact that Tibet and Tibetans are not entirely coterminous may seem overly pedantic. However, given the nonalignment of political and ethnic boundaries—and the inconstancy of such an alignment across history—the presence of Tibetans does not necessarily make any region a part of "Tibet." Although previous scholarship has repeatedly noted a need to differentiate between ethnographic and political Tibet, it has soft-pedaled the complexities of using the term "Tibetan." The following paragraphs are designed to throw into stark relief the need to interrogate what is meant by the term "Tibetan" so as to allow a clearer definition of what we mean when we speak of Tibetan Muslims.

*Böpa* (Tib. *bod pa*) is often suggested as the word most closely approximating the meaning of "Tibetan" in most Western languages. Like the distinction made above between a political and an ethnographic Tibet, however, the term *böpa* more often refers to Tibetans from the Tibetan central province of Ü-Tsang rather than all ethnic Tibetans.[27] Outside central Tibet, most ethnic Tibetans rarely refer to themselves as "böpa" but rather "people of Kham" or "people of Amdo" (e.g., Tib. *khams pa* or *amdo ba*). Even here, these terms are not as all-inclusive as one might initially believe. One of the early pioneers of Tibetan Studies, Rolf Stein, in his classic work, *Tibetan Civilizations,* implored his readers to recall "that since at least the eleventh century 'Tibetans' (*böpa*) have been contrasted with 'pasture-land people' (Tib. *'brog pa*) as though the latter were foreigners."[28] In this light, *böpa,* perhaps the closest literal analogue to "Tibetan" in English, conveys in Tibetan a very Lhasa-centric quality that is narrower in meaning than the broader and more flexible meaning than the term has in English.

Colloquially, the Tibetan term that is closest to the Anglophone usage "Tibetan" is *nang pa.* Translated literally, *nangpa* (Tib. *nang pa*) simply means 'insider"; however, it has a distinctly Buddhist overtone that is more accurately rendered as "Tibetan Buddhist." In this manner, the usage *böpa* is limited territorially, while *nangpa* carries a decidedly religious connotation. Again, speaking colloquially, if one is not *nangpa,* one would be, by definition, *chipa,* an "outsider" (Tib. *phyi pa*). Such conflicting terminology has led scholars, such as the Tibetologist Robert Ekvall, to conclude over half a century ago that to be non-Buddhist (*chipa*) would make one "no longer recognized by the Tibetans as being unequivocally Tibetan."[29] And yet Khache living in Kham or Amdo might not be either *nangpa* or *böpa* and still be ethnically Tibetan. The difficulty of finding appropriate cognates in English has led an increasing number of scholars to question more directly the imperfect nature of the term "Tibetan" as it is applied to the multiple terms employed by Tibetans themselves.

The Lhasa-centric nature of *böpa* and the Buddhist bias of *nangpa* are masked by the Anglophone term "Tibetan," as both meanings are often implicitly present in the popular conceptualizations of being Tibetan when outside of Tibet.[30] Sara Schneiderman, in an effort to decouple being Tibetan and being Buddhist, queries, "Just as there are Buddhists all over the world who are not Tibetan, why can there not be Tibetans who are not Buddhist?"[31] In this way, similar to the need to differentiate between ethnographic and political Tibet, although those from central Tibet would have called themselves *böpa,* they likely would not have applied the term to Amdo Tibetans and Kham Tibetans. In an eloquent critique of this unspoken bias, Françoise Pommaret observed that "one encounters an aspect of the culture of central Tibet which has not been addressed much so far: a certain condescending and despising attitude towards the surrounding regions which did not, in the eyes of the central Tibetans, reach what they considered to be the epitome of culture."[32]

On many levels, the obstacle lies less in the Tibetan definitions than in the English terms "Tibet" and "Tibetan." As Tsering Shakya has bluntly pointed out, the Tibetan language has "no indigenous term which encompasses the population denoted by Western usage."[33] Nor are there any clear alternatives. Emily Yeh, in her study of Tibetan indigeneity, accentuates this by pointing out that even today the "term *indigenous,* after all, is not widely used by Tibetans either within Tibet or in exile."[34] Nor is this an either / or question. There is a growing consensus that non-Buddhist Tibetans, including Tibetan Muslims, were seen as culturally, socially, and politically part of the larger Tibetan whole, even as they remained religious outsiders. Crucial to this understanding is that in the case of many non-Buddhist groups, the designation "outsiders" (*chipa*) did not mean they were deprived of all rights and privileges as Tibetans. Nor were those labeled *chipa* collectively branded as foreigners.

Even as the deep definitional fissures that make the terms "Tibet" and "Tibetan" unstable and imprecise, the lack of practical alternatives dictates that simply discarding them is equally impractical. Much like we knowingly accept the broad linguistic and regional diversity included in the label "Indian," the confusion unleashed by disposing of such a term hardly rectifies the situation. Instead, this brief examination cautions us to be mindful not to align the territory, the people, and the speakers of Tibetan under a single, unitary, and homogenizing umbrella of what it means to be Tibetan. More relevant to this study is the need to embrace this ambiguity in our efforts to delineate more carefully the category "Tibetan Muslim." Simply put, if being Tibetan has no direct cognate that neatly corresponds to the English term "Tibetan," similar regional and cultural biases have shaped the meaning of Khache and its English equivalent, "Tibetan Muslim."

To avoid confusion and yet embrace convention, the term "Tibetan Muslim" acknowledges many of the terminological fault lines discussed above. In my usage, the term refers to all Khaches who have resided permanently in Tibet and were accepted as Tibetan. It encompasses great spatial, linguistic, and even ethnic diversity. Though beyond the scope of this study, "Tibetan Muslims" can also refer to Tibetanized Chinese Muslims of Amdo, Tibetans who converted to Islam, or simply those communities of Kashmiri who have traveled to and from Tibet for centuries. Given the highly contested range of ethnic, religious, and cultural identities bound up in the term it is difficult to neatly align this process theoretically. Certainly, many of the traits raised below could be categorized as "invented traditions'" in the sense of Hobsbawm and Ranger.[35] Equally, the term is not meant to be employed strictly as an ethnonym suggesting Tibetan Muslims should be seen as an ethnic group, defined by Weber's emphasis on "common descent."[36] Historically the source base in Tibetan, Chinese, or any language remains so fraught that to engage in theoretical discussions of ethnicity, race, or identity becomes highly problematic particularly given the highly fragmentary and multilingual sources. The post-1950 situation of political and ethnographic Tibet has only clouded matters.

In light of the recent trend in Sinophone scholarship to employ the term "Zang-Hui," I agree with Gerald Roche that hyphenated terms, particularly those deployed along the Sino-Tibetan divide, tend to elide "local agency and marginalizes local distinctions as incomplete, failed, or hybrid byproducts of distant centers of purity."[37] Tibetan Muslims maintained an identity as Tibetans through shared symbols, stories, and practices while simultaneously accentuating a highly honed sense of relational alterity by emphasizing their different religious practices.[38]

Indeed, much of the confusion over the status of the Khache in Tibet has its roots in which process one emphasizes. Foreign travelers' accounts tended to stress identity maintenance through alterity, portraying the Khache as foreigners based on their Muslim beliefs, whereas the Tibetan sources reveal a focus on their shared Tibetan traits to a degree that the Khache were rarely even identified as a separate community. And so it is with the Tibetan Muslims, as Frederik Barth noted in his late-life musings on ethnicity and ethnic boundaries: "In a hall of mirrors, one needs to move with considerable circumspection."[39] My hope is that this study will orient future scholars with more familiarity of specific periods, areas, and groups within the Tibetan Muslim community to address the complex question of religious and ethnic identity.

## TO BE KHACHE AND TIBETAN

Most narratives of Tibet's past begin with one man, the Fifth Dalai Lama, in the early seventeenth century. With the military support of the Mongol leader Gushri Khan, the Fifth Dalai Lama not only unified Tibet, but became the irrefutable spiritual as well as a secular leader of Tibet. In the histories of Tibetan Muslims, as in the histories of their Buddhist Tibetan brethren, the "Great Fifth" Dalai Lama holds a central place in the mythos surrounding the Tibetan Muslims' arrival and inclusion in the cosmopolitan world of seventeenth-century Tibet.[40]

Tibetan Muslim foundation myths tend to be gently elaborated versions of more or less orthodox Tibetan history. A common chronicle told by Tibetan Muslims plays off the well-documented policy of the Fifth Dalai Lama to encourage foreign artisans, scholars, and traders to come to Tibet. When interviewed today, Tibetan Muslims generally all point to arriving under the reign of the Fifth Dalai Lama.[41] In a common telling, nearly fifty men and boys, sometimes more according to the teller, traveled to Lhasa as merchants. Upon demonstrating their skills, they were invited by the Fifth Dalai Lama to stay in Tibet and to receive a stipend to cover their expenses.[42]

These Khache oral histories neatly parallel the documented efforts of the Fifth Dalai Lama to recruit foreigners to come to seventeenth-century Lhasa.[43] All extant historical sources point to the Fifth Dalai Lama's reign as being the period when the earliest permanent Muslim settlements emerged across central Tibet. It is these Khaches who established a permanent community that has survived from that point in time in a direct line to the present who we can properly refer to as "Tibetan Muslims."

From the seventeenth until the twentieth century, the Khache consistently appear in foreign accounts of Tibet. During a multiyear sojourn in Lhasa, from 1686 to 1691, the Armenian merchant Hovhannes Joughayetsi listed numerous Khaches among his important clients.[44] In 1775, when the British emissary George Bogle arrived in the court of the Panchen Lama in Shigatse, he remarked that the Khache had "been long settled in this country" and were "mostly the offspring of Tibetans."[45] Songyun, a mid-eighteenth-century Manchu official appointed to Tibet, commented on the large Khache community, specifically pointing out that they "had taken up residence in Tibet making a living as traders many years ago."[46] Chinese gazetteers not only noted the presence of Khache but also included the Khache Garden Mosque on maps of significant landmarks in and around Lhasa.[47]

Tibetan Muslims appear with less frequency in Tibetan accounts, but in part that is due to the fact that most of the extant sources are religious, or religiously oriented (e.g., written by elite Buddhists). Regardless, few Tibetans or Tibetan documents dispute their presence. The Khache's linguistic facility made them highly sought after within the lay community, and it is not surprising that one of the greatest secular Tibetan works is *Advice on the Art of Living*. Almost certainly written by an eighteenth-century Tibetan Muslim by the name of Faizullah under the sobriquet Khache Phalu, it is among the most popular and classic Tibetan texts, remaining popular even today among Tibetans.

From the sparse details known about his life, Khache Phalu worked for the Seventh Panchen Lama (1782–1853), likely as the official in charge of the lama's stable of horses (Tib. *chibs dpon*).[48] The relatively short volume, consisting of eleven short chapters and roughly fifty-five pages, emulates the philosophical aphorisms of the Buddhist "Elegant Sayings" (Tib. *legs bsha*) literary tradition. Written in nine-syllable lines, it captures a quintessentially Tibetan view of the world, yet the author never seeks to conceal his Islamic beliefs. Unrivaled in its ability to create a hybrid of Islamic and Tibetan literary culture, it reflects the unique place that the Khache held in the Lhasa community, emulating but never becoming a lesser facsimile of high Tibetan culture. In *Advice on the Art of Living*, Khache Phalu deftly adopts metaphors and language that could as easily allude to Buddhist teachings as they do Islamic ones.

Referencing central Tibetan tropes like joke telling, local gossip, and even stories of immoral monks, it quickly became one of the most popular secular works in Tibet for well over a century.[49] In several instances when the author emphasizes his monotheism or invokes Allah, the tone of the text beautifully utilizes Tibetan patterns and allusions to make whatever might possibly be perceived as "un-Tibetan" into something undeniably Tibetan. His commentary on Buddhist ideals is often sharp, but similar in tone to denunciations that Tibetans themselves made, as when he laments at one point, "There are many who talk about the pursuit of right actions, but true followers are as scarce as gold" (Tib. *kha che pha'i sing gtam bshad yod do / nya na dang mi nyan so so'i bsam blo re*). Nor do his Islamic beliefs prevent him from exhorting his readers, by appropriating language generally understood to be Buddhist, to "pray with your body, speech and mind or to rely on the 'Three Precious Jewels' [the Buddha, the Dharma and the Sangha]."[50] More intriguing is when Khache Phalu seems to be defying both Buddhist and Muslim traditions. At one point he cautions against "eating the dirty food of the wicked butcher" (Tib. *las ngan shan pa'i dreg khu bza' ba la*), which could narrowly be read as only eating meat properly butchered (*halal*), but the term "wicked" (Tib. *las ngan*) here has the Buddhist connotation of "bad karma" commonly associated with being a butcher. Given that butchers were almost exclusively Khaches, most Tibetans (or Tibetan Muslims) would see this as a veiled reference to the Khache.

The very ability of Khache Phalu to capture such a Tibetan voice caused many to doubt his Islamic identity and speculate that he was actually a highly placed official or even the Seventh Panchen Lama himself. The enduring incredulity that a Muslim could write such a quintessentially Tibetan text remained in place well into the modern era, with one commentator insinuating, as late as 1981, that the work was the product of the Seventh Panchen Lama:

> The Panchen Lama had good relations with the Tibetan Muslims of Shigatse and since the Muslims had a very sweet style of speech that appealed to the masses, the Seventh Panchen Lama under the Muslim pseudonym deliberately wrote the book in their style of speech.[51]

The book's persistent popularity among Tibetans unsettled the Twelfth Dalai Lama (1857–75) enough that he ordered that all lines directly invoking Islamic beliefs be expurgated.[52] Such hearsay aside, the recognized literary prowess of Khache Phalu denotes a broader recognition of the Khaches' literary skill.

Perhaps not unsurprisingly, even today the most common attribute ascribed to the Khache by Tibetans is their facility with the Tibetan language. The noted Tibetologist Charles Ramble elegantly alludes to the subtle ways in which Tibetan Buddhists routinely would invoke the Khaches' Tibetan fluency as proof positive of their Tibetan identity, despite their religious differences:

> Adherence to Buddhism (or Bon) is generally regarded as being an integral element of Tibetan identity, although an exception is made for the Muslim minority. (The rather touching cliché that is commonly cited, apparently as a formula of acceptance, is that the Muslims "speak the best Tibetan," as if this linguistic excellence were satisfactory compensation for a religious deficiency.)[53]

The formulation of the Khache as Tibetan because they "speak the best Tibetan" remains strong today, even among the Tibetan exile community. In 2014, while visiting Los Angeles, the Fourteenth Dalai Lama mildly rebuked a largely Tibetan audience for not teaching their children to speak Tibetan, noting, "When I recently visited [exiled] Tibetan Muslims in Srinagar, I discovered their young children speak excellent Tibetan with a Lhasa accent. This is not the result of any instruction they receive at school, but of their parents' and grandparents' training."[54] His praise of the Khaches' linguistic ability was not simply another manifestation of the Fourteenth Dalai Lama's broad ecumenism but rather a subtle wink to the well-established maxim among Tibetans that Tibetan Muslims have elegant fluency. Emily Yeh similarly suggests that "given the great difficulty many young Tibetans in Lhasa today have speaking Tibetan without code-switching with Mandarin, the Barkor Khache . . . are admired for their ability to speak pure Tibetan."[55]

## FROM KASHMIRI TO KHACHE

By the sixteenth century, the Kashmiris were an already established presence in the Himalayan range. From Kashmir along the Himalayan front range to Nepal, Bhutan, and Sikkim in the east, Kashmiri merchant communities dominated trading. A prominent presence in virtually every large Himalayan trading entrepôt, the Kashmiri formed the backbone of trans-Himalayan trade. George Bogle, in describing Himalayan trade networks, referred to the Kashmiri as being "like the Jews in Europe, or the Armenians in the Turkish Empire, scatter[ing] themselves over the eastern kingdoms of Asia, and carry[ing] on an extensive traffic between the distant parts of it, hav[ing] formed establishments at Lhasa and all the principal towns in this country."[56]

While it is tempting to believe the Kashmiri traveled by the shortest route between Kashmir and Lhasa, the majority of the Kashmiris almost certainly traveled to Tibet from the key trading centers to the south via Kathmandu, Patna, and even Kolkata.[57] In the minds of the trans-Himalayan peoples and cultures, the term "Kashmiri" had an ethnoreligious rather than geographic or political association. That is to say, it is almost certain that the first Kashmiris were not explicitly Kashmiri from Kashmir but rather from Kashmiri communities outside of Kashmir and across the subcontinent.

Like many immigrant communities, it is difficult to determine the precise moment when the Kashmiri became Tibetan subjects. It appears most likely that the evolution occurred over a period of several decades in the late fifteenth century, and that evolution remains discernible in the multivalent nature of the term. For the past several centuries, the Tibetan term "Khache" has three broad connotations: it is a geographic marker, it is religious designation, or a specific term to denote a Tibetan Muslim. The meaning of "Khache" followed a terminological evolution that paralleled Tibet's own chronological interactions with Kashmir and with Islam.[58] In its earliest formulation, the Tibetan word *Khache* referred narrowly to the Himalayan region of Kashmir or to the Kashmiri people.[59] The second stage began several decades after the first permanent Kashmiri settlement with the arrival of Muslim immigrants from China who were also referred to as Khache. With this arrival of the Chinese Muslims, the dual meaning Kashmiri Muslim and Khache was quickly decoupled, and the term "Khache" evolved to mean all Muslims. The third stage occurred when the Khache communities settled, intermarried, and became Tibetan Muslims. In this final evolution, the term "Khache" came to refer to Tibetans rather than a foreign place or foreign religion. Tibetans have demonstrated little or no consternation over the multiple meanings of "Khache." As is common with ambiguous terminology, Tibetans had an array of terms that allowed one to distinguish between residential Tibetan Muslims and those transient Muslims from neighboring regions.

From the seventeenth century to 1959, the primary internal division among Tibetan Muslims fell along a South Asian–Chinese divide. The cultural, commercial, and linguistic specializations reflected each group's distinct geographic orientation. Since Muslims from South, Central, and East Asia all intermingled in the main cities of central Tibet, it was when Tibetan Muslims were spoken of in Tibetan that geographic prefixes were often affixed to indicate the communities' external orientation, place of residency, or ancestry (e.g., Chinese Khache [Tib. *rgya kha che*] or Ladakhi Khache [Tib. *la dwags kha che*]).[60] As explained in further detail below, these suffixes typically indicated the ancestral ties or cultural orientation, not that they were Chinese Muslim Hui or Ladakhi Muslims.

### Barkor and Wapaling Khache

Within Lhasa, the Khache community was divided into two main communities along linguistic and cultural lines, those of South Asian heritage and those of Chinese heritage.[61] This terminology eventually achieved even finer delineation within Lhasa and allowed for considerable specificity, referring to the neighborhoods in which they settled and built their mosques: the Barkor or the Wapaling.[62] By adding these modifiers the two communities were immediately distinguished from the other Khaches (or Kashmiri). The Barkor (South Asian) Khache, predominantly involved in commerce, clustered around the central Barkor market area near the Jokhang Temple.[63] The Wapaling (Chinese) Khache lived along Lhasa's Wapaling neighborhood in the southeastern corner of Lhasa, near the Lhasa River and closer to their fields and the areas in which they were allowed to butcher animals.[64] Tsarong Yangchen Dolkar, in her memoirs, described the Wapaling Khache community as primarily made up of vegetable sellers and butchers but having a good reputation as selling the best quality and widest variety.[65]

The striking aspect of this heterogeneity of Lhasa's two main groups was how rarely it was remarked on by outsiders. Even Xue Wenbo, a Muslim Chinese intellectual who arrived in Tibet in 1951, noted his initial confusion in attempting to differentiate between the Barkor and the Wapaling Khache:

> Just after arriving in Lhasa, I saw many Muslims on the streets, but I could not distinguish which were Wapaling Khache (Ch. *Huizu*) and which were Barkor Khache (Ch. *ka-shi-mi-er ren*). This was especially true with women who I could not even differentiate from Tibetan women. After sometime, when I concentrated, I began to see differences in their appearance and complexion, and also that some aspects of their manner of dress were different.[66]

If outsiders found it hard to grapple with the internal differences between the Wapaling and Barkor Khache, most struggled to come to grips with the other Khache communities that also flourished in Lhasa and many other central Tibetan towns.

### *Ladakhi Khache*

Of all the Tibetan Muslim communities, the Ladakhi Khache tended to be the most frequently conflated with the local Tibetan Muslims. Although the Ladakhi certainly were prominent traders and had strong ties with the central Tibetan government, by the 1920s it appears that aside from the subsidized triennial Lapchak (Tib. *lo phyag*) relatively little trade traveled directly between Lhasa and Ladakh. Central Tibetan trade, as British India flourished, oriented itself to the geographically closer and more lucrative India market.[67] As Janet Rizvi pointed out in her study of Ladakhi trade, Ladakh was "at best a staging-post between the Punjab and Sinkiang, and Leh an entrepôt for the exchange of goods produced and consumed hundreds of miles away."[68] The Ladakhi did retain an official representative in Lhasa, referred to as a consul in many Anglophone sources. In the eyes of the Tibetan government, those who retained their Ladakhi status were not considered Tibetan and were exempt from some taxes and obligations.[69] Twentieth-century sources suggest that the community was dwindling in size and influence from several dozen households in the early twentieth century to only a fraction of that by the early 1950s.[70]

### *Singpa Khache*

The Singpa Khache (Tib. *sing pa*; Ch. *senba*) have long existed as an identifiable subgroup of the Barkor Khache, but their name has caused considerable confusion in English, Chinese, and Tibetan.[71] Often misidentified as "Sikh," the Singpa Khache trace their origins to Muslim soldiers led by Zorawar Singh, who fought for the upstart Dogra state in the Kashmiri-Ladakhi-Jammu region. Having conquered Ladakh, the Dogra ruler in 1841 dispatched Singh to gain control over the trans-Himalayan region by invading Nepal through western Tibet. In an audacious assault, Zorawar Singh led his forces across western Tibet, running up a string of victories and controlling a broad swath of territory from Kashmir up to the Nepalese border near Mount Kailash. But with his supply lines stretched and his campaign being overtaken by winter storms, Zorawar Singh suddenly found himself on the defensive. In a stunning reversal of fortune, Tibetan forces attacked Zorawar Singh's much larger force in early December 1841, routed the Dogra army, killed the legendary general, and captured nearly a thousand soldiers in the process (all without the support or even tacit approval of Chinese forces).[72]

Unsure at first of what to do with such a large number of prisoners, the decision was made by the Tibetan authorities that since "it was not convenient to execute [the captured soldiers], it would be better to show mercy . . . and disperse them to various towns across Tibet."[73] Their continued presence is confirmed some years later, in the 1856 Nepal Tibet Treaty, where the Nepalese demanded that "the Tibetans are also to give back . . . [t]he [Singpa] prisoners of war who had been captured in 1841 in the war between Bhot [Tibet] and the Dogra ruler."[74] Exactly how many prisoners returned (or were returned) is unclear, though the Singpa Khache remained a prominent presence within the Khache community, by one estimate making up as much as 20 percent of the nearly two hundred Barkor Khache families living in Lhasa in the early 1950s.[75]

### Siling Khache

While the Barkor Khache likely settled in Lhasa prior to the arrival of their Wapaling counterparts, the Wapaling Khache grew demographically to be roughly as numerous as the Barkor Khache and served as key intermediaries for the Chinese officials serving in Lhasa. As the Qing brought Tibet increasingly into the Qing sphere of influence, Han and Hui Chinese, often first serving as soldiers or civil officials, settled in Lhasa, with the Hui typically marrying Wapaling Khache or Tibetan Buddhist women who converted. The primary exceptions to this were the Siling Khache, who were Tibetanized Hui from Qinghai, tracing their origins to the Amdo city of Siling (Tib. *zi ling*; Ch. *Xining*) in Qinghai province. They also tended to remain identifiable within the Lhasa Muslim communities. The Siling Khache aligned generally with the Wapaling Khache, but there were differences that allowed them to retain a separate identity from the other Wapaling Khache. By the twentieth century the Siling were a highly differentiated and identifiable group within the Wapaling Khache.[76]

### Gharib Khache

In addition to the above divisions, largely associated with a group's origin, a third group called "ghārib" (paupers) appears to have existed only in Lhasa.[77] The nineteenth-century account of Khwajah Gulam Muhammad describes a Muslim pauper's guild, composed exclusively of Khache, that paralleled (or perhaps was a subset) of the Ragyapa (Tib. *rags rgyab pa*).[78] The Ragyapa are a Tibetan hereditary class who carried out acts considered unclean or undesirable by Tibetans, such as disposing of corpses and animal remains, and they also served other functions like the guarding and execution of prisoners. Given the difficulty most non-Tibetans had differentiating between Khache and Kashmiri, it is not surprising that few non-Tibetan sources suggest the presence of the Khache Ragyapa.[79] For this reason Khwajah Gulam Muhammad's description from the late nineteenth century is invaluable, as it details a highly organized association having its own leaders and police. It is significant that he suggests they were recognized by the Tibetan government and even received a monthly stipend.

> The fifteenth of each month, a group of twelve to twenty or twenty-five gharīb present themselves at the Potala Palace, and with all their force howl and shout, and then receive each month eighteen tanka, that is to say the equivalent of twenty mohors [gold coins]. This is a stipend that they have received since ancient times.[80]

More recently, Tsarong Yangchen Dolkar has recounted that one of Lhasa's most famous beggers was a man call "Khache Powo" who used to beg by singing the lines, "happier than us is not even the gods of heaven."[81] The most recent indication of Ghārib Khache comes from Gaborieau, who while interviewing Tibetan Muslim refugees to India in 1961 confirmed the existence of such a class of Muslims and was told that a dozen or so of those families had fled from Tibet to India.[82]

The occupational definition of Ghārib Khache—butchers, waste collectors, and, in general, a surveillance force—was not unique among the Khache. While rarely as strongly enforced in the manner of the hereditary tasks assigned to the Ghārib Khache, each of the Khache groups tended to be defined, if only by reputation, by specific professions. The occupational orientation shaped where the various Khache communities congregated within Lhasa.

The numerous subgroups within the Khache community suggest that the Khache presence was not transient, ephemeral, or brief but that they were an integral and active element of Lhasa and Tibetan society. This historical commentary demonstrates that Tibetans across central Tibet were aware of the distinctions among the Khache and perceived them as being Tibetan. This awareness arose in part as a result of the Khache community's presence in commercial, social, and political fields pivotal to the functioning of Tibetan society. A clear definition of who the Khache are is inherently tied to a clear understanding of what it means to be Tibetan or even what we mean when we talk of Tibet.

## THE KHACHE: SEPARATE BUT TIBETAN

Early twentieth-century estimates consistently identify several thousand Khache across all central Tibetan communities. In 1934, a Chinese Muslim, Zhu Xiu, estimated that the Khache numbered roughly 800 households in a total Lhasa population of 6,500 lay households.[83] By the 1940s, several Chinese articles on the Tibetan Muslim community, reported that the Hui, originally from Shaanxi,

Sichuan, and Yunnan, "represent two-thirds of the Muslim (Ch. *Huimin*) community, while the Indian and Tibetan Muslims (Ch. *Huimin*) represent one-third."[84] In an article written a year later, a Muslim Chinese estimated that the Chinese Muslims "have 120 or so households," while the Barkor Khache, or as he called them the "Indian Hui" (Ch. *yindu Huimin*), "have 70 or so households."[85] In 1934, the Chinese envoy to Lhasa, Huang Musong, estimated the Lhasa population of "Han [Chinese] and Muslim [Chinese]" (Ch. *Han Hui renmin*) at 300 or 400 households. Almost certainly he was talking of the Wapaling Khache and the mixed Tibetan-Chinese population (Tib. *ko ko*).[86]

By the 1950s, more authoritative and precise population figures began to emerge. When a Beijing Chinese Muslim, Xue Wenbo, entered Lhasa with the People's Liberation Army in December 1951, he concluded that "the Lhasa Hui (Ch. *Huizu*) have 150 households, with a population of several thousand people."[87] His approximation accords with official estimates from 1953 that state the Khache (Ch. *kaji*) had 141 households.[88] This suggests that the number of Muslims in Lhasa by the mid-nineteenth century exceeded 3,000 individuals.[89] The population of smaller communities in Shigatse, Tsetang, and other small towns across central Tibet outside of Lhasa approached but did not surpass that of Lhasa proper (though in total these other communities likely did not surpass Lhasa's entire Muslim population).[90]

Perhaps the only single moment in time when we are able to confirm this estimate of roughly 3,000 Muslims living in central Tibet with a high degree of precision is in 1960 during the Tibetan Muslim Incident, examined in detail in chapter 5.[91] In that incident Chinese and Indian officials identified and allowed nearly 1,500 Barkor Khaches—men, women, and children—to leave China and enter India by virtue of their "Kashmiri" identity.[92] Several dozen others were allowed to leave for Nepal largely because of marriage to a Nepalese (or half Nepalese Khatsara). The Wapaling Khache, who remained behind, numbered more than 1,000 .[93]

All later estimates are hopelessly confused with the influx of Hui from the Chinese interior (including the northwestern provinces of Gansu) and the shifts in terminology brought about by China's ethnic classification project (Ch. *minzu shibie*). This resulted in Chinese making little differentiation between the Wapaling Khache and the in-migrating Muslim Chinese Hui. The matter was further confused by the arrival of large numbers of Muslim Chinese Hui. Due in part to this influx, the Wapaling Khache moved to the Small Mosque in the Barkor, relinquishing the Grand Mosque to the Chinese Hui.[94] According to the 1982 Chinese census for Tibet, Lhasa had 1,367 Muslim Chinese (Huizu), and given the strict residency limitations between 1960 and 1982, these were overwhelmingly the Wapaling Khache who were not allowed to emigrate to India. The 2000 census suggests that number had grown only to 1,741. This low number hints at the possibility that the Wapaling Khache might have registered themselves as

Tibetan rather than Hui in reaction to the influx of Han and Hui Chinese and the negative light in which such immigrants were perceived in Lhasa.[95]

If the presence of a substantial Tibetan Muslim community is incontrovertible, the ways in which that community integrated itself in mainstream Tibetan society also demonstrates how deeply acculturated and accepted the Khache were. It is instructive to draw attention to just how different they were from other foreign communities present in central Tibet. In the eighteenth and nineteenth centuries, representatives from four foreign states were granted official status by the Tibetan government and posted to Lhasa: Nepal, Ladakh, Bhutan, and China. The Chinese Qing court appointed Ambans, or Imperial Residents, in Tibet (Ch. *zhu zang dachen*).[96] The Nepalese were accorded the right by treaty to have an envoy (N. *bhardar*) stationed in Lhasa who was authorized to settle disputes involving Nepalese citizens.[97] The Bhutanese and Ladakhis had posted representatives in Lhasa from at least the early eighteenth century. Despite Qing China's insinuations to the contrary, neither sent tribute missions to the Qing court.[98] With the fall of the Qing Empire in 1911, the status of the Nepali, Ladakhi, and Bhutanese envoys remained unaltered. However, the representation of China's central government to Lhasa remained a mixed and highly contentious issue well into the 1940s, reflecting the political unrest within China proper.[99]

The only additional state accorded the right to post foreign envoys to Lhasa was Britain, which beginning in the first decades of the twentieth century and with a high degree of regularity dispatched delegations there. In 1936, Britain's informal relationship took on a more permanent status in response to the Nationalist Chinese sending a "condolence mission" to Lhasa after the death of the Thirteenth Dalai Lama. Instead of returning to China, this mission not only remained in Lhasa and installed Lhasa's first wireless radio transmitter, but then attempted to establish an official presence. Whether this office was a consulate or an office of the central government remained a point of contention. In response, the British swiftly sent their own delegation in 1936, establishing a permanent but technically unofficial mission under the leadership of Hugh Richardson, who became the first head of the British Mission in Lhasa.[100]

My emphasis on the presence of the foreign representatives in Tibet is to highlight the difference between these foreign envoys and the Khache leadership which was often erroneously grouped together with these foreign emissaries. The presence of Khache leaders did not escape the notice of foreign observers. Often erroneously believing the Khache were themselves foreign (and thus providing an accurate model of what rights and privileges the foreign visitors might be also accorded) often described with great accuracy the nature and powers of the Khache leadership. In 1845, the French Jesuit priest Evariste Huc remarked that the Khache "in Lhasa . . . [the Khache] have a chief who oversees their immediate needs, and whose authority is recognized by the Tibetan Government."[101] An early nineteenth-century Chinese gazetteer noted that the Wapaling (Ch. *chantou*)

Khache were governed by a council composed of four people: "three community leaders" (Ch. *datou ren*) representing those Khaches from in and around Lhasa (Ch. *qianzang*) and a "single community leader" (Ch. *datou ren*) for those Muslims in and around Shigatse.[102] The Barkor Khache had a single community leader (*datou ren*).[103]

A century later, George Sandberg explained correctly that the Khache "governor, who is chosen by the Tibetan Gye-po from among the [Khache] residents of Lhasa, decides all disputes between his own countrymen," but then he, incorrectly, attempted to suggest this is the same as "the Nepalese governor [who] exercises the same powers over the Nepalese inhabitants."[104] In 1916, Charles Bell also noted that "the Kashmiris at Lhasa are under the jurisdiction of their own headmen, these being appointed by the Tibetan Government."[105] Gaborieau, in his summary of the Khache *pöpo*, or community leaders (Tib. *dpon po*), summarizes the status precisely: "In effect, the kha-che 'go-pa was not a consul: he was not responsible to any foreign government, but rather to the za'idah [Tibetan-born Khaches] who constituted the majority of [Khaches] in Tibet, and retained ties neither to Kashmir, nor to any other region of India."[106] The significance of differentiating the status of the Khache headmen from the foreign consuls might appear minor, but it highlights an important distinction. The Khache headmen functioned as administrators entirely within the framework of the Tibetan bureaucracy. Instead of being seen as representatives of foreign missions from neighboring states, they served as representatives of community associations formally recognized by the Tibetan government and served at the behest of the Tibetan state at the lowest level of government.

Rebecca French describes, insightfully and more broadly, both the function and the force that such community associations wielded within Lhasa and central Tibet:

> Perhaps the most important interstitial and interconnecting networks of individuals in Tibet were the associations, *kyiduk dang tsokpa* (*skyid sdug dang tshogs pa*). As the fourth level [of the Tibetan bureaucracy], they constituted bounded social units that played an essential role in solving the disputes of their members and acted on behalf of their members in disputes with outsiders. Associations could be based on ethnic, religious, occupational or social similarities or formed around mutual-aid and special-purpose commonalities.[107]

Whether out of ignorance or unacknowledged bias, European accounts repeatedly grouped the Khache leadership with other foreign representatives.[108] Regardless, the administrative structure of the Lhasa municipal associations demonstrates a responsive and nuanced awareness of the complex subgroups within the Khache community and how they functioned within the central government.

Despite sharing many commonalities, often praying at the same mosque and frequently inter-marrying, the Khache were distinguished legally, culturally and socially by the Tibetan state. The distinct division between the communities is most apparent in the Tibetan government's treatment of them as separate communities, governed by discrete councils who reported to different ministries within the government. Each of the five Khache communities, including the Gharīb and Singpa, had their own separate headmen (Tib. *mgo pa*)."[109] In the case of the Barkor Tibetan Muslims, their self-selected leader reported to the Finance Ministry (Tib. *rtsis khang*) since they were engaged primarily in trade and commerce.[110] The Wapaling Tibetan Muslims' leader (Tib. *wapaling ponpo*) reported directly to the Agriculture Ministry (Tib. *so nam las khungs*).[111] While it is often assumed that the Wapaling Khache were assigned to the Agriculture Ministry because they were agriculturalists, Könchok Samden, an official in the Tibetan government, ascribed this to the fact that "people who came from other places such as from Kham, Amdo or from central Tibet and who did not thane a specific lord, in other words, who were people just roaming around, they all belonged to the Agriculture Office so it collected the *mibo* [Tib. *mi bogs,* "head tax"] from them. . . . [A]nd they also had a *gembo* [headman; Tib. *rgan po*] who was also appointed by the Agriculture Office itself."[112] Tibetan archival documents from 1938 describe the Barkor Khache committee as constituted of a leader, a primary assistant, a secondary assistant, and two members. Sometimes, though, there was an alternative description, specifying joint leadership by the Barkor and the Singpa *pönpo* plus three assistants.[113]

The precise powers and legal authority of the councils tended to be directed inward to the members of their own community. Abū Bakr Amīruddīn Tibbatī Nadvī's study of Tibetan Muslims described the powers of this five-member committee as "adjudicat[ing] all issues pertaining to Muslims, and the Tibetan government never interfered with its functions."[114] Khwajah Ghulam Muhammad describes the nature and powers such councils had during his visit in 1895:

> The verdict, in the majority of cases, is pronounced conforming to the injunctions of Islamic law. Though the sanctions for adultery and theft is neither stoning nor the amputation of the hand [as traditionally dictated by Islamic law], but other punishments are given. If the dispute is between a Muslim and a Tibetan, the case is heard by a mixed tribunal [of Khache and Tibetans].[115]

Even when a Muslim was found to be involved in theft or in a quarrel among Khaches, he was invariably handed over to this committee.[116]

Mirroring the Barkor Khache *pönpo*, the Wapaling also had a selected leader who served as the administrative head for their community. Perhaps because their community was not as diverse as the Barkor Khache, the Wapaling council had a more streamlined multimember committee. Both committees reported, paid their taxes, and confirmed the election of their head to the administrative ministries that were responsible for them.

The dilemma of trying to speak monolithically of "Tibetan Muslims" lies largely in the geographic positioning of Tibet. Almost all of the Tibetan Muslim communities that thrived within Tibet originally emigrated from non-Tibetan lands, most often as traders. As a result, unlike the Ladakhi, the Nepalese, and even the Chinese, the Khache considered themselves, and were treated as, fully Tibetan within decades after their arrival in central Tibet. In certain circles, many today seek to position the Muslim Tibetans as vital indicators of Tibet's internal and external relations. The Fourteenth Dalai Lama, for example, often cites the centuries-long cordial relationship between Tibetan Buddhists and Tibetan Muslims as a model for interreligious understanding.[117] Conversely, an emerging number of scholars are suggesting that the friction between "Tibetans and Muslims," said to have existed for centuries, is rarely historically accurate. More appropriate would be to note that the interethnic violence occurred in very specific periods of time and geographically delimited places, namely, in the eastern Tibetan Amdo region and during the violent warlord period.[118] Yet as the world began to increasingly encroach on Tibet's autonomy, it would challenge the multiple identities that the outside world read into the Tibetan Muslim communities.

3

# How Half-Tibetans Made Tibet Whole

On October 6, 1942, a brawl between two half Tibetans—one a half Nepalese (Tib. *kha tsa ra*) and the other a half Chinese (Tib. *ko ko*)—broke out in the center of Lhasa.[1] As it was later described by the British assistant political officer in Lhasa:

> A half-breed Chinaman and a half-breed Nepali started a quarrel outside the Cathedral [Jokhang]. The koko picked up a stone and hit the Nepali half-breed over the head. Four Tibetan constables now intervened. The koko flew, hotly pursued by the constables and sought refuge in the Chinese Mission. The constables followed, intending to arrest the koko, but were themselves arrested by Dr. Kong.[2]

Insisting the Koko merited the representation of the Chinese government, Dr. Kong Qingzong refused to release him to Tibetan officials and held the four Tibetan policemen for nearly five months.[3] It was only when the Tibetan government withdrew all of the government's assistance (including a translator and essential supplies for the Chinese Mission) and demanded that Kong be cashiered that the Chinese home government intervened and ordered Dr. Kong to release the policemen.

On the surface, this might appear a simple case of an overzealous foreign representative intervening to protect the rights of their citizens or China's representative in Tibet attempting to prevent Tibet from acting independently of the Chinese central government. Yet neither would be an accurate interpretation of the situation. By 1942, China had, for three decades, ceased to have oversight of Tibetan affairs. Tibet's laws were unequivocal on the matter. With few exceptions, those born in Tibet to a Tibetan mother were categorically treated as Tibetan subjects.

As far as the Chinese were concerned, however, China's control over Tibet could be demonstrated historically. This reasoning, then as today, was selectively applied

34

to regions formerly controlled by China that had slipped out of China's political control in the early twentieth century. Casually ignoring the geopolitical realities, the Nationalist government perpetuated the notion that "China" included Tibet by a tenuous reading of the past. Insisting that since both Tibet and China came under Mongolian rule in the thirteenth century, it argued that Tibet should be considered Chinese from that point forward. Such explications, while perhaps superficially plausible, crumble under more careful scrutiny. As the historian Warren W. Smith has written in his work on Tibet's relationship to China, after the fall of the Mongols in the late fourteenth century China "had no real interest in Tibet beyond Tibet's role in Ming relations with the Mongols." For the Tibetans, "Tibet's continuing relations with the Mongols were much more politically significant than Tibetan relations with the Ming."[4]

It was only three hundred years later, with the rise of the Qing, that China's more direct relationship with Tibet began under the Qing dynasty. But even then, its political oversight remained tenuous. As the Tibet scholar Fabienne Jagou provocatively contends, if one is speaking of Tibet as being part of China in the stricter sense of China having territorial control over Tibet, "it was only with the end of the 19th century that all three Tibetan provinces became a 'buffer zone' of overlapping international interests and a focal point of Inner China and the maintenance of the Qing Empire."[5] However, the end of the nineteenth century was precisely the period when the Qing central government was at its weakest, undermining the argument that there was an unending line of direct Chinese control.

By the twentieth century, though many of Tibet's distant neighbors schemed about ways to bring Tibet under their sphere of control, most treated Tibet as Metternich once famously described Italy, as merely a "geographical expression."[6] No two of Tibet's neighbors agreed on its political status, geographic delimitation, or international standing. Just as China insisted that Tibet remained part of China, the British perceived Tibet as it did many of the principalities in India, namely, professing the presence of native governance but appointing a British adviser to influence policy and deter others from doing the same. Both the Chinese and the British flattered themselves that Tibet remained in their sphere of influence while ignoring the mounting evidence of Tibet's independence.

Jagou's and Smith's comments reflect the scholarly predisposition to defend Tibet's independence primarily by examining its actions. Few studies have reversed the lens to question China's political fragmentation during this same period. Between the fall of the Qing in 1911 and the establishment of the People's Republic of China in 1949, China proper (typically defined as China's internal eighteen provinces) experienced multiple "central" governments, a nonstop succession of warlords, Japanese occupation, and a full-on civil war. One cannot identify any period from 1911 to 1950 when the Chinese central government could be described as exerting steady political, economic, or military control over the entirety of what today is understood as China. By comparison to China, Tibet appears the model of political stability, establishing its de facto independence over the course of four decades. If one can accuse Tibet of anything, it is that, as Melvyn Goldstein has stated, Tibet was "poorly prepared to defend its contested status."[7]

Given the considerable debate over Tibet's political status, it is surprising that so little attention has been paid to its relations with its Himalayan neighbors and their activities in central Tibet. Tibet's concern with regional, ethnic and occupational identity stems not from a misplaced elitism or ethnocentrism, rather it arises out of a long history of ethnic and religious tolerance of and interaction with its neighbors. According to traditional Tibetan historical accounts, Tibet's first ruler, King Songtsen Gampo (ca. 617–47), married both a Chinese and a Nepalese princess.[8] The elevated stature of the two princesses in Tibet's representation of its past can be measured in part by the fact that among their many accomplishments they are credited with bringing Buddhism to Tibet and founding two of Lhasa's most sacred sites, the Jokhang and Ramoche Buddhist Temples.

Although this idealized framing of the past illustrates Tibet's positive relations with its neighbors, it is with the fall of the Qing dynasty in 1911 that the Thirteenth Dalai Lama and many Tibetan elites began to recognize the need to clarify precisely who they were claiming as their subjects within the emerging modern definitions of statehood. In this reformulation, the memory of the two princesses continued to play a crucial role in their representation of their past. In 1923, the Tibetan regent, in a letter to the Nepalese government attempting to resolve a tense issue, sought to strike a conciliatory note by opening the correspondence by invoking the marriage between the Tibetan king and the Nepalese princess as evidence that "ever since, the two states treated each other as the members of one house" and that relations between Nepal and Tibet were thus the same as "the relations between two brothers."[9]

The relationship with China was presented quite differently. From a religio-spirtual perspective, in the priest-patron relationship between the Qing and Tibet during the seventeenth through nineteenth centuries, the Dalai Lama had been superior to the emperor, as this was the dominant perspective in the Tibetan theocracy. From a political point of view, the wobbly Chinese Republic that replaced the Qing had even less ability to enforce its will on Tibet.

With the establishment of the Republic of China in 1912, the Thirteenth Dalai Lama took formalized steps to demonstrate Tibet's status as an independent state, including standardizing the Tibetan flag, issuing postage stamps, and printing Tibet's first paper currency.[10] Despite the unrelenting rhetoric emanating from China, it is difficult to identify any official Chinese presence in Tibet. As discussed more fully in the next chapter, many scholars (largely historians of China) have taken the lack of Tibetan declarations of independence during this time as hard and fast evidence that Tibet remained part of China. Here I persue a highly visible on-the-ground perspective that demonstrates how Tibet perceived and protected those it treated as Tibetans subject to Tibetan governance. Such a shift in perspective also allows us to better understand precisely how the Khache community negotiated their positioning within this complex Himalayan context always retaining and emphasizing their status as Tibetan subjects.

The adoption of a more Tibetan-centric frame of reference, one that fully emphasizes the importance of the Himalayan context, is crucial to appreciating the many steps Tibet took to act as an independent state. The traditional framework in which the Tibetan government regulated foreigners, Tibetans, and half Tibetans—particularly in relation to their Himalayan neighbors—bears witness to its perception of itself as an independent state grappling with modern conceptualizations of citizenship, race, and statecraft. The efforts of Tibet in support of its independence certainly demonstrate that descriptions of it as a "fourth world state" mired in "statelessness" with "non-state actors" are exaggerated.[11] The specific cases also establish that many of the key examples used by those arguing for Chinese control—particularly the role of Liu Manqing, Huang Musong, Kong Qingzong, and Shen Zonglian—upon closer examination show how tenuous China's presence was in Lhasa. Rather what we find is a Tibetan government and society confident of their sovereignty and knowing precisely who fell under its rule.

At the heart of almost every challenge to Tibet's de facto independence were the communities that had existed as an integral part of Lhasa life for several centuries: the half-Nepalese (Khatsara), the half-Chinese (Koko), and the Khache.[12] The status of mixed-parentage offspring had concerned Tibetans and the Tibetan government long before issues of nationality and citizenship began to shape global relations, particularly in the post–Versailles Treaty and later postcolonial periods. By the early twentieth century, the Tibetan government had unambiguous definitions of who was and who was not Tibetan for the purposes of taxes, trade, and political rights.

The Khatsara and the Koko were two of most recognized and demographically significant groups within central Tibet. The Khatsara (Tib. *Kha tsa ra*; Newari, *Khacarā*; N. *khaccar*)[13] were children of mixed Nepali-Tibetan parentage, and the Kokos were children of Chinese-Tibetan parentage. The origins of both terms suggest an uncharitable view belied by the cordial acceptance and seamless integration of these individuals into Tibetan culture. "Khatsara" originates from a Nepali word for "mule," the infertile offspring of a donkey and a horse.[14] Most Tibetans remain unaware of the derogatory roots of this term, hinting at a more sustained Nepalese disdain for such mixed children than an innate negative opinion of the Khatsara by the Tibetans. The term for half-Chinese Tibetans, Koko, is derived from "Koko Yak" (Tib. *ko ko yak*), the offspring of a yak and a dzo (Tib. *mdzo*), a cross between yaks and domestic cattle.[15] The term's derivation emphasizes the commonly accepted notion of cross-breeding among Tibetans as a natural occurrence rather than the negative implication that the terms "mongrel" or "half-breed" inherently retain.

Nepalese picnic outside of Lhasa, 1921. Picnics were a common summertime activity of all groups in Lhasa. Note the diversity of the individuals in the photo, ranging from the clearly Newari hosts sitting at the table next to the phonograph but also the Chinese, Tibetan, and Khatsara individuals who were guests participating in the festivities. Copyright Pitt Rivers Museum, University of Oxford.

The populations of these mixed communities in Lhasa were estimated by the early twentieth century to be well over 1,000 individuals—a sizable presence in a city that was by most estimates no larger than 25,000 to 30,000 people in the first half of the twentieth century. Similar to the Khache communities, the Khatsaras and Kokos, while not limited to living in Lhasa, were largely concentrated in central Tibet's urban centers, thus amplifying their role in central Tibetan life.[16]

## THE POLITICS OF MIXED PARENTAGE IN TIBET

For centuries, Lhasa attracted foreigners who, as merchants, soldiers, or laborer, found themselves in Tibet for extended but finite periods of time. Given the transient nature of their postings to Tibet, these foreign communities were unique in ways that altered the manner in which they were treated, understood, and distinguished by most Tibetans. Lhasa's foreign communities varied in significant ways from the diasporic communities found across Asia. Unlike overseas Indian and Chinese communities, very few foreigners permanently settled in Lhasa.

The foreign sojourners, mostly from Nepal and China but also Kashmir, Bhutan, and Sikkim, tended to be overwhelmingly transient, young, and male.[17] Combined with central Tibet's gender imbalance due to the large number of males joining monasteries, many of these foreign men formed relationships, and in some cases established households, with Tibetan women. It was the children of these mixed unions who emerged as clearly identifiable cores of the foreign communities in the central Tibetan cities of Lhasa, Shigatse, and Gyantse and to a lesser extent in the eastern Tibetan cities of Dartsedo (Ch. *Kangding*) and Siling (Ch. *Xining*). As a result, while foreign observers, particularly in the twentieth century, viewed them as non-Tibetan, the Khatsara, Koko, and Khache were uniformly perceived as Tibetan by Tibetans.

Out of this ethnic and cultural mix, a consistently used nomenclature emerged for the offspring of mixed parentage: Tibetan Muslim (Khache), half-Nepalese (Khatsara), half-Chinese (Koko). Like the Khache, the Khatsara and the Koko played a prominent role in Lhasa society. Confusion arose as outsiders consistently conflated the "mixed parentage" term to mean non-Tibetan. Yet with the majority of these half-Tibetans being raised by Tibetan mothers, the mixed offspring retained strong cultural and, as we will see, legal ties to Tibet. In this way, and on a daily basis within Tibetan society, the Khatsara, Koko, and Khache tended to be treated not as outsiders but as identifiable Tibetan subgroups.

Of the three communities, only the Khatsara retained vestigial legal rights of citizenship as a result of their foreign mixed parentage.[18] This legal status, sharply delineated in ways quite different from the Koko and the Khache, arose largely from the fact that of all Tibet's neighbors none remained so consistently engaged and demographically present in Tibetan society as the Nepalese. Nepalese merchants were semipermanent residents, often taking Tibetan wives, as early as the seventeenth century.[19] The growing number of incidents over the Khatsaras' rights emerged as a point of conflict by the mid-nineteenth century, leading to the Nepalese inserting a clause in the Treaty of Thapathali of 1856. In a treaty with only ten articles, three deal directly with Nepalese subjects in Tibet. Specifically, Nepal gained the right to post an envoy (N. *bhardar* or *vakil*) in Lhasa who was given legal oversight over all Nepalese residents in Tibet, including half Nepalese and "Nepalese Khache" (N. *Nepal ka Kashmiri*).[20] The emphasis on granting male Khatsaras legal protection in Tibet reflected an acknowledgment by the Nepalese community that such children had virtually no legal standing back in Nepal.

At the same time, Nepalese traders relied on their half-Tibetan offspring to help them maintain a commercial presence in Tibet during their extended absences. While the Nepalese may have held children of these mixed marriages in contempt, they relied enough on the Khatsaras' role as guardians of lucrative Nepalese business interests to jealously guard their legal status within Tibet. It is significant that the term "Khatsara," while highly derogatory in Nepalese, retains little of those pejorative overtones in Tibetan. From the nineteenth century on, these conflicting perceptions of the Khatsara caused the Khatsara population to remain a primary cause of tension between Tibet and Nepal.

With the departure of the Chinese in 1912, the Nepalese, and consequently the Khatsara, became the most dominant foreign presence in Lhasa, and they increasingly leveraged their privileged position to their economic benefit. Such economic activity resulted in the Khatsara becoming an increasingly vilified group by their Tibetan business rivals. After 1912, Tibetans accused the Khatsara of minor but persistent acts of fraud and theft. These offenses were often undertaken with the open protection of the Nepalese consul. The growing bias against the Khatsara often boiled over during the Great Prayer Festival (Tib. *smon lam chen mo*).

The Great Prayer Festival was one of Lhasa's prominent celebrations. Tibetans from across the region flocked to the city. Monks flowed into Lhasa from the surrounding monasteries. The population of the city doubled, and according to tradition monks took administrative control of the city for the duration of the festival. The monk officials, who were notoriously stringent in punishing any infraction, accused Khatsaras on numerous occasions of refusing payment on goods or, alternately, of demanding that goods be sold to them at extortionately low prices. When confronted with their crimes, Khatsaras would inevitably maintain their innocence and seek protection from the Nepalese consul, which only further inflamed the large crowds. In numerous instances the public outcry spiraled into violence, with rioting and the frequent destruction of Nepalese shops.[21]

The popular disdain of the Khatsara did not arise out of ethnic bias, religious prejudice, or Tibetan nationalism. Accounts from early twentieth-century Tibet are rife with anecdotes clearly explaining that the animosity towards Khatsara were based on their unfair business practices and the perception they were hiding behind their Nepalese foreign parentage.[22] Foreign visitors often remarked on the tension. In 1921, Charles Bell observed in his characteristically laconic manner that "disputes between the Tibetan and Nepalese Governments are not uncommon, and sometimes reach an acute stage."[23] A few years later the political officer posted to Lhasa, Major F. M. Bailey, succinctly summarized the popular perceptions:

> The Newars who settled in Tibet as traders married Tibetan women and all their halfbreed sons are Nepalese subjects. This arrangement was peacefully observed for many years and in case of any disputes arising between the subjects of the two States, the subjects report[ed] the case to their respective authorities, who decided the case at once to the satisfaction of both. Since sometime, some of the khachars [Khatsaras] have been breaking the law, and in defiance of the laws of Tibet they make big cases out of trifling matters with the help of the Captain, the Agent of the Maharaja of Nepal.... In spite of our [the British] efforts, the Nepalese officer desires the khachars [Khatsaras] to win their cases although they are in fault.[24]

The animosity toward the Khatsaras tended to cluster around the excessive privileges, perceived and real, that the Nepalese and Khatsaras garnered as a result of their special status. Fearful of disrupting relations between Nepal and Tibet, the Tibetan authorities rarely pressed the privileges held by the Nepalese. Instead Tibet repeatedly sought to reclassify the Khatsara as Tibetans, to be treated like the Khache and Koko: as Tibetans, subject to Tibet's laws, taxes, and regulations.[25] The Nepalese government adamantly and repeatedly rejected any overture by the Tibetan government to change the Khatsaras' status.

Despite Nepal's pressing for protection of the Khatsaras' legal status in Tibet, the Khatsaras occupied a very tenuous legal position in Nepal. According to the Nepalese scholar Tirtha Mishra, until the mid-twentieth century Khatsaras held no legal claim to their fathers' Nepalese property, even if they were the only living heirs.[26] The Newari's strict caste-class system considered the Khatsaras, who were often practicing Buddhists, unclean. Thus, prior to 1950, they were rarely invited (or ritually allowed) to return to Nepal to the embrace of the larger family.[27] In addition, Nepalese officials levied an annual tax on Khatsaras living in Tibet, forced them to pay a surcharge when obtaining a Nepalese passport, and charged them the same tariffs as foreigners. Notwithstanding Nepal's dismissive attitude towards the Khatsaras and despite repeated attempts by Tibetan authorities to bring the Khatsaras back under their direct rule with promises to collect and deliver taxes to Nepal at five times the normal rate, the Nepalese government preferred the status quo.[28]

Tensions continued to grow as the Khatsaras continued to abuse their special privileges, as did Tibetan outrage that a group they considered Tibetan were allowed to persist in such obviously inappropriate behavior. Some Tibetans suggested that the level of benefits and protection had grown to the extent that even non-Khatsaras were claiming themselves to be Khatsara. In one such incident, which occurred during the Great Prayer Festival in the late 1920s, Chabdam Ugen, a Tibetan monk acting in his role as a monastic warden during the festival, overheard a Khatsara monk telling a confidant about a crime he had committed. Understanding Nepalese, the elder monk immediately arrested him, only to have the younger monk protest his innocence and declare his immunity as a Khatsara. Unable to contain his indignation, Chabdam Ugen replied, "If you are a Khatsara I am a *na-tsara*" (Tib. *khyoe Khatsara yina nga natsara yin*)," with "na-tsara" being a nonsensical made-up term implying the man was an imposter.[29] Though the arrest is said to have caused a minor diplomatic row, Chabdam Ugen became a minor celebrity for his actions. The tendency of Khatsaras to abuse their immunity fueled growing popular indignation against the half-Nepalese community.

The growing outrage over the legal protection given the Khatsara culminated in the infamous "Gyalpo Affair" of 1929. Sherpa Gyalpo, sixty-five years old at the time of the incident, was born in Tibet and raised from the age of five in Nepal by his Nepalese uncle. According to court documents, Gyalpo married a Nepalese Sherpa woman and worked for a decade as a tenant farmer in Nepal, then took a series of odd jobs before finally becoming an itinerant curio dealer trading items between Lhasa, Darjeeling, and Kathmandu. The strong relationships he forged while in this trade gave rise to rumors of sordid activities he conducted under cover of this ostensible trade in rare objects and jewelry. Many Tibetans accused him of being a Nepalese spy who used his supply of high-end (and highly desirable) coral and turquoise to gain entry into many of Lhasa's elite households.[30] As was common among many Nepalese and Khatsara men, he took a local Tibetan woman as a second wife to help run his affairs during his absence. His status as a Khatsara allowed him to avoid paying taxes on many of his goods, which fostered considerable resentment among Tibetan traders, a reaction only exacerbated by Gyalpo's imperious behavior toward others in Lhasa's trading circles.[31]

It is unclear exactly why Tibetan authorities charged Gyalpo in early 1928 with a "series of alleged offenses ranging from the illicit trade in cigarettes and tobacco, minting counterfeit Tibetan copper coins, . . . and above all furnishing secret information to the Nepalese *Vakil* in Lhasa."[32] These scattershot accusations led some to speculate that the charges were fabricated and that the Tibetan government simply wanted a scapegoat to soothe local discontent and to deflect blame for the years of ineffectual efforts to resolve the Khatsara issues. Others suggested that his arrest would be better characterized as a backlash against the Khatsaras' growing immunity in the Tibetan legal system. Gyalpo's arrogance and high-profile behavior made him a perfect target in the eyes of many Tibetans. The incident might have ended there if public resentment had simply faded and government officials had quietly resolved any differences. However, popular opinion within Lhasa clamored for a harsh sentence, and the Nepalese government refused to accept any blame and rejected anything less than complete exoneration of Gyalpo, on the basis that Tibetan courts had no jurisdiction over Nepalese citizens.[33]

Held in custody for more than a year, Gyalpo managed to flee to the Nepalese legation in September 1929. The drama of his escape, and the swift sanctuary provided by the Nepalese consul, caused many to suspect collusion between the two governments, thus reigniting popular resentment. The Nepalese reasserted their claims that it was perfectly legal for a Nepalese resident, a Khatsara, to seek sanctuary. They refused to turn him over to the Tibetans until it was agreed that his case would be settled by a joint judicial proceeding.[34] Tibetan authorities replied that Gyalpo was simply a Tibetan trying to avoid government oversight and taxation by falsely asserting to be a Khatsara. They twice summoned the Nepalese *vakil* before the Kashag, but he stubbornly refused to release Gyalpo until the question of his nationality was settled.

With public pressure mounting, the government acted. On August 25, two weeks after his escape, over a thousand Tibetan police and soldiers stormed the legation and forcibly removed Gyalpo. Gyalpo found himself again placed in detention, now with round-the-clock guards.[35] Nepalese sources claim that following his return to Tibetan custody, his jailers alternately caned and scalded him with boiling water until he died from his injuries some days later.[36] Tibetan sources asserted that he succumbed to pneumonia and that they were blameless in his death. British accounts tend to support the Nepalese claims. They indicate he died a slow, painful death from his injuries and that he ultimately succumbed to gangrene, for "pieces of flesh have begun to drop out of the affected parts."[37] All three sources agree that until his death, Gyalpo refused to sign a statement attesting to his Tibetan nationality.

In most Tibetan accounts, the case of Sherpa Gyalpo is cast as a prime example of the excesses occurring under Tibetan governance in the 1930s, in particular, due to the influence of the Tibetan official, Lungshar. Representing an ultraconservative and reactionary side of Tibetan politics, Lungshar is typically presented as a villain who pushed Tibet to the brink of war with Nepal.[38] But the Gyalpo case suggests considerably more was at stake.

More than a singular case of an individual attempting to falsely hide behind his Nepalese citizenship, the Gyalpo Affair offers insight into the complex stance Tibetan authorities adopted in distinguishing between those who were clearly foreigners (e.g., the Nepalese, Bhutanese, Ladakhi, and Chinese) and those who were often confused with foreigners but considered Tibetan (e.g., the Khache and Koko) and the Khatasara, who tended to play both sides against the middle.[39] In fact, Sherpa Gyalpo's ambiguous status was the exception to the norm in the treatment of the Khatsara. With the strong Nepalese bias against the Khatsara hindering their return to Nepal and commercial incentives enticing them to remain in Tibet, it was rare for the Khatsara to leave Tibet. According to local perceptions, the Khatsara were considered Tibetan in all but their citizenship.

As the Nepalese scholar Prem R. Uprety has demonstrated, documents uncovered in the Nepalese archives almost certainly certify Gyalpo's status as a Khatsara. From the perspective of the Tibetan government, its case was equally ironclad, for it maintained that since the matter of his birth in Tibet was undisputed, little else mattered. (It should be noted that at the time considerable emphasis was also placed on the signed affidavits of nine witnesses who swore that Gyalpo was not Nepalese, although their motives in making the sworn statements were deemed dubious).[40]

The Gyalpo Affair also illustrates the shifting measures used by governments to assert, authenticate, and endorse citizenship in the twentieth century, as well as the increasing difficulties individuals faced when seeking to verify their citizenship in a world without clear national boundaries, passports, or identity papers. As Gyalpo's case demonstrated, it was community confirmation, not state documents, that remained the central determiner of the validity of such cases.[41] An established Nepali merchant and his Khatsara son who lived in Lhasa their entire lives were likely to have had little difficulty establishing their provenance. It was harder for someone like Gyalpo who led a peripatetic life with relatives and property both inside and outside of Tibet. Marital relations figured prominently in establishing one's Himalayan identity, and that also complicated Gyalpo's case: his first wife being Sherpa suggested he was Nepalese, while his second wife being Tibetan led many to believe he was Tibetan. Though the details of Gyalpo's case remained in dispute between the Nepalese and Tibetan governments, the Tibetan government had the more difficult task of proving he was not Khatsara in spite of the strong evidence of his Nepalese upbringing, his Sherpa wife, and his self-identification as a Khatsara.

Gyalpo's arrest and death, far from a marginal footnote, took Nepal and Tibet to the brink of war. In February 1930, the Nepalese prime minister mobilized troops, and Tibet quickly followed suit.[42] With Gyalpo's death, however, relations between the two countries eased. Not wanting to see Tibet get engaged in a war with their protectorate state, British officials worked to deescalate the situation. On March 7 the Thirteenth Dalai Lama wrote a formal apology acknowledging that Tibetan police had entered the Nepalese legation. He wrote, "Once more for the sake of unity, with deep regret I submit this apology to the Maharaja [of Nepal]."[43] Given the diplomatic discord, the rumors of war, and the tales that circulated among Tibetan tea and beer houses about this and other cases for many years afterward, one can understand how outsiders new to Lhasa misinterpreted the incident as a series of border issues rather than an issue of nationality.

Treated primarily as a border incident in the nationalist histories of India, Nepal, and China, the Gyalpo case highlights the manner in which individuals of mixed parentage shaped the definition of Tibetan citizenship in distinct ways. The confusion and tensions over Sherpa Gyalpo's nationality highlights a seldom acknowledged but common facet of Tibetan society. His case is important for gaining an understanding of the evolution of twentieth-century Tibetan notions of citizenship. Unfortunately, this incident only served to muddle the position of the Khatsara, Koko, and Khache in Tibetan society because many outside observers assumed all three groups held the same rights and privileges in Tibet.[44]

Efforts to treat Khatsaras, Kokos, and Khaches as synonyms for Nepalese, Chinese, and Kashmiris effectively masked the central role these mixed communities played in Tibet, despite the fact that the latter two groups were without question subject to Tibetan law. The resentment toward the Khatsara largely stemmed from the fact only male Khatsaras could claim Nepalese citizenship and thus were the only individuals of mixed parentage who could claim foreign status.[45] Female Khatsaras, that is, women with a Nepalese father and Tibetan mother, were, for all intents and purposes, considered Tibetan (though still referred to as Khatsara). The fact that only male offspring could claim foreign citizenship became a central indicator of the Khatsara status to many outside observers. The confusion arose when outsiders, believing that the Koko and the Khache held the same status, incorrectly assumed that Koko and Khache men were foreign but that their women remained Tibetan. Some accounts took this a step further to suggest that the status of Khache children as Tibetan or foreign depended on the gender of the offspring (e.g., daughters being Buddhist and sons, Muslim).[46]

At the heart of such confusion lay the unmistakable fact that all Khatsara, Koko, and Khache were originally offspring of marriages between Tibetans and non-Tibetans. As Khatsaras were, by definition, the children of Nepalese men and Tibetan women, many accounts sought to assert that this was equally the case with the Koko and Khache. One such account suggested that "all [Khache] Muslims marry Tibetan women."[47] At the same time, some visitors insisted that for religious reasons Khaches only married other Khaches, accepting at face value the common Muslim assertion that the Khache were entirely endogamous.[48] This was likely a misconception stemming from the fact that Muslims are expected to only marry Muslims. All this means is that the Tibetan women who married Khache men were expected to convert prior to marriage; it did not prohibit Khaches from marrying ethnic Tibetans.[49] The central point here is that among the Khatsara, Koko, and Khache, only Khatsara men had the right of extraterritoriality.

The demographic inference of these claims—that all Khache women *only* married Khache men, while Khache men tended to marry Tibetan women—is that the community would have consistently grown in size over the centuries rather than remain, as it did, at approximately three thousand individuals. It is far more likely that the Khache engaged in exogamous marriage with Tibetans in greater numbers than the other two groups in order to maintain a more or less numerically stable Khache community over several centuries.[50] Even as early as the eighteenth century, Bogle noted that "the Kashmiris settled in Tibet are mostly the offspring of Tibetans."[51] Evidence points heavily toward the conclusion that intermarriage between Khache and their Tibetan Buddhist neighbors caused little consternation among either group. Certainly, historical evidence suggests that Khache men and Tibetan women married frequently enough that it was not viewed as atypical or objectionable.[52]

Perhaps the most extreme such characterization is that of Ghulam Muhammad in early 1933. Almost certainly motivated by the attempt to curry favor with the British (and elicit direct British support), he maintained, "The Muslims had long been taking Buddhist girls in marriage. A few months ago, the Tibetan authorities gave orders that all such women should revert to their former religion."[53] Perhaps fearing that the British would soon learn no such law was enacted, he quickly added that the Dalai Lama had rescinded that order. Then, rather bewilderingly, he insisted that the "Tibetans confiscated the mosque of the Muslims," but it was later restored by the Dalai Lama. His most peculiar assertion was that the "Chinese Muslims who reside in Lhasa are not treated this way." Muhammad's entire letter, with its numerous contradictions, is most sensibly read not as an accurate description of Khache marriage practices but as an effort on his part to play to the British interest in retaining influence in Tibet and to be offered direct oversight of the Barkor Khache.[54] His statements suggest that anxieties over mixed marriages were of greater concern to foreigners trying to maintain their preformed notions of a pure Buddhist land than they were to Tibetans themselves.

By the 1940s, when we have a far greater number of personal memoirs, anecdotal evidence suggests there were few if any barriers to intermarriage between Khache, Nepalese, or Chinese with Tibetans. Phünwang Wangye, a founding member of the Tibetan Communist Party, married a Wapaling Khache named Tsilila (Tib. *mdzes legs lags*).[55] Abdul Wahid Radhu, a Ladakhi Khache who traveled to Lhasa in the 1940s, noted that "intermarriages were common," and he detailed a number of intermarriages within his family across three generations.[56] In a more systematic study, the Chinese scholar Chen Bo confirms this practice by citing Tibetan archival records from 1960 that estimate Khache intermarriage constituted roughly 85 percent of all Khache marriages.[57]

Significantly, although many foreign sources tend to characterize the Khache, Khatsara, and Koko as foreigners, the reality was almost the exact opposite. Outside observers consistently played on the notion of Tibet as a homogeneous Buddhist society intent on preserving its purity by resisting the reality of mixed parentage. Even when confronted with mixed marriages, non-Tibetans failed to see the communities as anything other than foreign. While post-1950 documents sometimes acknowledge the existence of "mixed Chinese" (Ch. *hunxue;* lit., "mixed-blooded") the documents of the Nationalist Chinese period stubbornly clung, with patent self-interest, to the belief that the Koko and Khache remained Chinese (Han or Hui).[58] The situation had hardly changed after 1959. The facts became so muddied that a Wapaling Khache interviewed in the late 1980s suggested that in pre-1950s' Tibet "the *Kha-che* were considered as Indian citizens, thus having the status of foreigners. In the case of a mixed marriage the son was considered as an Indian citizen and the daughter as a Tibetan."[59] Despite confusion, false assertions, and a misremembered past, the Khache, throughout all this, remained unambiguously Tibetan and together with the Khatsara and Koko, occupied a distinct and acknowledged position within Tibetan society. However, like the Khatsara and the Khache, the Koko were also caught between foreign assertions and a Tibetan reality.

## BEING HALF-TIBETAN AND ALL CHINESE

Even with the dramatic diplomatic consequences of the Gyalpo Affair, no group faced more pressure from an outside force than did the Koko. After the Chinese Revolution of 1911 and the expulsion of the Chinese forces in 1912, virtually no Chinese representative was stationed or sent to Lhasa in a formal capacity until after the formation of the Nationalist government in 1927. Among the first was a young woman of Chinese-Tibetan parentage who helped usher in a new phase in China's efforts to reassert control over Tibet.[60] Born in Lhasa to a Wapaling Khache father and a Kham Khache mother, Liu Manqing, or Yudhona (Tib. *Dbyangs can*),[61] lived in Lhasa before moving with her family to the Himalayan hill town of Darjeeling when she was five or six years old. Despite being commonly referred to as "Chinese" or "Chinese Muslim Hui," Liu's father was born and raised in Lhasa and spoke fluent Tibetan, and, although he served as a clerk in the Amban's office in the early twentieth century, all indications suggest he was Wapaling Khache.[62] After first moving to Darjeeling, India, Liu's father, in 1918, relocated his family to Beijing. There he enrolled his daughter in a Chinese primary school, and she quickly became fluent in Chinese.[63] Coming of age in the heady political activism of the May Fourth era (ca. 1917–21), she sought to pursue a path that allowed her to help the Tibetan people in the context of the new Chinese nation. In 1927, she arrived in Nanjing and was embraced by the politically active Kham Tibetan community, which had been swept into a position of influence by the newly established Nationalist regime. As she would later recount, it was this serendipitous sequence of events that led to her return to her birthplace: "I was in Nanjing for two years. In 1929, because the Tibetan and central [Chinese] governments had absolutely no lines of communication, the Nationalist government decided to send me to serve as an envoy to Tibet in order to reestablish relations."[64] The precise powers the Nationalist government granted her remain unclear, but late that summer, when she was twenty-three years old, she set off overland to Lhasa through Kham (eastern Tibet), a longer and more precarious route than traveling by sea and then overland via India. Upon her arrival in Lhasa, the Wapaling Khache community received her as one of their own. It was through these local connections that she succeeded in achieving numerous interviews with the Thirteenth Dalai Lama.[65] Staying a little over three months, Liu returned to Nanjing as the first quasi-governmental delegate to travel to Lhasa and publicly write about her travels.

The Chinese media showered Liu with praise. In 1930, the *China Weekly Review* led with a story, "Miss Liu—China's Hero," that aptly captured the excitement elicited by Liu's visit to Lhasa. The media also broached the awkward fact that "one president came after another but no attention had ever been given to Tibetan Affairs."[66] One report stated that "it has been 20 years since a special envoy was sent by the Chinese government to Lhassa."[67] The discontent over the discernible gap between the Nationalist government's words and their deeds with regard to Tibet had not gone unnoticed by the Chinese public. Aside from quasi-governmental and private goodwill missions carried out by individuals like Liu Manqing, nearly two decades had passed with no official Chinese representative in Lhasa. Despite the enduring fiction that China's territorial integrity remained much as it had under the Qing, the public readily could see that Tibet (much like Xinjiang, Mongolia, and Manchuria) had been independent from any Chinese oversight since 1912.[68] The power of Liu Manqing's mission to Lhasa lay in its ability to spark a new optimism and interest among the Chinese public, who hoped to end the two-decade break between the central governments of Tibet and China.[69]

That Liu had traveled through the large swath of eastern Tibet claimed by both the Tibetan and Chinese central governments—tantalizingly outside the reach of both—only accentuated the belief that perhaps the moment had arrived for peaceful reconciliation.[70] Liu Manqing's book-length account of her trip, *Overland Travel to Xikang and Tibet* (Ch. *Kang-Zang yaozheng*), captivated Chinese audiences and sealed her celebrity status. Her book was so popular that it went through three editions and was translated into five languages. Much of the book's charm for the Chinese public came from the manner in which Liu downplayed the implications of her parents' mixed ethnicity, referred to herself as Han Chinese, and promoted China's presence in Tibet. In this manner, her journey back to Tibet represented the journey that many Chinese hoped their government was embarking on. In fact, it was nothing of the sort.

The primary barrier to the normalizing of Sino-Tibetan relations was China's lingering inability to accept that Tibet no longer considered itself under Chinese authority. Throughout the first decades after the Republic of China was founded in 1912, no phrase captured the idealized vision of China better than "Unity of the Five Races" (Ch. *wuzu gonghe*).[71] A powerful rhetorical device, it presented a territorially and ethnically unified China that is sometimes also translated as the "Republic of Five Races" or "Five Races Harmoniously Joined." As the historian Gray Tuttle has remarked, "The discrepancy between translations shows that the concept could be understood both as a political system in which five races were joined in a single state structure, or as a racial ideal, in which case the 'harmonious' links took priority over any particular conception of state structure."[72] The dilemma was less the danger that the term was understood in only racial or ethnic terms than that in public discourse it could seamlessly pivot from one meaning to the other or mean both at once.[73]

The ethno-territorial logic inherent in the term suggested a Chinese nation with a Han Chinese core surrounded by Tibetan, Muslim, Mongolian, and Manchu peoples or territories. "Unity of the Five Races" was virtually omnipresent in the rhetoric of the Chinese Republic, as illustrated by the original flag of the republic under Sun Yat-sen, which contained five different-colored stripes, and the academic discussions of the archaeological discoveries of Peking man, which posited that they demonstrated that the "five races" all descended directly from a single ancient people.[74] Although Chinese leaders spoke of a China that maintained the territorial boundaries of the Qing Empire, a considerable disconnect existed between the idealized rhetoric and the reality.

China's paramount leader at the time, Chiang Kai-shek, had been propelled to prominence as a result of his leadership role in the Northern Expedition, which reunified much of southern and central China primarily through the use of military force and the forging of political allegiances with local power brokers. He had defeated or co-opted many of his rivals in southern and central China, creating a functioning central government based in Nanjing. His support in western China relied on a tenuous patchwork of regional warlords who agreed to acknowledge the Nationalist government in exchange for near-complete autonomy. Japan's invasion of Manchuria and the creation of the Japanese-backed puppet state of Manchukuo in 1931 only highlighted the deeply flawed premise of a Chinese state that embodied the Unity of the Five Races. The Nationalist government's principal concern now focused on defending its already precarious position against further territorial incursions while stabilizing its political grip onr those areas they did control.

The Tibet question for the Nationalist leadership in the 1930s was not a matter of how to reintegrate Tibet into the Chinese nation-state but how it would prevent Tibet from openly declaring itself independent. Of even greater concern was the fear that any actions against Lhasa would exacerbate the situation in eastern Tibet and western Sichuan, further degrading the Nationalists' already negligible influence there. No high-ranking Nationalist official had dared step foot in Kham or Tibetan Sichuan since 1928, and the entire region was openly governed by local warlords who might take Tibet's public expression of independence as a sign that they too could openly do away with the thin pretense of loyalty to the Nationalist government.[75] If the central Chinese government had hoped that Liu Manqing's visit would lead to Tibet formally relinquishing all claims of independence in the early 1930s, it failed. More to the point, the Chinese government simply did not have the resources, the expertise, or even any direct oversight of the territories abutting Tibet to pressure Tibet into an open admission of being under Chinese sovereignty.

Just when it seemed no avenue forward existed, the death of the Thirteenth Dalai Lama on December 17, 1933, provide just the opening the Nanjing government needed. As the historian Hsiao-ting Ling noted in his description of their subsequent efforts, it was the death of the Dalai Lama in Tibet coupled with the fact that the Eighth Panchen Lama remained in China proper (a result of a political dispute with the Lhasa government) that the Tibetan theocracy found itself without its two most prominent leaders. The requisite multiyear search for the Dalai Lama's reincarnation allowed the Chinese government a rare window of opportunity that proved too tempting to resist.

Measuring what goals the Nanjing government believed feasible at this juncture is largely an exercise in conjecture. Almost certainly Chiang Kai-shek saw his primary objective as the establishment of direct political control over the informally allied provincial leaders of southwest China through the settlement of the eastern Tibet boundary. The likelihood of convincing the Tibetan leadership to accept formal reintegration under Chinese sovereignty, while certainly desirable from the Chinese standpoint, remained so improbable that few believed such an outcome plausible and the dangers of aggravating the situation too great. More pressing was finding an experienced and senior official who could undertake such a sensitive mission with grace and vision. The official eventually selected, General Huang Musong, would prove to have neither grace nor vision.[76]

Appointed special commissioner to Tibet in 1934, Huang, from the Nationalist perspective, seemed the perfect choice. A member of Chiang Kai-shek's inner circle and deputy chief of staff in Nanjing, he was a trusted insider. He also understood the government's precarious position in the ethnically diverse borderlands. However, the previous year when Huang had served as "pacification commissioner" to Xinjiang he demonstrated a harrowingly bad sense of judgment. Aggressively pushing a pro-Nationalist agenda, Huang so alienated the Xinjiang warlord Sheng Shicai that he barely escaped with his life. It was only after Chiang succumbed to Sheng's extortionate demands that Huang was even allowed to return to Nanjing. But Huang's ham-fisted efforts resulted in Sheng purging and executing several key pro-Nationalist sympathizers after his release.[77]

Perhaps apprehensive of a repeat of that failed intervention, prior to Huang's departure to Lhasa Chiang Kai-shek explicitly instructed him to adopt a conciliatory tone. Specifically, Huang was cautioned to be sensitive to any points relating to Tibet's sovereignty and advised not to push for border delimitation in eastern Tibet unless Tibet broached it first.[78] Huang chose to follow neither piece of advice.

In the late spring of 1934, Huang's small platoon of eighty staff, porters, and translators set out from Chengdu. Instead of going via the faster, cheaper, and safer India route, Huang chose to travel overland through poorly mapped territory and areas of questionable political allegiance.[79] Almost from the start, Huang reverted to his old habits. An advance team of Chinese officials, traveling via India, had arrived in Lhasa several weeks ahead of Huang and were instructed to post notices written in both Chinese and Tibetan throughout Lhasa advising the Tibetans to place their trust in "the Chinese government that can ensure the comfort and happiness [of all Tibetans] forever."[80] The patronizing tenor of these notices, not to mention the obviously misplaced political message, incensed the Tibetans.

Arriving in Lhasa on August 28, Huang stubbornly ignored the advice proffered by Tibetan officials, insisting instead on a flamboyant procession and public ceremony to present China's gifts. The Tibetan officials demurred, suggesting Huang's proposed memorial ceremony for the Dalai Lama was inappropriate given that the Tibetan people were still in mourning for him. Huang refused to be dissuaded and insisted on publishing "a panegyric to the late Dalai Lama" that included an "invitation to the Tibetan people to join the family of nations and rely on the Chinese Government."[81]

Huang, perhaps taking the wrong message from the Tibetans' reluctant consent to the ceremony began to strong-arm Tibet into formally acknowledging Chinese sovereignty over the country. His actions resulted in the Tibetans systematically stonewalling his proposals. Headstrong and not realizing how damaging his actions were to his larger goal, Huang blamed his lack of progress in the negotiations with the Tibetan officials on their lack of ability or appreciation of the benefits China could offer Tibet in his reports back to Nanjing.[82] Only when the Tibetan authorities were pressed to reply formally to his queries did they finally deliver a carefully translated response to Huang. The October 17 communiqué, written in spare but precise language, indicated that Tibet, a "self-governing, independent country" (Tib. *rangda gyekab*; Ch. *zizhu zhiguo*), was governed by a religious-political system incompatible with that of the Chinese Republican government. In a veiled rebuke to Huang's pretentious assertions about Tibet being part of the same family as China, the document asserted that "there was no reason for China to interfere in its affairs or to station civil and military officials in Lhasa."[83]

Taken aback by the unequivocal tone of their reply, Huang refused to accept the Tibetan government's response as the last word on the subject. Concerned, perhaps, with the continued presence of British officials in Lhasa, he pressed for assurances from the Kashag that the Tibetan government would at least agree to consult with and then follow China's counsel with regard to external affairs. He could not have been pleased with their response, which arrived in early November. The Kashag's ten-point memorandum politely but forcefully rebutted each point Huang had raised in support of increased Chinese presence. It reiterated that the Chinese government retained no legal powers within Tibet. It restricted the number of formal Chinese representatives in Lhasa to one, with a retinue no larger than twenty-five, before going on to explicitly state that "those Chinese (Ch. *Hanmin*) who have resided in Tibet since 1912 shall continue to be governed by the Tibetan Government's Agricultural Ministry."[84]

Almost certainly realizing that his gambit to push Tibet to recognize Chinese sovereignty had backfired, it dawned on Huang, certainly more slowly than it should have, that he had wildly exceeded his government's initial directives. A swift exit was his only option. As a last request before hurriedly crossing the Himalayan passes before the winter snows, Huang received permission from the Tibetan authorities to allow two members of his delegation, Jiang Zhiyu and Liu Puchen, to remain behind to set up a permanent wireless radio station.[85]

In most accounts, this is where the narrative of the Huang Mission ends.[86] Chinese newspapers heralded Huang's return from Lhasa with glowing praise. Public reports, left uncorrected by Huang, gave the impression that his mission had single-handedly reversed the slow decline of Chinese influence in Tibet. Most accounts not only failed to mention that the Tibetan government had only allowed Liu Puchen to remain in Lhasa to run the wireless radio station, but suggested he was the new head of the Chinese Mission.[87] This led the world to assume, as the *New York Times* reported, that "Tibet, after twenty-two years of estrangement, has pledged its support to the Nanjing Government."[88] For these successes, Huang was promoted to the position of head of the Mongolian and Tibetan Affairs Office.

In Lhasa, China's position appeared far less promising. In early January 1935, Liu Puchen died after a short illness. As a result, sole authority in Lhasa fell to Jiang Zhiyu, who became the first permanently stationed Chinese official in Lhasa in more than two decades.[89] Despite the world press proclaiming a Chinese victory, Jiang had no formal title, no background in Tibetan affairs, and, other than running the wireless station, no clear directives from Nanjing. To make matters worse, Huang's aggressive pressure tactics had greatly increased anti-Chinese resentment.[90]

Tibet's decision to permit a Chinese official to remain in Tibet, if only to run the wireless radio, reflects inconsistencies that would typify Tibet's international policy for the next decade. As Melvyn Goldstein remarks in his study of the Huang Mission, the "decision again reflects the paradox of Tibet's China policy": Tibet neither clearly asserted its de facto independence nor endeavored to make a complete break with China.[91]

Perhaps seeing no other path forward, Jiang continued where Huang left off, by following an unabashed pro-China agenda. With no secular public schools available in Lhasa and with the Nationalist government's strong tradition of promoting public education across China, Jiang focused on establishing a Chinese school in Lhasa. To Jiang, the proposition seemed an appropriate starting place and one that would not cause any displeasure among his superiors in Nanjing. One could argue that by shifting from hard to soft diplomacy Jiang was bound to succeed where Huang had failed. Yet Jiang's efforts to make Lhasa conform to China's perception of Tibet, rather than respecting Tibet as it was, typified the attitude of almost every Chinese official posted to Tibet until the late 1940s.

Jiang demonstrated his shallow understanding of Tibetan society almost immediately. Perhaps by falsely concluding that the Wapaling Khaches were Hui Chinese Muslims, Jiang hastily targeted the Wapaling Khache half day school as the best place to begin his school reform. He demanded that the school be turned into his new Chinese school. In February 1935, Jiang instructed the Wapaling Khache in charge of the mosque to close it. According to Derrick Williamson, a British political officer visiting Lhasa at the time, Jiang then ordered it to be "opened 'by the Chinese Government' as a school for the study of Tibetan."[92] Mistaking the Khaches' Chinese linguistic and cultural proficiency for Chinese support, he must have been shocked when the Wapaling Khache immediately and effectively blocked his efforts.

As soon as Jiang attempted to have the mosque closed, a group of Wapaling Khaches, led by a senior Khache named Isi Shah, openly objected to the mosque's conversion and "refused to agree that the mosque should be used as such a school."[93] Jiang's scheme encountered a further setback when his plan became known to the Tibetan National Assembly (Tib. *tshogs 'du*), which swiftly ordered representatives from both sides to appear before them. When the appointed day arrived, only the Wapaling representative appeared, and the case was referred to the Kashag. But before the Kashag could begin its inquiry, several Chinese soldiers apprehended and then forcibly escorted Isi Shah to the Chinese Residency where he was interrogated and severely beaten. Soon thereafter, soldiers went to Isi Shah's home, and upon their arrival they "broke open the house and shot Isi Shah's son dead."[94] In less than a week, Jiang's actions had, remarkably, surpassed Huang's inept legacy by reinvigorating the "very strong feeling in Lhasa against the Chinese."[95]

After its formal inquiry, the Kashag ordered Jiang's school closed and demanded he pay retribution to Isi Shah and his family. Unfazed, Jiang set up lessons at his own residence. Teaching in both Chinese and Tibetan (as well as Qur'anic Arabic) for several decades, the school succeeded in attracting a handful of both Muslim and non-Muslim Tibetan students.[96] Despite being asked repeatedly by the Tibetan government to shut his school, Jiang took "no notice of the warning," and the school remained open throughout the remainder of his tenure in Lhasa.[97] When he finally left Lhasa in 1937, after more than three years in the Tibetan capital, he was despised by the Tibetans and derogated by his superiors, who felt he had diminished rather than advanced China's stature in Tibet.[98]

After Jiang's departure, British officials noted that attendance at the school quickly diminished to only 20 or more half-Chinese children.[99] It is surprising then that both the Huang Mission and Jiang Zhiyu's tenure in Lhasa are consistently cited as evidence in support of China's claims of solid influence in Tibet. After the fall of the Qing in 1912, there were no Chinese officials present in Tibet, and though the coming of Huang and Jiang signified an increase in Chinese involvement in Lhasa, their presence hardly demonstrated a robust Chinese influence in that city, let alone more broadly in Tibet.

## TIBET'S RHETORICAL PLACE WITHIN CHINA'S NATIONALIST IMAGES

In their governmental and private correspondence, Huang Musong and Jiang Zhiyu rarely indicated how the Tibet they encountered differed from how it was represented in China. They employed the standard China-as-center terminology as they doggedly reinforced China's claim to Tibet through distorted representations of the past. Huang, in his published writings about his time in Lhasa, stated that when the Chinese army departed in 1912, "three hundred to four hundred Han and Hui households remained in Lhasa."[100] At best, such assertions should be dismissed as half-truths, since few Chinese soldiers, let alone hundreds of households, chose to stay behind. The larger problem is that his statements have uncritically been accepted to mean that there was a considerable population of native Chinese who resided in Lhasa. Not a single extant source points to even half that number of Chinese living in central Tibet. Such claims are relevant to this discussion of the half-Tibetan populations because one soon realizes that Huang and Jiang presumably believed and erroneously presented the highly assimilated Wapaling Khache and Koko as Chinese citizens.

In his writings, Huang went to great lengths to simultaneously assert China's cultural superiority and its presence in Tibet. In his description of Lhasa, he disingenuously tried to suggest that a local proverb stated, "A skilled Tibetan official was not as good as an incompetent Chinese official" (Ch. *yi hao zangguan buru yi huai hanguan*).[101] In his efforts to rewrite the rather shameful behavior of the Chinese army in 1912, he asserted that the Khache had protected three hundred of their "Han and Hui brothers" (Ch. *Han Hui bao*) against the Tibetans.[102] It became increasingly clear that in ignoring the historical and ethnic realities of central Tibet, Chinese officials were playing to their home audience and not offering an accurate reflection of central Tibet's ethnic makeup. Although there were certainly Han and Hui Chinese in Lhasa prior to 1951, these individuals represented but a small number of the total population.[103] The mischaracterization of the half-Tibetans by Huang and Jiang and, as we will see, by subsequent Chinese officials posted to Lhasa was simply a thinly veiled effort to exaggerate China's presence in the country. Chinese officials began to base Chinese policy on this poorly constructed notion of Tibetan society, and by the mid-twentieth century their policy demonstrated a rejection of Tibet's highly nuanced conception of what constituted Tibetan citizenship.

Chinese claims of a prominent Chinese population are unreliable for several reasons. Almost all Chinese accounts, in adopting the "five groups" (*wuzu*) taxonomy, divided Tibet's population into only three groups: Tibetans, Han Chinese, and Hui Muslims. This simple act, one that seemed (and still seems to most Chinese today) completely appropriate, largely suppresses the nuanced realities of Tibet's cosmopolitanism. To adopt a more legalistic tone, such statements defiantly ignore the Tibetan government's repeated admonition that any Chinese citizens who remained in Lhasa after Chinese forces departed in 1912 had, by virtue of staying, accepted Tibetan citizenship. One could argue this was an issue of semantics by all parties, but the descriptions of both Huang and Jiang seem to be at odds with all other accounts of the period. The few firsthand accounts that remain indicate that all the Chinese in Lhasa realized that to remain was tantamount to becoming Tibetan citizens.[104] More significantly, no permanent Chinese population existed in Lhasa that considered itself Chinese citizens or, as in the manner of Sherpa Gyalpo, sought protection from the Chinese. The groups that Chinese officials inevitably attempted to categorize as Han and Hui Chinese—the Koko and the Wapaling Khache—were, by cultural, linguistic, and legal definition, Tibetan. What one is left with is the realization that for the Chinese officials to admit no native Chinese remained in Lhasa was tantamount to admitting that Tibet was no longer Chinese. As that was an unacceptable conclusion, they simply identified the closest thing to Chinese in Lhasa, the Kokos and the Khaches, as Chinese.

Such a stance played well with virtually all segments of the population in Central China. The Chinese press, the Nationalist leaders, and most Chinese continued to cling to the convenient fiction that Tibet remained a part of China and that all people there were Chinese. In the face of all the evidence to the contrary, such assertions were just that, assertions. The historian Hsiao-ting Lin's recent analysis of China's frontier policies finds him equally at a loss to explain the disconnect between the reality of China's extremely tenuous presence in Tibet and the image of Tibet as a part of China held by the Chinese. He concludes that "regardless of how brilliantly Huang's visit to Lhasa impressed [the Chinese] people, . . . [t]he mission can by no means be deemed a victory."[105] Lin's harsh verdict is equally true with regard to the manner in which Huang and Jiang's narratives had neatly created the illusion of a continuous Chinese presence in Tibet from 1912 until 1949, an illusion often uncritically accepted as the final word on that period.

At the heart of this misrepresentation of China's presence in Tibet is the repeated portrayal of the Koko and Khache as Chinese. Unlike the Qing imperial officials who wrestled with adopting the correct Chinese terminology to delineate the divisions within the Khache community, Huang and Jiang rarely acknowledged the Tibetanized nature of Muslims and repeatedly declared the Koko were Han Chinese. By ignoring how the Tibetan groups perceived their nationality, the descriptions of these two groups as Chinese lent deeper credibility to the notion that a Chinese community, and thus Chinese sovereignty, endured in Tibet over the centuries.

Particularly because of the Chinese tendency to treat Tibetan, Han, and Hui as impermeable categories, Huang and Jiang rarely acknowledged the notion of mixed parentage as the British did. Instead, the reports by Chinese officials from Lhasa routinely divided the population into Tibetan, Han, and Hui, conforming to and neatly glossing over the knotty ethno-territorial contradiction implicit in the Republican-era definitions of China. As a result, China was able to sidestep the reality that in the context of central Tibet those three groups reported by Huang and Jiang as Tibetan (Ch. *Zang*), Chinese Han, and Hui all considered themselves Tibetan, not Chinese.

One gets the distinct sense that many Chinese accounts attempted to treat the Koko and Khache populations in Tibet in a manner quite similar to how the Overseas Chinese populations were treated. The adoption of the once-a-Chinese-always-a-Chinese logic that had tied Overseas Chinese communities to their ancestral homeland despite centuries of intermarriage with non-Chinese reflected an ethnocentric petulance that when applied to Tibet was entirely wrong. Unlike the Overseas Chinese, few of the Khache or Koko identified themselves as Chinese. As Chris Vasantkumar's research on the ethnocentric and homogenizing power of "Overseas Chinese" demonstrates, Chinese categories of citizenship often elided any ethnic contradictions within such categories. Although in English "we can write Han Chinese, . . . it is impossible to hyphenate other nationalities with Chinese."[106] In other words, of the other four of the "five races" that ostensibly constituted China, none is easily delineated as "Chinese" in English. Conversely, when speaking of the Overseas Chinese communities across much of Southeast Asia and the Indian Ocean world, neither the passage of centuries nor the generations of intermarriage with non-Chinese altered the deep-rooted cultural chauvinism underpinning the notion of what it meant to be Chinese. Crucially, it was the strict maintenance of their Chinese identity, so typical of the Overseas Chinese, that was missing in Tibet. Tibetans openly accepted the half-Tibetans as Tibetan unless, as demonstrated by the Khatsaras, when explicitly forced to relinquish such a standpoint.

The ethnic chauvinism demonstrated by Nationalist China in the 1930s and 1940s is further compounded when it is placed within the prevailing political rhetoric of the period, as in the Unity of the Five Races, which was a cornerstone of China's identity as an independent nation. Most Chinese, throughout the mid-twentieth century and despite a lack of political control, never relinquished their idealized notion of China as territorially retaining the same borders as it had in the Qing dynasty. As a result, political rhetoric obscured the considerable gap between being a Chinese citizen and being an ethno-cultural Han Chinese. The selective manner in which the term "Chinese" (Ch. *Zhongguo ren*), could omit the non-Han in some instances, such as with the term "Overseas Chinese," and yet incorporate them in others, such as in the concept of the Unity of the Five Races, remained an unquestioned pillar of Chinese identity within mainstream Chinese culture throughout the twentieth century. If, during this period, a Chinese were to speak in Chinese of a Mongolian, Manchu, Hui, or Tibetan, the language used would make clear that one was speaking of them as Chinese citizens.

The ethnonationalist formulations offered up by Huang and Jiang provide rare insight into the limitations of the Chinese concepts of ethnic and political Chineseness during the first decades of the twentieth century. It is not surprising, though still wrong, that many of the Chinese officials appointed to Lhasa were unfamiliar with Tibetan culture, and because they rarely spoke Tibetan, they erroneously promoted the notion of the Wapaling Khache and Koko as having never stopped being Chinese. In many ways, by designating the Khache and Koko as Hui and Han Chinese, the Chinese officials were not simply fulfilling their own expectations, but were attempting to make Tibet conform to the political discourse of the center. The fact that Lhasa preserved its cosmopolitan structure and that other semipermanent communities of Bhutanese, Nepalese, and Ladakhi retained their legal standing seemed, at least to the Chinese, to lend their claims a veneer of plausibility. In reality, however, China's assertions flaunted the very clear definitions of who the Tibetan state considered citizens of Tibet. As the soccer matches that opened the book aptly captured, even in a recreational milieu the division between Tibetan and non-Tibetan remained clearly self-evident to those living in Lhasa society.

The irony is that Chinese officials, by seeking to impose an inaccurate definition of "foreigners" in a Tibetan context, only highlighted how Tibet administratively defined itself as independent from China—a stance the Chinese officials desperately wanted to stifle and not amplify. Huang Musong, for example, attempted to contrast the situation of the Han Chinese with that of the Nepalese by asserting, "The Han in Tibet are required to provide corvée labor while the Nepalese are not. Thus, we can see that the Tibetan Government is afraid of the Nepalese and are in harmony with us."[107] Huang's claim is peculiar on several levels. Corvée labor was a tax imposed on citizens of Tibet. The Nepalese, among all the communities residing in Lhasa, were unambiguously foreign. Nepal, Britain, and Tibet all recognized their foreign status in Tibet. Huang's claim suggests, if anything, that the Han, by virtue of providing corvée labor to the Tibetan government, are Tibetans fulfilling their duties as Tibetan subjects, not that they are Chinese.[108]

The consistent inclination to consider the Khache and Koko Chinese had specific implications for the Khache communities in Lhasa. Jiang's usage "Hui" in his efforts to commandeer the Grand Mosque stemmed directly from a misapprehension of the Wapaling Khache as Chinese. Nor was the Chinese misreading of Tibetan citizenship limited to those communities. In examining Tibet's relations with Nepal, Chinese officials and the Chinese press presented the Gyalpo Affair primarily as a territorial dispute over a border between China and Nepal rather than a test of wills over the issue of citizenship. The disconnect between China's complete absence from Tibet at that time and its assertions of sovereignty over Tibet are particularly striking given the utter lack of documentation for its claims. In one 1930 press account, an article concluded that "unless strong detachments of Chinese troops are immediately dispatched [to the Nepalese border], it is feared that southern Tibet may soon be lost to China."[109] While this may have been a convenient ploy for maintaining the fiction of a unified China in the face of multiple external threats (foremost, from the Japanese) as credible policy, it borders on delusional. Already by 1930 the military reach of the Chinese central government could barely maintain control over much of Central China let alone having the resources to mount, supply, and finance sending troops to the Nepalese-Tibetan border. Yet such press accounts neatly capture the mind-set that Huang, Jiang, and subsequent Chinese officials brought to their positions. Their approach seemingly left them with the unsavory choice of perpetuating a reality entirely of China's own making or openly conceding Tibet's independence. With the latter option untenable, they were left with only the former. And by making such a choice, their actions and their interpretation of Tibet remained unalterably skewed.

## FRACTIONAL POLITICS: A HALF-CHINESE IS BETTER THAN NONE

On August 27, 1942, a Lhasa policeman came upon a Koko beating his wife in the middle of a Lhasa street. When the policeman attempted to intervene, the Koko responded by assaulting the policeman. He was swiftly arrested, imprisoned, and the next day tried and sentenced to one hundred lashes. Learning of the man's arrest and punishment, the new Chinese representative in Lhasa, Dr. Kong Qingzong, "intervened and demanded the release of the Koko," insisting that he had the right to impose punishment on the Chinese. This occurred six weeks prior to the incident that opened this chapter, and it was the first indication that Kong intended to impose China's ethnonationalist categories in central Tibet in a manner that far exceeded those imposed by Huang and Jiang.

Well acquainted with this strategy, Tibetan authorities rebuffed his appeal by once again patiently explaining that in 1912 all half-Chinese were given the choice to return to China as Chinese citizens under the terms of the truce with the Chinese military forces. Those half-Chinese who chose to remain agreed to accept Tibetan authority, including adhering to all Tibetan laws and paying taxes. The Lhasa government, confident in the question of jurisdiction and the appropriateness of the sentence, duly applied the one hundred lashes to the Koko. Seemingly more incensed by the lack of respect Kong felt due to him by the Tibetan government than by the actual punishment, he attempted to create a political firestorm over the event. He demanded photographs of the man's bloody back be forwarded to his superiors in the central government.[110]

Kong's efforts to interfere in the Koko's sentencing did not emerge solely out of a desire to protect the rights of a Chinese citizen. Frank Ludlow, the British political officer posted to Lhasa at the time, noted that Kong had made multiple requests the previous month to the Tibetan government and "was very hurt at thus being ignored."[111] Ludlow did note that up to that point Kong had cooperated with the Tibetan government, and in a previous incident "when a Koko (half-Chinese) committed an offense, Dr. Kong always used to hand them over to the Do-de Minpon [city magistrate] for trial."[112] All this suggests a level of awareness that abruptly disappeared when his political ambition took a new direction.

Some weeks after Kong's arrival, the Tibetan government took the formal step of establishing the Foreign Affairs Bureau. As part of this process, it demanded credentials from all foreigners, including the Chinese who traveled to Tibet. The Tibetan government's decision stemmed from an unmistakable desire to formalize its independence on the world stage. It instructed all foreign governments to cease addressing their concerns through the Kashag and instead communicate through the Foreign Affairs Bureau. An exception was made for the Nepalese (and Khatsara) since an office already existed to deal with their needs and demands.[113] This change, and the exception made for Nepal but not China, triggered a sudden change of heart and interpretation of policy by Kong. In a fit of pique, and without specific instructions from Central China, he insisted that his "instructions were to deal with the Kashag only."[114]

Born in Sichuan in 1898 and educated at the University of Brussels, Belgium, Kong had been a professor at the National Sichuan University and National Central University in Nanjing. In the years leading up to his appointment to Lhasa, he had served as counselor to the Mongolian and Tibetan Affairs Commission.[115] A member of the Wu Zhongxin Mission to Lhasa in 1940, Kong attended the induction of the Fourteenth Dalai Lama. After the ceremonies concluded, he was selected to remain in Lhasa and to assume the new post of China's representative to Tibet.

Whether this was a foreign or domestic posting was a point of contention that remained unresolved, though the Chinese made their perspective clear on the sign over the mission's main gate: "Tibet Office of the Tibetan Mongolian Affairs Commission of China."

Kong faced a dilemma. Desperate to challenge the treatment of the half-Chinese Koko, he was equally adamant that he would not acknowledge Tibet's sovereignty by filing his charges, as the Tibetan government required, in the new Foreign Affairs Bureau. If he agreed that the Koko was a Tibetan, he would be tacitly acknowledging Tibet's independence and his own status as a foreign representative. Yet to file a complaint he would need to adhere to the new protocol, tacitly accepting that Tibet was not part of China. If he agreed, he would be accepting his status as a foreigner, an act that was at variance with the very outcome he was attempting to achieve.[116] Unsure how to both file a complaint and not undermine his position, he alerted his superiors and let the matter drop. A little over a month later, when another incident involving a Koko came about, Kong decided to act.

On October 6, 1942, a scuffle, this time between a half-Nepalese Khatsara and a half-Chinese Koko, occurred.[117] According to bystanders, the Koko and the Khatsara were engaged in a verbal dispute in front of the Jokhang Temple when, to borrow from the British version of the incident, the Koko "picked up a stone and hit the Nepali half-breed over the head." Four Tibetan policemen witnessed the altercation and immediately tried to intervene. Fearing arrest, the Koko took flight and sought refuge at the Chinese Mission. There, Kong offered him sanctuary, and when the police entered the mission to arrest the Koko, they instead found "themselves arrested by Dr. Kong."[118]

Desperate not to let an opportunity slip through his fingers again, Kong hurried, not to the Foreign Affairs Bureau, but to the Norbulingka Palace to seek an audience with the regent. It was already very late, and he arrived to find the gate shut. Breaking with propriety, he pounded loudly on the doors and demanded to be allowed to meet with the regent. He was informed that the regent would not meet with him and told to return in the morning.[119] The following day the National Assembly convened and immediately censured Dr. Kong for his actions. Incensed over his interference in the street fight between two Tibetans, as well as his arrest of the four Tibetan policemen in deliberate defiance of Tibetan rule of law, the government demanded that the Nationalist government in Chongqing recall him and replace him with a more suitable candidate. More pointedly, and quite likely with more effect, the Tibetan government withdrew their liaison officer, ceased delivery of firewood to the Chinese Mission, and halted all government provisions for them. Without these services, Dr. Kong was stripped of all Tibetan assistance, an act that effectively denied him any formal standing while not formally expelling him.

Resentful of his treatment, Kong stubbornly held the policemen for five months. Initially the Chinese home government had accepted his interpretation of the events as yet another tactic by the Tibetans to force China to accept Tibetan independence. But the recognition that Kong had instigated the incident became increasingly difficult to ignore. In the end, and desperate not to let Tibetan-Chinese relations slide into endless bickering, Chiang Kai-shek ordered Dr. Kong to immediately release the four policemen he still detained within the Chinese Mission.[120] Although Dr. Kong and his staff would remain in Lhasa until 1944, largely due to the exigencies of the war against Japan, he and almost all his staff were formally notified that they would be recalled to Chongqing and replaced.[121]

As the actions above suggest, Dr. Kong was not an endearing individual. Secretive, impulsive, and overbearing, he frequently insisted that the Tibetan government had no right to treat him as a foreign representative. He repeatedly asserted that Tibet was part of China and that he, a Chinese official, should have the right to address the Kashag directly. Within Lhasa, his assertions gained little traction. It vexed him that the Tibetan leadership had rejected China's many offers for Tibet to return to China's protection. His vision of Tibet was unambiguously one where Tibet remained firmly rooted within the Chinese sphere of influence, as it had been under the Qing Empire. In offering counsel to Nanjing, Dr. Kong appealed to his superiors to accept the notion that "Chinese affairs should be dealt with in the same way as they were in the days of the Manchu emperors." In essence he was advocating that Tibet return to a protectorate status and promoting himself to the status of an Amban, the imperial official appointed to Tibet during the Qing dynasty.[122] The Nanjing government, slightly more circumspect in their efforts to reassert control over Tibet, repeatedly rebuffed his requests. Within Lhasa, his imperious attitude caused his prestige to fall to a new low. He became a social pariah, rarely invited into, visited by, or allowed to participate in elite Tibetan social circles.

As World War II wound to an end, the influential Wellington Koo, serving as ambassador to the United Kingdom at the time, urged Chiang Kai-shek to address the deteriorating relationship between Lhasa and China by appointing a more level-headed official.[123] The appointment of Shen Zonglian, a graduate of Qinghua and Harvard Universities and a powerful Ministry of Foreign Affairs official, appeared to be the perfect antidote to Kong's calamitous tenure. Shen's well-oiled network of acquaintances and allies allowed him to dictate his own terms of engagement. He hand-picked a team of officials to accompany him to Lhasa, including individuals with specialties in sociology, engineering, and geology—several of whom could speak Tibetan.[124]

Shen and his team's arrival in Lhasa on August 8, 1944, ushered in a new direction in both Chinese policy and on-the-ground diplomacy. Shen adopted a conciliatory and friendly tone in his general interactions with Tibetan officials, including hosting popular dinner parties. The Tibetan government immediately responded in kind, relaxing their harsh treatment of the Chinese officials and resuming delivery of supplies to the Chinese Mission, which had been cut off since Kong's unfortunate 1942 incident. With access to discretionary funds far exceeding those available to Kong, Shen's appointment marked the beginning of what one historian termed an escalating "cash diplomacy" between China and Britain, including increasing China's annual donations to the Tibetan monasteries surrounding Lhasa by nearly 20 percent.[125]

A prominent concern with educational reforms is one area where one can see continuity between Shen and his predecessors. Although the Chinese school had remained in operation since Jiang established it in the late 1930s, Shen sought to make it a showpiece of his office's initiatives. Within weeks teachers' salaries were increased, students were provided with free khaki uniforms, and Shen personally instructed that cash gifts be distributed to the poorer students' parents.[126] The support of the Wapaling Khache during Shen's tenure is unmistakable.

Topics taught at his school consisted of the normal curriculum of any Chinese school, including the Chinese language and arithmetic, in addition to, not surprisingly, Tibetan. It was, however, inclusion of a course on the Qur'an, among several additional optional courses, that signaled the considerable influence and presence of the Khache. Officially the Chinese school was referred to in documents as the Lhasa National Elementary School (Ch. *guoli xiaoxue*). However, it was perceived by most in Lhasa and central Tibet—and even Tibetan Muslims interviewed decades later—as the Wapaling Khache mosque school.[127] British estimates suggest enrollment of nearly a hundred students of whom nearly half were Khaches, with only ten listed as Chinese.[128] The remainder was made up of Tibetans and Khatsaras.[129] Perhaps indicative of the socioeconomic backgrounds of the students, none of the children of Tibetan officials attended the school (although several were tutored privately in Chinese).

Far from mounting a simple cash-infused charm offensive, Shen assiduously adhered to Chiang Kai-shek's explicit threefold directive: "not interfering with Tibetan internal affairs," ensuring that Tibet "not lose any part of her territory to other powers," and respecting Tibetan jurisdiction over "Chinese half castes and other Chinese nationals in Lhasa."[130] Such directives, while deviating from Sun Yat-sen's Unity of the Five Races of the early Republican period, also digressed considerably from the position Chiang Kai-shek had laid out in *China's Destiny* only two years earlier, in 1943. Shen's actions did, however, reflect a broader Nationalist postwar effort to pursue a policy of borderland autonomy. Most likely stemming from Shen's success in Tibet, Chiang went as far as to articulate, in a major policy speech, the promise that "if the Tibetans should at this time express a wish for self-government, our government would, in conformity with our sincere traditions, accord it a very high degree of autonomy."[131]

Yet even as Shen greatly ameliorated Sino-Tibetan tensions in Lhasa, Tibetan attitudes towards the Chinese generally remained negative. The lingering distaste for the Chinese presence and for their political messages was most obvious when Shen organized several hundred Chinese, half-Chinese, and Wapaling Khaches in August 1945 to celebrate China's victory over Japan. Bearing Chinese flags and a large photograph of Chiang Kai-shek and accompanied by a Chinese band, the procession marched around the Barkor. Mistaking the march for a display of pro-Chinese nationalism, Tibetans lined the route "booing, hooting and hissing."[132] Even with Tibetan policemen accompanying the procession, many in the crowd threw stones and at one point damaged decorative lanterns carried in the parade. Several months later, in early 1946, Shen returned to China, bringing to an end the era of Nationalist efforts in Lhasa. His tenure signaled the high-water mark of Chinese influence in Tibet in the first half of the twentieth century, a mark that would be dramatically overtaken with the arrival of the People's Liberation Army five years later.

Khatsaras, Kokos, and Khaches featured prominently in Tibet's confrontations with its neighbors during the 1912–50 period. While most of the incidents discussed above are well documented, the role of half-Tibetan communities is frequently obscured, overlooked, or glossed over in favor of narratives that highlight the non-Tibetan perspectives of their neighbors or outsiders. In part, this is because historical interpretations of the period overwhelmingly emphasize the question of Tibet's independence. Throughout the 1930s and 1940s, Tibet displayed a reluctance to openly declare itself independent or to be drawn into discussions on the matter with either British or Chinese officials. British and Chinese representatives repeatedly approached Tibetan officials to seek clarification. Tibet repeatedly demurred.

As late as 1945, Shen Zonglian, a Chinese representative who had engendered considerable goodwill in Lhasa, appealed for advice from all levels of his Tibetan contacts as to how to get a definitive response about Tibet's status. Even as he "heard that most of the Tibetans are very keen on 'Tibet's independence,'"[133] few would discuss it with him. During casual conversations with high Tibetan officials, "they either evade[d] the question or decline[d] to give any answer."[134] The British Foreign Office concluded in 1950 that all evidence demonstrated that Tibet was not part of China but rather "had a clear international identity of her own."[135]

If Tibet displayed some hesitancy in declaring itself independent on the international stage, internally it openly defended itself against all external attempts to declare that half-Tibetans were not Tibetan. Tibet's defense of the Khatsaras, Kokos, and Khaches as Tibetan citizens demonstrates how these three communities lay solidly within Tibet's traditional definition of itself. The significance of Tibet's proactive stance on citizenship has seldom been explored because of the ambiguity surrounding its status as an independent state, yet the clarity with which Tibet delineated and defended the status of these groups suggests a confidence not previously recognized. When one accepts the premise that these groups were unequivocally Tibetan, as Tibetans typically did, the incidents involving Khatsaras, Kokos, and Khaches discussed above take on a new significance.

In this broader context, it appears that in practice Tibetans—and other subcategories such as Khatsaras, Kokos, and Khaches—had little difficulty traveling between Tibet and India. Indeed, it was harder for Chinese to travel to Tibet than it was for Tibetans to travel to India. By the 1940s, particularly after the war, increasing numbers of Tibetans, including Tibetan Muslims, were traveling to the hill town schools of Darjeeling and Kalimpong in India and elsewhere to continue their education. Although monitored, most such travel occurred without any formal border control. At the same time, Tibetans also traveled to the interior parts of China with equally limited oversight. Finally, Tibetan Muslims traveled freely to the Middle East on hajj via both China and India and typically did so by taking the fastest route, via Bombay.[136] In each case, there appears to have been a willingness, a customary acceptance, and a desire to maintain the status quo of freedom of travel, such that travel rarely precipitated diplomatic protocols such as the carrying of passports, let alone documents proving one's residence or citizenship.[137] The expectation that such documents were unwarranted would later, after the arrival of Chinese governance, prove to be an unexpected shock.

The breadth of Tibet's (and similarly British India's) acceptance of the many Muslim groups entering India is apparent in the well-documented maneuvers by the Tibetan government to extricate the Fourteenth Dalai Lama from the grip of the Muslim Chinese warlord Ma Bufang. In a complicated negotiation, culminating in a payment of large bribes to Ma Bufang from the Chinese Nationalist and Tibetan governments, the Dalai Lama was released to a group of rich Siling (Ch. *Xining*) Tibetan Muslim merchants who intended to travel via Lhasa to India and on to Mecca to carry out their hajj.[138] Acting as guarantors in the transaction, the Tibetan Muslims would first advance Ma Bufang the promised payment, with the Lhasa government repaying the merchants upon the young reincarnation's arrival in Lhasa. Several months later, the Muslim traders, with several Chinese escorts, arrived and were duly paid in Indian rupees at an advantageous rate before continuing to India and then Mecca. Their onward travel to India was sanctioned, and it was even expressly indicated that they were traveling "without valid passports."[139] The Tibetan government, acknowledging their crucial role in escorting the new Dalai Lama out of harm's way, diligently facilitated the Qinghai Khaches' travels in their communications with the British officials. For all parties, the prosaic nature of Tibetan Muslim merchants made them the most dependable option for Ma Bufang, the Chinese Nationalists, and the Tibetan and British governments.

These merchants were part of a rarely remarked on branch of the large number of Muslims from Tibet and Central Asia who traveled via Indian ports on the hajj. Between 1930 and 1938, the annual number of Muslim pilgrims traveling via India who were classified as Tibetan, Nepalese, or Turkestani averaged nearly a thousand individuals per year—a number confirmed by official hajj figures of pilgrims arriving by sea.[140] Issues of mixed parentage, cross-border identity, and Himalayan interstate relations played key roles in how Tibet defined itself, a definition very often inconsistent with the interpretation applied by China but accepted by most other nations the Tibetans passed through. It was Tibet's cosmopolitan populace that lay at the intersection of the various notions of citizenship, notions that were quickly hardening with the Chinese occupation and taking on new and untraditional meanings. Typical of most Himalayan states, Tibet remained far less concerned with what it considered an abstract demarcation of formal territorial boundaries and more concerned with retaining and delimiting the peoples who populated its urban centers. The consistency with which Tibet maintained that focus for nearly four decades suggests that Tibet was forcefully and successfully able to assert its independence primarily through its definition of Tibetan citizenship, in all its complexity.

Even as such crossing of international borders remained commonplace, the concern over the individual's precise status began to slowly change in the postwar years. The ability to delineate and categorize individuals according to their country of residence, which had been put aside during World War II, arose again, more prominently, after the war. Hugh Richardson, who had remained in Lhasa after Indian independence in 1947, to serve as the Indian consul-general, somewhat presciently noted in an annual report that "except for Government servants, there are few Indian subjects in Lhasa, etc., and those others who can technically claim that status are Ladakhi Muslims at present somewhat undecided about their allegiances."[141] Concerns about nationality were superseded by the arrival of the People's Liberation Army in Lhasa in October 1950. With the army's appearance, the question of what being Tibetan meant began, abruptly and forcibly, to bend to the Chinese conceptualizations, ones that the Nationalists could only express but never impose.[142]

4

------

# Himalayan Asia

In late 1951, over eight thousand Chinese soldiers arrived in Lhasa, marking a new era for the capital.[1] During this time, Lhasa, like many cities in the early phases of occupation by a new political force, was a city of contradictions, political machinations, and cultural clashes. Following Mao Zedong's explicit instructions, the Chinese government adopted a gradualist approach. As Goldstein describes it, the Chinese officials in Lhasa "set out to develop cooperative and cordial relationships with the elite and to convince them that these officials had come to Tibet to help them modernize and develop, not to oppress and exploit them, as previous Chinese regimes had done."[2]

Although post-1951 Tibet is often presented either as a case of state-sponsored Chinese "liberation" or as a case of Tibetan oppression and resistance, recent scholarship has begun to avoid such polarized interpretations.[3] Nowhere is this revisionist perspective on Tibet's past more visible than in the years immediately following the arrival of Chinese forces.[4] New evidence and oral histories from this period suggest that Tibetan autonomy in many spheres of life persisted well into the mid-1950s. Lhasa's social calendar—Tibetan Buddhist rituals, daily prayers, and constant flow of pilgrims—proceeded largely unabated. The Kashag, the Tibetan governing council, and Tibetan monasteries persevered institutionally. The Dalai Lama carried on in his central role in the institutional and cultural life of the city while serving as the primary mediator between the realities of Chinese control and the limitations of Tibetan authority. Republican-era Chinese silver dollars continued to serve as the legal tender in central Tibet, making Tibet the only administrative region in the People's Republic of China (PRC) not to have "People's money" (Ch. *renminbi*) as its primary currency.[5] In many ways, life improved. Spared the monetary transition to Chinese currency, Chinese officials and soldiers generally received wages in and paid for goods with silver dollars, adding a new stream of revenue for central Tibet.[6] Yet even as these recent perspectives have become more widely accepted, Tibet's experiences typically are seen in isolation from China's post-liberation and more broadly Asia's postcolonial history.[7]

The lingering tendency to isolate narratives of Tibet's past from mainstream accounts of Asia's past is peculiar, since many of the seminal forces that shaped Tibet, particularly in the 1950s, emerged out of the same complex postcolonial historical trends that swept across Asia after World War II. Unlike the experiences of Europe and the United States, where victory over Nazi Germany in May 1945 marked the beginning of the Cold War era, in Asia the defeat of Japan ushered in an extended period of decolonization and political change. There was China's civil war between Nationalist and Communist forces, culminating in a sweeping Communist victory in 1949; India's independence from Great Britain, precipitating the traumatic partition of India and Pakistan in 1947; and the creation of nearly a dozen new nations in Southeast Asia, ushering in a period of intense patriotic nationalism. In each of these instances, the citizens of these newly formed nations grappled anew with what it meant to be Chinese, Indian, Malaysian, Indonesian, or Thai. Similarly, overseas populations of peoples who had permanently settled outside their ancestral homelands found their identities challenged in new and often fraught ways. While becoming manifest in different ways, 1950s Tibet's responses to the newly delineated territorial, religious, and national identities had much in common with the broader Asian experience.

## NEW CHINA, NEW TIBET, AND A NEW ERA FOR THE KHACHE

A quick succession of events unfolded in the spring of 1951 that would establish Tibet's political trajectory for the next decade and beyond. The Indian, British, and U.S. governments in the early months of 1951, after years of vague promises of support, signaled that they would not be willing to defend Tibet against a Chinese invasion or even provide a safe haven for the Dalai Lama's government. Tibetan government officials, seeing little or no alternative, met with officials from the Chinese government on May 23, 1951, and signed the 17-Point Agreement for the Peaceful Liberation of Tibet. The agreement affirmed Chinese sovereignty over Tibet, although it stated it would "not alter the existing political system in Tibet." Ending months of speculation about his plans, the Dalai Lama returned to Lhasa from the Indian border town of Kalimpong, arriving in the Tibetan capital on August 17, 1951. Finally, on September 9, the *People's Daily* reported that with "the warm Tibetan sun" shining down on the spectacle, "Tibetan crowds flowed into the main avenues, sitting on the walls surrounding the city's many densely wooded *lin-ka* (parks) dressed in their best Tibetan attire" to greet with requisite enthusiasm the several-thousand-strong vanguard of the People's Liberation Army (PLA).

The People's Republic of China, like the Nationalists before them, insisted that Tibet was historically an integral and unalienable part of China, but they often emphasized Tibet's Asian and Himalayan positioning. In a *People's Daily* article published on September 7, 1949, just weeks prior to the formal founding of the PRC, the government laid out what would become one of several core rationales for China's liberation of Tibet: "That British-American Imperialist efforts to invade Tibet is unmistakable. . . . British Imperialists through the Indian Nehru government, gained control of the protectorates (Ch. *tubang*) of Sikkim and Bhutan positioned between Tibet and India as a means by which to threaten the Tibetan regional authorities into taking one more step towards to submitting to Western governments."[8] The inclusion of Sikkim and Bhutan in its justification for liberating Tibet highlights China's sensitivity to Tibet's Himalayan standing while disingenuously sidestepping the Chinese government's own tenuous position on the Tibetan plateau.

It was not simply that the PRC refused to acknowledge that the Tibetan government had functioned entirely independently of the Chinese government since 1912. It was also the fact that, even as China consolidated its rule over Tibet, the traditional ties the Dalai Lama's government had with Nepal, Bhutan, and Sikkim remained in place. More startling is the equally telling fact that the Himalayan states, all with prior ties to Qing China, had resolutely refused to officially recognize the new Chinese Communist government.

The PRC's swift occupation of Tibet caused speculation across the Himalayan region over China's ultimate intentions. This concern included how China might alter the status, rights, and position of Nepalese, Bhutanese, and Kashmiri, as well as the Khatsara, Koko, and Khache. For the Tibetan Muslims, the 1950s marked an era of opportunity as well as unaccustomed scrutiny by both Tibetans and Chinese. The Khache quickly sought to indicate their loyalty, with one Wapaling Khache explaining to a Chinese official, "We Hui-Hui support (Ch. *qingxiang*) the motherland. We often were at the receiving end of the [Tibetan] government's pro-English group's wrath. At this old age, what do I have to be afraid of? Before I would not dare do many things, now that we have freedom and equality, what am I to be afraid of?"[9] Although the political discourse certainly changed with the establishment of the PRC, Chinese characterization of Lhasa in the public media remained remarkably similar to that presented by the Nationalist officials during the previous decade. In newspapers, magazines, and radio broadcasts, all Muslims were monolithically labeled "Hui." The repeated articulation of Muslims as Hui, Tibetans as Zang, and Chinese as Han was a formula used to demonstrate the government's support of ethnic diversity but also to emphasize Tibet's similarity to China. Deliberately fastidious in their efforts to appear ethnically neutral, Chinese officials pursued ethnic parity at all levels of the government (even though the Han and Hui represented a tiny proportion of Tibet's population). To take one example, the Patriotic Cultural Youth League membership in 1955 was reportedly composed of 100 Tibetans, 100 Chinese, 80 Wapaling Khaches, and 20 Barkor Khaches.[10]

Portraying the Khache in this manner proved useful to the Chinese in multiple ways. The Chinese could avoid the appearance of exclusively promoting the interests of the Han if their policies and public works also included the Hui. The Chinese Communists, however, differed from the Nationalists in one critical way. In unofficial writings by early Chinese officials sent into Lhasa, following the initial vanguard, one encounters both an understanding of and a concern with the divisions within and among the various Muslim communities—particularly the differences between the Barkor and Wapaling Khache communities. The recognition of the Barkor Khache as aligned with India proved to be an early concern for many Chinese officials. It was also of concern that the Barkor Khache remained more strongly allied with the Tibetan government than did their Wapaling Khache neighbors. Yet both groups remained monolithically Hui in the writings of the period.

Similar to the Nationalists' dispatching of the Lhasa-born Liu Manqing in 1927 to serve as an early envoy for the government, Beijing identified and included cadres whose knowledge of Muslim affairs would shape China's early efforts to realign Tibetan attitudes with those of Central China. Foremost among these figures was the Beijing native Xue Wenbo. As the historian Wlodzimierz Cieciura has neatly presented, Xue was a Hui scholar active in Republican intellectual circles during the 1930s who had "advocated pan-Muslim nationalism, defining *Huizu* as encompassing all the Muslims in the world, not only in China."[11] A pro-Muslim activist with a global perspective, Xue had been hand-picked to serve on a five-member Nationalist Chinese Muslim delegation to the Near East in the 1930s.[12] With a strong record of assisting the Communist government in Qinghai and Gansu, Xue possessed the skills and political background to make him a natural fit to join the Tibet Working Research Team attached to the PLA forces departing for Lhasa in 1951.[13] His presence in Lhasa, beginning in early December, denotes a sophisticated awareness by the Chinese central government of Lhasa society.

In his memoirs Xue indicates his mandate was vague but stemmed from the leadership's concern that the two Khache communities remained divided in some ways. Realizing the essential role they played in Lhasa, Xue "was ordered by [his] superiors to unify them into a single group."[14] The Barkor Khaches' stature in Lhasa was not lost on Xue. Their standing as traders "was second only to the Nepalese, and only after them do the Han and Hui appear."[15] It was Chinese officials, including Xue, who demonstrated how difficult it was for outsiders to comprehend the subtle differences within the Lhasa Muslim community.

Even though he had traveled throughout the Muslim world and had a deep personal and intellectual familiarity with divisions among the Chinese Hui,

Xue indicated upon his arrival that he had difficulty not only differentiating the Barkor from the Wapaling Khache but also distinguishing both groups from the Tibetans. Eventually he came to be able to tell the Barkor and Wapaling apart by their sartorial preferences, noting that "Barkor (Ch. *Ke-shi-mi-er*) prefer wearing a red and black hat that is taller and longer while the Wapaling (Ch. *Hui*) prefer a smaller and flatter black and white hat."[16] In spite of his awareness of internal differences, journal entries from his time in Lhasa tend to characterize the Khache on the whole as more ideologically aligned with China than with the Tibetans. Differing in tone from the *People's Daily* account above, Xue's journal recounts that "when the People's Liberation Army arrived in Lhasa, the Lhasa Tibetans, as a result of the pro-British propaganda, were not terribly welcoming (Ch. *qinre*), but the long-oppressed Hui already believed themselves to be closer to the motherland, and were willing to come out and support us in our efforts."[17] Like many Chinese tasked to work in Tibet in the early years of the PRC, Xue tackled his duties with considerable enthusiasm and blamed the differences within the Muslim community on the lack of progressive influences in the traditional Tibetan society. Xue focused on recruiting the Khache as essential interlocutors and supporters of government-desired reforms in Lhasa, a task that gained considerably more urgency in the face of inflation and the unanticipated shortfall of supplies that occurred with the arrival of the Chinese in the Tibetan capital.

Descriptions of Lhasa in the 1950s often highlight the rapid inflation that occurred immediately after the arrival of the Chinese.[18] Less often emphasized is that the worst of this inflation was a short-lived result of the influx of Chinese soldiers and officials without a commensurate level of supplies being sent with them, creating a scarcity of goods.[19] During the first six months, the price of grain quadrupled. However, Goldstein's detailed study of the 1951–55 period argues that the extreme shortages and inflation were mostly transitory. Tibetan and Chinese officials resolved the acute grain shortage, caused by improper accounting and communications, within a year. The larger food-supply issues were partially dealt with by planting and harvesting barley and vegetables from reclaimed swampland outside of Lhasa. By and large, the worst of the food shortages had been rectified by the summer of 1952.[20]

As inflation became a fact of life during the early months of Chinese rule, the dramatic influx of silver dollars made a deep impression on many Tibetans. The noted Tibetan historian Dawa Norbu recalled a saying popular in Lhasa at the time, "The Chinese Communist Party is like a kind parent / To whom we owe a great debt of gratitude / They give us silver dollars like showers of rain" (Tib. *rgya gung khran drin chen pha ma red dngul da yangs char pa babs babs red*).[21] The Chinese government paid for all goods in silver dollars, and the soldiers and government officials who were posted to Lhasa drew their salaries in silver dollars. As most of the Chinese had their daily needs met by eating and living in government quarters, they had considerable disposable income to spend on items not available in China proper, and at a much cheaper price.[22] As a result of the 17-Point Agreement signed in 1951, traders were still permitted to import goods from India that were scarce, extremely expensive, or even banned in other parts of China. In addition, luxury goods remained tax-free (or were taxed at a greatly reduced rate) as compared with other inland Chinese cities.[23] These conflicting forces—inflation and monetary policy—simultaneously created both a scarcity of basic foodstuffs and a market for luxury goods inconceivable in China.

In the first months following his arrival in late 1951, Xue Wenbo remarked on the difference between the goods available in Lhasa and the markets in Qinghai. In his memoirs he noted that during his six-month stay in Lhasa, "life was quite good. We had access to American powdered milk and ornately wrapped candies, and I was even able to buy an Omega brand watch."[24] Several years later, in 1956, the Xinhua News Agency photographer Chen Zonglie recalled his surprise, soon after being posted to Lhasa, at being escorted to the Barkor and seeing the stalls "fully stocked with goods that one almost never saw in interior China such as brand-name Swiss watches, French perfume, Italian accordions, German cameras, American Kodak film, . . . Indian silk, spices, condensed milk and desserts, as well as Nepalese Buddhist figurines and ceremonial instruments, etc."[25]

With the large number of Chinese officials and soldiers in Tibet, demand swiftly outstripped supply. In interviews years later, Tibetan Muslim caravaneers boasted of selling off their complete inventory within days of arriving in Lhasa. Realizing the remunerative potential, the Barkor Tibetan Muslim traders quickly abandoned the importation of textiles, cigarettes, and kerosene and branched out into high-value, low-bulk luxury items such as European pens, watches, and even batteries. The scale and scope of goods being imported from India into Tibet, even as the availability of dry goods and the wool trade shrank, caused profits to soar for most traders. A British Embassy official traveling in northwestern and central China shared a train compartment with a Chinese Air Force major who was returning from an assignment in Lhasa:

> He was wearing a new Rolex watch and explained that he had bought it in Lhasa where watches and pens are tax-free. He had therefore paid only ¥130 instead of ¥480 in Beijing. In Lhasa there are apparently large numbers of Omega, Rolex, Longines and even American watches together with a plentiful supply of Parker '51 pens, all imported from India. Members of the Chinese forces are allowed to buy one watch and one pen each.[26]

Even as late as 1958, an Indian trade agent, K. C. Johorey, who was posted at the Indian-Tibetan border town of Yatung (Tib. *Dromo*; Ch. *Yadong*), reported that there remained "a heavy demand for radios, cameras and watches as the Chinese were buying these in the hundreds and thousands."[27]

The plethora of luxury goods was in stark contrast to the dearth of daily necessities. It was during this period that the Chinese government, having few local options, had to ship in needed supplies such as medicines, construction materials, and even rice from outside Tibet. This allowed the Khaches, as well as Tibetan and Nepalese traders, to make unprecedented profits.[28] These profits meant many more Barkor Khaches could, and did, bear the expense of sending their children to study in the Indian hill stations of Kalimpong and Darjeeling, or even Delhi. It was against this backdrop of a significantly altered political situation, as well as acute shortages of food, fuel, and housing, that the Barkor Khaches found their economic circumstances in the 1950s far exceeding what they had experienced in the 1930s and 1940s.

With profits rising and business good in 1956, as many as forty-one Tibetan Muslims were able to afford the high cost associated with going on pilgrimage to Mecca—more than double the number who went ten years earlier.[29] These Khaches did not travel with the official Chinese Islamic Association delegation (and thus do not appear in national statistics). They traveled by their own means via India, demonstrating a rarely remarked autonomy from the PRC's control over all religious associations and international travel.[30] China had attempted to send a group of Chinese Muslims on the hajj via Pakistan as early as 1952, only to be denied entry by Saudi Arabia with whom the People's Republic of China did not have diplomatic relations. Indian officials in Lhasa reported concern in 1956 among the Wapaling Khache over whether Saudi Arabia would accept Chinese passports, for it created "considerable anxiety as to whether they would be granted entry." They were told, however, by Chinese officials that "by the kindness of Chairman Mao, the Muslims had been able to proceed to Mekka."[31] More likely, the Tibetan Muslims simply joined Indian Muslims traveling from Bombay. Relatively large numbers of Khaches took the hajj during the 1950s. As Yusuf Naik indicated, many Barkor Khaches went several times, his father, for example, in 1953 and 1958.[32]

The ongoing contact with India and the Middle East, prevalent among the Barkor Khache, raised concerns among Chinese officials regarding that community's loyaltyy. Xue Wenbo was delighted that both the Barkor and the Wapaling Khache participated in the first May Day celebrations in Lhasa, excitedly describing them "carrying the national flag, enthusiastically shouting slogans." The Khaches' patriotism, however, remained an open question for many of the newly arrived Chinese authorities.[33]

If the Barkor Khaches were prospering economically through their trade and other commercial ventures, the Wapaling Khaches profited as linguistic, cultural, and political brokers between the Chinese and Tibetans. From the perspective of the Chinese, the Wapaling Khaches were crucial interlocutors. This affinity between these two groups did not always sit with well with the Tibetans. Some Tibetans even suggested that the Wapaling Khaches viewed the liberation of Tibet as a personal windfall, well deserved for their having suffered under the pro-British Tibetan government.

The Wapaling Khaches' rapport with Chinese officials stemmed from years of cultural and linguistic linkages, yet, as discussed in chapter 3, there exists little evidence that such connections caused the Wapaling Khaches to perceive themselves as "Chinese" or even "Hui." Rather, the local Wapaling Khaches, even in 1952, tended to describe themselves as common Tibetans (Ch. *Xizang de baixing*).[34] However, the pro-Chinese stance of the Wapaling Khaches gradually came to annoy many local Tibetans. This vexation most likely stemmed from the seeming favoritism shown them by the Chinese.[35] A former Tibetan government official, Tubten Khétsun, with a bitterness undiminished by the intervening decades, recalled that the Wapaling Khaches "immediately after the invasion welcomed and cooperated with [the Chinese Communists] like a baby embracing its mother" (Tib. *btsan 'dzul byas ma thag a ma yin shag dang nu ma 'thung shag*).[36] It was certainly not just the Wapaling Khaches who benefited from the arrival of the Chinese. As Dawa Norbu has noted, it was during the 1950s that "for about seven years the Chinese invaders literally [gave] away *dayin* (silver dollars). Every man has his price, and I do not think that there was any Tibetan heroic enough to refuse."[37] But the perception of the Wapaling Khache both benefiting from the Chinese and assisting them is likely accurate.

With a dearth of Tibetan-Chinese translators available in Lhasa, the Wapaling Khaches emerged as critical intermediaries for Chinese officials and soldiers. They were in high demand as a result of the political and economic forces in play, and these forces most likely proved too enticing to resist.[38] Like the Barkor Khache who profited from the new trade in luxury goods being purchased by the newly arrived Chinese officials and soldiers, the Wapaling Khache appear to have displayed little disquiet over any moral, political, or ethnic dilemmas that were presented by aligning themselves with the new Chinese presence in Lhasa.

The Wapaling Khaches' linguistic abilities also led the Chinese Communist officials to replicate early Nationalist policy by introducing state-approved curricula and engaging the Wapaling Khaches as natural partners in that venture. In 1952, two elementary schools were established, one was Tibetan and the other was Chinese. In the Chinese school, Wapaling Khaches held key positions and ran the school with the Wapaling *ahong* (a Chinese term for "imam") serving as the principal. A previous Wapaling Khache Council leader, Wang Chunshen, was appointed assistant principal. As had occurred in the 1930s and 1940s when the mosque became the Chinese school, the classes held on the grounds of the Grand Mosque offered instruction in Chinese, Tibetan, and Arabic.[39] While it may seem that an Islamic presence in Lhasa's first public schools under Communist rule would be an issue, in the near term, like the earlier efforts by the Nationalists, the Chinese officials had few options for instructors fluent in Tibetan and Chinese or for appropriate alternative school sites.

The more immediate problem appeared to be how to classify the Khache. Chinese officials and cadres admitted they were undeniably Tibetan, as demonstrated by their dress, language, and social traits, but they consistently referred to the Khache as Hui. The Communist government saw being Muslim as sufficient to designate them as Hui. The Chinese approached the question through the lens of whether or not Tibetans were Chinese citizens, reasoning that if both the Wapaling and the Barkor Khache had been treated as Tibetan and Tibet was now part of China, then the Khache were Chinese citizens.[40]

The primacy of Tibet as Chinese, while adequate to resolve questions of citizenship, was less effective in dealing with the question of understanding the Khache ethnically as either Hui or Tibetan. The default interpretation of treating them as Hui hints at the larger problem the Chinese had with individuals of mixed parentage and heritage or marriages between Tibetans and foreign nationals, as existed with the Nepalese and Ladakhi. Such questions were not simply academic, given that for several years the Tibeto-Nepalese Treaty of 1856 granting the Khatsara Nepalese citizenship had not been officially abrogated.[41] As groups like the Ladakhi, Nepalese, Indians, and other Himalayan peoples continued to traverse the Tibetan borders, as they had prior to Chinese control, the difference between Tibet's continued relationship with its neighbors, on the one hand, and the Dalai Lama's acknowledgment of Chinese rule, on the other, became an increasingly awkward issue for the Chinese in both predictable and unpredictable ways.

## LOST CITIZENS OF THE HIMALAYAS

What is often forgotten in much of Chinese scholarship on Tibet is that regardless of whether one accepts China's claim that Tibet has been part of China since the Yuan dynasty is the fact that Tibet remained far more embedded in Himalayan and Central Asian politics than the politics of central China. Tibet's de facto independence after the fall of the Qing in 1911 only amplified Tibet's Himalayan ties, allowing Tibet to reestablish itself as a political, religious, and commercial center among its Himalayan neighbors.

Although Nepal occasionally sent missions to the Qing court and Qing documents described the relations of Bhutan, Nepal, and Sikkim with China as tributary states (Ch. *jingong*), each of these states had far closer ties with Tibet than with China.[42] Complicating the picture is the fact that these same Himalayan states, in addition to Kashmir and other lesser Himalayan states, had all experienced varying degrees of British control, making them essentially British protectorates. At one extreme, in Sikkim, the British gained "direct and exclusive control over internal administration and foreign relations."[43] At the other extreme, in Nepal, Nepalese officials retained internal autonomy during the nineteenth and early twentieth century, although Britain often dictated the country's foreign policy.[44] Bhutan evolved from a quasi-protectorate in the late nineteenth century to being forced to cede much of its external affairs to Britain by the early twentieth century.

Regardless of this British influence, it was throughout the nineteenth and early twentieth century that all three Himalayan states continued to dispatch permanent and semipermanent representatives to Lhasa. Annual tribute payments were exchanged between Tibet and its neighbors, demonstrating the continuing relationship between them. The resilience of these relationships, in light of the tumultuous events in Asia during the 1930s and 1940s, is impressive. Although it is true that by the postwar 1940s, Nepal, Bhutan, and Sikkim were paid little heed by India and China, for Tibet they remained key nodes of external contact. Only with the People's Republic of China's decision to invade and declare Tibet part of sovereign China in 1951 did the position of the Himalayan states slowly demonstrate their relevance.

The 1950s were a time of careful Sino-Indian diplomacy, a diplomacy emerging out of these nations' shared struggle for independence and liberation from an imperialist past. As the Cold War heated up, both China and India sought to cooperate in the pursuit of a new Asian era, unfettered by the former colonial or new Cold War powers. Nehru had deftly negotiated India's independence from British rule and became the first prime minister of independent India in 1947. Similarly, Mao cast the victory of the Chinese Communist Party in 1949 as one of China having finally "stood up" after a century of humiliation.

Although both Nehru and Mao certainly aspired to become dominant Asian leaders and wield the informal prestige that would spring from such a role, both intuitively grasped the strategic benefits of jointly forging postcolonial solidarity in Asia. On numerous occasions following Indian independence, Nehru advocated on China's behalf, including consistent support of the PRC's claim to China's seat in the United Nations. China's invasion of Tibet did not alter his stance. Staunchly pro-Tibet, Nehru hewed to a distinctly pragmatic line, realizing that China's leaders seemed intent on reclaiming Tibet and that most of the other world powers were determined not to get involved. Nehru remarked, "I think it may be taken for granted that China will take possession, in a political sense at least, of the whole of Tibet. There is no likelihood whatever of Tibet being able to resist this or stop it. It is equally unlikely that any foreign power can prevent it. We cannot do so."[45]

After the arrival of Chinese troops in Tibet, and even after it was clear Nehru would not intervene, Tibet's neighbors did not immediately relinquish their extraterritorial ties with Tibet. Bhutan, for example, continued to post a permanent representative to Lhasa through 1960, even as it refused formal diplomatic ties with Beijing.[46] China's permissiveness towards Tibet's relations with its neighbors neatly correlates with the central government's initial commitment to Tibetan autonomy. Similarly, China, initially at least, allowed the Tibeto-Nepalese Treaty of 1856 to remain in force. This included allowing Tibet, with China's acquiescence, to continue making its annual 1856 treaty payments of 10,000 rupees to Nepal.[47] The government's early forbearance stemmed largely from its categorization of the Tibetan government's actions as ceremonial rather than political in nature. However, Nepal, Bhutan, and Sikkim, as well as the Dalai Lama and his Tibetan government, quickly demonstrated that they saw them as more tangible.

A year after Tibet and China signed the 17-Point Agreement, China could not have been happy to see Indian press reports of a letter from the Dalai Lama to the Nepalese representative in Lhasa (N. *vikil*) stating, "[I have] every hope that there will be no hindrance to continuing the age-old relations between my Government and yours. I pray to God that our relations may become stronger than ever."[48] A year later, in 1953, China finally informed the Lhasa government that it should cease the annual tribute payments to Nepal as stipulated in the 1856 treaty. But that seems not to have put the matter to rest, as two years later Nepalese prime minister M. P. Koirala asserted that "Nepal would approach the Dalai Lama and not Beijing, for Nepal even now acknowledged the Dalai Lama as the sovereign of Tibet."[49] As the political scientist Leo Rose correctly pointed out, Nepal's stance "by implication, at least, seem[s] to question China's claim to sovereignty in Tibet."[50]

It is odd that despite China telling the Tibetan government to cease its relations with Nepal, neither the Tibetan nor the Chinese government notified Nepal of the intention to abrogate the treaty, which left Nepalese officials simply waiting for the tribute mission to arrive in 1954. This expectation is somewhat more understandable given that China and Nepal had yet to establish formal diplomatic ties. Nepal's surprise at this measure is palpable when the Nepalese prime minister somewhat plaintively conceded in 1954 that the "tribute-bearing emissary of the Dalai Lama does not seem to have left Lhasa."[51] The following month when the Nepalese representative in Lhasa was again instructed by his government to query the Dalai Lama about the matter, he was told "to refer all questions about Nepalese-Tibetan relations to the Chinese Government."[52] China's swift, decisive, yet unexplained actions alerted the Himalayan states to the intentions of the Chinese Communists in ways that troubled many across the Asian subcontinent.

Headlines such as "Reds Next Move Near India's Border" were common in newspapers, in government debates, and on street corners across the region in the early 1950s. Such concerns, when read in the context of global Cold War anxiety, appear unremarkable. Given that China seldom mentioned any of the Himalayan states, let alone made provocative statements about them, the number of entirely fabricated reports that circulated in the Indian and Western press was extraordinary.[53]

Many newspaper articles, politicians' speeches, and diplomatic reports citing a wide variety of sources (including Mao's own writings) began to assert that Nepal, Sikkim, and Bhutan, like Tibet, had been part of China and would soon be reclaimed in a similar manner.[54] A prominent promoter of such notions was George Patterson, a Scottish medical missionary who had lived in the Kham region of eastern Tibet for several years in the late 1940s. Forced to flee the region in 1949, he took up residence in the hill towns of Kalimpong and Darjeeling, earning a living writing stories describing China's ill treatment of Tibetans. In his first book, *God's Fools,* he claimed that China's occupation of Tibet was part of a larger plan to "liberate" all of Asia, asserting that "within one year Tibet would be liberated, within three years Nepal, Sikkim and Bhutan would be liberated and in five years India would be liberated."[55] Preying on Cold War anxiety, he promoted the phrase "Tibet's Five Fingers" to describe the designs China had on Kashmir, Nepal, Sikkim, and the North East Frontier Agency of Assam as natural targets stemming from their invasion of Tibet.

> Certainly as Mao Zedong has gone on record as saying that Nepal must return to China as part of her former territories annexed by the imperialists and he has also said that Nepal and China must work together to liberate their "oppressed brothers in India." But in China's long-term plan it is Sikkim, the middle finger, the NEFA, the thumb, which will play the key pressure parts in China's larger ambitions in these areas.[56]

There was one small problem with Patterson's assertions. They were entirely fabricated. No Chinese documents, and in particular none of Mao's writings, ever made any claim for territorial expansion into the Himalayan states. There was certainly nothing approaching the very clear claims the Chinese Communists had indicated for Tibet.[57]

## DR. SINGH AND REDEFINING HIMALAYAN ASIA

The active imagination of Patterson and others regarding China's interest in the Himalayan front range, however, should not suggest that the events in Nepal, Bhutan, and Sikkim were not of interest or did not affect Tibet and China more broadly. The extraordinary experiences of Dr. K. I. (Kunwar Inderjit) Singh reflect how little attention is given to the Himalayan context in which these events occurred.[58] Singh was a Nepalese politician who in the course of five years would be called a revolutionary, a populist, a communist, and a rebel, and yet he was a man who also gained the title of prime minister of Nepal for four months in 1957. His experience demonstrates the risk of viewing this period purely through a Cold War lens, a lens that focuses solely on nationalist or ideological themes to the exclusion of the still-present traditional interstate ties.

Raised in western Nepal, Singh led a peripatetic life that included growing up in rural western Nepal, fighting for (and being dishonorably discharged from) the Indian National Army (INA), fleeing Burma on the eve of the Japanese invasion just prior to his becoming a practitioner of homeopathy back in Nepal. An early member of the Nepali Congress Party in western Nepal, Singh promoted a reformist agenda that pushed rural relief to the forefront of Nepal's political consciousness. Singh's grassroots organizational skills and his ability to speak in blunt and coarse language that resonated with Nepal's broad underclass rocketed him to political prominence. The same qualities quickly attracted the attention of the government, which, threatened by his success, accused him of banditry and other crimes against the regime.

In the course of six months in late 1951, Singh was arrested, imprisoned, and escaped; he was ultimately rearrested and transferred to Kathmandu, where in January 1952 he awaited trial. A result of the ruling Rana family's oligarchic excesses, Nepal in this period was already experiencing a constitutional crisis. Singh was a popular leader, and his presence in the capital prompted sympathetic members of the paramilitary police to carry out a coup d'état.

Late on January 21, Singh's supporters released and immediately declared Singh the leader of a new parallel government. In a poorly coordinated set of maneuvers, the rebels raced to seize key governmental offices, to gain control over the nation's communications centers, and to round up top ministers, all in a bid to spur the reform-minded King Tribhuwan to call for an all-party representative government.[59] Instead, the state army, tipped off in advance, whisked the leading government officials to safe havens, quickly recaptured many of the key state buildings, and effectively forestalled the prospect of negotiations with the king. Less than twelve hours after it had begun, the coup had failed.

Realizing their fate, Singh and a small group of his closest associates, in the dead of winter, fled Kathmandu and headed north towards Tibet.[60] Exactly why Singh chose to flee to Tibet remains an enigma. His base of support lay in western Nepal near the southern Indian border. Politically, he had never allied himself with any communist movements or demonstrated strong interest in Chinese Communism. The decision to flee to Tibet must have been relatively spontaneous. Given the almost certain ruthless reception he would face upon capture, Tibet's proximity (roughly a hundred miles from Kathmandu) and misplaced optimism that the Chinese would support any anti-establishment movement likely seemed a better option.[61]

The sheer audacity of the escape combined with Singh's larger-than-life personality fueled wide-ranging rumors that soon filled the front pages of newspapers across the Himalayan front range to Delhi and beyond. By February, the Nepalese government, clinging to power and seeking to use the threat of extremist and radical political parties to gain public support for their government, insinuated that "the Chinese Communists with the help of the rebel leader Dr. K. I. Singh would take advantage of this [lack of peace] and enlarge their field of activity."[62] Weeks turned into months with no clear intelligence about what had happened to Singh, and the rumors grew. In March, reports speculated that Singh, with roughly "50 followers, fully armed, and a large amount of cash looted from the Nepalese treasury," had used the funds to make "substantial payment to local Tibetan officials for protection and safe passage to Lhasa."[63]

By April 1952, the stories began to take a slightly different tack. Some asserted that Singh had been invited to Beijing, his men had enlisted in the People's Liberation Army, and all were involved in a plan for Singh "to take a leading part in the 'liberation' of Nepal.[64] Shortly thereafter, it was suggested that Singh and his followers had been captured near Shigatse, with the Nepalese trade agent stationed there assisting in "negotiations between the Tibetan and Nepal Governments."[65] By July, a newspaper article highlighting disturbances in western Nepal speculated that the leader must be "a follower of K. I. Singh," since the "trouble-makers" were "either Communist-led groups or the rightist Rana elements or a combination of both."[66] Nor were these rumors simply gossip published by the papers to sell more copy. When Nepalese general Bijaya briefed British officials in May, he informed them that there was "no doubt that K. I. Singh had turned completely Communist . . . [and] that he was gathering some of his followers and [there was] a risk that he might stage an armed uprising in Nepal."[67] With the benefit of hindsight, we now know that the accusations claiming Singh and his men had joined the Chinese army or had participated in plans to "liberate" Nepal or that Singh had become "completely Communist" were entirely untrue. In some ways, the true story of Singh's time in China is equally interesting if not quite as politically expedient for those attempting to use his flight to Tibet for their own political ends.

In an odd twist of fate, on January 21, 1952, at the very moment that Singh and his men, desperate to escape pursuing Nepalese troops, were racing north to Tibet after their failed coup, Peter Aufschnaiter, grateful to have escaped from Communist-controlled Tibet into Nepal, was headed south along the same road. Aufschnaiter, the sardonic friend of Heinrich Harrer, whose book *Seven Years in Tibet* would make them both household names later that year, had fled Lhasa ahead of the arrival of the People's Liberation Army. In Aufschnaiter's telling, "K. I. Singh had escaped northwards along the road I was traveling down. His group crossed the river at Shabru, throwing the middle section of the bridge into the water to hinder pursuers, and then crossed over the [Rasua Garhi] Pass from Chilime to Chang in Tibet continuing to Kyirong."[68] Forgoing the main road for the less patrolled mountain paths, Singh eluded efforts by Nepalese troops to block his progress at Rasua Garhi pass (elev. 16,500 ft.).[69] His band of brothers fared badly. Without proper clothing or supplies, several of the nearly forty men who began the journey died in the crossing. On January 31, 1952, Singh and his remaining followers emerged in Tibet frostbitten and famished.[70] Singh later indicated that they did not reach Shigatse until March 20, 1952, where they remained for four months, before moving on to Lhasa in June.[71]

From all accounts, the Chinese were as surprised as the rest of the world about Singh's arrival in Tibet. It should be remembered that the first Chinese officials and soldiers of any significant number had just arrived in Lhasa months earlier, in September 1951, followed by the main forces in December. The first months of their occupation had not gone smoothly, as they grappled with rampant inflation, dwindling food supplies, and with having only a tenuous political grip on the country, outside of Lhasa and Shigatse. Although desperate to improve their image, the Chinese seemed at a loss as to what to do about Singh and his men, particularly as the Nepalese government, still treating the Tibetan government as an autonomous entity, communicated only with Tibetan officials in their effort to locate and repatriate Singh.[72] Given that the Nepalese and Chinese governments would not establish diplomatic ties for another four years (1956), the Nepalese actions were not completely irrational. Desperate to get control of the situation, Chinese officials went to great pains to have Singh and his men apprehended, even procuring a photo of Singh and providing it to the local Tibetan government. Given the political ambiguities of this situation, it is intriguing that the Chinese did not simply order Singh and his men back to Nepal. They chose instead to order the local Tibetan officials to hand him over to them so that he could be transferred "on to China."[73]

That Singh did not arrive in Lhasa until midsummer, five months after his arrival in Tibet, is indicative of the limits of Chinese control in those early months. As late as June, the Nepalese representative in Lhasa continued to effectively canvas "senior [Tibetan] officials to secure the handing over of K. I. Singh to Nepal."[74] Only in early August, half a year after fleeing Kathmandu, did Singh and his nearly forty followers leave Lhasa for the southwestern China city of Chengdu, which traditionally served as the administrative hub for Tibetan-related activities.[75] While Singh and his men were likely to have welcomed the Chinese intervention on their behalf, the questions of jurisdiction still being sorted out between the Tibetans and the recently arrived Chinese suggest the limited reach of the Chinese authority, or as one British official speculated, it could have simply represented "the procrastination of Tibetan officials."[76]

Singh appeared delighted to be in China. According to Chinese accounts, he repeatedly compared his journey from Kathmandu to China as his own personal "Long March," asking on his arrival to be taken to Beijing to meet with Mao Zedong. This request would be politely deflected and never fulfilled during his nearly four-year sojourn in China. After arriving in Chengdu, he and his men were provided with housing, language instruction, and the occasional outing. It was not until the following May 1953 that Chinese officials invited Singh to Beijing; the forty men who had come with him remained in Chengdu.[77] In Beijing he led the life of an honored visiting guest, living in a government guest house and meeting with a string of minor foreign office and friendship association officials.[78] From his treatment, it is clear that the Chinese perceived Singh more as a political fugitive for whom they had generously provided asylum than as a revolutionary leader whose presence could serve a domestic or international purpose.

The Chinese rarely, if ever, publicized his arrival or used him in politically motivated ways. No articles appeared touting his support of China, nor was his presence used to demonstrate the weakness of "lackeys of western imperialism." There also does not seem to be any evidence that they contemplated at any point benefiting from his presence in fomenting Communist activity in Nepal.[79] Several years later, in one of his rare public comments about his time in China, Singh simply stated, "The Communist countries have their own rules to regulate the movement of foreign visitors and political refugees. I was governed by those rules."[80] Even after Singh returned to Nepal to become prime minister for a brief period in 1957, the Chinese state media never alluded to his time in China, even though numerous reports of his term as prime minister appeared in Chinese newspapers.[81] While Singh's motives for his actions remained opaque, it seems likely the Chinese were primarily intent on keeping him from further destabilizing Nepal and, potentially, Tibet.

China's strategy to control the international framing of Singh's visit appears to have had some merit. Although all evidence suggests that China had given diplomatic relations with Nepal little consideration prior to 1952, China could hardly ignore Nepal's repeated efforts to maintain the terms of the 1856 Nepal-Tibet Treaty in which Tibet was considered an independent government. Nepal's expectation of annual tributes and the prime minister's reference in 1954 to the Dalai Lama as "the sovereign of Tibet" suggested that Nepal had no intention of accepting China's presence in Tibet.[82] Nor was China entirely sure of India's stance in the matter. Nepal had long been under the mantle of India. Nehru repeatedly asserted that the "Himalayas are the guardians and sentinels of India and Nepal and their white-capped peaks welcome friends and are a warning to those of hostile intents," going on to conclude that he considered "the fate of India and Nepal linked closely together."[83]

In early 1954, several disparate elements of China's broader plan began to move toward a delicate alignment with India, Nepal, and Tibet. Only months after Singh crossed into Tibet, India and China finally concluded a Sino-Indian agreement, which was signed on April 29, 1954. The agreement included elements that satisfied both China and India. Foremost of these was that India explicitly recognized China's sovereignty in Tibet and forfeited all former privileges that it held in Tibet. Despite considerable domestic opposition, Nehru had reason to be pleased with the outcome. The agreement's preamble included, for the first time, his Five Principles of Peaceful Coexistence (Panchsheel), a blueprint he believed would usher in a period of peace and stability in Asia. The principles the agreement envisaged were (1) mutual respect for each other's territorial integrity and sovereignty, (2) mutual nonaggression, (3) mutual noninterference in each other's internal affairs, (4) equality and mutual benefit, and (5) peaceful coexistence.[84] Speaking before the Indian Parliament and clearly defensive over claims he had been soft on China, he said, "In my opinion, we have done no better thing than this since we became independent. . . . I think it is right for our country, for Asia, and for the world."[85]

In the weeks after the agreement, India and China both, independently, sought to resolve the respective ambiguities in their relationship with Nepal. In Beijing, Singh was summoned for a forty-minute meeting with Zhou, who proceeded to tell Singh that while China supported the Nepalese People's Revolution (Ch. *Nipoer Renmin Gemin*), Singh should understand that "China would never send even one soldier [to Nepal]."[86] It would seem that now, with the Sino-Indian Agreement signed, Singh's usefulness was coming to an end. Soon after Zhou met with Singh, Nehru summoned the Nepalese foreign minister to meet with him in New Delhi. In their meeting, and in equally explicit language, Nehru explained that the "old Treaty between Nepal and Tibet had no force or relevance today" and that "in effect Nepal should recognize the change in Tibet and not seek to exercise any of its previous rights."[87] Nepal's efforts to perpetuate its advantageous status with Tibet had come to an end, and neither China nor India was about to let Nepal's wishes get in the way of their larger plans.

Singh's significance in the larger picture became apparent several months later, in October 1954, when Nehru broached Singh's presence in China during his first state visit to Beijing:

> There is a very small thing [I would like to raise]. . . . One man named K. I. Singh had created some trouble in Nepal some time ago, fled to Tibet. He was then reported to be in China. Later on, news came that he was being openly entertained. When persons who are traitors to their countries are thus openly feted then people naturally get apprehensive.[88]

After assuring Nehru that China had no intention of asking Singh to engage "in any activity for overthrow of [the] Nepal Government," Zhou and Nehru continued to discuss China's need for diplomatic relations with Nepal. Zhou willingly conceded India's "special position in Nepal" and agreed that diplomatic representation for Nepal "could probably be dealt with by the Chinese Ambassador in Delhi, who was also accredited to Kathmandu."[89]

As the discussion came to a close, Zhou Enlai raised the possibility of China being included in the Asian-African Conference championed by Nehru, which would later be known as the Bandung Conference. This was a moment that Nehru had been waiting for, for he emerged from the meeting with Zhou believing himself vindicated for engaging rather than resisting China's presence in Tibet. With Zhou's expressed interest in attending the Bandung Conference, Nehru had his faith in his Principles of Peaceful Coexistence confirmed.

Heavily criticized by his detractors at home for pursuing a policy of appeasement towards China, Nehru's efforts were seen by many of India's Asian neighbors as a masterful maneuver to break out of the dualistic Cold War geopolitics. Aware of the dangers presented by China's occupation of Tibet, Nehru clearly believed that the Sino-Indian Agreement and his successful state visit to Beijing validated his decision not to contest China's control of Tibet. It appeared to justify his policy, dating to 1950, when he first asserted "that neither the U.K. nor the U.S.A., nor indeed any other Power, is particularly interested in Tibet or the future of that country. What they are interested in is embarrassing China. Our interest, on the other hand, is Tibet, and if we cannot serve that interest, we fail."[90]

This stark evaluation of the options available to India in this instance reflected an unabashed pragmatism, even as Nehru remained optimistic about avoiding the high stakes politics of the era. Much of his political philosophy is referred to obliquely, using a terminological shorthand that is rarely fully defined—"third way," "non-aligned movement," or Panchsheel. His philosophy did, however, capture the ethos of the period among the newly independent Asian and African nations. In the end, twenty-nine nations, including Nepal, India, and China, came together in Bandung, Indonesia, to lay the groundwork for a future free from their former colonial rulers and to explore ways to avoid the emerging divisions being imposed by the Cold War.

A tentative postcolonial expression of Afro-Asian unity, the Bandung Conference sought to forge a Third World alliance independent of the First World powers and to create a neutral space between Communist and non-Communist nations. Indonesian president Sukarno captured the boundless optimism of the conference in his opening speech when he set out the task of the twenty-nine African and Asian participant nations as nothing less than to "demonstrate to the minority of the world which lives on the other continents that we, the majority, are for peace, not for war."[91] Yet the mere fact that Nehru had convinced the attendant nations to allow the PRC to attend, which was still unrecognized by the United Nations, was a major step in demonstrating India's commitment to facilitate China's role in Asia. The conference fostered an Asia-centered discussion of issues facing the newly established nations—not one governed by colonial powers with permanent seats on the U.N. Security Council. Nehru hoped that the involvement of China with Asian initiatives would distance China from the Soviet Union while nurturing the possibility that India and China would emerge as the centers of Asian authority, free of external oversight. For its part, China believed that attending the conference would advance its efforts to manage relations among non-Western countries, to develop Islamic connections, and to promote the rights of Overseas Chinese even if they had not been citizens of China for generations.[92]

A central dilemma for both India and China was that these communities of Indians and Chinese, many of whom had lived outside their homelands for generations, were perceived by their host countries as retaining enduring if ambiguous ties to their homelands. In many countries across Asia, the Indian and Chinese populations were seen as "a source of internal conflict and threat."[93] The sense of threat was particularly present in Malaysia, Singapore, and Thailand, where the Chinese made up a significant portion of the population, and Indonesia, where Overseas Chinese controlled considerable commercial and financial assets.

While all parties agreed that the implicit dual nationality of these communities posed a problem, the obvious solutions required multilateral agreements across Asia. Extremely sensitive to the accusation of fostering neo-imperialism, China and India sought to acknowledge their ethnocultural ties to these communities while advocating that they accept citizenship in their country of residence. Achieving such a solution would not only provide Asia's many newly founded states with a much-needed ethnic stability, but, as India and China recognized, if left unresolved such discontent would be redirected back at them and potentially prevent either or both from taking a much desired leadership role in Asia.

Nor was it simply demographic influence in elections or financial leverage that these newly formed nations most feared. In the case of Overseas Chinese, the question remained highly politicized. On the one hand, the Beijing government was concerned that many Overseas Chinese, particularly in India and Burma, might still be politically aligned with the Nationalist Chinese government which was still a prominent threat even if largely contained to the island of Taiwan. On the other hand, many countries in Southeast Asia worried that their Overseas Chinese populations might be susceptible to the Communist propaganda of mainland China and thus could serve as a fifth column within new nations. When this issue again emerged in talks in Beijing in 1954, Zhou Enlai stated quite categorically that China believes "there should be no dual nationality. An individual is either Chinese or a national of the country where he resides. It is a question left to us by history. But we would like to make it clear that it should be decided voluntarily and on the basis of parentage. If you remain Chinese then you cannot participate in the activities of the country where you reside."[94]

With this question of citizenship still unanswered and with a deep desire to offer tangible evidence of a triumph fostered by the "Bandung spirit," China and Indonesia sought to bring resolution to the question of the citizenship of Indonesia's large Overseas Chinese population. In 1955 roughly 1.1 million Chinese still held dual nationality.[95] Since Indonesia's independence, and China's liberation, a central concern for both nations was the citizenship status of Overseas Chinese, essentially persons of Chinese descent, who at the end of Dutch rule in 1946 had passively acquired Indonesian nationality while still being considered ethnically alien by the Indonesians. Such a choice was not a patently obvious one at that time for most Overseas Chinese in Indonesia, given the strong anti-Chinese sentiments in many parts of the country. As the historian Philip Kuhn pointed out, "For an ethnic Chinese to renounce Chinese nationality and choose Indonesian offered scant protection."[96] Agreeing that the dilemma needed resolution, China and Indonesia met and emerged from the meeting with a bilateral accord on dual citizenship: those individuals who held dual citizenship would be allowed two years to choose citizenship in one or the other. In the context of the Bandung Conference, this protocol captured the resolve to address the undesirable and lingering vestige of colonialism in a peaceful and collective manner. Many took the agreement as proof that these newly formed nations could broker their own agreements without the assistance of the former colonial and new Cold War powers. It also appeared to herald a broader resolution of the persistent concerns held by many Southeast Asian nations over the ambiguous status of Indian and Chinese communities outside of India and China.

The Bandung Conference also offered an interesting denouement for Singh. On the eve of the conference, the Nepalese king, Tribhuvan, died and his young son, Mahendra, ascended the throne. Hardly a reformist, King Mahendra, like many young Nepalese, still sought to guide Nepal away from India's overwhelming influence. He instructed his envoy to openly endorse the Principles of Peaceful Coexistence, and he fully embraced the goals of the conference. Sensing the appropriate moment had arrived, Zhou Enlai approached the Nepalese delegate and conveyed that "Dr. K. I. Singh and his followers were anxious to return to Nepal, if the Nepalese Government assured them that they would not be prosecuted or otherwise victimized."[97] Despite the shift in political mood since his hasty departure, Singh had remained a popular figure in Nepal's political landscape. After the message was relayed to the king and Singh's return agreed to, the Nepalese government asked only for assurances that Singh and his men pledge to forsake any form of violence.

By September 1955, Singh and his followers arrived at the Tibet-Nepal border. Singh was escorted back into Nepal and ultimately pardoned by the king. He received a hero's welcome, as described at the beginning of this chapter. Even the international press took note. *Time* magazine labeled him the "Robin Hood of the Himalayas."[98] The question of Singh's political agenda and aspirations remained unknown, though many assumed that Singh would be sympathetic to Chinese values. After several weeks of reflection, Singh astonished the mainstream political establishment by announcing a political philosophy built on a pro-India and pro-monarchy platform underpinned by a vociferous denial of any Communist ties. Nehru remained unimpressed. After meeting Singh some weeks later in New Delhi, he described him, with his characteristic sharp wit, as "not a communist, just a freebooter."[99]

With Singh's declaration of his pro-India beliefs, Nepal had become less anxious over China's territorial interests in Nepal. The following year, on September 20, 1956, Nepal and China signed the eight-year Agreement to Maintain the Friendly Relations between China and Nepal. The treaty not only officially abrogated the Nepal treaty of 1856 but also abolished all the privileges that Nepal and its citizens had previously enjoyed in Tibet.[100] The swiftness of this change is difficult to fully appreciate. On one level, the treaty simply brought the Nepal-China relationship to a modern diplomatic standard by replacing Nepal's representative with a consul. Yet there were other seemingly anodyne clauses in the treaty, such as the stipulation that all those "who travel across the border between the Tibet Region of China and Nepal, shall hold passports," that marked a rather sharp deviation from

Dr. K. I. Singh's triumphant welcome in Kathmandu, Nepal, on October 5, 1955, after having spent more than three years in the People's Republic of China. Copyright Bettmann / Getty Images.

the traditional ways in which Nepal, Tibet, and the other Himalayan states had interacted.[101] Given the centrality of the concepts of citizenship, ethnicity, and nation at the Bandung Conference, it is striking how little attention was paid in the agreement to the complexities of Tibet's Himalayan relations and multiethnic population. In many ways the post-Bandung period generally, and the year 1956 specifically, signaled a high-water mark in China's attitude towards Tibet.

The Bandung Conference, Nehru's Five Principles, and K. I. Singh's escape to China all reflect a shared activism rooted in dissatisfaction with the political limitations of post-independence Asia. As Singh's experience epitomizes, his quixotic choice to seek refuge in China ultimately led back to his championing the traditional pillars of Nepalese politics: supporting the Nepalese monarchy and the Indian alliance. Similarly, the treaties signed between China, India, and Nepal were greeted with considerable enthusiasm precisely because they sought to usher in a new Asian order, one that transcended both Cold War divisions and the long-established status quo between Himalayan states and their neighbors. Yet in the rush to move forward, many elements of the past were forgotten. The Bandung Conference sought to facilitate, in different ways, an inter-Asian communication that would allow such changes to occur. The confident optimism of the early 1950s quickly succumbed to stiff conservatism, particularly with regard to the concepts of indigeneity and citizenship. The seemingly simple solutions defining citizenship through the philosophy advanced at Bandung or by treaties at the state-to-state level became difficult to enact on the ground given the highly situational and often ambiguous definitions of identity. No ideological optimism was able to paper over those challenges. The lingering Himalayan relations combined with the hardening notions of state boundaries and identity caused considerable consternation for the residents of central Tibet. The Himalayan manner in which the Khache, Khatsara, and Koko had thrived increasingly faded, leaving few options in the new postcolonial era.

## THE BEGINNING OF THE END: 1956–1958

Much of China's early success in Tibet had been built on China's willingness to preserve, or in some cases simply to not prohibit, much of Tibetan culture, society, and, in some instances, government. In its depiction as a "forbidden kingdom," pristine and morally pure, pre-1951 Tibet has been cast as the epitome of an idealized version of premodern society. The few Western visitors in the 1940s often described screening movies to delighted Tibetan crowds as if seeing a film for the first time, suggesting that Tibet had remained untouched by such common "modern" experiences. There is, in fact, considerable evidence that the Tibetan elite were avid early adopters of motion pictures, and Tibetans in general were ardent consumers. Among the earliest of these enthusiasts was Tibetan commander-in-chief Tsarong Dasang Dadul who in 1936, after serving a sumptuous forty-course dinner to the British head of mission, Charles Bell, proceeded to give Bell a screening of an "8-millimeter cinema film which he had taken himself" on his "small electrically driven projector."[102] Similarly, the Dalai Lama, from an early age, had been fascinated with movies ever since he discovered two hand-crank projectors belonging to the Thirteenth Dalai Lama. The German visitor Heinrich Harrer and the English officer Frank Ludlow, serving the British Mission in Lhasa, encouraged the popularity of film in private and public screenings.[103] Although such examples suggest that movies were a private affair of the elite, in fact, a Barkor Khache, Abdul Aziz, opened the first commercial cinema hall in Lhasa in the early 1930s, screening well-known Indian movies to considerable popular acclaim (and profit).[104]

By the arrival of the Chinese in 1951, Lhasa residents had enjoyed the delights provided by cinema for several decades. The number, topic, and style of foreign films permitted in Central China in the 1950s, though perceived as a key avenue for the new regime to educate and indoctrinate its populace, was highly regulated. They tended to be limited to Chinese films or those from China's closest allies such as the Soviet Union. Chinese officials in Tibet decided quite early on to make exceptions there in an effort to woo favor among Tibetan residents for whom Indian films remained immensely popular. Within weeks of the Chinese arrival in Lhasa, Abdul Aziz's two younger brothers, Muhammad Asghar and Sirajuddin (commonly called the Tsakhur brothers), were, with little fuss, granted the necessary permits to show films at their private cinema.[105] Over the next few years, the Chinese authorities attempted to combine propaganda with entertainment, allowing the brothers to show Hindi films and even films borrowed from the Indian consulate, with the simple demand that all material be previewed for objectionable content by Chinese officials. As late as 1955, Chinese authorities still demanded that all Indian films be prescreened by them, though they had seemingly never censored or banned a single Indian film (leading many Tibetans to speculate the Chinese simply wanted a free screening of the Indian films).[106]

In 1956, a subtle shift began to occur. Although the cinema remained as popular as ever and was still being allowed to show Chinese and Indian films, in late 1955, the Chinese central authorities procured three Indian films (*Do Bigha Zamin, Awara,* and *Toofan*), dubbed them into Chinese, and offered screenings to "select audiences." Clearly, the screenings were an effort by the Chinese authorities to tap into the undeniable success and popularity of Indian films. There appears to have also been some resentment among the Chinese over the fact that Tibetans found Chinese films lacking. According to an Indian consular report, many Tibetans had remarked "about the higher technical standards and aesthetic qualities of [Indian] films as compared with Chinese films, which are mostly of a propagandist nature."[107] Perhaps Chinese officials began to tire of these unfavorable comparisons, one being that, according to the Indian consul, despite several years of exposure to Chinese movies, it was those from India that remained "extremely popular among the Tibetans."[108]

Business continued to be profitable and the political situation amenable enough for the Tsakhur brothers to decide to construct Lhasa's first public cinema hall on June 8, 1958. The Happy Light Movie Theater (Tib. *bde skyid od snang*) opened to great fanfare with a showing of *Jhanak Jhank Payal Baje* and included the screening of several newsreels of the Dalai Lama's visit to China in 1954. The audience that night included important Tibetan officials, "a few Chinese officials," and the Indian consul general and his staff.[109] This grand opening, however, marked not the start of an era of superior cinematic experience but the beginning of increased Chinese censorship.

Soon after the grand opening, the Chinese informed the management that moving forward they would only be allowed to screen ten Indian movies per year. "The remaining pictures," they were advised, "should be either Chinese or Russian."[110] By the end of 1958, Chinese officials reduced that number to "only six Indian pictures a year instead of ten, and they would have to get the films through them and not direct from India as being done by them at present." As the Indian consul general at the time remarked, "The Chinese notice that the India pictures are very popular and they draw full houses, while their own [Chinese] pictures fail to attract Tibetans."[111]

Finally, in January 1959, the managing director of the theater was informed he would not be allowed to show any Indian films in the future but only Chinese and Russian films provided to them by the Ministry of Culture (Ch. *wenhua bu*).[112] The Tsakhur brothers grew increasingly concerned. Not only were they down to one Indian film every two months, they could only select Indian films from those made officially available by the Chinese government, with no access to the more popular ones available in India. To make matters worse, they were required to pay the Chinese government 40 percent of all ticket sales, as a rental fee, even though Chinese and Russian pictures attracted only fifty to sixty persons per showing and Indian movies "attract[ed] full houses."[113] Although Indian consulate officials indicated their distress and were "completely at loss to understand as to why the Chinese have passed this order," the signs of change were all around them.

The Chinese treatment of the Tsakhur brothers could be seen in many other areas of Lhasa life. Beginning in 1956, Chinese officials began to stress the need for Tibetan traders to "concentrate on internal trade and to gradually lessen dependence on foreign trade."[114] At the same time, Chinese officials promised "financial assistance" to local Khache traders if they would begin to challenge Nepali traders.[115] Several months later, Abdul Aziz, the original owner of the Lhasa cinema, sensing the shifting balance of trade, began withdrawing assets from Tibet and transferring them to India. The Indian consul, in his monthly update on Tibet to the home office in New Dehli, remarked that such a step indicated something larger afoot, since "usually these Muslim traders have a shrewd idea of the shape of things to come and their precautions give us some clue to the possibility of greater control over trade in the near future."[116]

The following year, the Indian trade agent apprised his superiors of the fact that the "Chinese were trying their very best to push their [Chinese] consumer goods into the Tibetan markets by requiring Indian traders to pay exorbitant rents for shops and storehouses," while the Chinese were allowed to "merely requisition such houses and godowns [warehouses] at a very nominal rent."[117] At the same time, the Chinese government began to wean the Tibetan region from Tibetan currency by attempting to set the official conversion rate at an artificially high exchange rate, over and above its market-determined value. Their clumsy attempt to favor their Chinese silver dollars as a half-step to ultimately introduce Chinese paper currency floundered in the face of near-uniform displeasure from the Tibetan populace. As Goldstein described the failed effort, "The opposition was led by the abbots of the Big Three Monasteries, who were the money lenders in Tibet, and who did not want the Tibetan government to lose the ability to print and regulate Tibetan currency. Tibet therefore, continued to print and use its own money until the uprising of 1959."[118] Though the Chinese efforts were temporarily thwarted, they demonstrated China's increasing desire to reintegrate Tibet into China in very real ways.[119]

In 1956, as the government in Tibet began to impose the regulations initiated by the treaties with India and Nepal, passports began to be required to leave or enter Tibet's border with India and Nepal. Previously such a requirement had rarely been imposed. As a reaction to the crackdown, the Indian consulate in Lhasa saw a year-on-year 400 percent increase in visa requests between 1955 and 1956.[120] That same year the consul registered five Ladakhi Khaches and two Nepalese as Indian citizens. The Nepalese consul general started issuing passports in November 1958.[121]

Individuals whose identity did not fit neatly into the national categories Nepal, China, or India began to express their concern.[122] The first were the Khatsara and the Tibetan wives of Nepalese citizens who were not consulted or even identified in the 1956 Sino-Nepalese Treaty (a notable oversight since significant consideration was given to them in the previous treaty with Tibet). Not surprisingly, such changes were not popular with the three hundred to four hundred Nepalese nationals who remained in Lhasa despite the economic downturn. Originally told they would be "given the choice to decide their future [citizenship]," by 1959, the Chinese government insisted that such individuals would first "be issued passports from the Chinese [government]." This was a significant shift: it meant they would need to accept Chinese citizenship before being allowed to leave Tibet in order to be granted Nepalese citizenship.[123]

For smaller communities, like the Ladakhi Muslims in Lhasa, the new regulations put them in a challenging position. Many Ladakhi Muslims had registered as Indian citizens at the consulate, but nonetheless they deliberately attempted not to advertise their foreign status in order to be allowed to trade as Tibetans. Since the Sino-Indian Agreement of 1954 did not designate Lhasa and Shigatse as trade marts for Indians, it was illegal for them to carry on their livelihood as non-Tibetans.[124] The point often lost regarding the momentous events of 1959 is how few foreign nationals living in Lhasa pursued passports since they did not intend to return to their home countries. Aside from the Khaches, Nepalese, Ladakhis, Khatsaras, and Indians who did travel back and forth with considerable consistency and ease between 1957 and 1958, few thought to procure a passport even as a safety precaution. In addition, given the swift downturn in foreign trade and the diminished number of foreign traders active in the trade that remained, the number of individuals needing passports remained quite limited.[125]

As discussed in chapter 3, the Tibetan designations of ethnicity, identity, and mixed parentage were seldom employed or well understood by the Chinese, making it difficult for the affected individuals to know the proper actions to take for their specific status. The transition from the traditional context, where such definitions were rarely disputed or challenged, as in the case of Sherpa Gyalpo, to one where such categories were now being demanded by the government was challenging. That this transition occurred with the swiftness it did, essentially between 1957 and 1959, and without any mechanisms to identify those groups who did not fit neatly into the newly established national categories—or those who preferred to retain their pre-1951 Tibetan categories as long as they could under the regional Tibetan government—resulted in very few individuals conforming to the categories now imposed by the central government.

The fact is that this very question—the ambiguity that lay at the intersection of ethnicity, nation, and regional identity—was what prompted China's participation in the Bandung Conference. That this troublesome ambiguity facilitated its single most prominent diplomatic outcome, in the form of the agreement with Indonesia about the Overseas Chinese, suggests that such issues were not completely absent from the concerns of the central Chinese leadership. Yet China appears to have been working with two standards. There was one for defining and classifying Chinese outside of China, primarily with an eye to entice them to declare themselves as Chinese. There was another for defining ethnically different Chinese inside of China, primarily with an eye to prevent them from declaring themselves as anything other than Chinese. For the Overseas Chinese, ethnicity trumped any assertion of nationality as defined by place of birth, since China wanted as many Overseas Chinese as possible to have the option of selecting China as their nationality. Domestically, Chinese officials were especially sensitive to assertions that Tibet and Tibetans were not part of China (or were not Chinese). Given this heightened concern over Tibet being portrayed as not Chinese, the Chinese authorities sought to invert that logic by suggesting that, except in clear-cut situations in which individuals could prove their foreign identity (usually by birth), they would be treated as Chinese. To put this in a slightly different way, the Chinese government, although using similar logic in both situations, insisted that Chinese with dual citizenship abroad should be allowed to select their citizenship while those with similar cases in Tibet should not. In Indonesia, it did not matter to the Chinese government if the Overseas Chinese had arrived centuries earlier or just last week; all Overseas Chinese should be given the opportunity to select their nationality based on their Chinese ethnicity. In Tibet, if you had foreign ancestry but had lived in Tibet, you were considered Chinese. Only if you had just arrived from a foreign country would you possibly be considered alien.

As demonstrated by the Chinese officials' increasing concern with the number and origin of Indian films being shown in Tibet and with their intent to exert control of them, the outward facade of normality that had been assiduously adhered to after their arrival in 1951 began by 1958 to crack. Internally, other indicators began to alert the residents of central Tibet to new political winds. Increasing numbers of Kham Tibetans from eastern Tibet began appearing in Lhasa, fleeing the increasingly harsh political reforms occurring outside of the administrative borders of the Tibet Autonomous Region. As the broader situation became clear, many in Lhasa, including the Dalai Lama, reevaluated Tibet's relationship with China's central government. It became clear that Tibet's limited autonomy was at an end.

# The Tibetan Muslim Incident of 1960

In January 1959, Mao Zedong remarked ominously that " in the Tibetan area over the next several years, the enemy side and our side will compete for the [support of the] masses and test the ability of the armed forces. . . . [I]t is inevitable that a great showdown will occur."[1] After eight years of pursuing a policy of accommodation within Tibet, the Chinese were growing weary of what they perceived as Tibetan resistance to Chinese rule.[2] Predictably, as the Chinese tightened their controls, the number of Tibetan "pro-independence" and "self-determination" demonstrations rose dramatically.[3]

S. L. Chhibber, who arrived in 1956 as Indian consul general, was one of only a few foreign officials who had long-standing familiarity with Lhasa.[4] Since 1936, the British Mission in Lhasa had resided in a traditional Lhasa-style compound on the outskirts of the city known as the Dekyi Lingka (Garden of Happiness). In the years that Chhibber had been in Lhasa, he witnessed firsthand the slow rise in tensions between the Tibetans and the Chinese. He was also accustomed to the short periods of agitation exhibited by one side or the other followed by a tense reconciliation.

In January 1959, something different was in the air. Chhibber grew concerned enough that he began to offer detailed reports to his superiors in Delhi on the unmistakable vigilance and readiness being displayed by the Chinese in what seemed to him to be preparations for a clash. All around the city, stone watchtowers were suddenly constructed at intersections and other strategic points as the Chinese became "feverishly busy in strengthening their defense."[5] These fortifications were erected on the top of the buildings where Chinese worked or lived. A sense of urgency permeated their actions, and when progress was deemed too slow, Chinese officials "requisitioned the services of their [Chinese] civilians, like barbers, hotel keepers, tailors, etc. to help them in making these [defenses]."[6] Rumors began to circulate of the Chinese stocking emergency rations and digging wells inside their courtyards. In tandem with these defensive preparations, the Chinese officials also began to exert pressure on the Kashag to expel the Khampas who had been flowing in from eastern Tibet and who were perceived to be undermining the city's stability. The general inaction of the Kashag on the matter made an already tense situation worse.

Speculation surrounding impending Chinese troop reinforcements and the increased swirl of rumors suggesting Chinese plans to seize the Dalai Lama exacerbated the already unsettled mood in Lhasa. On March 10, 1959, amidst swirling accusations and denials between the Tibetan and Chinese authorities, large demonstrations by Tibetans became commonplace. Both Chinese and Tibetans seemed to be at the end of their patience. Tibetan groups, including government officials, monks, and heads of monasteries, as well as an assembly of several thousand women, began to organize themselves. A deputized committee approached the Nepalese and Indian consuls in Lhasa seeking their support, advice, and protection. In each instance the foreign officials indicated, apologetically, that despite their obvious distress they could not interfere in the domestic affairs of China.[7] In response, Tibetans began to dress conspicuously in only Tibetan attire. Tibetan volunteers took up positions around strategic points. Tibetan employees of Chinese schools (and the Tibetans who attended them) were pressured to not attend work or school. Finally, the Dalai Lama and his closest advisers, unable to discern Chinese intentions and fearful of public consternation over the possibility of his being abducted, fled Lhasa on March 17, 1959, crossing the Himalayas and arriving in India two weeks later.[8]

On March 19, as news of the Dalai Lama's departure became known, Tibetans and Chinese, already tense, angry, and suspicious of one another, began a fierce fight for control of the city.[9] The fighting that occurred in the 1959 March Uprising has been portrayed primarily in Anglo-European literature as Tibetan resistance and Chinese suppression. And seen broadly, such a description is not inaccurate. Yet as the historian Tsering Shakya has described, the reality was much more complicated. That complexity was due in part to the considerable anger Tibetans directed against the "Tibetan ruling élite who, they believed, had betrayed their leader [the Dalai Lama]."[10] This anger, in the twenty-four hours after news of the Dalai Lama's departure became public, was not particularly rational, nor was it predominantly directed against the Chinese. Rather in these first hours the pent-up outrage tended to occur as unpremeditated attacks on pro-Chinese Tibetan elites at traditional Tibetan centers.

The first individual to be attacked was Sampho (Tib. Sampho Tsewang Rinzin), and it would appear his assault came about not as political targeting but an unfortunate decision to wear Chinese rather than Tibetan-style clothing. He was a member of the original Tibetan delegation who had agreed in 1951 to the increasingly unpopular 17-Point Agreement that led to Chinese control of Tibet. At the time of his 1959 attack, Sampho held concurrent posts as Tibetan Army commander-in-chief and as the PLA Tibet Military Command vice-commander. As he approached the Norbulingka Summer Palace in Lhasa, dressed in a PLA uniform and riding in a military jeep driven by a Chinese driver, a large crowd surrounding the Summer Palace assumed he had pro-Chinese sympathies and began throwing stones. As he exited the jeep, a rock hit Sampho on the head. Injured and fearful of further violence, he fled to the nearby Indian Mission Hospital for treatment.[11]

The next pro-Chinese Tibetan to be attacked was a prominent member of the Chamdo Liberation Committee, Khunchung Sonam Gyamtso. He had entered the Norbulingka wearing traditional Tibetan clothing but later left in trousers, a white shirt, and with a white surgical mask covering his face—attire commonly worn by the Chinese.[12] In Tsering Shakya's telling, "this simple act seems to have enraged the public, who attacked him and beat him to death."[13] According to another account, he was "shot dead and his body taken round the streets of Lhasa in the most humiliating manner."[14] The day ended, however, without overt military actions from either side.

The following day, March 20, began very differently. Tibetan rebels took up defensive positions at various points across the city, with the violence now deliberately targeting Chinese military forces and government buildings. At 10 A.M., in response to this provocation, the Chinese PLA was given the order "to take punitive action against the traitorous clique who had committed monstrous crimes."[15] Clashes erupted across the city. Particularly bloody clashes occurred west of Lhasa around the Norbulingka Summer Palace and the Potala Palace, as Tibetan centers of resistance struggled to defend these important Lhasa landmarks and repel the organized Chinese military assault. Given the overwhelming firepower of the well-trained Chinese troops, the opposition had little chance of success. During the fighting, the Indian consulate, situated between Norbulingka and the center of Lhasa, was caught in the crossfire, with bullets striking the building, killing a Tibetan staff member.[16] As the fighting spread into areas in and around the Barkor, the second story of the Nepalese consulate was also hit and damaged.[17] The Chinese government gave no figures of Chinese or Tibetans killed, but it estimated that "more than 4,000 rebel troops were taken prisoner."[18]

Almost as quickly as the fighting had begun, it drew to a close. Within twenty-four hours the Chinese flag flew over the Potala, dead Chinese soldiers and Tibetans littered the streets, and virtually all the Tibetan resistance had melted away. As a result, many Lhasans decided to follow the Dalai Lama over the Himalayas to India.

Rarely remarked is the fact that during the clashes on March 20, in addition to the "anti-collaborationist" violence at the Norbulingka and Potala, Tibetan groups attacked the Wapaling Khache community at the southeastern edge of Lhasa. This was unlike the attacks on individual Tibetans, for the violence directed at the Wapaling Khaches resulted in the destruction of their personal property, their homes, and their place of worship. By the end of the day, the centuries-old Grand Mosque and several dozen Wapaling Khache residences were burned to the ground. Wapaling Khache homes and shops along the market street were looted and ransacked. Despite the widespread attacks, not a single Chinese soldier was dispatched to protect the Wapaling Khaches or their property. Fearing for their lives, many Wapaling Khaches sought out the Chinese soldiers and took shelter in the PLA encampment outside the city.[19]

It is tempting to characterize the attacks on the Wapaling Muslims as a case of a minority population being caught in the crossfire of a violent insurgency, but that does not seem to be the case. The Wapaling Khaches had over the previous decade, in the eyes of many Tibetans, clearly become identified as colluding with the Chinese and thus became early targets of Tibetan violence.[20] Tibetans made no secret of their open displeasure with the Wapaling Khaches' pro-Chinese stance. Some Tibetans suggested that not only did they offer aid to the PLA and Chinese officials, but when approached by Tibetans to help in the uprising, they were said to have staunchly refused. Nor did the violence against their community alter this attitude. According to the historian Tubten Khétsun, "During the subsequent violent suppression, many Muslim youths took up arms and accompanied the Chinese soldiers as translators, oppressing and terrorizing the Tibetans."[21]

With the departure of the Dalai Lama, with broad-based Tibetan resistance spent, and with the Chinese government abandoning all pretense of policies of accommodation, the period of the Wapaling Khache remaining politically ambivalent while benefiting from the Chinese came to an end. Deciding if one was Chinese or Tibetan became, for the Khache, a decision with far-reaching consequences. From this point forward, there would be no middle ground, and from the perspective of the Chinese government, there was only one choice: to embrace their Chinese identity or be labeled as a traitor.

Immediately following the 1959 March Uprising, the Beijing central government feared that its suppression of the uprising would be used to fuel accusations of the state being antireligious. They quickly sought to portray themselves as protectors of religion and denounced the Tibetan rebel attacks on the Wapaling Khaches as evidence of religious intolerance. Early state media reports of the Uprising portrayed the Wapaling Khaches as valiant defenders of the Chinese state against the treasonous and desperate measures of Tibetan rebels. Between the end of March and early May 1959, the *People's Daily* conspicuously featured the Wapaling Khache in a half-dozen front-page articles detailing the Uprising. The earliest article, on March 31, characterized them as local supporters of China's military response to the uprising. Wang Peisheng, a Lhasa-born Wapaling Khache and a prominent pro-Chinese Khache, was quoted as asserting, "The overwhelming majority of

Lhasa's Hui are patriotic, and we, the entire Hui people, will steadfastly follow the Communist Party."[22] Two days later, on April 2, a front-page article appeared with the headline, "The People of Tibet Enthusiastically Uphold Suppression of Rebels," in which two senior Wapaling imams decried "the rebels' monstrous crimes of looting and burning Lhasa." The article noted that the rebels' "crimes reached up to the heavens and brought calamity to both the country and the people."[23]

Two weeks later, in mid-April, a front-page article denounced the Tibetan rebels, profiling over two hundred Wapaling Khaches and highlighting the harm done to them. In the article one Wapaling Khache, Ma Mingliang, berated the Tibetan rebels, insisting, not inaccurately, that the Khaches had been targeted "only because they were opposed to the rebellion and refused to participate in the pro-uprising rallies."[24] In late April, two more *People's Daily* articles appeared. By this point, the thrust of the articles shifted from the trauma endured by "normal Tibetans" at the hands of Tibetan rebels to the rebels' purported heartless behavior towards the Khache. The articles, far from defending the Khache, primarily were interested in undermining the commonly held view of Tibetans as peace-loving Buddhists.

By twisting the manner in which the rebel violence had affected the Tibetan Muslims who had lived in Tibet for generations, the state press sought to subvert the commonly held notion that Tibetans generally, and the rebels specifically, were innately harmonious and nonviolent. The first article was titled "Inhuman! Deplorable! Tibetan Rebels Heinously Murder by Ripping Out Hearts!" In an accompanying photo, Muslims are shown holding Friday prayers in the burned-out shell of the Grand Mosque. The headline of the second article, "Tibetan Rebel's 'Protect Religion Army,'" deliberately underscored the irony of the rebel's moniker by demonstrating their antireligious actions against Muslims. The article is juxtaposed to a photo of a Wapaling Khache standing forlornly in the remnants of his burned-out home.[25] Employed in this manner, the Wapaling Khache remained powerful instruments of the Chinese central government's claim that the Tibetan rebels were a minority intent on reversing the positive achievements of the People's Republic since its arrival in Lhasa.

In the weeks and months after the uprising, many Tibetan leaders were arrested, imprisoned, and often publicly criticized for their crimes during mandatory public rallies. All citizens of Lhasa were expected to show their support of the Chinese by insulting, spitting on, and, in some cases, beating the former leaders. Often individuals selected to lead such demonstrations were those who had personal grudges against the ones who were imprisoned. In one case, Chinese authorities selected Ghulam Muhammad, a well-known Wapaling Khache, to publicly criticize a Tibetan accused of crimes against the state.[26]

By early May, the prominent reporting of the Wapaling in Chinese state media suddenly ended. This dramatic change reflected the broader shift in Chinese central government's strategy, which shifted the focus away from the Tibetan rebels' antirevolutionary actions towards one establishing India's central role in organizing the uprising.[27] On May 6, the day after the last article in which Tibetan Muslims were prominently featured, this new anti-India offensive began with the *People's Daily* banner headline reading, "The Revolution in Tibet and the Philosophy of Nehru."[28] The long, 18,000-character editorial filled the entire first two pages of the paper. While saying little about Nehru's philosophy, the article articulately, and with choice use of Nehru's own words, attacked the Indian leader's views on Tibet's autonomy. Taking particular issue with how some Indians characterized "Tibetan autonomy," the editorial scathingly rebutted commonly held Indian perceptions of Tibet as a protectorate or buffer state of China:

> Some politicians in India regard China's "suzerainty" over Tibet like that inherited from the British tradition of the past: suggesting China's so-called "suzerainty" over Tibet is like India's "suzerainty" over Bhutan and Sikkim. . . . It is true that Tibet is not a province but an autonomous region of the People's Republic of China. An autonomous region has more constitutional and legal rights than provinces. The province has more authority under the Constitution and the law. But Tibet is definitely not a protectorate—neither a protectorate of China nor a protectorate of India, nor a joint Chinese-Indian protectorate, nor is it a so-called buffer state between India and China. The People's Republic of China enjoys full sovereignty over Tibet, just like it does over Inner Mongolia, Xinjiang, Guangxi, Ningxia [autonomous regions]. These facts are not even in the slightest degree in question, and no foreign country or the United Nations are allowed to interfere in any name or form.[29]

Alternating between deeply polemical language and scathing sarcasm, the editorial advised Nehru to pay more attention to his own country's problems and leave those of Tibet to China.

One also finds a subtle degree of introspective self-criticism. It went as far as to suggest that the Chinese government had waited too long, coddling the misguided efforts of Tibet's errant traditional elite. Only now, by listening to the will of Tibet's lower classes, was the Chinese leadership going to alter Tibet for the better:

> In Tibet, we displayed especially great patience in order to win the cooperation of Tibetan upper strata elements. For eight long years since the liberation of Tibet we maintained intact the former Tibet Local Government, its complete system, its army and even its currency and persuaded the people of Tibet not to carry out for the time being the reforms they urgently demand.[30]

While China's dissatisfaction with India emerged from many quarters, there is little doubt that by late May, the Khaches' claim of Indian citizenship had unexpectedly become a potential liability for the Chinese government.

Observant Chinese, now quite attuned to such rapid shifts in the political winds, would have realized that the Khache's absence from the state media was a clear sign their political stock had plummeted. However, it would have been difficult for any but those intimately familiar with Tibet to understand the continued role the Khache played in the Chinese government's growing unease over the situation. Part of the difficulty lies in the *People's Daily's* choice to refer to the Khache, generically and uniformly, as Hui (Muslim Chinese). As in the years leading up to the 1959 March Uprising, no mention or distinction was ever publicly made of the diversity within the Lhasa Muslim community.[31] Never, for example, did the media reports divulge that while Tibetans did raze the Wapaling Khache mosque, they neither desecrated the Barkor Small Mosque nor damaged a single Barkor Khache home. Not surprisingly, Chinese government coverage avoided mentioning the Wapaling Khaches' role as translators for Chinese soldiers and officials or that Tibetans accused them of "behav[ing] with unlimited arrogance."[32]

In the state newspapers, the Khaches' swift descent from fame to obscurity was a result of deliberate expediency, not unintended ignorance. In the hours after the uprising, and as quickly as the government acted to promote the victimization of the Wapaling Khache, they also moved to suppress what they considered to be the Barkor Khache threat to the city's tenuous calm. On March 21, the very day they secured control of Lhasa after the uprising, the Chinese detained and arrested Hamidulla (Rapse) Masle, senior leader (Tib. *kha che dpon po*) of the traditional Khache council.[33] This action was followed by two other arrests, and the entire council was in prison by the end of the year. Within the week, Chinese officials informed the Barkor Khache that all "previous laws and documents [regarding their Indian citizenship] were to be deemed as cancelled, and no claim was to be accepted unless it was backed by fresh documentary proof."[34]

On April 1, Chinese officials went to the Barkor Khache residences and businesses inquiring about their "race and nationality" while demanding at the same time that they declare themselves Chinese. Those who refused were taken for extended interrogation sessions that resulted in several Barkor Khaches being forcibly coerced into declaring themselves Chinese citizens.[35] Throughout this period, the Barkor Khache were forbidden from gathering in groups of more than three people.[36] Even as they disputed their citizenship, officials demanded they participate in various indoctrination and propaganda meetings, under the threat of being taken into custody.[37]

## TO BE TIBETAN IS NOT TO BE CHINESE

The Indian consulate was one of only three foreign missions in Lhasa, along with the Nepalese consul general and the Bhutan Mission. It was in 1947, with India's independence, that the consulate was transferred from British to Indian control, and a succession of Indian consuls had occupied the post over the next decade. Since his posting to Lhasa in 1956, Chhibber had made it a point to become familiar with the Khache community, and their decision to approach him was not unexpected.[38] In the face of these aggressive tactics, as Ramadan came to an end in early April, the Barkor Khache leaders "approached the Indian Consulate for aid, whereby they hoped to bring about the migration of the whole [community to India]."[39] Having traveled back and forth to India for decades if not centuries, the Barkor Khache were familiar with Indian culture, customs, and government. Many Khaches sent their children to school in India, and a small but substantial minority had moved to Kalimpong, Darjeeling, and elsewhere there.

Presciently, Chhibber had addressed the question of the Tibetan Muslims' nationality on April 27, 1958. Nearly a year before the Dalai Lama left Tibet, the Indian consul general in Lhasa and his Chinese counterpart, the director of the Foreign Affairs Bureau in Tibet, had discussed the issue.[40] That autumn, Chhibber again informed his superiors in Delhi that the "Muslims in Lhasa, especially those who have origin in Kashmir, are worried about their future. Some of them have approached us for registration as Indian citizens."[41] The 1959 March Uprising had both raised the stakes and dramatically altered the context of this issue.

Taking up the issue again in a note to the Chinese dated May 1959, Chhibber contended that his own investigation into the matter had led him to conclude that "the Kashmiri Muslims and other Indians living in Lhasa and Shigatse should be treated as Indian nationals."[42] Two months later, when the Chinese finally offered a response, it was equally concise and unequivocal: "These assertions are opposed to the historical facts and I cannot agree with them."[43] Not deterred by China's position, the Barkor Khache approached the Foreign Affairs Bureau to ask how to legally declare themselves Indian citizens and were told they needed to present Indian passports. Then, according to Chhibber's account, about "four to five hundred Muslims of Kashmir origin, who had never approached us earlier" came to him asking to register as Indian citizens.[44] After asking for and receiving his government's approval, he distributed forms to register them as Indian citizens. Just as the Barkor Khache prepared to submit the forms, the Chinese officials seized all their documents and declared them null and void. The Barkor Khache were then informed that any further efforts to prove their foreign citizenship would be considered illegal.[45] The local Chinese authorities then posted guards outside the consulate to prevent further communication between the Khache and the consul general. Throughout July and August 1959, groups of Barkor Khache that approached the Indian consulate were repeatedly "turned away by force."[46]

Adding a new wrinkle to the Chinese state's insistence that Tibet had been an integral part of China since the Yuan dynasty, Chinese officials maintained that all the residents of Tibet were Chinese citizens regardless of origin. While the Barkor Khaches were the obvious target of this policy, several hundred Ladakhi Buddhists who had never required passports or papers to cross the border into India were now detained and told they needed to produce documentary evidence of their country of origin. In a testy response to Chhibber, the director of the Foreign Affairs Bureau in Tibet lectured the Indian government:

> As everybody knows, among the inhabitants in Tibet of our country, there are a number of people of Islamic faith. Besides the Hui from such provinces as Yu[n]nan and Sichuan these are some whom we call Kachis [Khache]. Although their forefathers were from Kashmir, yet as early as the 17th century, during the time of the Dalai Lama, their forefathers had already chosen the Chinese nationality and had thus become a component part of the Tibetan people of China.[47]

These historical assertions did little to clarify why the Chinese government had not instituted such steps earlier or how such a view accommodated the realities of Tibetan autonomy under the Nationalists in the first half of the century. Nor does it explain how, according to the memoirs of the Chinese diplomat Yang Gongsu, the Khache had for many years been raising the question of their "Indian ancestry" (Ch. *yindu ji*). In his account, the Khache had first approached the Kashag in 1956, who in turn referred them to the Chinese Foreign Affairs Bureau. The Foreign Affairs Bureau rejected their request because it was "in violation of China's foreign policy," and also because the "Kashag had in the past consistently treated them as Tibetan."[48]

These specific inconsistencies added to the more general impression that the Chinese government had suddenly, in 1959, adopted a blanket policy forcing all individuals, with or without proof of foreign citizenship, to accept Chinese citizenship. The Chinese officials in the post-Uprising period seemed to be primarily interested in establishing a policy that would uphold their contention that all residents of Tibet were Chinese. They preferred this to sorting through the complicated pastiche of citizenship claims they faced, fearing that such a process would result in Tibetans claiming non-Chinese citizenship and make an already awkward situation worse.

The problem with the Chinese government's efforts to impose a one-size-fits-all solution on Tibet was that even in obvious cases of foreign citizenship, China's own national interpretations of citizenship laws were being ignored. In one instance, eight Nepalese, whose government had a recognized diplomatic mission and a representative in Lhasa, were arrested and held without charge. When the Nepalese consul general demanded their release, the Chinese replied that "there was no special law for foreigners and that their cases would be taken up under the law of the land."[49] Even those Nepalese who were not arrested, such as Nepali traders, were given the choice of returning to Nepal or remaining in Tibet, recognizing that if they remained their movements would be restricted to Lhasa, severely hindering their livelihood as traders.

By August, the constantly fluctuating situation for Lhasa's Khache, Nepalese, and mixed-nationality populations reflected China's new autocratic stance toward Tibet. China's new posture and policy were unambiguous. Tibet was a part of China, and no concessions were to be sanctioned. The consequences were immediate and pervasive. Chhibber disconsolately summarized this in his monthly report at the end of summer 1959, "With the overwhelming number of Chinese troops and cadres the local opposition has completely been overcome. The younger generation in particular have been taking active part in the pro-Chinese programs and activities."[50] Chinese authorities began to tighten control over every aspect of life in the city. All residents of Lhasa were rounded up and over the course of three days fingerprinted, cataloged, and issued identity cards.[51]

During this period, disinformation was rampant. Chinese officials and residents began circulating a rumor that the Dalai Lama was being detained against his will in India, and this led to a group of nearly five hundred Tibetan women storming the Indian consulate, "refusing to leave the premises unless some proof of the Dalai Lama's free movement was shown to them."[52] In June, the Chinese government circulated the news that Chinese currency would become the only legal tender; foreign and Tibetan currency would no longer be accepted.[53] Two months later, officials formally instituted the currency regulations but would convert Tibetan currency at only 20 percent of its face value.[54] With little or no advance warning, the foreign and Tibetan traders, who had been commercially prosperous until March, were faced with financial ruin, as most of their assets were in Indian rupees or silver dollars. When the news of China's actions reached India, silver prices shot up as bullion traders panicked over the prospect of a curtailed supply of silver from Tibet.[55]

By August, China and India appeared to be at loggerheads over the Barkor Khache. In mid-August, India's ambassador delivered a diplomatic note to the Foreign Ministry in Beijing. In the note he accused local Lhasa officials of arresting a Barkor Khache on August 6 who had refused to attend a neighborhood meeting intended for local residents. In response to the Barkor Khache's arrest, "two to three hundred of his compatriots went in protest to the Foreign [Affairs] Bureau." Later, when fifty to sixty Barkor Khaches "endeavored to come to the Indian Consulate," they were "prevented by the Chinese guards at the point of weapons."[56] While Chhibber assiduously maintained very careful relations with all Tibetans, the Chinese expressed unhappiness with the Indian consul general's behavior. Having already served for nearly three years, longer than any of his predecessors, the Indian government made the judicious decision to move Chhibber to a new post.

While not exactly unanticipated, Chhibber's departure was warmly welcomed by the Chinese. If the Chinese believed that his replacement would be less troublesome, they were to be disappointed. The appointment of P. N. Kaul, a career diplomat hastily transferred in from Romania, marked an astute shift in tactics by India in Tibet. With his arrival, the Barkor Khaches' status became a central concern of the Indian government.

## INDIA AND THE "KASHMIRI MUSLIMS"

If the question of whether the Barkor Khache were Tibetan, and thus Chinese, dominated the discourse in Lhasa, in India the question initially centered on the dilemma of whether they should be considered Kashmiri and thus Indian citizens. Indian diplomats, politicians, and reporters tended to use a hodgepodge of terminology to refer to them. Consul General Chhibber, in his May 1959 communication to his Chinese counterpart in the Tibetan Foreign Bureau, refers to them as "Indian Muslims from Kashmir," or "Muslims of Jammu and Kashmir origin," or "Kashmiri Muslims."[57] The Indian press, and even the *New York Times,* repeatedly referred to the Barkor Khaches simply as "Indian nationals" or as "Indian traders," emphasizing their rights as Indians. From the Chinese perspective, all Muslims in Tibet, whether they were Barkor Khache, Wapaling Khache, or Muslims from Beijing living in Tibet, were all Hui and without exception were considered Chinese citizens.

Initially, the Barkor Khache mustered historical evidence to put their case in the best light possible, even if the proofs they chose to use were selective, fragmentary, or deliberately taken out of context. At first, in seeking to prove that they were foreign, not simply of foreign ancestry, they often purposely conflated their position with that of the Ladakhi community by playing into the ongoing confusion over Khache/Kashmiri terminology. Given their clear-cut pre-1951 status as Tibetan, the Barkor Khache appeared to be unsure of the best path forward to prove their Indian ancestry. In the face of the persistent Chinese assertion that to be Tibetan is to be Chinese, they sought to play to the common (albeit false) notion that in the eyes of the Tibetan government they had been like the Ladakhi in order to prove their claims. The "evidence" they provided was a mixture of half-truths and white lies that played to the Chinese ignorance of Tibetan society, including that they were "tax exempt," that they were self-ruled by the Khache council, and, citing a Tibetan dictionary, that they were defined as "Kashmiri."[58] The Chinese never directly refuted the Barkor Khaches' argument but simply indicated that none of this definitively proved they were not Tibetan and thus were Chinese.

In the months immediately after the Uprising, Indian officials were equally at a loss as to how to prove that the Khache were Kashmiri and thus Indian. In the Indian parliament, Nehru's response to queries about Indian citizens arrested by Chinese forces at first suggested it was just a matter of clarification: "We have approached the Chinese authorities to permit Muslims from Kashmir as well as Ladakhi Lamas to contact our Consulate in Lhasa and to allow them to return to India if they so wish." When immediately pressed for more details, Nehru could only state:

> Two types of Indians went there [Tibet]; the one were the [Buddhist] Lamas and they went for study there; the other were Ladakhi Muslims who sued to go for trade. According to our old practice nobody need get the papers and most of them did not. So, we had no record. . . . The Chinese authorities have raised the point that these people are no longer Indian citizens if ever they were because many of the Kashmiris—Ladakhi Muslims—have been there for a long time. That is a matter on which we are conferring with them.[59]

Yet, when immediately pressed again, Nehru elucidated with even greater clarity:

> There is no question of mistaken identity. It is a question of a person establishing his nationality, not identity. Nationality is normally established by papers, passports etc. Now, they have no papers and passports except such oral or other evidence they might give. Immediately it becomes a little less definite although it might be established. It depends upon the authorities taking a strict view or a flexible view about it. They [Khache] have said quite definitely that they are Indian nationals from Kashmir.[60]

Clearly, Nehru, by September 1959, had already concluded that the Barkor Khache met the criteria to be considered Indian citizens.

Despite Nehru's newfound confidence, it was only months earlier that Indian and Chinese officials appeared far less sanguine about their positions vis-à-vis the Khache. In May 1959, a group of Tibetan Muslims on hajj found themselves stranded in Bombay and without international travel documents. Having left Lhasa prior to the political tensions, the pilgrims, as customary for several decades, had been allowed to cross the Indian border with the simple notation that they were pilgrims traveling to Mecca via Bombay.[61] For many years Bombay had functioned as the primary exit port for Muslims traveling to Jeddah by boat on their hajj to Mecca. The presence of Tibetan Muslims would not have attracted attention in the past, but as this group attempted to board the boat, Indian agents discovered their lack of international travel papers and they were stopped. A progressively stringent enforcement of hajj travelers' identity had begun under the British in the 1930s, making their plight a not uncommon occurrence. What made this story newsworthy was the fact that when the Tibetan Muslims approached the Chinese consulate in Bombay, the Chinese refused to issue them passports or to claim them as Chinese citizens.

Alerted to their plight when he saw a picture of them in a newspaper, Nehru personally raised the matter with his foreign secretary, Subimal Dutt, asking him to intervene on their behalf. Several days later, Morarji Desai, the Indian finance minister, was dispatched to meet with them at the hajj Pilgrims Welfare Committee office in Bombay and facilitated their departure.[62] Nehru's growing interest in the Khache issue almost certainly stemmed from the immense domestic and international acclaim he had received because of his treatment of the Dalai Lama. In early July, he would write again to Dutt regarding China's increasingly belligerent behavior towards India's consulate officials and the continuing anti-India abuse in the Chinese media: "I have been wondering if we have done all we could in these matters. The impression created in my mind is that the Chinese authorities in Tibet are behaving very badly and are trying to squeeze out our people."[63] As Nehru began to orchestrate a state response to resolve the Khache issue in Tibet, other Tibetan Muslims in India also began to mobilize their resources.

A small Tibetan Muslim community had existed in Kalimpong since at least the 1930s and had retained strong connections to the Barkor Khache in Lhasa. As the situation deteriorated in Lhasa, they were the first group that the Lhasa Khache attempted to contact for assistance. Their first letter, written in Urdu to escape Chinese detection and smuggled out by Tibetan traders, arrived in late April. This letter outlined the basis for their claim to be Indian citizens, almost as if to signal their strategy with a single voice to those Khache in India:

> It is vitally important for us to let you know that the Chinese Government, after the recent trouble in Lhasa, has threateningly asked us about our ancestry. In reply we have declared ourselves with cogent evidence as Kashmiris and subjects of INDIA. The Chinese Government is trying its best to subjugate us and make us Chinese Nationals. With great perseverance and sacrifice we reported the matter to the Chinese Government as well as to the Indian Counsel in DEKILINGA. The Indian Counsel at Dikilinga is also striving hard for us by representing to the Chinese Government that we are INDIAN NATIONALS, and you might have heard it on the Radio.[64]

The overall tone of the letter is one of extreme urgency. It repeatedly emphasized their dire circumstances in Lhasa and ardently demanded the assistance of those Khaches living in Kalimpong. The authors of the letter cast their appeal in multiple registers, including their obligation as Muslims: "It is a question of the entire generation whether it will cling to its faith or turn infidel. . . . Muslims and specifically our own kith and kin must not sit idly by enjoying comfort and remaining indifferent."[65] The letter concludes by addressing the two Khaches in Kalimpong by name and calling their request a "test from Allah." A second letter from them was received several months later and said plaintively, clearly at their wits' end, "we were hopeful after our last letter that you would surely do something for us. But we sadly noted that nothing was done."[66] In spite of their concern, many among the Khache in Kalimpong had taken up their cause, none more than Fazullah Chisti. Chisti, a prominent citizen of Kalimpong had in the past aided Khaches in securing needed Indian transit permits and passage on the annual hajj boats from Bombay. Immediately after receiving the first letter, Chisti had approached Indian officials with memoranda and face-to-face meetings.[67]

By late August 1959, several factors converged to facilitate the Kalimpong efforts to raise awareness of their fellow Khaches' plight in Lhasa. Chisti led a four-member delegation from Kalimpong to New Delhi to "meet Mr. Nehru and other members of the Cabinet and . . . apprise them of the difficulties being faced by Indian traders in Tibet."[68] As noted above, his timing coincided fortuitously with the Indian government's renewed efforts to discover a process by which to resolve the issue. Indian public opinion also became more interested as a result of a flurry of front-page articles in early to mid-August that pushed for a resolution to the Khaches' situation.[69]

Tibetan Muslims at the Haj Pilgrims Welfare Committee office in Bombay, India, pleading with Morarji Desai, Indian finance minister, May 28, 1959. Copyright AP Photo.

From spring to late summer of 1959, the parameters of the dispute over the Barkor Khache remained for all parties involved—Indian, Chinese, and the Khache—largely a reiteration of previous assertions about (1) the historical status of the Khache under the Tibetan government prior to 1950, (2) the issuing agency of the Khaches' passport or visa to travel to Mecca on the hajj, and, often, (3) the assertion that the term "Khache" meant Kashmiri and thus, ipso facto, the Khache should be adjudged to be Indian citizens.[70] In late August, however, two seemingly unconnected events—a skirmish at the Sino-Indian border outpost of Longju and an anti-Chinese trade ban in Indonesia—preceding the ratification of the Dual Nationality Treaty between Indonesia and the People's Republic of China dramatically altered the context and rationale with which both China and India would interpret and portray the Lhasa Khache.

## BANDUNG'S REVENGE

The Bandung Conference had achieved considerable goodwill across Asia in 1955. All participant countries were deeply committed to a wide range of issues; however, only China and Indonesia had emerged at the end of the meeting with a bilateral accord on dual citizenship. The agreement sought to clarify for both nations the citizenship status of Overseas Chinese who had, at the end of Dutch rule in 1946, passively acquired Indonesian citizenship while still being considered ethnically alien. This protocol captured the goal of the Bandung Conference to resolve the undesirable and lingering vestiges of colonialism. It also appeared to proclaim a broader resolution of the persisting concerns many Southeast Asian nations held regarding the ambiguous status of Indian and Chinese communities outside of India and China. While both nations agreed on the desired outcomes, they very quickly discovered they did not see eye to eye on the means by which they sought to achieve that goal.

The unbounded hopefulness that characterized Indonesian president Sukarno's welcoming speech in Bandung in 1955 expressed his desire to "demonstrate to the minority of the world which lives on the other continents that we, the majority, are for peace, not for war." Four years later, this optimism appeared naive.[71] Particularly in the Indonesian context, the lingering anti-Chinese sentiments combined with Sukarno's strong anti-Communist tendencies caused Indonesia to fear that China's actual intention was to spread Communism among Indonesia's Overseas Chinese population.

In the years following the Bandung Conference, the social priorities and political convictions had undergone substantial evolutions in both China and Indonesia. As a result, the ratification process for the bilateral accord on dual citizenship exposed the difficulty of transforming lofty sentiments into meaningful actions. In the summer of 1959, a complex combination of religious, ethnic, and political tensions culminated in the Indonesian government placing a ban on all alien-owned (overwhelmingly Chinese) rural retail stores.[72] In response, the Chinese government dispatched embassy employees to impede the ban's implementation by seeking to intimidate Indonesia into reversing its decisions. At an impasse, both nations dug in their heels.

Sensing little movement by the Indonesian government and believing they were winning over international public opinion, China dispatched merchant flotillas to repatriate the Overseas Chinese in Indonesia, culminating in more than 100,000 Chinese returning to China by early 1960. With both sides believing they had won domestically, Chinese and Indonesian officials finally agreed on terms and, in 1960, ratified a mutually amenable treaty.[73] Yet China's broad and assertive actions on behalf of the Overseas Chinese in Indonesia were now proclaimed in headline news around the world and began to intermingle in perplexing and unexpected ways for the Khache in Lhasa.

India, by late September 1959, realized that China's handling of its overseas population in Indonesia had created an opening for them in the standoff over the Khache in Tibet.[74] In the preceding decade, China had deftly managed to organize its domestic ethnic diversity into a state-approved set of fifty-six ethnicities (Ch. *minzu shibie*) that neatly existed under an overarching framework of Chinese citizenship.[75] But even as the classification had resolved the thorny issue of internal ethnic differences, China's traditional definition of "Overseas Chinese" remained unaltered. As so forcefully demonstrated in Indonesia, this rubric applied only to ethnically Han Chinese. As most Chinese understood the term, Overseas Chinese were those Han Chinese who had lived outside their ancestral homeland for generations but remained Chinese.[76] As China openly and aggressively demonstrated in their standoff with Indonesia, no amount of time, distance, or even intermarriage with non-Chinese diminished China's ability to declare Overseas Chinese citizens of the People's Republic of China.

The stark differences in China's definition of citizenship in Indonesia from that in Tibet demonstrated to Nehru that Mao's strategy, far from following the Bandung Spirit as a way to lead Asia away from the ideological quarrels of the Cold War, remained at its base an ideological cover to be used selectively to serve China's best interests. As the Indian government began to see the inherent contradictions in the PRC's policies, Nehru hastily seized upon the contradiction between China's once-a-Chinese-always-a-Chinese reasoning inherent in their definition of Overseas Chinese and the refusal to allow the Khache to assert themselves as citizens of India. India now confronted the Chinese government with the fact that having already admitted that the Khache were once Indian, China must allow the Khache, as "overseas Indians," an opportunity to declare themselves Indian citizens.

The first appearance of this diplomatic end run was in Nehru's answers to questions in the Indian Parliament's Upper House (Rajya Sabha) about the status of the Barkor Khache in August 1959 when he succinctly explained: "There is an argument going on between the Chinese government and ourselves as to whether they are to be considered Indian nationals or not. I do not want to take up in answer to the question the story of this argument. We think they are Indian nationals; they claim to be Indian Nationals; they want to be Indian Nationals."[77] A little over a month later, on September 24, 1959, the Indian government delivered a 2,500-word note to the Chinese embassy in New Delhi that fully explicated their position on the matter. Marking a major shift in Indian tactics as well as tone, the Tibetan Muslim issue was presented not as hinging on whether the Khache had been classified as Tibetan subjects but as the need to equally apply a single policy by two liberated Asian partners. More specifically, India began to use China's demands for its Overseas Chinese population in Indonesia as a criterion by which the Khache in Tibet should be evaluated:

> As is well known, a large number of persons of Chinese origin have been resident for decades, if not generations in the various countries of South-East Asia without having actually accepted the nationality of the countries in which they reside. In the Agreement which has been concluded by the People's Republic of China with the Republic of Indonesia, to take only one example, persons of Chinese origin have been given the option to choose between Chinese nationality or the nationality of Indonesia. The Government of India seeks no greater concession in respect of persons

of Indian origin in the Tibet region of China than the application to them of a principle which the People's Republic of China have accepted in respect of persons of Chinese origin resident outside China.[78]

Realizing that China's primary justification for not recognizing the Khache as Indian had been their historical claim of Chinese control over Tibet, the Indian government's note neatly exposed the intellectual lacuna between China's territorial-based definition of being Tibetan and thus Chinese and the extraterritorial logic deployed to assert Chinese citizenship in Indonesia. The note also explicitly pointed out that the Chinese government's earlier claim that "the Kashmiri Muslims were subject to the jurisdiction of the Tibetan courts, that the selection of their leader was confirmed by the Dalai Lama, that they recognized the Fifth Dalai Lama, and further, that they sometimes fought alongside Tibetan forces" was not in itself enough to "constitute conclusive evidence regarding their Chinese/Tibetan nationality."[79] In this elegant maneuver, India forced China to acknowledge in the Khache case that ethnic heritage trumped sovereignty. With this tactic, India had limited China's options to two basic choices: (1) either reverse themselves and surrender the ideological high ground to India but relinquish the rights of Chinese in Indonesia or (2) to insist that national boundaries alone defined Chinese citizenship and concede that the Overseas Chinese in Indonesia could not be considered Chinese.

China initially refused to concede either point. Instead, it adopted a two-pronged response to stymie India's change of tactics. Internationally, China denied that any double standard existed, insisting that "the Chinese Government cannot agree to the fact that the Government of India should lodge a so-called strong protest against this matter which is purely within the scope of China's internal affairs."[80] Feigning complete innocence, the Chinese maintained that "it is a fact known to all, that foreign nationals in the Tibetan region or any other part of China who desire to return to their country are always given permission" when they apply to the relevant departments.[81] Most telling, though, was China's meticulous avoidance of being drawn into India's comparison between the Khache in Tibet and the Chinese in Indonesia. Treating this statement as their final word, and despite repeated and insistent requests from India for dialogue, the Chinese refused all of India's attempts to draw them into any further discussion of the topic. Nearly seven months passed before China would again deign to respond to India's repeated questions regarding the Khache.

Internally, however, the Chinese adopted a rather more strident tone and course of action. At the same time that formal communications were being exchanged between the two central governments, inside China officials from both countries were taunting each other, using slights, snubs, and only slightly veiled insults. In particular, the Chinese singled out the Indian consul general, Chhibber, for his role in aiding the Khache. Having served nearly four years in Lhasa, his transfer to Sikkim was highly anticipated by the Chinese authorities stationed in Lhasa.

In early September, as the day of his departure approached, Chinese officials collectively declined to attend a farewell ceremony in his honor. To make their insult explicit and before his actual departure, Chinese officials came out in full force to attend a welcome party for his replacement, P. N. Kaul.[82] The Chinese government also ramped up its unambiguously explicit internal attacks against India. Both in the media and as topics for study in political meetings, Indians were repeatedly described as "expansionists" and "interventionists," with the Indian consul and his staff in Lhasa labeled "agents of Imperialists."[83]

If the situation became unpleasant for the Barkor Khache in the first months after the 1959 Uprising, by the end of the summer it became even more so. There was a marked increase in the intensity of an all-out campaign begun with renewed vigor by local Chinese officials to convince the Khache to give up their claims to Indian citizenship. This coercion resumed in earnest on October 21, 1959, when all Khaches were summoned by China's local Lhasa authorities and told they should attend the daily meetings required of all Lhasa residents. They were also "warned that failing compliance they would be subjected to punishment."[84] Over the next four days, Khache men and women were repeatedly held, individually interrogated, and "harassed and pressed" to accept Chinese nationality. When none agreed, one Khache family was placed under house arrest.[85]

As 1959 came to an end, the Barkor Khache adopted far more exacting and precise measures in their efforts to prove their Indian nationality. They cited instances where the Chinese themselves had acknowledged their foreign status, and they noted how they had educated their children in separate schools (madrasa) from those of the Tibetans prior to 1951. Initially such arguments seemed, at least in Lhasa and Tibet, to gain traction. Quickly, though, the Chinese again altered their tactics and attempted to compel the Khache to abandon their claims, regardless of precedent, and to accept Chinese citizenship.[86] The Chinese insisted on documentation, not only of Indian ancestry, but of Indian residency or citizenship. This was a requirement that just months earlier the Chinese had not enforced for traders crossing the border and had pointedly resisted in the case of the Overseas Chinese in Indonesia.

As a result, the Khache also changed tactics. Instead of working to provide evidence of their Indian origin, they endeavored to avoid taking any steps, administratively, politically, or socially, that the Chinese could construe as accepting their status as Chinese.[87] The Khache avoided all meetings that were expressly for Chinese citizens (e.g., not work related or required for other foreign citizens such as the Nepalese) and all large events of a political nature. As Indian consul general Kaul noted, the Khache became cautious when filling out forms that required them to include their ethnicity (Ch. *minzu*) or documents that were "obviously meant for the Tibetan nationals so as to have a census of them and enable them to prove their bona fides as citizens in every-day transactions."[88]

A new dynamic emerged that made an already unpleasant state of affairs even worse. Realizing that being considered Tibetan would be tantamount to accepting Chinese citizenship, Barkor Khache could no longer allow themselves to be treated as equals by their Tibetan neighbors, who were often their relatives. To this end, the Khache increasingly looked to how the Chinese government oversaw the Nepalese living in Lhasa. They insisted on being treated as noncitizens and rejected any administrative designation that grouped them with the local population. As the Chinese slowly began to impose more restrictive administrative control in Lhasa, the Khache could only resist passively and accept harsh sacrifices in order to continue their fight to make their claim to be Indian citizens. In 1959 when the government had begun to control foodstuffs in the capital by issuing ration cards, the Barkor Khache as a group refused to accept the cards because theirs were to be issued by the office for local residents, unlike the Nepalese, whose ration cards were issued by the Lhasa Foreigners Administration Department. Initially, the community dipped into its communal funds to supplement their supplies, but by December, goods on the open market gradually became unavailable, which caused the community considerable privation.[89]

The free-flowing Lhasa that had been so prominent in the early 1950s was now completely absent. In August 1959, Chinese paper currency became the only legal tender. Even though the purchasing value of Tibetan currency was a fraction of its face value, as fixed by the Chinese government, Tibetans continued to circulate it among themselves, and they still calculated prices with it. The Chinese responded by "flooding the market with their paper currency and withdraw[ing] the silver dollars." This action halted one of the last ways in which the Khache could procure goods and food.[90] The Chinese opened their own stores and prohibited all Chinese officials and soldiers and their families from purchasing foodstuffs from non-state-owned shops and shops selling foreign commodities. Such regulations were strictly enforced. If any Chinese soldier or official made a purchase from a nonapproved source and were "noticed by Chinese watch-dogs [they] were made to return their purchases and asked to buy those things from the Government shop."[91]

Nor were the Khaches alone in feeling the new restrictions. Over 1,500 Nepalese and Khatsaras and their Tibetan spouses remained in central Tibet.[92] The few dozen Nepalese traders remaining in Lhasa who were able to import luxury goods continued to thrive, and "Chinese soldiers and cadres flock[ed] to a few Nepalese shops for purchase of watches, cameras and similar luxury [goods]."[93] However, for the majority of the Nepalese traders who made their living selling essential goods, life was difficult given that the Chinese had banned the public sale of commodities. Even the sale of yak dung cakes and firewood was prohibited. Even those "pavement hawkers" who plied their goods on the streets of Lhasa were forced off those streets by a variety of tactics. As a result, Nepalese traders were increasingly closing their shops and returning to Nepal.

Returning to Nepal, however, turned out to be more difficult than it had been only a year earlier. The few Nepalese traders who attempted to return to Nepal found their way blocked by the Chinese, who refused to give them exit visas. Worried they were only making a bad situation worse, some Nepalese tried a more positive approach. Instead of filing protests through their government representatives, they sought to work with, instead of against, the Chinese. At the invitation of the local Chinese authorities, a growing number of Nepalese participated in the various cultural events and public rallies. Roundly praised by the Chinese officials at the time, the Nepalese were sorely disappointed when their participation had little or no effect on their status. The discriminatory pro-Chinese exchange rates, the preferential policies for Chinese traders, and the restrictive trade tariffs all remained immutably in place.

Nor were the Chinese authorities more generous in their dealings with Nepalese officials posted to Tibet. When the Nepalese trade agent posted to Gyantse attempted to travel to Shigatse in June 1959, he was denied transport by the Chinese and forced to travel by horse-drawn cart. Also, if Nepalese traders had Tibetan wives, which included about twenty of the one hundred Nepali traders in Lhasa, the Chinese were prepared to allow their spouses to leave the country on an ordinary exit permit, with one condition. The exit permits would be granted only when the Nepalese consul general certified that "in the case of death of either parent the property would devolve [to] their [Khatsara Tibetan] children."[94] At issue was the fact that the traders often had two families, one in Tibet and one in Nepal. The consul general refused to agree to the Chinese terms because Nepali law specified that inheritance "went to the legitimate collateral descendants living in Nepal rather than the direct descendants of the deceased living together in a family in Tibet."[95] Those Khatsaras who declared themselves Nepali and were granted exit permits for their return to Nepal were often shunned by their Newari in-laws and their "stepmother" (the Nepali trader's Newari wife).[96] Facing such a difficult decision, the Nepali community remained subdued, unsettled, and concerned about their shifting political status in Tibet.

On October 1, 1959, Lhasa, like towns across China, celebrated National Day. If the PRC's tenth anniversary gave Mao confidence in the path he had forged as the nation's primary architect, his meeting with Khrushchev in early October likely left him feeling deflated. The Soviet Union had remained uncharacteristically silent about events in Tibet and had openly sought to disassociate its India policy from that of China's.[97] When Khrushchev had visited China in early 1958, he responded to Mao's risk-taking brinksmanship with a shared Cold War comradery. When he visited China a year later, in early October 1959, Khrushchev was in a distinctly different mood.

Coming off of two seminal diplomatic triumphs, the visit of British prime minister Harold Macmillan to Moscow and his own visit to the United States the previous month, Khrushchev felt that the Soviet Union understood how to navigate the deep waters of the Cold War. Compared to China's more petulant brinksmanship with India and Taiwan (China shelled the Taiwanese islands without notifying the Soviet Union), Khrushchev's diplomatic maneuvers seemed to be paying dividends that irritated the thin-skinned Mao. Deploying his characteristic bluntness in a conversation with Mao, Khrushchev said, "If you let me, I will tell you what a guest should not say—the events in Tibet are your fault."[98] To which Mao, clearly peeved, replied, "Nehru also says that the events in Tibet that occurred [are] our fault."[99] Khrushchev, not willing to let the issue drop, needled Mao further by asking him, "If you allow [the Dalai Lama] an opportunity to flee to India, then what has Nehru to do with it? We believe that the events in Tibet are the fault of the Communist Party of China, not Nehru's fault."[100]

Though both men eventually let the matter drop, Mao's reluctance to let Khrushchev and the Soviets call out his actions in Tibet suggests that Mao himself realized that he was not entirely blameless in his handling of the events in Lhasa.

## LAST STANDS / NEW BEGINNINGS

By the spring of 1960 tensions between the Chinese and the local Lhasa Khaches had reached a fever pitch. At least twenty-two Barkor Khaches were imprisoned, the community was under increasing pressure to relinquish their claims as Indians, and the stress of the past year was beginning to show.[101] Chinese authorities, offering no explanation, searched eight Khache residences in the middle of the night. In Lhasa, the rationed food publicly for sale without ration cards was of bad quality and in extremely short supply. Staples like mutton and butter formerly available were virtually unobtainable. In spite of these hardships, the Barkor Khache remained steadfast in their refusal of ration cards, even as the last of their stockpiled supplies were depleted. In early April, they again approached Chinese authorities for permission to emigrate to India. The government officials responded that as Chinese nationals they would not be given permission to travel to India "except on regular [Chinese] passports for trade or meeting relations."[102]

On April 13, the Indian Ministry of External Affairs delivered a withering note to the Chinese embassy in India. It dealt exclusively with Chinese intransigence in resolving the issue of "Kashmiri Indians." The Indian note, written in the curt tone of a schoolmaster scolding a recalcitrant student, did not simply refute the past arguments of the Chinese, but demonstrated the inconsistency of China's policy with regard to the Khache. The Indians pointed out that the Chinese definition of nationality appeared to be "based on principles of *jus sanguinis;* that is, every descendent of Chinese nationals, irrespective of residence, was considered to be of Chinese nationality."[103] Following this logic, the Indian government found it baffling that "the Chinese Government should endeavor to challenge the right to Indian citizenship of Indian origin" since it is based on a principle to which the Chinese "have traditionally and specifically subscribed, and even now continue to subscribe."[104]

Citing that international law and international opinion were on their side, India's note preemptively refuted three common assertions repeatedly employed by the Chinese to stonewall Indian efforts to break the diplomatic deadlock. First, in answer to the Chinese contention that some Khaches held Chinese documents, the Indians observed that even if Indian nationals have "for the sake of convenience and out of ignorance, taken Chinese papers, the Government of India believe that such assertion does not apply to the bulk of Kashmiri Muslims, " and it should not deprive them of their Indian nationality.[105] Second, the Indians asserted that even if the Khaches had been in Tibet for more than a generation, they have retained a separate identity and there is no evidence that they "expressly renounced their right to Indian citizenship." Thus it is "unfair and illegal" to force such people to renounce their "assumed" Chinese nationality, given that there is no evidence to suggest they had ever "acquired Chinese nationality much less that they had surrendered it."[106] And third, the Indian government politely but firmly stated that "it may be expedient to recall the Treaty between the People's Republic of China and the Republic of Indonesia on the question of dual nationality." At its core the treaty affirmed the "principle that all persons who simultaneously hold the nationality of two signatory countries have the right to choose according to their own will which nationality they would wish to adopt."[107] The note concluded by stating simply that a list of "Kashmiri Muslims" had already been furnished and that "in the spirit of friendship" and "in accordance with International law and custom," "the Chinese Government will facilitate the return to India of persons of Indian origin should they so desire and that local authorities in Tibet will be instructed to remove obstruction in the way of their doing so."[108]

Later that same month, Zhou Enlai arrived in New Delhi for his first visit since 1956. In advance of this summit, the Tibetan Muslims living in Kalimpong sent a telegram to Nehru urging that "your excellency will also take the opportunity to talk about those miserable and deprived of human rights 135 families numbering about 600 people . . . [w]ho are still detained in Lhasa and Shigatsi [sic] by the Chinese government."[109] With tensions running high over border disputes between the two countries, neither side appeared to be in a mood to make concessions. Nehru was under extreme domestic pressure not to concede anything to the Chinese. Although Zhou and Nehru's discussions largely focused on finding a way to avoid aggravating the border disputes between the two countries, India took the opportunity to press China on the Khaches' situation, delivering an informal diplomatic note again stating strongly that in accordance with the Bandung Treaty of Dual Nationality (1955), India maintained that "regardless of the period of their residence abroad, these persons of Indian origin are entitled to Indian nationality."[110]

In spite of all these overtures and oral assurances given to Prime Minister Nehru by Zhou Enlai during his visit, China's home government remained silent on the matter.

Perhaps more disconcerting than the lack of diplomatic progress at the summit was the fact that the Chinese authorities in Lhasa appeared to redouble their efforts to coerce the Khaches to renounce their claims. On May 2, 1960, a young Barkor Khache, Abdul Ghani Shakuli, was initially charged with failing to have the proper licenses for his shop. It quickly became known, though, that the Chinese were in fact accusing him of being responsible for a series of anti-Chinese posters that had been posted anonymously on walls around central Lhasa.[111] Later that month, Shigatse leader Muhammad Sayeed was arrested after nine Shigatse Khache families refused to be strong-armed into attending daily political meetings.

It was on May 19 that Haji Habibullah, a wealthy Lhasa trader, was arrested after a search of his house uncovered a considerable sum of Indian currency hidden inside a quilt. That same day a second Khache, Gulam Muhammad Nyangroo, was also arrested. Although the Chinese found no incriminating evidence, they accused him of also concealing caches of illegal currency. The absence of such currency, the authorities decided, was evidence enough to prove that he must have illegally sent his profits to India.[112]

The intimidation and arrests continued into the next month. On the morning of June 20 and with virtually no advance notice, Chinese officials notified all local Lhasa residents, including the Barkor Khache, of a mandatory rally at the newly constructed Athletic Stadium. All Lhasa residents were instructed to gather at the stadium and to split up into their neighborhood units. When the Barkor Khache insisted they were not "local" and wished to remain as a single unit, they were "told they were not wanted at the meeting and should leave forthwith."[113] Later they learned that after they had left the stadium, seven Chinese and five Barkor Khache prisoners were paraded before the crowd in the manner of a show trial. Sentences for the Chinese were announced first, with six receiving lengthy prison sentences and the seventh receiving a death sentence. The Chinese prisoner was marched away at once and executed.

The Barkor Khache prisoners were then paraded out before the crowd "handcuffed, and with their heads bent, [to] hear the sentences passed on them." Two of the four prisoners were charged with "incitement of the [Khache] to claim a foreign nationality" and received prison sentences of eleven years. The third, Abdul Ghani Shakuli, the young Khache arrested in May, had the additional charge of illegally affixing anonymous posters with pro-India slogans on walls in the city and received a fifteen-year sentence. The fourth prisoner, Muhammad Umar Nyangroo, was acquitted and immediately freed after it was announced his father had publicly accepted Chinese citizenship. The message to the other Khaches was unmistakable, yet no other Khaches succumbed to the temptation of avoiding prison by agreeing to declare themselves Chinese.[114]

By early July, the local authorities were again escalating their campaign of terror tactics, as the Chinese broadened their efforts to menace, bully, and harass key members of the community. Already having shut down the Khaches' shops, the government now attempted to extract as much of their wealth, property, and assets as possible. They were "called every day to area offices, subjected to severe abuse and then admonished to line up with other Tibetans and attend indoctrination meetings."[115] On July 8 and 9, they were summoned by Chinese authorities and told to provide lists of all their property. Then the Barkor Khaches were ordered to pay, retroactively, six months of sales tax set at an inflated rate. This arbitrarily high tax rate was undoubtedly punitive, and the action was especially galling given that the private exchange and sale of goods with India had been at a standstill for almost a year. In most cases, the shops had been closed since May 2.

Although the Khaches agreed to pay the taxes, a day later they were ordered to return to the municipal offices where, according to Indian consul Kaul's sources, they were subjected to aggressive interrogation and beatings. Two of the Barkor Khache leaders, Barkat Ullah Shahkali and Ibrahim Naik, were singled out and charged with spearheading the "movement in the community for claiming Indian nationality."[116] The two then were beaten repeatedly, forced to stand bent forward with their arms behind their backs for hours on end while rifles were aimed at them, and were told that if they did not acquiesce and accept Chinese nationality "they would be shot dead."[117] Refusing to back down, they were released; however, as they left, officials told them to abandon their claims for Indian nationality and to attend the political meetings. If they did not, they were threatened, the "worst offenders would be shot" and the others imprisoned. Personal accounts describe the Lhasa Muslims as living "in constant terror" and in "constant fear of being deported or even executed." Others describe how "living conditions were very difficult in Lhasa" because rations were "fixed at ten kilos of cereals a month and one or two pounds of meat every two months."[118] Kaul informed his home office that the consulate, acknowledging their deprivations, quietly sold them food on the side, but even this only amounted to half rations.[119]

All summer long the Chinese had been mobilizing parades, political meetings, and propaganda sessions in Lhasa to promote the attempt by Chinese climbers to summit the Chinese (North) face of Mount Everest. On May 27, when news of a successful climb reached the city, the *People's Daily* reported that "over 30,000 people from all walks of life ebulliently poured into Lhasa's stadium."[120] Banners declared, "The summiting of Everest is a victory of Mao Zedong Thought!" Over ten thousand of Lhasa's residents lined the streets to welcome the climbers to Lhasa with a banner reading, "The conquest of Everest is the victory of the [Chinese Communist] Party's general line."[121]

At the same time, a new media campaign emerged spotlighting Tibetans who returned to Tibet from India after discovering that life there was worse than in Tibet.[122] In addition, local cadres, speaking out in neighborhood meetings, began suggesting that leaving for Nepal, Sikkim, and Kalimpong was a short-term solution with long-term consequences, since these areas would "eventually fall into Chinese hands."[123] In the local schools, anti-Khache instruction was included in the children's daily lessons.[124] All of this occurred against a backdrop of increasing political radicalization, including the emergence of communal organization, such as the creation of common dining halls and day care centers.[125] A Radio Tibet broadcast called for all Tibetans residing abroad to return to Tibet, claiming that the situation in Tibet had been normalized and that by returning they could "devote their creative energies for the development of their fatherland."[126]

The Chinese attacks on the Khache peaked in the second week of July with meetings called ostensibly to deal with the new sales tax on traders. At these meetings a dozen Barkor Khaches were subjected to extreme harassment after being accused of crimes and were assaulted for four to five hours at a stretch. Then, almost as suddenly as it had begun, it stopped. In his monthly report for August, Kaul stated, in some bewilderment, that "after the extreme harassment of Kashmiri Muslims during the second week of July, there has been a complete lull in the Chinese attitude towards [them]."[127]

## THE ROAD BACK TO INDIA

On September 2, 1960, with no advance notice, the top Chinese leaders from the Foreign Bureau in Lhasa convened a meeting of the Barkor Khache and informed them that although they were still considered Chinese nationals, "they would be allowed to proceed to India provided they put in requests voluntarily stating that they wanted to change their nationality from Chinese to Indian."[128] Acknowledging that their earlier actions had had a dire effect on the Barkor Khaches' food rations, Chinese officials discreetly issued provisions to tide them over until arrangements could be organized for their departure. The Chinese authorities also quickly facilitated the return to Lhasa of three Khache boys who had been studying at minority institutes in Shayan and Beijing so that they could leave China with their families.

Two weeks later, the Chinese Ministry of Foreign Affairs delivered a succinct four-point diplomatic memo to the Indian ambassador in Beijing. The memo characterized the yearlong deadlock over the Khaches' nationality as a misunderstanding entirely of India's own making. It asserted that "the Indian Government repeatedly ignored and distorted the theses of the Chinese government, flagrantly rejected the proposal for a sensible and rational settlement of the question of the nationality of the [Khache]."[129] The Ministry then insisted that while the Khache had always been treated as Chinese, the "Chinese Government would naturally respect the wishes of the concerned [Khaches] who do not want to remain Chinese." The note went on to suggest that "should they, out of their own will, apply to the Chinese Government for exit or ask to settle their nationality, the Ministry of Foreign Affairs believes that the Chinese Government, in view of the friendship between the Chinese and Indian people, will as before effect a sensible and rational settlement of their questions, and will be prepared to give whatever possible consideration to those who apply for exit."[130] The only caveat to this concession was that the Chinese would not release the five Khache leaders who had "committed offenses against the law."[131] In essence and in the face of mounting international pressure, the Chinese government conceded every point of the Barkor Khaches' claim of Indian nationality. Within several days' time, Indian consul general P. N. Kaul quickly drew up a list of the Barkor Khaches and issued identification cards with his seal and signature.

The Chinese, perhaps in an attempt to put a good face on what was capitulation on their part or as a final gesture of goodwill prior to the departure of the Barkor Khache community, compensated them almost 40,000 yuan for their destroyed mosque, for the other buildings they owned in central Lhasa, and for any immovable property they left behind. It should be noted, however, that the government drew the line at offering them any payment for the other Lhasa mosques and the thirty acres of property that constituted the Khache Lingka (Ch. *kaqi yuan*). Perhaps peeved by this treatment, when government officials attempted to present the few destitute families with rations for the journey to India, the Khache council intervened, rejected the government's offer, and instead paid for their food out of council funds.

The Chinese process of arbitrating who was a "Kashmiri Indian," however, immediately became more fraught than originally anticipated. Although the Barkor Khache community initially provided lists of individuals to Kaul, all these individuals had first to receive approval from the Chinese authorities. All three entities—the Khache, the Chinese, and the Indian consulate—initially appeared relatively lenient, allowing most Khaches who identified themselves as Barkor Khache to be issued documentation. This approval included those Khaches who had declared themselves Chinese. Several individuals who had actively and openly advocated for the Chinese against the Barkor Khache also managed to be included. As did two Khaches with Tibetan parents who supported the March Uprising. In the end, the Chinese authorities permitted each of these cases to be allowed to leave for India.[132] Perhaps the biggest act of leniency was made for a Barkor Khache woman whose husband had worked at the *Tibetan Daily* and was arrested and imprisoned under "suspicion of their pro-KMT [Guomindang Nationalist] tendencies."[133] While he was not released and despite the politically charged circumstances, she and her children were allowed to register as "Kashmiri" and depart to India.[134]

In the early phase of implementing the departures, it appears that several Wapaling Khaches received Chinese approval to leave by asserting some distant relationship to the Barkor Khache. In one case, a Muslim from Xinjiang attempted to claim to be of Khache descent.[135] But as the Chinese leniency became known, the Foreign Bureau soon began to be increasingly vigilant and to demand explicit and demonstrable proof of a relationship to the Barkor Khache.[136] To be fair, the selection process was complicated. Chinese officials complained that "many people claiming they are of Kaji [Khache] descent are fake. *But we have no way of checking.*"[137]

Given that Khaches lived in most of the cities in central Tibet, living in Lhasa was not a prerequisite for being allowed to leave. Five Khache families in Tsetang and nine families from Shigatse also came to Lhasa to be processed and were adjudged to be of Barkor Khache ancestry and allowed to leave.[138] Conversely, some Barkor Khaches adamantly refused to leave. In one case, the daughter of one of the Tsetang Khache families who had been working in Lhasa for two years, "point blank refused [to leave Tibet] saying she was happier here."[139]

## LEAVING TIBET AND RETURNING "HOME"

In the third week of September, the first group of Barkor Khaches and their families departed from Lhasa. By early October, nearly five hundred Barkor Khache were transported by Chinese military trucks to Nathula Pass and the border of still-independent Sikkim, where they were met by Indian transport and eventually relocated to the Himalayan hill town of Kalimpong. Over the course of the next six months, nearly a thousand men, women, and children left Tibet, virtually emptying the Barkor Tibetan Muslim communities in Lhasa, Shigatse, and all central Tibetan urban centers.[140]

For those unable to depart with the Barkor Khache, the situation was often bitter. There were others, though, who chose to believe the Chinese press and the rhetoric of the near-constant political meetings that told of India's poor economic conditions. They mocked the departing Khaches, telling them that they were making a horrible mistake and that they were better off in Tibet. Kaul heard that one Chinese official told a teacher applying to leave that "it was no use proceeding to India now as eventually the Chinese would be there in a decade's time."[141] Inevitably, as each group of Khaches departed from Lhasa, some of those left behind grew envious and despondent. Others, primarily the younger children who had received the greatest degree of Chinese political education, displayed a more "defiant demeanor."[142]

Having altered their stance toward the Khache, the Chinese government then attempted to deal with the even more complicated issue of Nepalese and Khatsara residents. Despite relatively clear terms in the Sino-Nepalese Treaty of 1956, the Chinese had initially refused to issue exit visas to Tibetan wives of Nepalis and Khatsaras. In May, the Chinese authorities finally agreed to issue passports and Nepalese visas to Tibetan spouses of Nepalese men. In August, the Chinese consented to provide passports for the Tibetan wives of Khatsaras even taking the extra effort to issue them transit visas which allowed them to proceed to Nepal via India.[143] On September 20, 1960, about 250 Nepalese and Khatsaras and their Tibetan families left for Nepal via India.[144] All told, under the terms of the Sino-Nepalese Treaty of 1956, roughly a thousand Khatsara opted for Nepalese nationality.[145] A decade and a half later, Dor Bohador Bista, serving as Nepal's consul general, estimated that the "Nepali population of Lhasa proper is about 350" and the total in central Tibet close to 500 individuals, with only roughly 40 having been born in Nepal.[146]

However, despite the fact that intermarriage with Tibetans was well documented among both the Nepalese Khatsara and the Khache communities, the Chinese refused to grant Indian citizenship to the few cases of half-Indians whose Indian parent was no longer resident in Tibet. The explanation given to the Indian officials was that "a child born of either father or mother who is a Chinese (now Tibetans are called Chinese) will acquire Chinese nationality."[147] If the manner in which the Chinese handled the Nepalese was protracted and resistant, it still appeared far more cordial than the manner in which they dealt with the Indian officials.[148]

By the end of the year, most of the Lhasa, Shigatse, and Tsetang Khaches who were declared eligible had departed for India.[149] All that remained in the Barkor Khache neighborhoods were those who had decided to stay behind in Tibet, those Khaches who were imprisoned by the Chinese, and perhaps a dozen Khache families whom the Chinese had rejected as not adequately demonstrating their case for Indian nationality.[150] The dozen families who remained were often cases of mixed marriages with Tibetans or whose relationship the Chinese authorities adjudged to be too distant from the Barkor Khache. Most continued to receive the support of the Indian consulate to press their case with the Chinese authorities but with little success.[151]

The case of the Khaches who had been arrested was far less clear. The Chinese had asserted in their September note, "As to the few [Khaches] who committed offenses against the law, it is entirely correct for the Government to deal with them in accordance with the law." [152] Initially, the Chinese resolutely refused to release any Tibetan Muslims who had been arrested even if their only "crime" was to have asserted their Indian citizenship, a status the Chinese government now agreed was correct. It was a decision made purely out of spite. Nor was there consistency even in this decision. Perhaps seeing the incongruity of their stance, a slow trickle of Khaches who had not been formally tried were released between October and December.[153]

On March 30, 1961, the last group of Barkor Khache, composed primarily of the families of prisoners, left Lhasa. Just moments before the group left Yatung for the Nathula Pass, Habibullah Naik was released from prison and allowed to join them.[154] On the same day, forty Nepalese and twenty Khatsaras also left.[155] The border crossing of these two large groups marked the end of the two-year ordeal for over a thousand Khaches and some two thousand Nepalese. Left behind were five prisoners: Hamibullah Shamo, Abdul Gani Shahkali, Hamidullah Maslie, Haji Abdul Kadir Malik, and Abdul Gani Naik. None would ever see their families again, and all but one, Abdul Gani Naik, would die in prison.[156]

## KHACHE BUT NOT "KASHMIRI"

In a sad coda, just as the last Khaches were making their way over the Nathula Pass and into India, the Wapaling Khaches also began demanding to be allowed to emigrate to India. Witnessing the success of the Barkor Khache departures, many Wapaling Khaches immediately petitioned to be allowed to leave as well—and some had succeeded, which only increased their aspirations. Given the large number of intermarriages and the complex family trees among the various Khache and Buddhist Tibetan communities, the maneuver is not as devious as might have appeared. However, Chinese officials quickly limited the criteria by which one could claim to be "Kashmiri Indian."[157]

As 1960 came to an end, increasing numbers of Wapaling Khaches came to the Indian consulate to consult with Kaul, even though there was the risk of having one's name (and number of visits) noted by the ever-present Chinese guard. The Wapaling continued to press, using the legal channels that had succeeded for the Barkor Khache. From the outset, Kaul declared quite openly that "there is no question of their being Indian citizens."[161]

Throughout the spring, the Wapaling Khache slowly escalated their demands. They boycotted praying at the Grand Mosque (only just reconstructed after its destruction in the 1959 Uprising), with a majority of them beginning to carry out their prayers and activities in the Small Mosque in the Barkor neighborhood.[162] By May they realized that the Chinese government had more or less finished processing all the individuals they intended to allow to leave for India. It was then that a group of ninety Wapaling Khache families, roughly two-thirds of the thousand-strong community, began adopting the same tactics as their now-departed neighbors. The remaining families resigned themselves to their circumstances and refused to join the increasingly belligerent actions of their neighbors.[163]

The Chinese government, realizing perhaps that they had the upper hand now that the worst of the crisis had passed, consistently told them that there was absolutely no chance they would be allowed to leave. However, the government officials never reverted to the pattern of harassment and intimidation that had typified their actions in the past year, even opening a Muslim *halal* (Ch. *qingzhen*) bakery in the Wapaling neighborhood in an attempt to ingratiate themselves with the Wapaling Khaches.[164]

Such efforts by the Chinese did little to alter their stance. Desperate to obtain a positive response to their request, nearly fifty Wapaling Khaches resigned their government positions in August 1961, refused their ration cards, rejected the Chinese household registration (Ch. *hukou*), and moved north of Lhasa to the

Muslim cemetery and small mosque in Dokdé (Tib. *dog sde*; Ch. *Duodi*).[165] There they pitched their tents and began a campaign of passive resistance. Other accounts describe protests in front of government offices, some Wapaling children being removed from the schools, and several older students, at university elsewhere in China, returning to join in their family's protest efforts. Kaul stated that "local authorities have recently been warning Tibetan hawkers and others not to help the [Wapaling] with the sale of food and loan of tents as long as they continued to live in the said garden."[166] Local Chinese officials, showing continued restraint, labeled their actions simply as a "contradiction amongst the masses" rather than the much more severe designation "enemies of the state."

As political tensions rose the sudden shift in the Chinese government's position led to accusations of Chinese infiltrators among those early Wabaling Khaches allowed to leave for India. In India, concern centered on several pro-Chinese Wapaling Khaches who were suspiciously, some felt, included among the Barkor Khaches approved by the Chinese government's Foreign Bureau in Lhasa to be allowed to emigrate to India. This struck many Khaches as particularly odd because other individuals with much stronger cases for Barkor Khache identity had been denied permission to leave Tibet. Attention quickly focused on the Wapaling Khache Habibullah Batt and his Nepalese Khatsara wife.[158] With no close ties in the Barkor Khache community, distrust of his actual motives was accentuated by the fact that the Chinese government had granted him an exit permit with other Tibetan Muslims instead of assigning him the seemingly more appropriate designation of Nepalese and returned to Nepal. The questionable circumstances surrounding his status, along with the highly charged political atmosphere, caused Batt and his family to be cast out of the Tibetan Muslim community and forced to leave Kalimpong only weeks after their arrival.

Batt's swift return to Lhasa after leaving Kalimpong suggests that such suspicions were not misplaced. In late 1961, Batt immediately came to the attention of Arvind Deo, who had just arrived in Lhasa to replace P. N. Kaul as consul general for India. In his monthly report Deo identified Batt as a Wapaling Khache who repeatedly met with the disgruntled Wapaling Khaches attempting to leave India. In these meetings, Batt painted "a grim picture of life in India" and spoke of "grave reprisals" by the Chinese authorities if they continued to claim Indian nationality.[159] Batt's special status seems to be confirmed by the fact that he received "special permission" to hold on to his Nepalese passport and "carried on his [religious] work even when the Grand Mosque was closed from 1966 to 1981."[160]

In November, Habibullah Batt led a group of thirty Wapalings out to the Dokdé group in an attempt to convince those Wapaling holdouts to cease any further resistance and return to their homes. Habibullah Batt's leadership role is significant, given that as a Wapaling Khache (married to a Khatsara) he had managed to be among those allowed to join the Barkor Khaches in emigrating to India the year before, and, it was believed among Chinese officials, his voice might help convince the demonstrating Khache that they would be better off remaining in China.[167] When his efforts to convince the renegade Wapalings failed, he and his allies issued thinly veiled warnings of Chinese retaliation if they persisted in their claims of Indian nationality. As the Wapaling protests continued, the Chinese officials began to grow weary of the movement and to fear political reprisals from their superiors if the protests were discovered. The authorities began to bring the Wapaling leaders to Lhasa in order to interrogate them, and Habibullah Batt continued to be dispatched by Chinese officials in increasingly futile efforts to persuade the Wapalings to return to their homes in Lhasa.[168]

It was at this point, in mid-December 1961, that the State Council (Ch. *guowuyuan*) became involved. According to Chinese Foreign Ministry Archive documents, the Wapaling Khaches had become increasingly disruptive, embarrassing Chinese officials by interrupting a banquet hosted for them at the Nepali consulate.[169] The Lhasa municipal government and the Party committee met to discuss how to proceed. They agreed that the Khaches should be fully investigated and arrested if found guilty of resisting the government's call for them to cease their demonstrations.[170] In what became known as the Lhasa Muslim Incident of 1961 (Tib. *hu'i rigs kyi rnyog gra*), the government's patience came to an end.

More than a dozen individuals were arrested and threatened with the use of military force to compel the remaining families to return to the city. In the end, without food, deprived of income, and forced to beg to stave off starvation, they slowly returned to their homes, destitute and defeated.[171] In his account of the period, Tubten Khétsun suggested that some Wapalings persisted in their resistance into 1963: "a few families were still stubbornly refusing ration cards, and their children were among the beggars along the Lingkor path during the fourth month Saga Dawa (Buddha's Birthday) holiday (Tib. *sa ga zla ba dus chen*) that year."[172]

The Wapaling Khaches' lingering reputation as collaborators and pro-Chinese diminished over the years, partly as a result of the manner in which the larger Khache community was split but also because of the hardships they had faced in 1961–62. But even two decades later when Catriona Bass arrived in Lhasa as an English teacher and the topic came up among her Tibetan friends, they expressed sympathy and even pity, noting, "Life has been difficult for them. . . . In the beginning of the Sixties, their situation was almost worse than ours."[173] Perhaps like many lingering prejudices, those past disputes, rifts, and altercations were forgotten when the violent political campaigns of the Cultural Revolution reached Tibet and in their brutality erased many of the earlier, now seemingly less important disagreements.

6

## Prisoners of Shangri-La

Late on March 17, 1959, the Fourteenth Dalai Lama changed out of his customary maroon robes into khaki pants and a long black coat. Knowing he could carry little, he hastily rolled up a favorite *thangka* of the Second Dalai Lama and slid it into a small bag. With this in hand, he slipped out the main gates of the Norbulinka Palace under the cover of darkness. Several trusted officials whisked him through the crowds, which had gathered there in an attempt to protect their revered leader, and down to the banks of the Kyichu River where several small coracles awaited to row him and his small group across the river. Early the next morning, having reached the 16,000-foot Che-la Pass overlooking the Lhasa valley, he paused, turned, and cast a long last glance over the Tibetan capital. Implored to hurry by his small guard unit, he quickly began the descent and his march south to the Indian border.[1] It would be the last time he would see his city.

Two weeks later, on March 31, having traversed some of Asia's most treacherous terrain and protected by an escort that at times was more than several hundred strong, the Dalai Lama arrived at the Indian border.[2] With the details of the March Uprising still largely unknown and with the Dalai Lama's arrival along with the tens of thousands of Tibetans who eventually followed him, Sino-Indian relations entered a new era.

After working for more than a decade to establish a constructive relationship with China, Prime Minister Nehru was forced to make a choice he had long hoped to avoid. Nehru, facing extreme domestic hostility to his policy of promoting engagement with China, remained skeptical of calls to alter his strategy. A mainstay of his Tibet policy was his conviction that only by maintaining friendly relations with China could India preserve its deep "sympathy for the people of Tibet."[3] Wary of taking any step that might create an atmosphere of "unfriendliness with China," he initially "rejected the suggestion that India should open her doors to all those Tibetans who might like to seek refuge in India."[4] His restrained stance stemmed primarily from his initial belief that the Chinese military presence in Tibet would prevent a mass exodus of Tibetans, and he was convinced that "it is not easy to move about from one place to another . . . and the few passes to India will probably be guarded by [Chinese soldiers]."[5] By the end of April, China intensified its rhetoric. As Tibetan refugees, first in the hundreds, then in the thousands, began to pour into India, Nehru finally realized his decade-long formulation of peaceful coexistence had become untenable.

Nehru's initial reluctance to modify his China policy lay in the dearth of solid information available regarding the 1959 March Uprising in Lhasa. Even weeks after the event, the outside world's understanding remained largely limited to what S. L. Chhibber, India's consul general in Lhasa, could glean from rumors, observable troop movements, and other basic information, all garnered while he was restricted to the consulate just outside the city. Many in India's press, and Nehru himself, were quick to compare the situation to Alfred Hitchcock's thriller *Rear Window*. When asked about Chinese reports admonishing India to "take an objective view on the Tibetan situation," Nehru, in a press conference, obliquely likened Chhibber to Jimmy Stewart's character in the film who is confined to his apartment and believes he has witnessed a murder. He said amidst laughter, "He takes an objective view. He sits near a window and looks at Lhasa. I think all these days he has been sitting there and taking this objective view."[6] India's most famous political satirist, R. K. Laxman, captured the powerful allusion, lost in the actual transcription of Nehru's comment, and also amplified it by placing Nehru himself in the window.

Few would have missed Laxman's and Nehru's broader point in comparing *Rear Window* to the situation in Tibet since the film's denouement turned on the fact that people initially dismissed his claims only to discover that a murder had actually occurred. Although Chhibber, like the film's star, Jimmy Stewart, finally succeeded in relaying the details of the uprising to India and the world, Nehru's position remained tentative, as the details emerged slowly to paint a fuller picture of life in Tibet.

By early May 1959, it became clear that the Chinese could not stem the tide of refugees, nor would they passively accept that India was offering sanctuary to the Dalai Lama and thousands of Tibetan refugees. It was then that Nehru, for the first time as prime minister, candidly asserted that India had to adhere to its basic values and beliefs "even though the Chinese do not like it."[7] With this assertion, and in the face of China's virulent anti-Indian rhetoric, Nehru assented to providing accommodation and material relief to the Tibetan refugees who had begun to find their way into India. Within the month, the Indian government had begun to issue "Indian Registration Certificates" to the more than 15,000 Tibetans who had entered the country. By the end of 1962, when the Chinese had effectively sealed the Indo-Tibetan border, no fewer than 80,000 Tibetans had traveled by foot from Tibet, with most of them settling as resident refugees in India.[8] China regarded India's actions in providing asylum for the Dalai Lama and the multitude of refugees who flowed into India in the months and years following the March Uprising as prima facie evidence of India promoting Tibetan independence.

Nehru's support of the refugees swiftly completed China's turn away from India diplomatically. In the early 1950s, India had been a key non-Communist ally, but now in its internal propaganda China began to cast it as a pawn of Western imperialist powers. This about-face in attitude left Nehru few avenues to explore the international relations he had so desperately sought to achieve by diplomacy through his Panchsheel Five Principles, the Bandung Conference, and the 1954 treaty between China and India.

The Dalai Lama remained appreciative of the steps Nehru took to welcome him and was fully aware that the position of the Tibetan refugees would be untenable without the Government of India's help.[9] In the Dalai Lama's later writings about those first weeks in India, he recalled that Nehru initially "made it quite clear that the Government of India still could not contemplate taking issue with the Chinese over the question of Tibetan rights," even reprimanding him, "You say you want independence and in the same breath you say you do not want bloodshed. Impossible!"[10] The Dalai Lama's early meetings with the prime minister produced a "profound feeling of disappointment."[11] He realized Nehru's position offered little room for negotiation as he faced intense domestic opposition on the handling of the Tibet question in the Indian Parliament, as well as daily criticism by the press of his allowing China to seize control of Tibet. However, despite Nehru's attitude, the Dalai Lama and the Tibetan leadership emerged from those first few weeks in India with an even deeper resolve to shape their own future.[12]

Central to this vision was the determination among Tibetans to form a functioning Government in Exile, a decision that both eased and challenged the Indian government's efforts to accommodate them. The exiled government, ultimately centered in Dharamsala and officially known as the Central Tibetan Administration (CTA), offered an organizational framework that gave coherence to the refugee community. More specifically, it established "a government-like structure that is able to negotiate with the Indian government."[13] Despite India's initially tepid response (going as far as to issue a communiqué stating it did not officially recognize the Government in Exile), India did nothing to prevent the political activism of the Tibetans and continued to provide considerable material support to the Tibetan refugees. The fact that India had neither ratified the United Nation's 1951 Convention Relating to the Status of Refugees nor enacted domestic legislation regarding the status of refugees meant that "Tibetans in India do not enjoy the official status of refugees under either international or India law."[14] The Dalai Lama, the CTA, and the Tibetan refugee population realized that all protections and agreements operated at the pleasure and consent of the Indian government.

The Dalai Lama and the Tibetan refugees' primary objective remained the pursuit of an independent Tibet. In part, the lack of security with respect to their status in India mattered little because their main goal remained "to ensure the preservation of Tibetan identity and culture, and give a proper education to our younger generation."[15] Instead of seeking to bolster and stabilize their status as Indian citizens, they sought to embrace their status as refugees. By remaining refugees, they defined themselves as displaced persons whose homeland remained Tibet. Their time in India was, they asserted, temporary. To suggest otherwise would be to propose that they intended to permanently abandon Tibet. Within weeks, the exiled Tibetans had quickly fused the definition of being Tibetan with that of being a refugee. The question few asked was if it was possible to be Tibetan and not be a refugee—until, that is, there emerged in fall 1960 a group of Tibetans who were not refugees.

## FROM TIBETAN MUSLIMS TO INDIAN CITIZENS

In September 1960, when the Chinese government abruptly consented to the Barkor Khaches' request for Indian citizenship, Faizullah Chisti, president of the Indian Tibetan Muslim Evacuees Welfare Association (IKMWA) immediately set in motion the work needed to welcome the dozens of—on some days, over a hundred—Khache refugees traveling over Nathula Pass through Sikkim and, ultimately, into Kalimpong, India. Unlike the thousands of refugees who had fled Tibet in the wake of the March Uprising, the Khaches who crossed over into India did so with the direct cooperation of the Chinese and Indian governments. Unlike many of their Tibetan Buddhist compatriots who faced a violent Chinese backlash to the March Uprising, many Khaches had chosen to remain in Tibet and to challenge the Chinese government. In this way they achieved a rare direct victory over the increasingly intransigent Chinese central government. The Khaches argued that, based on their Indian ancestry, they should be allowed to return to India. In the language of the time, the Khaches had not fled as refugees struggling across the Himalayas but as "evacuees."

The Khache journey to India was an arduous one. On prescribed dates, the Chinese provided transportation for each group from Lhasa to Yatung before they made the slow climb in military trucks to the Sikkim-Chinese border at the top of Nathula Pass (14,000 ft.). At the border, Indian vehicles met them, and they were immediately transferred the thirty-five miles down to Gangtok. There they were quickly processed and allowed to proceed to Kalimpong. In Lhasa, Indian consul general P. N. Kaul had registered and issued each family an exit document with their photograph, certified with the consulate seal and Kaul's signature. To prevent them from being unduly delayed at the border, Kaul also provided detailed lists of their luggage, including contents, to be presented at the border check post.[16] The Khaches from Lhasa arrived in groups varying in size from several dozen to nearly a hundred at the height of their departures from Tibet. In the first week of October 1960, more than 500 Khaches arrived in Kalimpong.[17] In early 1961, the last remaining Khache trickled in. When these were added to the hundred or so Khache boarding school students already in India for several years, the total number of those who had permanently left Tibet exceeded 1,500 men, women, and children.[18]

It is hard to imagine their thoughts as they were driven into Kalimpong, a city familiar to most of them, at least by reputation. As Tina Harris explains in her study of the Tibetan wool trade, "The economic connections between Kalimpong and Tibet were so important to the local geographical imagination that many Tibetans would use the word 'Kalimpong' to refer to India as a whole."[19] For more than a century Kalimpong, the last commercial center before the major pass into Tibet, had emerged as the primary trading center for Indian-Tibet trade. Traditionally, the town's populace of 10,000 or 20,000 had long been composed of Tibetans, Nepalis, lowlander Indians, and a diverse mix of other Himalayan peoples.[20] But with the influx first of Tibetans in the immediate aftermath of the March Uprising and now the Khaches, the trading town had been utterly transformed.

Initially a small trading town, Kalimpong was ill equipped to handle such an inundation of new residents. As the weeks of their stay in Kalimpong turned to months, the Khaches' concerns over their dwindling resources and no viable source of income led many to consider selling their valuable Tibetan jewelry or other sacred objects they had brought with them. Unfortunately, the Tibetan refugees who had arrived in Darjeeling and Kalimpong months earlier had already saturated the market for such goods. The result was that only the most desperate sold their valuables, and only then at predatorily low prices.[21] Added to this, at least 10 percent of the Khaches arrived widowed or destitute.[22] Finally, despite the Indian consul's repeated requests to the Chinese government for compensation "for all property left behind by Indian nationals in Tibet due to causes beyond their control," the Chinese adamantly refused, suggesting that it was a "completely unwarranted demand."[23]

At the end of 1960, the local newspaper, citing a recently completed census, estimated that the population of Kalimpong included over 4,000 Tibetans as well as "nearly seven hundred [Khache] and four hundred Chinese nationals."[24] Another report described "3,390 refugees queued up" to receive free powdered milk, and in the neighboring town of Darjeeling, though the Dalai Lama's representative in charge of relief reported that only "1,200 destitute people came regularly for the twice-weekly distribution of powdered milk and a little rice."[25] The indeterminate status of the Khaches as "evacuees" did little to mitigate their situation.

As incursions along the Chinese-India border increased in frequency and as Cold War fears heightened tensions, the situation in the towns of Darjeeling and Kalimpong remained politically tense. Still fearful that the Chinese government would use refugees as cover for infiltrating India, the accusations of Chinese spies coming across the border were common.[26] In the progressive weekly *Thought,* an editorial reflected ongoing concern with the possibility of continued Chinese territorial expansion in the Himalayas. Dismissing as irrelevant China's protests over India's offer of sanctuary for the Dalai Lama and refugees, the opinion piece warned that China would be unsatisfied with simply occupying Tibet:

> The Chinese obviously have their eyes fixed elsewhere. . . . Their dream of a so-called federation of Himalayan States will ever remain unrealized unless Nepal has first been bagged. The rare promptitude they have shown in ratifying their so-called border and aid agreements with Kathmandu is an eloquent testimony of their resolve to push ahead in the Himalayan Kingdom, with or without an understanding with India. In truth they have in Nepal a wide field for practicing mock-generosity, whether it be the quantum of economic aid or concession on Mount Everest. To be wise, India cannot afford to trust either chance or the Chinese. Sedulous flirtation is not the same as genuine friendship.[27]

As Nepalese, Chinese, and Tibetans had all commonly called Kalimpong home for centuries, it is not surprising that accusations of collaboration with the Chinese soon began to appear.

Perched on the edge of Tibet and India, the city, since the founding of the People's Republic of China, had attracted a wide array of those agents interested in "listening-in to the echoes from Communist-occupied Tibet."[28] Nehru famously described the small community as a "nest of spies," like a "detective story unraveling itself there," with individuals of "every variety and every shade of color."[29] The Sino-Indian tensions and the near-constant stream of Tibetan refugees had completed the transformation of Kalimpong from a sleepy backwater to a cosmopolitan town bursting at the seams with people with a hundred different political agendas. George Patterson, the former Scottish missionary in eastern Tibet who had made Kalimpong his home, described how "within a few months of the Chinese Communist attack on Tibet I had as my immediate neighbors in Kalimpong one of the Shapës, or Cabinet Ministers of Tibet, the Finance Minister, the Dalai Lama's mother, sister, brother and brother-in-law and several other leading members of the Tibetan Government."[30]

The Chinese government even accused India of allowing pro-Tibet agents to transform Kalimpong into a command center of the Tibet revolt.[31] The Chinese protested repeatedly that pro-Tibet demonstrations were occurring there (and elsewhere in India) with the Indian government doing nothing to stop them. The Chinese government took India's inaction as tantamount to encouraging them.

The Indian government patiently explained that in India free speech and demonstrations were protected rights, and if carried out in a legal and legitimate manner, the Indian government could not intervene or prohibit them. The Indian government, for its part, ultimately arrested and deported the Chinese headmaster of the local Chinese school and his wife for unidentified "undesirable activities."[32] It was into this toxic mix that the Tibetan Muslim evacuees arrived.

## HELLO INDIA! GOOD-BYE TIBET?

In late November 1960, amid the business of greeting the arriving Khaches, registering their presence, and sorting out their next steps, the president of the Tibetan Welfare Association, Faizullah Chisti, received a letter, addressed with only his name and marked "SECRET." Chisti, who had corresponded with many high officials, must have been slightly astonished upon opening the envelope to see the Dalai Lama's red seal. Written in an elegant Tibetan script, the letter began by addressing "all the Khache and their leaders who came recently to India from Tibet." Like others who had followed the tribulations of the Khaches over the previous year, the Dalai Lama expressed his distress over "how the Khache were subjected to the Chinese's inhuman behavior, maltreatment, unlawful occupation of Tibet and their intolerable suppression and endless torture and had to evacuate to India." The Dalai Lama's letter then exhorted them to join the Tibetans in India to free Tibet from China and "to make other peace-loving countries of the world better understand our case." Given the still tenuous situation of Tibetans in India, the Dalai Lama counseled Chisti, "[If] in recognizing the difference between a friend and an enemy you could support our case, it would be a great help and useful for better understanding our case by the other peace loving countries of the world." The Dalai Lama concluded by urging the Khaches to remain in touch and to "write me without hesitation."[33]

While the letter underscores what would later become the Dalai Lama's hallmark trait of initiating interfaith dialogue in order to achieve common goals, his open and intimate manner also demonstrates just how close and familiar the two communities had become over the preceding centuries. Both parties understood the Khache to be Tibetan. Yet the letter appears to have unnerved Chisti with its open references to the Khache as his subjects, demonstrating just how quickly the experiences of the Tibetan Buddhists and the Khache had diverged in crossing from Tibet to India. Not daring to transgress an issue of Indian political sensitivity so soon after the Khache had arrived, Chisti immediately wrote to the Indian political officer in Gangtok asking for counsel.[34] After two months, the office finally responded, simply instructing them that any correspondence to "H.H. the Dalai Lama is entirely a matter between you and H.H. The Dalai Lama and we are unable to give any advice on the matter." The two-month response time to compose two sentences suggests Chisti's initial concern about India's stance was well founded.[35]

In early February 1961, Chisti's eventual reply to the Dalai Lama, sent on behalf of the Khaches in Kalimpong, was equally careful. Certainly, Chisti's response matches the Dalai Lama's original missive in its affection and respect. He begins by assuring him that "we are sure that these difficulties are only temporary and one day the time will come that your Majesty's holy steps will land on the sacred soil of Tibet and once again the peace-loving Tibetan people will inspire under the honest leadership of your Majesty."[36] Remarkable also is Chisti's conviction of the Dalai Lama's ecumenical tolerance when he adds that the Khache "earnestly pray that the Almighty Allah may fulfill the aspiration of thousands of peace loving Tibetan people."[37]

The letter is filled with polite compliments, thanking the Dalai Lama for remembering the "few humble Khache (Kashmiri Muslims) amids[t] your Majesty's countless other problems" and expressing gratitude to the "kind-hearted Nehru" for saving them from the "hands of tyrant Red China." And yet Chisti seems far more cautious about how to negotiate the Khaches' newfound status as citizens of India.

The letter concluded with what might at first glance seem innocuous, yet in fact it broaches what weighs most on Chisti's mind. Namely, he seeks to remind the Dalai Lama of both communities' reliance on the good offices of the Indian government for their present circumstances:

> We with all our abilities are with your Majesty and your Majesty's fellow Tibetan people in the task of li[b]eration of Tibet from the Red Chinese's unlawful occupation or their tyrant hands. And we are pleasure [*sic*] to inform your Majesty that every member of our community are very thankful for the facilities and hospitalities given by your Majesty's Government in the past in Tibet to us as honest guests of your Majesty's Government.[38]

Chisti's closing comments hint at the uncomfortable balancing act the Khache had to maintain after their escape from Tibet.

It was not just the manner of their arrival—traveling in government-assigned trucks instead of stealing across the Himalayan passes on foot—that separated them from their Tibetan Buddhist compatriots. Certainly, both groups shared a desire to extricate themselves from their desperate situation in Tibet, but the manner in which they were received in India quickly divided them. The Tibetan Muslims, by asserting and receiving formal acknowledgment of their Indian ancestry, arrived in India effectively as Indians, not Tibetan refugees. The consequences of this differentiation began to be manifested almost instantly, as they crossed over the mountainous pass into India. Greeted as Indians, not Tibetans, as citizens, not refugees, as Muslims, not Buddhists, the Khache faced a very different set of circumstances, choices, and reception in post-Partition India than did the Buddhist followers of the Dalai Lama.

On the one hand, the very criteria by which they exited China was that they were *not* Tibetan. On the other hand, by almost every measure—language, culture, centuries of intermarriage, and their recognition of the Dalai Lama as their ruler—they were Tibetan. The Dalai Lama's tone in his letter to the Khaches was to fellow Tibetans. This was not a letter that could have been sent to others who might have witnessed the excesses of the Chinese, such as the Nepalese, Ladakhis, or Bhutanese. The Dalai Lama approached the Khaches as Tibetans, as the Tibetan government had for centuries. Yet it is the seeming immutability of such a relationship that made Chisti most uneasy. Chisti desperately wanted to reciprocate the Dalai Lama's deep affection. However, he felt compelled to send the Dalai Lama a signal of the Khaches' present status by adopting a new narrative denoting the Khache as outsiders or "guests" of the Dalai Lama's government. Their status had changed. Chisti's language confirms the awkward struggle of the Khaches as they sought to make sense of the new world in which they found themselves.

The speed with which their experiences diverged from those of the Tibetan Buddhists who had fled Tibet only months ahead of their exodus underscores the pull of factors beyond their control. The Khaches left Tibet by virtue of being Kashmiri. By claiming Kashmiri ancestry, they arrived as Indian citizens; by accepting Indian citizenship, they forfeited any claim as Tibetan refugees (or exiles); and finally, they left behind a life as a beloved and respected minority and entered the post-Partition landscape of India. Each of these changes occurred inadvertently. The repercussions were swift and largely unanticipated. The clearest and most agonizing consequence took somewhat longer to become manifest: in the eyes of most of the world, the Khaches were no longer Tibetan.

To suggest it was only external circumstances that both the Tibetan Buddhists and the Khaches wrestled with upon their arrival in India does not fully articulate the complexity of the challenges that faced both communities. Internally both groups retained strong and visible ties to each other, ties that were evident even a half century after their desperate flights from Tibet. Carole McGranahan's nuanced study of the impact of exile on Tibetan identity deftly articulates a central element of this dynamic when she suggests that "in exile Tibet, a nationalist identity both flourishes and flattens. The perceived need for internal cohesion, given the current political state of Tibet, resulted in the devaluing of diversity in the exile community."[39] While McGranahan's comment refers specifically to the Tibetan Buddhist exile community, the perception that their circumstances demanded uniformity at the expense of diversity is indisputably true for the Tibetan Muslims as well. The road to such a flattening and narrowing of identity can be seen by choices that began with their departure from Tibet in 1960.

## NEW BEGINNINGS, OLD LESSONS

Minor political setbacks aside, Faizullah Chisti and the other local Khache leaders quickly set about to establish the IKMWA in order to work through decisions about their futures. In its first weeks, the association faced not only the difficult task of finding accommodation for the displaced Khaches but also helping with the psychological stress they felt from the strain of the previous two years. In the days and weeks after their departure from Lhasa, the Khaches began to realize that in the eyes of the Indian government, and increasingly the Tibetan Buddhists, they had ceased to be considered Tibetan. They could not openly declare their intention to return to Tibet one day in the indeterminate future as the Dalai Lama and his followers were–doing. The Khaches' dilemma was an entirely different one. United in their desire to leave Lhasa, they were soon divided as to how to begin their new lives as Kashmiri Muslims in India. The stark and unanticipated choices now facing the Khaches served as a reminder of how their abrupt departure from Tibet had altered both their circumstances and their identity.

This sudden imposition of Indian citizenship was manifested in bewildering but consequential ways. Immediately following the 1959 March Uprising, as detailed in the previous chapter, the Khaches successfully asserted that as Kashmiri they should be allowed to declare themselves Indian. Yet when interviewed several decades later, many Khaches admitted this was far less an expression of a long-held belief in their "Kashmiri" identity than a maneuver to extricate themselves from China. In the months before the Chinese finally acceded to their claims, many among them (under considerable pressure from the Chinese) did renounce their claim to be Kashmiri Indian, and others, even as they exited Tibet, became confused about their nationality. Prior to their departure, the Chinese government had insisted that the Khaches be issued Chinese passports. But when numerous Khaches crossing the border into India were asked about their nationality, they replied they were Indian, believing that this was the answer they had worked for the past eighteen months to achieve. As a result, they were given the wrong forms, and their efforts to apply for Indian citizenship were made much more complicated.[40] Others, who had family members who were Khatsara or Nepalese, responded to the immigration officials honestly by stating they were Nepalese.[41] This blend of externally confusing but internally legible Tibetan labels, Khache, Koko, and Khatsara, did not neatly fit into any of the available nation-state divisions now being imposed by India.

The choices facing the Khache once they arrived were even more bewildering. Despite their claim to be Indian Kashmiri, most of them continued to identify themselves as Tibetan. In documents from the period and in talking with elder members of the community today, a profound apprehension had gripped the Khaches, much like that which Chisti expressed in his letter to the Dalai Lama.

They felt that they had to conform to the identity that had allowed them to escape Tibet. The problem was that few, including most Tibetans, treated them as "Tibetan refugees." More pressing, although rarely stated explicitly at the time, the Khache did not want to appear deceptive or ungrateful to the nation that had championed their harrowing escape from Tibet.

The scars of their last months in Lhasa did not diminish quickly, and daily concerns weighed on them, causing the community to question just how to begin to rebuild their lives. Within weeks after the first group's arrival in Kalimpong, three general schools of thought on how best to push forward emerged. Each envisioned a starkly different vision of the Khaches' future, correlating directly with the three major ways the Khaches began to perceive of themselves. The first group, headed by Chisti and others who had deep experience in India, implored the group to remain in the Himalayan hill towns of Darjeeling and Kalimpong, where they would have commercial opportunities and could remain geographically and culturally close to Tibet. Others, caught up in the notion of their Kashmiri heritage and having safely preserved their community, exhorted their brethren to "return" to Kashmir (their ostensible homeland). The third group, embracing their identity as Muslims, urged settlement in Saudi Arabia (the birthplace of Islam).

The question of what the Khache should do was taken up in a spirited two-day meeting at the end of November 1960 with all the heads of the refugee families in attendance. A vote was taken, and the majority (roughly 600) decided to move to Srinagar in Kashmir. The motion and vote summarized the choice in this manner: "This meeting conveys to the Government of India that [a] majority of the members Indian Muslims of Kashmiri-Ladakhi origin prefer the soil, climate, weather and scope of trade in Kashmir within the Indian Union, to be quite suitable for their health, habit, hygiene."[42] The vote was not binding on the group as a whole, and many of the elders, in particular, had been convinced by several Ladakhi Khaches of the merits of settling in Kashmir, even though they had visited but never lived in Srinagar. Still, more than a third of the Khaches, typically those who were younger and more cosmopolitan, stood firm and decided to remain in Kalimpong and Darjeeling.[43] The remaining members hoped to emigrate to the Middle East.[44] The final motion of the meeting voted Faizullah Chisti the "leader of the delegation" and "President-cum-secretary," despite his personal opposition to settling in Kashmir.

Chisti's job was not easy, though his selection was inspired given his intimate knowledge of Indian bureaucracy and his tireless work ethic, even when it meant pursuing ends with which he personally disagreed. Chisti displayed an amazing degree of administrative acumen by keeping highly detailed lists of people, organized and enumerated by individual and by family. The day after the vote, Chisti contacted government officials asking that arrangements for the first groups be set in place so that their travel could be completed in time for them to celebrate Ramadan in Srinagar. However, the bureaucratic wheels of India turned very slowly, with each administrative office referring the request to another, until the delay was so great that the departure had to be postponed until after Ramadan.[45]

Within weeks, Chisti began the complicated process of moving the six hundred Khache, of varying financial means, to Kashmir from Kalimpong across northern India to Srinagar. He separated those who were going to Srinagar into three groups, and between March 28 and April 4 he personally oversaw each group board the bus in Kalimpong early on their appointed morning so as to ensure each of them made the journey down the steep twisting road to Siliguiri. In Siliguri each person in the group was issued a third-class railway ticket, boarded the first of three train journeys, and only at the end of the third day make the final stage of their trip to Srinagar by bus.[46] While the bulk of the Khaches who desired to move to Kashmir had left Kalimpong by April, other groups continued to be organized for several more months. It was not until August 1961 that the very last group, which Chisti described as "quite ignorant, illiterate, and helpless," departed. Chisti requested special attention from the government to help the group join those who had gone on ahead.[47]

Those Khaches who remained in Kalimpong and Darjeeling began to realize firsthand how precarious their documented status was. Despite the considerable and sustained involvement of the Indian government in facilitating their move from Tibet to India, it was at this moment that the Indian government almost instantaneously turned its attention elsewhere. The Tibetan Muslims did not receive any of the high-level, prolonged attention given to the Dalai Lama and Tibetan Buddhists, and they encountered sustained and widespread resistance from Indian and Kashmiri officials, who hindered their efforts to process their applications for full Indian citizenship.

As they sought to begin the process of buying property and setting up shops, "the authorities concerned ask[ed] such persons to produce proof of Indian Citizenship."[48] Nearly two years later, in 1962, local officials had still not taken action on the Khaches' applications for citizenship.[49] Chisti, courteous until the end, wrote to the deputy commissioner of Darjeeling District, "I regret to point out that so far nothing has been done. . . . [Khaches] are being subjected to unnecessary harassment and embarrassments at check posts and elsewhere."[50] In August 1963, P. N. Kaul, now serving in the central government, wrote to Chisti indicating that he had reached out to "concerned authorities" and "presume[d] they will investigate it through the West Bengal Government."[51] Only then, nearly three years after their arrival, did the three hundred Khaches who had stayed behind in Kalimpong and Darjeeling begin to be properly registered and to receive their Indian Citizenship Certificates. All except Faizullah Chisti, whose application the deputy commissioner purposely delayed for another year, peeved at being made to look bad by going over his head.[52]

Even after the departure of nearly two-thirds of the Khaches, Chisti continued to press for the Indian government's support of those who remained behind.[53] He appealed for government intervention regarding Sanaullah Shahkuli, an eighteen-year-old Khache student in Beijing who was unable to return to Lhasa in time to join his family and was being detained in Lhasa despite promises that he would be allowed to join his family in India. Chisti kept in nearly continuous contact with the two Indian consul generals, Kaul and Chhibber, even after they moved on from their posts in Tibet. In addition, he organized classes for the Khache children at the Anjuman Islamia School in Kalimpong and then, with government assistance, placed them in nearly a dozen schools. The degree to which he set aside his personal needs for the greater good of the community appears in his correspondence for one small, heartbreaking moment. In a letter to an Indian official, seeking assistance yet again for the Khache prisoners held in Lhasa, he apologizes for the delay of his response, due to the "sad demise of my beloved wife."[54] In the very next sentence he returns to the matter at hand, not letting the death of his wife diminish his pursuit of government assistance. Perhaps feeling the need to continue for the greater good of the community, he remained in the position of president of the association and was the community's foremost advocate until near the very end of his life.

Foremost in the minds of most Tibetan Muslims were the five Khaches who had been arrested and tried in June 1960 and who remained imprisoned in Lhasa. (Diplomatic records sometimes include a sixth, Abdul Ahat, whose father, an Indian, was the cook at the Indian consulate in Lhasa.) Their families had waited until the very last moment to leave Lhasa, but in the end they had been convinced there was little they could accomplish by remaining behind. Survivor's guilt and witnessing, on a daily basis, the grief of those families prompted Chisti to continue to appeal and to actively seek ways to tangibly extend assistance to them. In a petition to the Ministry of External Affairs, he stated that the "wives and relatives . . . at the present moment steeped in deep worries and anxieties constantly brooding over the conditions of their men at Lhasa in Tibet and such worries and anxieties have seriously told upon their health."[55] Chisti organized a package of items to be sent to the prisoners, everything from shirts, trousers, and caps to items such as tea, biscuits, and cigarettes—items that allowed them a modicum of comfort they would otherwise have been denied.[56]

As relations deteriorated between China and India and as numerous small incidents of ill treatment of Chinese in India came to the fore, the issue of the five remaining prisoners slipped from view. At the end of 1962, India closed its Lhasa consulate, citing constant "restrictions of various kinds which were intensified after Chinese forces launched massive attacks on Indian territory. . . . Food was difficult to obtain, communications were cut off and the personnel were harassed."[57] In this atmosphere, Chinese responses to all queries about the remaining Khaches became tediously repetitive. Chinese officials repeatedly circled back to their original September 23, 1960, communication in which they had stated that the "Chinese Government had always considered the [Khache] to be Chinese."[58] In October 1963, the Indian officials seemed at their wit's end after finding "patently illogical" the Chinese government's response indicating it had investigated the matter and "found there were no Indians in Tibet."[59]

The following year, the Indian government again attempted to reason with the Chinese, stating that their stance on the Khache prisoners was "at variance with their own policy on the question of nationality of overseas Chinese" and noting that the only crime they committed was that they insisted they were Indian nationals and desired to emigrate India.[60] Chisti continued to plead for government intervention as late as 1967 but to no avail.[61] A month after that, he received a reply explaining that although the Indian government had made repeated claims for their release, the Chinese government had now "refused to enter into further correspondence with the Government of India" on the matter and that no communication had been received since China's last reply on December 5, 1964.[62]

If the road to Indian citizenship had been an uneven and difficult one for those Khaches who remained in Kalimpong and Darjeeling, their lives by 1964 had begun to assume a sense of normalcy. Their children were attending quality local schools. Many of the Khaches had become leading citizens in the two cities. Realizing that the Indo-Tibetan trade, from which many of them had made their livelihood, was not likely to return any time soon, given the 1962 Sino-Indian border conflict, they invested their capital in opening shops and hotels or becoming tailors and hat-makers—skills that had served them well in Lhasa. Their success and general contentment contrasted sharply with those who chose to leave for Srinagar in 1961.[63]

## HARD LESSONS: KASHMIR

For those Khaches who chose to settle in Kashmir, arrival in Srinagar in the late spring and summer of 1961 was far from idyllic. While awaiting construction of forty two-bedroom apartments, intended to house roughly eighty to a hundred families, the Khache endured their first Srinagar winter in a tent city on the Numaishi Exhibition Grounds.[64] Their expectation that Kashmir would bring a return to a life as peaceful as they had once had in Tibet was quickly dashed. They were unable to speak the Kashmiri language, unfamiliar with local customs, and completely unaware of the complex political situation into which they suddenly found themselves. Claimed by both Pakistan and India, after the Partition in 1947, Srinagar's political status remained a controversial and unsettled question when the Khaches arrived in 1960, as it remains today.

When British governance ended in 1947, Kashmir had, in a complicated set of still disputed steps, attempted to remain independent of both Pakistan and

India. Like many other princely states under British rule, Kashmir had remained officially autonomous but had largely adhered to British colonial leadership. Its position along the Indian-Pakistan border, with its complex Hindu-Muslim history, reflects the highly amalgamated past of many Himalayan states, their distinctive legacies shaped by multiple influences and rulers. In the nineteenth century, Kashmir was ruled by Punjabi Sikhs before coming under the rule of a Hindu Dogra king. By the early twentieth century, Kashmir, along with Tibet, Sikkim, Bhutan, and Nepal, served as strategic Himalayan buffer states among the more powerful regional political forces. Their status, however, remained elusive and debatable. As a result, Kashmir never fit neatly into the religio-political categories of the lowlands; rather it reflected the typically diverse hybrid status found of other Himalayan states.

In 1947, under the British formula of partition, which viewed the future success of their former colony through an almost exclusively Hindu-Muslim lens, Kashmir was offered the choice of joining either a Muslim-majority Pakistan or a Hindu-majority India. Such a choice made little sense for a Kashmir that was a Muslim-majority state with a still vibrant Buddhist historical tradition ruled by a Hindu ruler. The Kashmiris resisted being forced into a choice along religious lines, given that neither option reflected their culture or their political values. Thus Kashmir's initial choice was to remain independent. This did not sit well with either India or Pakistan, both of which sought to claim the territory as their own.

Faced with the choice of military occupation by Pakistan or signing an "instrument of accession" with India (in exchange for military protection), Kashmir chose to join the India Union under a strict set of conditions set out under Article 370 of the Indian Constitution.[65] This constitutional provision created a special status for Kashmir by placing it directly under the control of India's president and by restricting the central Indian government's powers to three areas: foreign affairs, defense, and communications. All other rights were retained by the state of Jammu and Kashmir. To further clarify and institute an unambiguous and asymmetric federalist relationship with India, the Jammu and Kashmir government, on January 26, 1957, promulgated the Constitution of Jammu and Kashmir. The constitution, among other things, declared that "permanent residents" were defined as those individuals who were resident in the state prior to May 14, 1954. This provision explicitly sought to maintain the precarious Hindu-Muslim demographic balance and to prevent in-migration that might swing the state in one direction or the other. The Khache who arrived in Kashmir had little understanding of the legal hurdles, religious complexities, and almost insurmountable identity politics that awaited them.

The consequences of this lack of understanding for the Khache were immediate and absolute. Many of those who decided to settle in Kashmir had based their decisions on the claims of just a few Khaches about weather, topography, and the belief that they were fulfilling the Indian government's claim to their Kashmiri ancestry. Almost every positive assumption the Khache held when they chose to settle in Kashmir was dashed on their arrival in Srinagar. Perhaps most dispiriting was the realization that in the eyes of the Kashmiri government, and under local laws, they were not welcomed as long-lost brethren but were forcefully and definitively designated as non-Kashmiri Muslim immigrants.

From the moment of their arrival, Kashmiri officials, through small measures and large, made the Khaches' efforts to settle permanently in Kashmir difficult, unpleasant, and stressful. It was the Kashmiri's sense at the time that to offer the Khache permanent residency might set a precedent that would flood the state with other non-Kashmiri Muslims. It is an irony rarely touched on that the Khache, though technically retaining a pathway to Indian citizenship, would, if they settled in Kashmir, remain non-state subjects. And in the eyes of most Kashmiri, they would be treated as Tibetan refugees.[66] This conundrum of being Indian citizens but not a state subject of Kashmir is a critical facet of the Khache experience in India that, if disregarded, renders their more recent past incomprehensible.

Initially, it was local Kashmiri officials who resisted allowing them to register as Indian citizens.[67] In part, this resistance was a legacy of those immigrants who had preceded them. The Khaches' arrival a decade after thousands of Uyghur and Kazak refugees from Xinjiang had descended on Kashmir complicated their reception. Many Kashmiri officials erroneously equated the Khaches' status with the Xinjiang and Tibetan stateless peoples who had preceded them to Srinagar.[68] After nearly a year, desperate for resolution, Khache representatives contacted Nehru, who had been vacationing in Kashmir, asking him to personally intervene, to no avail.[69] To the many Khache it appeared that the Indian government, after working diligently on their behalf to secure their release from China, had become indifferent to their situation now that they had arrived in India.

The situation became far more serious on July 1, 1962, when local police notified the Khache that failure to "get all the Tibetan Muslim refugees" registered (as foreigners) within two weeks' time would lead to the state taking "legal action against them under the Foreigners' Act and Rules."[70] Attempts to approach the superintendent of police to apprise him of the fact that as repatriated "Indian Kashmiri Muslims" the Foreigners' Act and Rules did not apply to them were fruitless. Faced with immediate arrest, the Khaches in Srinagar were forcibly registered as foreigners and classified as Tibetans. Only at this point did the Khache leaders in Srinagar reach out to contact Faizullah Chisti in Kalimpong. He told them of the July 7 memo from Kaul advising them to "approach local Registering Authority for the grant of Indian Citizenship."[71] Even with his aid, it took until late 1963 and only with the forceful intervention of the central Indian authorities for the Khache to be properly registered as Indian citizens, like the Khache in Darjeeling and Kalimpong. While they had achieved Indian citizenship, the fact remained that as long as they stayed in the state of Kashmir and Jammu, they would be "non-state subjects."

Without state subjects' status, the Khache continued to be ineligible for key documents, such as identity cards for Kashmiri elections and ration cards, the lack of which accentuated their outsider status. Being denied state citizenship also had broader implications. As non-state subjects in Kashmir, the Khache could not gain access to the many other privileges: they could not acquire immovable property, were deemed ineligible for government employment, and were disqualified from applying to receive bank loans. Khache youth were denied access to state-run Kashmiri higher technical and professional education.

This was in stark contrast to the benefits granted to the Khache children who remained in Darjeeling and Kalimpong. There the Khache successfully registered as Bhotia, a scheduled tribe eligible for local postgraduate education benefits, such as lower admissions requirements. Any Khache youth who settled in Srinagar who was interested in pursuing a university education had to do so by incurring the high costs associated with going to other Indian states, an expense beyond the means of most Khache families. In the face of these obstacles, the Kashmir Khache established their own school and maintained their cohesive identity over the next several decades. Yet as the Tibetan Muslim Masood Butt would write in a fiftieth-anniversary retrospective, for those Khache in Kashmir, the "lack of proper guidance and leadership proved to be an obstacle in their development."[72] Without ways to earn their livelihood, the increasingly desperate community began to look for alternative solutions.[73]

Their harsh reception in Kashmir unsettled the many Khaches who had come to believe a myth of their own making, that as Khache they were Kashmiri. The contradiction between the case the Indian government made for their departure from Tibet, based explicitly on their Kashmiri heritage, and what they encountered when Kashmir refused to accept them as Kashmiri deeply disoriented the entire Khache community.

## PURSUING MUSLIM ROOTS

By 1969, the Khache in Srinagar, Kalimpong, and Darjeeling became increasingly disenchanted with the lack of opportunities available to them in Kashmir, and more broadly in India. Many younger Khache were striking out in search of work and education in Nepal and elsewhere. Deep disillusionment over their inability to re-create or build on the previous lives they had had in Tibet was manifest. Unlike the difference of opinion between various Khache groups over where to settle that had occurred in November 1960, now, almost a decade later, an overwhelming majority were of a single mind: to make a move to Saudi Arabia. Much of the impetus for this move came about because several groups of Tibetan Muslims and

Chinese Muslims had successfully established numerous small communities in Saudi Arabia and in the Middle East.

The Khache based their wish to move on information from those who had already migrated to the Middle East. The Barkor Khache leaders in 1961 had noted Nehru's assistance to a large group of Khaches who had become stranded in Bombay two years earlier. Even more influential in the Khaches' resolve to move was the example of a second group of a hundred or so Khaches, led by Ghulam Muhammad, who decided in 1960 not to move with the bulk of the Khaches to Kashmir but instead to emigrate directly, or so they believed, to Saudi Arabia.[74] This group joined but soon outnumbered other Muslims who had immigrated to Saudi Arabia from China.

In a little known fact, many Muslims from China, Xinjiang, and Tibet had chosen to settle in Saudi Arabia, often out of political expediency, and appeared to be prospering. According to a Republic of China 1961 survey of Chinese living in Saudi Arabia, only the Muslims from Qinghai and Gansu outnumbered those from Tibet.[75] Though different from the Khache, many Uyghur, Kazakh, and Hui Muslims from northwest China fled China and settled in Saudi Arabia after the fall of the Nationalist Chinese government in 1949. Of the some 400 surveyed, nearly 300 had become Saudi citizens or permanent residents. The immigration to Saudi Arabia was largely accomplished through the assistance of Ma Bufang, a Qinghai Muslim who served as the Republic of China's ambassador to Saudi Arabia from 1957 until 1961 and who would himself ultimately obtain Saudi citizenship.[76] The welcome they received and the commercial success they achieved there remained well known because many of those who fled had traveled through India (often specifically Kashmir).[77]

Contrary to the beliefs of those Khaches who promoted the move to Saudi Arabia, these early groups had not had an entirely easy path to settlement. Both the Qinghai group and the group led by Ghulam Muhammad had arrived on Hajj visas that allowed them to stay only for one year. As their pilgrimage ended, these groups approached Saudi officials asking to be allowed to settle permanently. As the Saudi government had done with most such requests, it denied their appeal. The timing of their appeal proved fortuitous, though, since the inroads made by the People's Republic of China in the Middle East had caused representatives of the Republic of China to redouble their efforts in the region, particularly in 1957 after the PRC had persuaded Egypt to sever relations with Taiwan and recognize the PRC. The rising prominence of the PRC in the Middle East intersected with the Tibetan Muslims fleeing Tibet. The Nationalist government saw an opportunity in supporting the Tibetans: a means to foment broader internal dissent within Tibet and, in their calculus, aid their long-term plan to retake the Chinese mainland.[78]

In an effort to encourage the uprising in Tibet, U.S. State Department officials in 1959 urged Chiang to offer recognition of "Tibet as an independent state" to solidify anti-Communist activities in Tibet.[79] While Chiang did not in the end agree to this, the Nationalists did offer the roughly one hundred Khaches ROC citizenship and passports (they had left India prior to being granted Indian citizenship).[80] While this resolved the Khaches' immediate dilemma of being stateless persons, it did not alter the fact that the Saudi government still refused to grant them permanent residency. In the end, after being granted residency by other neighboring states, it was the initiative of several Tibetan Muslim students who were enrolled at Medina University that convinced the Pakistani Islamic scholar, Imam Maulana Abu Ala Maududi, to assist them in writing and delivering a petition to the Saudi king.[81]

Adopting a compelling religious strategy, Maududi advised them to contrast their situation with that of the increasing global visibility of Tibetan Buddhists. At the heart of the appeal was the portrayal of the Tibetans' flight from "Chinese-occupied Tibet" as consisting of two peoples: the Buddhists who had successfully founded a new community and government in Dharamsala; and the Khache Muslims who remained stateless. Maududi personally took the appeal to the king, and two months later, thirty Tibetan Muslim families received an invitation from the king to move to Saudi Arabia. The community quickly decided to settle in the Jabal Bazim area of Taif. Located in the Sarawat Mountains about 62 miles southeast of Mecca, it was the city that served as the unofficial summer capital of the Saudi government. There the Tibetan Muslims quickly established themselves as proficient tailors and hat makers. Although allowed to reside there permanently, their status as foreigners deprived them of many rights given to Saudi citizens. Several years later, after the discovery of oil, the requirements for obtaining citizenship, even for those Tibetan Muslims born in Saudi Arabia, became ever more circumscribed.

It is likely that at least some of the Khaches back in India knew some of these facts, though most deemed their options in the Middle East no worse than the situation they faced in Srinagar. The Khache leader Muhammad Ramzan Butt arranged a meeting with the Indian government to broach the idea of their assisting the Tibetan Muslims to emigrate to Saudi Arabia. Realizing they were unhappy and that perhaps such a move would make things easier for the Indian government, an Indian official advised Butt to collect a list of those individuals wishing to leave India and to once again approach Kaul for his guidance and assistance. In their appeal to Kaul, the hardships of the Khache became apparent. The 1969 letter first explained that the "main reason of our desire to migrate in Saudi Arabia is for easy earning of our livelihood" and then went on to explain that "because most of our community members are tailors and it is reliably learnt that the tailoring business particularly cap making, etc. (which is easy for us) is one of the best means of earning in Saudi Arabia, and also our old aged men desires are this, that ending of the life be in that holy place."[82] The letter described how the Khache, with limited but not insubstantial capital, had "started business[es] of shoes, caps and many other items" while others "opened restaurants, hotels, etc."[83] According to the letter, within the first five years most Khaches in India had run through the bulk of their capital assets. Over 120 of the original families who arrived in India in 1960 included their names on the petition asking to be allowed to leave India to resettle in Saudi Arabia.[84]

With no objection from the Indian government, the Khache communities appealed directly to the king of Saudi Arabia through the offices of the Saudi embassy in India. Playing to Saudi Arabia's anti-PRC stance, the letter began, "With due deference we the helpless Muslim Tibetans who have migrated to India from Tibet, forcibly occupied by the Red China, beseech your Majesty kindly grant us permission to migrate from India to Saudi Arabia and settle down there permanently."[85] The letter stressed that due to their faith, the Chinese in Tibet had "plundered and tortured" them, that their honor had been "robbed," and "the irreligious Chinese threatened us with dire consequences if we did not give up our faith in God and the Holy Prophet."[86] The Dalai Lama's representative, Thupten Ninje, also wrote a three-sentence note to the Saudi embassy on their behalf asking the Saudi government to permit them to settle in Saudi Arabia. The exact response from the Saudi government was not recorded, but the gist was clear: the Khache would not be welcome. With their final appeal to leave India dashed, the Khache, by and large, turned to making the best of a life there.

THE GIFT OF CITIZENSHIP AND THE PRICE OF BEING
TIBETAN

Leaving Tibet in 1960 and accepting Indian citizenship affected the Khache in ways that they could never have anticipated. The most unexpected consequence of that choice was how quickly they ceased to be Tibetan in the eyes of other Tibetans, Indians, and the international community. As McGranahan has compellingly explored, citizenship for refugees is often conceived of as a "gift" bestowed by the host countries.[87] Often the host nations, focusing on the presumed benefits, rarely consider the consequences that citizenship may bestow. So while Indian citizenship played a key role in the Khaches' ability to leave Tibet, the Tibetan Buddhist refugees had long refused citizenship. For the Khache, the acquisition of Indian citizenship had indeed been a gift. It was the means by which to escape the untenable circumstances they had found in Tibet after the March Uprising. Rarely addressed is the fact that for the Khache, the gift of citizenship was not presented in a manner that could be refused, and it came with the immediate consequences of losing the Tibetan identity held by many of their fellow Tibetans.

While the Khaches regarded their Indian citizenship as a political means to a desired end, the Tibetan Buddhists saw their refusal of Indian citizenship as evidence of their commitment to an independent Tibet. Their defiant rejection of citizenship served as a means by which their loyalty to Tibet was authenticated. Not surprisingly, then, to be a refugee was, by definition for the Tibetan Buddhists (and their supporters), to be a Tibetan. The exiled Tibetan community's emphatic rejection of citizenship is overshadowed by the fact that India never publicly offered them citizenship. As McGranahan pointedly concludes, "One cannot receive a gift that is not offered."[88] In this formulation, then, it might be correct to suggest that Tibetan Buddhists who flowed into India "refused and were refused citizenship in South Asia."[89] The Khache, by accepting the "gift" of Indian citizenship that was offered to them, were thus perceived as rejecting the privileged label of refugee, and subsequently they were refused the right to be Tibetan, at least among the Tibetans in exile community.

This is not to say that the two groups avoided each other. In Darjeeling and Kalimpong there were individuals, like Faizullah Chisti, who spoke all three key languages of the Himalayan front range, Nepali, Tibetan, and English, and who aided both the Khaches and the Tibetan Buddhists in their daily commercial, political, and social interactions. Yet the swiftness with which the Khache pursued the Kashmiri/Indian and Muslim dimensions of their identities and the response of the Tibetan Buddhists in distancing themselves from fellow Tibetan Khaches was, while perhaps predictable, startling. Predictable because the rationale by which they exited Tibet was based on their Indian, not Tibetan, ancestry. Startling because they remained culturally Tibetan and highly integrated with other Tibetans and the Tibetan government up to the moment of their departure.

While the Indian government undeniably championed the Khaches' exit from central Tibet, it was Tibetan Buddhists, not the Khache, who received the bulk of the Indian government's attention and resources, largely as a result of the swift international repercussions that accepting them into their country had for India. In the face of an ever-increasing number of refugees, the Indian government grew concerned over the very real need for housing, disease prevention, and infrastructure in the refugee camps. With few options, the Indian government coordinated a response with the Dalai Lama, a response that resulted in the creation of permanent Tibetan Buddhist settlements.[90] By 1969, more than twenty agricultural, industrial, and handicraft settlements involving more than 30,000 refugees were established in India, Nepal, and Bhutan.[91] India took other actions that indicated their strong pro-Tibetan stance, such as choosing in 1962 not to renew the Sino-Indian 1954 Agreement in which India acknowledged China's sovereignty over Tibet, thus intimating, but never formally stating, that the nation had changed its position on Tibetan independence.

The benefits of being Tibetan in India initially appeared to be advantageous but slowly became a point of contention within the exiled Tibetan community. Their refugee status often limited their ability to purchase property, to vote, and to travel internationally. In the eyes of many exiled Tibetans, however, keeping their refugee status became a litmus test for remaining politically committed to a "Free Tibet" and/or being committed to an eventual return to their homeland.

To be labeled "refugee" made a political statement, one that would be greatly diminished by acquiring citizenship. Since the 1970s the issue of accepting Indian citizenship has been a highly contentious one. The question of the status of the Tibetan refugees has been a charged topic full of conflicting realities. On a very basic level, refugee status represented one's personal views on Tibetan politics, that is, one's commitment to a free Tibet. More broadly, there was the Dalai Lama's "Middle Way" and the political meanings it held for the Central Tibetan Administration. Finally, there were the myriad legal ramifications that, in India at least, restricted one's movements and limited one's legal rights. As one Tibetan refugee put it, "We aren't Indians. We don't get benefits. We can't buy land. There is no Indian citizenship for us. There is only a residential certificate that we have to renew once a year. We can't take loans, no buying land, and we can't get good jobs."[92]

To be a refugee was to be a Tibetan patriot, yet it rarely translated into an easy life. And regardless of the spectrum of beliefs among the Tibetan refugee community, most Tibetan refugees perceived the Khaches' acceptance of Indian citizenship as a sign of their disloyalty to Tibet. What is overlooked with such a perspective is how similar the Khaches' non-state status in Kashmir was to that of the Tibetans-in-exile refugee status in India.

The clearest indication of the Khaches' new status as non-Tibetan seems to be the decision by the newly established Tibetan government in exile not to actively include them in their early elections, thus limiting their ability to acquire representation in that governmental body. Many have noted that the exile government was dominated by Gelug followers but that the other branches of Tibetan Buddhism (e.g., Sakya, Nyingma, Kagyu) were only given a small amount of representation. Little or no representation, however, was given to the non-Buddhist Bon, the Christian, or the Muslim Tibetans.[93] The exclusion of the Khache, even if it was a result of expediency rather than doctrinal purity, runs counter to the more secular position in which they were held by the Dalai Lama, the ruler of Tibet for non-Buddhist Tibetans.

Why the Khache, as a group, never approached the Dalai Lama and why the CTA never officially invited the Khache to participate in their Tibetan governance in exile were, in the end, not so much conscious decisions as a series of misunderstandings. From the Tibetan perspective, the Khache seemed to repeatedly show little loyalty to Tibet and Tibetans, first by declaring themselves Indian and then by seeking to immigrate to the Middle East. From the Khache perspective, many older Khache point to the fact that when the national assembly was formed, the "body gave equal representation to each of Tibet's three regions and four Buddhist sects" but not to Muslims.[94] This is not to suggest that Tibetan Muslims were uniformly excluded, for several Khaches were recruited to work in the CTA.[95] Trine Brox's research on the exile government has demonstrated that the bottom line is that although Tibetan Muslims have been allowed to hold offices in the Dharamsala administration, "they are otherwise excluded from receiving special treatment or representation in the [Tibetan Government-in-Exile] parliament."[96]

When Khaches were asked about the Dalai Lama in interviews carried out in the past decade, they were uniformly positive, yet they often expressed confusion over the reluctance by the CTA to issue Green Books (Tib. *lag deb ljang khu*) to the Khache. Also commonly referred to as "Freedom Books" (Tib. *rang btsan lag deb*), the Green Books serve as the primary marker of the exiled Tibetans' affiliation with the government in exile and are sometimes referred to as a pseudo-passport. A primary requirement of the Green Book is that the holder pay an annual contribution to the Tibetan Government-in-Exile, and those Tibetans who have income are expected to make an extra contribution equivalent to 2 percent of their salary.

The Green Books are far more than a simple indication of support for the CTA, for they also serve as a condition of admission to Tibetan schools and of access to scholarships.[97] Limiting voting to Green Book holders runs counter to the broader definition of Tibetan "citizenship" often touted by the CTA. In its 1991 Charter, the CTA defines being Tibetan as follows: "All Tibetans born within the territory of Tibet and those born in other countries . . . [w]hose biological mother or biological father is of Tibetan descent has the right to become a citizen of Tibet."[98] As many have noted, the Tibetans-in-exile have created a Tibetan identity that projects itself outwardly as a singular entity, but internally it is limited to those who embrace the collective goal of returning to a "future self-ruled and democratic Tibet."[99]

The fact that the Khaches resisted association with any of the other Tibetans living in India is striking, as it contrasts with the deep respect that the Khaches hold for the Dalai Lama. In his 1960 reply to the Dalai Lama, Chisti wrote on behalf of the entire community, "We, with all our abilities are with your Majesty and your Majesty's fellow Tibetan people in the task of li[ber]ation of Tibet from Red Chinese's unlawful occupation or their tyrant hands."[100] If there is one constant across the twentieth century, it would be the Khaches' clear and ardent regard for both the Thirteenth and Fourteenth Dalai Lamas. Yet it is clear that the Khache leaders did not see their reverence for the Fourteenth Dalai Lama as affecting their status in the eyes of the CTA. They seemed to abstain rather than to engage, not out of disdain for their fellow Tibetans, but because of a harsh pragmatism and recognition that the two communities faced starkly different challenges.

By 1970, the Dalai Lama began to reach out to the Khaches in Srinagar in an overt attempt to rekindle and repair their relationship. In his first visit to a Tibetan Muslim community since his arrival in India in 1959, the Dalai Lama visited the Khache settlements and donated 10,000 rupees to the "refugee camp" at Idgah. The following year, the *Tibetan Review* published its first full-length article on the Khache in India. Adopting an openly supportive tone, the article highlighted the harsh Khache experience in terms that must have deeply resonated with the Tibetan Buddhist readership, quoting extensively from an unnamed Khache:

> Sixteen years have now lapsed and these years speak a story of adaptation, re-structuring and of conditioning to new social mores and a language distinct from our own. The road has not lacked its trials, but it would have been rougher had it not been for the Indian government's initial assistance to us on our arrival in India, and to them we issue our grateful thanks. Through these years, we Tibetan Muslims have invested every energy in trying to salvage what would otherwise seem wrecked lives, and have attempted to rebuild and reorganize an integrated life. But even superhuman powers would not have helped us tide over financial and educational crisis.[101]

Clearly seeking to break down the refugee-citizen division, the article consistently referred to the Khaches as "refugees." While the term was not totally inappropriate for the Khaches living in Srinagar, it was technically incorrect given that legally they remained Indian citizens. The reference by a Tibetan Buddhist author for a Tibetan audience appears to be a deliberate attempt to link the Tibetan Muslim experience with that of the Tibetan refugees. In the article's conclusion the author finally comes out and makes the connection explicit:

> The Tibetan Muslims were not very different from the rest of the Tibetan refugees who sought shelter in India since 1959. But quite unlike their refugee counterparts the Tibetan Muslims entered India as Indian citizens. . . . Though the Tibetan Muslims were genuine refugees, yet their status designating Indian citizenship preempted them from being included in rehabilitation schemes, organized for the host of other Tibetan refugees, as they did not fall within the category of Tibetan refugees.[102]

By making being a refugee a virtue, the Dalai Lama not only invoked compassion, but sought to bridge the divide between the two communities.

Despite the relationship with the Dalai Lama and these seemingly genuine overtures, the two communities remained estranged. Over the next decade the Dalai Lama made several more visits to Srinagar and used the leverage of his growing international prestige even more explicitly in pressuring the government of India "to sanction [additional] land for settlement somewhere in Srinagar."[103] There were periodic attempts at inclusion, such as the admission of a small number of Tibetan Muslims to schools run by the CTA and an invitation to Tibetan Muslims to visit Dharamsala.[104] Yet it would not be until 1995 that the CTA invited thirty Khache leaders and scholars to Dharamsala in an attempt to delve into the various reasons such a division between the communities still existed. When queried as to why more Khache had not become active in the Tibetan community, the invited Khache leaders, clearly embarrassed, "agreed that the main reason [was] their inability to pay the monthly voluntary contribution" required by Green Book holders. The meeting concluded with an agreement to hold conferences every two years "to review progress and exchange ideas." No meeting of Tibetan Muslims by the CTA was ever reconvened.[105]

In 2012, after an absence of nearly twenty-five years, the Dalai Lama again returned to Srinagar, a visit that marked a true renaissance in Tibetan and Tibetan Muslim relations. In his speech he "recalled that in the past there had been Tibetan Muslims working in the Central Tibetan Administration in Dharamsala. . . . As this arrangement has lapsed, . . . it would be very good if any among them would like to come and work in Dharamsala again."[106] Two years later he returned and in a warm speech reminded the community, "In the small village where I was born near Kumbum Monastery there were Muslim families so I have long been familiar with people of Islam. When I reached Lhasa at the age of five, about 1,000 Muslims lived there and whenever there were government functions Muslim representatives took part." He continued by saying that for many years he had been unable to visit them and had "renewed his acquaintance" with them two years earlier. He "spoke of being surprised and touched to discover that their young children spoke good Tibetan with a Lhasa dialect, an indication that they still use Tibetan within their families."[107]

The Fourteenth Dalai Lama has always had a close relationship with Tibetan Muslims. Equally, Tibetan Muslims continue to accord him a high level of respect. When asked, during the Dalai Lama's latest visit to Kashmir in 2012, why Tibetan Muslims supported his visit, one Tibetan Muslim replied, "His Holiness, the Dalai Lama, is our king, our leader. We all love him. That is why we are here."[108] The Khaches' continued reverence for the Dalai Lama accentuates his traditional secular role as a leader for all Tibetans, regardless of religious orientation. However, his high-profile visits aside, the communities remain distant. In the spring of 2016 when a four-day conference titled "Freedom, Justice and Equality" was being organized, a conference expressly focused on dissidents from China's ethnic and religious minorities, Tibetan Muslims were again left off the initial invitation list. This led Masood Bhat, one of the few Tibetan Muslims to have worked in Dharmsala, to remark that while they were aware of the conference, "none of us have received any invitation."[109]

If relations between the Muslim and Buddhist Tibetan communities have improved after nearly half a century, the improvement most likely comes from realizing that their experiences, up to the present day, were along two different but parallel paths. As Alfiani Fadzakir noted in his study of one Tibetan Muslim family that had first gone to Kashmir, then to Saudi Arabia, before finally settling in Kathmandu, their experiences "in two 'homelands'—Kashmir and Mecca— taught them that they could not deny or abandon their Tibetan identity."[110]

The Tibetan Muslims who greeted the Dalai Lama in Srinagar are still facing many of the same obstacles they found on their arrival. A recent survey of Tibetan Muslim housing in Srinagar noted that "about one-fifth of the houses were in a dilapidated condition." The population has grown roughly threefold since their arrival, from about 600 persons in 1960 to some 1,600 in 2000 and to 2,000 in 2011. A new settlement of 125 apartments, located in the Hawal (Sangeen Darwaza) area of Srinagar, has considerably relieved the pressure for housing within Tibetan Muslim settlements.[111]

On one level, this reawakening of the relationship between the refugees in India and the Khaches in Srinagar is related to the fact that the Srinagar Tibetan Muslims have, through their status in Kashmir as "non-state subjects," come as close as one can to being refugees. Despite having lived in Srinagar for over six decades, the Khache still remain outsiders, owing to the political constraints that have made their acceptance by the Kashmiri community difficult. While always citizens of India, they are refused "citizenship" in Kashmir. Their status as citizens of India but refugees in Kashmir has caused many Kashmiri to confuse the Khaches' situation with that of the Uyghurs and Kazaks who had arrived as refugees in the early 1950s, suggesting it was the Kashmiri government in 1959 that granted the Khache citizenship and settled them in Srinagar.[112] There is great irony in noting that it was in Lhasa that foreigners often cast the Khache as Kashmiri and now, having settled in their ancestral homeland of Kashmir, they are treated as Tibetan.

Today, most Khaches in Srinagar prefer to be called "Kashmiri," and they bristle at any implication that they are Tibetan. As one Tibetan Muslim explained, "In Tibet we are called Kashmiris and in Kashmir we are being called Tibetan."[113] When asked to comment further by a Kashmiri newspaper reporter, one elder Khache explained, "We are basically Kashmiri, but people still call us Tibetans, which hurts us."[114] Another puts an even a sharper edge to his response, "Don't call us Tibetans. We are not refugees. We are Kashmiris."[115] One could perhaps dismiss these responses as a reflection of lingering fears from a bygone era if such distinctions did not remain of consequence. When asked, many younger Kashmiris expressed disbelief and even exasperation about their parents' or grandparents' decision to settle in Kashmir, a place where they were unwelcome, even as other Khaches lead relatively more prosperous lives in Kathmandu, Kalimpong, and Darjeeling. Like many second-generation immigrants, this younger generation feels only a distant tie to their grandparents' homeland. "Even if tomorrow Tibet might be liberated from China, we will stay here only," said twenty-year-old Irfan Trumboo.[116]

The paths of the Tibetan refugees in India and the Tibetan Muslims in Kashmir seem to have come full circle. In both communities they are separate, and they are both often contentious in their pursuit of full rights in India and Kashmir. Indian courts had long ruled that they were unable to intervene in the rights of non-state subjects because Article 370 of the Indian Constitution dictates that the state of Jammu and Kashmir govern all matters except those surrendered to the Union of India. Recently, however, in a case challenging the limitations of Indian federal guidlines as they relate to federal finance laws, the court asserted broadly (and against decades of legal precedent) that the constitution of Jammu and Kashmir did not supersede that of India:

> It is rather disturbing to note that various parts of the judgment speak of the absolute sovereign power of the State of Jammu & Kashmir. It is necessary to reiterate that Section 3 of the Constitution of Jammu & Kashmir, which was framed by a Constituent Assembly elected on the basis of universal adult franchise, makes a ringing declaration that the State of Jammu & Kashmir is and shall be an integral part of the Union of India.[117]

The judgment went on to assert that Jammu and Kashmir residents are "first and foremost citizens of India" and that "there is no dual citizenship as is contemplated by some other federal Constitutions in other parts of the world."[118]

Faced with the choice of clinging to a Tibetan past or a future in Kashmir, the Khaches who have lived most of their lives in Kashmir have chosen to marry Kashmiris to ease the lives of their children, and they have pressed to be accepted by Kashmiris. But as the Dalai Lama noted on one of his recent visits, the Tibetan Muslims of Srinagar, to a far greater degree than the Tibetan refugees spread across South Asia, Europe, and the United States, have managed to stave off acculturation and maintained Tibetan as their language of communication. If the litmus test of citizenship lay at the heart of differences between the two communities, the dilemma facing Tibetan Buddhists over the ideological benefits of retaining their refugee status has also worn thin.

It is not that this renewed affinity between the two groups can be attributed to any political shift as much as that both groups have seemingly arrived at a common position by two totally different routes. After more than a half century of living in India, there is an increasing difference of opinion among Tibetan refugees over whether the refusal of citizenship comes at too high a price.

India has remained undeniably generous to the Tibetans who reside in exile in India, though they remain only by the grace of executive policy. As a recent report by the Tibet Justice Center on Tibetan refugees in India concluded, "In India, most undocumented Tibetans and their children remain stateless: India does not recognize them, legally speaking, as refugees under either international law or its own national laws, which do not provide for the adjudication of refugee status."[119] Under a special arrangement known as the Gentleman's Agreement, Tibetans, once they are in India, are recognized as "foreigners" and are required to hold a valid Registration Certificate that must be renewed every six months for a period of up to five years. The status of Registration Certificate holders is inherently precarious. It is by its very nature temporary, and it legally provides the holder with only an informal status that exists largely at the discretion of local officials (and varies by state). The certificate is also a prerequisite for acquiring an Identity Certificate that allows its holder to travel internationally to those countries that accept it as a legitimate travel document (currently the United States and Switzerland and several other states in Europe).

It is often suggested that the Tibetan Government-in-Exile, in an implicit accord with the government of India, has promoted a policy of Tibetans retaining their position as "stateless" refugees. More complicated is the fact that as holders of Green Cards, they are registered "nationals" of the government in exile and its formal CTA government. Karma Yeshi, a member of the Tibetan parliament-in-exile, stated that the CTA would not prevent Tibetans from seeking Indian citizenship but acknowledged, "Our aim is not to settle in India, but eventually go back to Tibet."[120] And yet as the decades have passed, many Tibetan refugees have grown weary of the uncertain nature of living in the stateless netherworld the exiled community demands. As Tenzin Pelky pointed out, it is with few clear-cut legal protections for Tibetan refugees that the "harsh penalties, including incidents of arrest for the mere failure to renew these documents have further heightened fears over the tenuous nature of exile in the settlements."[121]

Beginning in 2010, several younger Tibetans (most born in India to Tibetan refugee parents) began to challenge the ostensible legal barriers preventing them from their theoretical birthright citizenship under Indian laws. Similar to the Tibetan Muslims' dilemma in Kashmir, many within the Tibetan community still sensed the pursuit of Indian citizenship as being irreconcilable with retaining one's support of the government in exile's claim to Tibet. For decades, the unspoken agreement between the government in exile and India was the notion that pursuing citizenship was a sacrilege for Tibetans. But in a series of legal challenges brought by young Tibetans, cracks began to appear in that belief. In 2010, Namgyal Dolkar, born in India, denied citizenship, and officially "stateless," wondered how "according to the Citizenship (Amendment) Act 1986, any person born in India on or after January 26, 1950 but prior to the commencement of the 1986 Act on July 1, 1987, is a citizen of India by birth."[122] In the verdict in favor of her application, the court noted that Dolkar's description of herself as "a Tibetan 'national' is really of no legal consequence as far as the CA [Citizenship (Amendment) Act, 2003][123] is concerned, or for that matter from the point of view of the policy of the Ministry of External Affairs."[124]

India's Ministry of Home Affairs remained opposed to giving voting rights to Tibetan refugees, and in 2014 it asked the Ministry of External Affairs to express an opinion on the impact such a decision would have on India-China relations.[125] Although Dolkar won her case, the Indian government continued to resist. In 2016, three Tibetans, all born in India prior to 1987 (or born to parents born in India), were denied Indian passports and again took their case to trial. The court's verdict decided definitively in favor of the Tibetans. Its opinion explicitly cited the Dolkar verdict, brushed aside internal ministerial objections, and directed the Ministry of External Affairs to "issue the India passports to the petitioners, who have been declared to be Indian citizens, within a period of four weeks."[126] The question of citizenship being a "gift" remains awkward, however, among the Tibetans, with the verdict eliciting considerable consternation among many exile Tibetan leaders. By and large, those who are against Indian citizenship cling to the notion that accepting it would "dilute the struggle" for a free Tibet. The Tibetan activist Tenzin Tsundue suggested that that those who accepted citizenship in another country would "continue to be culturally Tibetan, but now they can be supporters not claimants for Tibet."[127] Yet such ideological differences aside, the tribulations of living as stateless persons in India seem to be winning the day, as many younger Tibetans seek to decouple their ideological beliefs in a free Tibet from the security of having Indian citizenship. Perhaps as more Tibetans in exile accept Indian citizenship, the relationship between the Tibetan Buddhists and the Khaches will again grow strong.

## AMBIGUOUS, ANONYMOUS, AND OVERSHADOWED

For three centuries the Khache lived as Tibetans among Tibetans. Their place within Tibetan society was never disputed. The arrival of Chinese Communist forces, officials, and cadres in 1951 created, particularly in the traditional Chinese ethnic categorization and the narrower PRC framing of Hui, a semantic breech between being Tibetan and being Muslim. The Wapaling Khaches who remained in Tibet continued to be a vibrant community, but they faced a large influx of Hui in-migrants who altered the face of Islam in central Tibet. As a result, the definition of "Tibetan Muslim" became more "Muslim-in-Tibet" (or more recently "Hui-in-Tibet"), leading to the common but ambiguous term, Zang-Hui, being employed to designate all Muslims in Tibet. The conflation in the minds of many Chinese that being a Hui-in-Tibet and a Khache were one and the same creates new divisions between the Tibetans and Tibetan Muslims since the Hui are increasingly perceived as working alongside the Han and Chinese government to undermine and overwhelm traditional Tibetan culture. According to research carried out in the past decade, Hui migrants who arrived in Tibet, in comparison to their Han migrant counterparts, tended to stay longer than the Han. As a result, most Khache have adopted Tibetan (Ch. *zangzu*) as their official ethnicity, largely out of a growing hostility to the in-migration of Chinese from Central China.[128]

Adding to this confusion, all Muslims tended to be uniformly referred to as Hui in the Chinese language, a linguistic twist that only furthered a conflation of the terms "Wapaling" with "Barkor Khache." It also served to emphasize the assertion that the Barkor Khache were not Tibetan. In the wake of the Barkor Khaches' departure for India, when the Wapaling moved from the Grand Mosque in the Wapaling neighborhood and began praying in and caring for both the Barkor Small Mosque and the Khache Lingka Mosque outside of Lhasa, the strong Barkor and Wapaling neighborhood subidentities among Lhasa Khache became distorted and increasingly forgotten. This move led many to believe that all Khaches were, in the absence of the original Barkor Khache, "Chinese" to some degree or another.

The dramatic shift in attitudes became clear in 2008, when Lhasa again erupted in anti-Chinese violence. Tibetan demonstrators attempted to once again burn down the Grand Mosque. Many articles in the mainstream press linked the

Positioned at the southern edge of the Barkor, the Small Mosque faced the sacred Linkor circumambulation route. After 1960, many of the Wapaling Muslims began to use it for their daily prayers. Hui from outside of Tibet had an increased presence in the Grand Mosque. Source: Kevin Bubriski.

violence to the 1959 March Uprising, when the Grand Mosque in the Wapaling neighborhood was first burned to the ground. These reports inferred the violence was long-standing anti-Muslim in nature without understanding how the circumstances had changed. In both cases, the violence was not anti-Muslim but anti-Chinese, or, perhaps more accurately, anti-collaborationist. For our purposes, the distinction that should be made is that the 2008 hostility was anti-Hui in its orientation, not anti-Khache.

Not only had the primary occupants changed, but the new, often semipermanent Chinese Muslim Hui residents of the Grand Mosque were perceived to be handmaidens of the Chinese state. Since the Wapaling Khache had moved to the Small Mosque, the symbolism of the 1959 and 2008 attacks seemed similar, but the occupants were no longer the same and the circumstances were fundamentally different. As one Tibetan Muslim put it, in recent years there continues to be a division between "Tibetan Muslims whose families have lived in Tibet for generations" and "Hui and other Muslims who have migrated to Tibetan areas to work."[129] If the Barkor Khache lost their Tibetan identity by leaving Tibet, those Khache who remained behind suffered the similar, if different, indignity of being forced to choose between being Tibetan or being Hui. For most Khache, the choice to be Tibetan was the more obvious one.

Since 1959, the Tibetan Muslims have remained frustratingly illusive in the historical treatments of Tibet and Tibetans because they fail to conform to the internal Chinese notions of what it means to be Tibetan or Hui, or because of the increasingly narrow external definition of a Tibetan-in-exile as only being a Buddhist refugee living in India. Although the Tibetan Buddhists who followed the Dalai Lama to India did face numerous hardships, their situation differed substantially from that of the Tibetan Muslims. Due to a variety of economic and political factors, the exiled Tibetan Buddhists became increasingly dependent on Indian and Western support, and they often found themselves compelled to play to romanticized Western ideas of Tibetan Buddhism. Tibetan Muslims escaped the fate of the Tibetans-in-exile community who successfully fled Tibet, only to become, in the words of Donald Lopez, "prisoners of Shangri-la."[130] The fate of the Tibetan Muslims, on the other hand, was to quickly lose any claim to being Tibetan in the face of this newly popular globalized version of Tibet. It was through their participation in the Indian government's political artifices as that government negotiated with China that the Tibetan Muslims earned Indian citizenship and lost, in the eyes of the Tibetan Buddhists, their claim to be Tibetan citizens.

India and China's increasingly fraught relationship reached its nadir with the 1962 Sino-Indian Border Conflict. Scholars of this period tend to characterize Sino-Indian relations in terms of either security concerns or conflicting worldviews. On the surface, it is tempting to see China and India as two regional powers battling for ideological and territorial supremacy: as in the Dalai Lama's harrowing escape from Communist China to a democratic India or as in escalating clashes over a geopolitically significant boundary. Such explanations tend to be overly deterministic as a result of a narrow, selective, and even teleological ordering of events. Positioning the Lhasa Khaches' claim for Indian citizenship and that claim's importance to the Indian government and its Indian citizenry among these other events of the time—those that were creating front-page headlines in both China and India (and around the globe) for many months—suggests something different was at work.

This excision of the Tibetan Muslims from historical treatments of the period is more than an overly deterministic and selective ordering of events. In the Asian context, transnational histories are particularly prone to the nation-state's interpretation of its past as a result of systemic deficiencies, or alternatively, as an exploitation of the periphery by the center. The political scientist Manjari Chatterjee Miller has recently suggested an alternative reading of Chinese-Indian relations with an emphasis on "post-imperial ideology." As she describes it, "The goal of victimhood led both countries to emphasize their past suffering and anti-colonial credentials . . . [in order to] become a key player in the newly decolonized Third World community."[131] Seen through this corrective lens, China and India perceived any major encounter, meeting, or incident as an opening for them to demonstrate to Asia and the broader world how one might hold a preeminent position over the other.

Miller's postimperial ideology creates a space that previous Cold War or conflict-centered analyses did not. The ascendency of such interpretations of the period also explains, in part, the speed with which the Khache quickly dropped out of sight in scholarly analyses. The swiftness with which the Tibetan Muslims faded from general conversation among the public, the media, and governments is, in retrospect, striking. While victimhood might have been a potent strategy against former colonizers, it was less effective among the colonized. It was this dilemma on which China and India's relationship ran aground, as the Bandung Conference clearly demonstrated that both sought to be the dominant leader among the Asian nations.

Nehru's objective was to guide the newly independent nations of Asia and Africa, through an amorphous combination of the Panchsheel Five Principles, nonviolence, and ideological neutrality, in order to avoid serving as proxies in the larger Cold War. Mao chafed at the idea of Soviet and U.S. dominance of the global political dialogue. However, Mao sought to position China as an appealing alternative leader to these same nations in anticipation of, not in an effort to avoid, a coming global conflict. Both men realized that politics was a messy business, but the two diverged over the manner in which they sought, through their influence, to precipitate change. Nehru's influence was one founded on dialogue and compromise. Mao's interpretation viewed the world as a more zero-sum formula whereby were China to gain influence, another must lose it. In this light, the Sino-Indian solidarity of the 1950s, based as it was on the outward deployment of victimhood and influence, collapsed in the 1960s when such strategies proved incapable of resolving conflicts between themselves.

Similar to the ways in which the Bandung Conference is often dismissed as having largely achieved only symbolic outcomes, the 1960 Tibetan Muslim Incident, when it is remembered, is often cast as subsidiary to the more substantive 1962 Sino-Indian Border Conflict. Framed in this manner, the history of Tibetan

Muslims reveals how the ethnic, religious, and political categories of postcolonial Asian nationhood often conceal significant dimensions of Asia's past. The Khaches' experiences in the post-independence period bring into sharp relief those—often minority peoples—who reside in regions that fall outside both the former colonial regimes and the "new" Asian nations. Even the oddly oxymoronic sense of the ethnonym "Tibetan Muslims," as applied in these more modern analyses, points to the tremendous pressures the Khache resisted in order to retain their identity, an identity that had prevailed for centuries within premodern Tibet. Inherently transnational, inter-Asian, and transcultural, the Khache, by simply stepping across the political border of Tibet into India, had their existing South Asian narrative of community rewritten in a manner that repositioned them primarily, not as Tibetans, but as Muslims. In this modern age of complex and highly politicized post-Partition ethnic, subnational, and religious identities, they found none that could accommodate the Tibetan dimension of their identity.[132] Stripped of their hybrid Tibetan identity, excluded from any formal position in the government in exile that emerged in Dharamsala, and shunned in Kashmir, the Khache became exiles manqué—recognized neither by the land they had left nor by the "homeland" to which they had fled.

# GLOSSARY

| ENGLISH | TRANSLITERATION | TIBETAN | CHINESE |
| --- | --- | --- | --- |
| | THL (*Wylie*) | | |
| **Agriculture Ministry** | sonam lekhung (*so nam las khungs*) | བོ་ནམ་ལས་ཁུངས་ | 农业局 |
| **Aristocrat** | ku drak (*sku drag*) | སྐུ་དྲག | 贵族 |
| **Barbarian** | lalo (*kla klo*) | ཀླ་ཀློ་ | 夷 |
| **Barkor** | barkör (*bar skor*) | བར་སྐོར་ | 八廓/帕廓 |
| **Blond ("golden head")** | goser (*mgo gser*) | མགོ་གསེར་ | ———— |
| **Council head** | pönpo (*dpon po*) | དཔོན་པོ་ | 官吏, 头目 |
| **Drapchi (Prison)** | drazhi (*grwa bzhi*) | གྲྭ་བཞི་ | 拉萨第一监狱 |
| **European (English)** | pérang (*phe rang*) | ཕེ་རང་ | 披愣 |
| **Finance Ministry** | tsi khang (*rtsis khang*) | རྩིས་ཁང་ | 财政部 |
| **Foreign Office** | chi gyel lé khung (*phyi rgyal las khungs*) | ཕྱི་རྒྱལ་ལས་ཁུངས་ | 外交部 |
| **Ganden Podrang** | ganden podrang (*dga' ldan pho brang*) | དགའ་ལྡན་ཕོ་བྲང་ | 噶丹颇章 |
| **Happy Light Theater** | dekyi ö-nang (*bde skyid 'od snang*) | བདེ་སྐྱིད་འོད་སྣང་ | 幸福剧场 |
| **honorific Tibetan** | zhesa (*zhe sa*) | ཞེ་ས་ | 敬语 |
| **Hui (Huizu)** | hürik (*hu'i rigs*) [haérik (*ha'e rigs*)] | ཧུའི་ཧུའི་རིགས། | 回民/回族 |
| **Hui-Hui** | hühü (*hus hus*) | ཧུས་ཧུས་ | 回回 [忽忽] |
| **Chinese Hui (Amdo)** | gya haé (*rgya ha'e*) | རྒྱ་ཧའེ་ | [内地回民] |
| **Tibetan Hui (Amdo)** | bö haé (*bod ha'e*) | བོད་ཧའེ་ | 藏回 |

| ENGLISH | TRANSLITERATION THL (*Wylie*) | TIBETAN | CHINESE |
|---|---|---|---|
| Infidel | mutekpa (*mu stegs pa*) | མུ་སྟེགས་པ་ | 异教徒 |
| Insider (Buddhist) | nangpa (*nang pa*) | ནང་པ་ | 佛教徒 |
| Jokhang | jo khang (*jo khang*) | ཇོ་ཁང་ | 大昭寺 |
| Kashag | kashak (*bka' shag*) | བཀའ་ཤག | 噶厦 |
| Khache | khaché (*kha che*) | ཁ་ཆེ་ | 卡契/卡基 |
| – Chinese | gya khaché (*rgya kha che*) | རྒྱ་ཁ་ཆེ་ | 加卡契/甲卡基 |
| – Barkor (Chinese) | barkör khaché (*bar skor kha che*) | བར་སྐོར་ཁ་ཆེ་ | 八廓卡契 |
| – Wapaling (South Asian) | wapaling khaché (*wa pa gling kha che*) | ཝ་པ་གླིང་ཁ་ཆེ་ | 河坝林卡契 |
| – Ladakhi | ladak khaché (*la dwags kha che*) | ལ་དྭགས་ཁ་ཆེ་ | 拉达克卡契 |
| Khache Lingkha | khaché lingkha (*kha che gling kha*) | ཁ་ཆེ་གླིང་ཁ་ | 卡契园/卡基林卡 |
| Khache Phalu | khaché palü (*kha che pha lu*) | ཁ་ཆེ་ཕ་ལུ་ | 卡其帕鲁 |
| Kham (person) | Khampa (*khams pa*) | ཁམས་པ་ | 康巴人 |
| Khatsara | kha tsa ra (*kha tsa ra*) | ཁ་ཙ་ར་ | 卡扎拉 |
| Koko | ko ko (*ko ko*) | ཀོ་ཀོ་ | 汉藏混血 |
| Leader, head | gopa (*mgo pa*) | མགོ་པ་ | 首领 |
| 1961 Lhasa Muslim Incident | hürik kyi nyokdra (*hu'i rigs kyi rnyog gra*) | ཧུའི་རིགས་ཀྱི་རྙོག་གྲ་ | 回民闹事 |

| ENGLISH | TRANSLITERATION | TIBETAN | CHINESE |
| --- | --- | --- | --- |
| | THL (*Wylie*) | | |
| **Lingkor** | ling kor (*gling skor*) | གྲིང་སྐོར | 林廓 |
| **Lochak (Lapchak)** | lo chak (*lo phyag*) | ལོ་ཕྱག | 洛恰 |
| **Muslim (lit., white hat)** | gokar (*mgo dkar*) | མགོ་དཀར | 缠头回回/戴白帽 |
| **Great Prayer Festival** | mönlam chenmo (*smon lam chen mo*) | སྨོན་ལམ་ཆེན་མོ | 大祈祷节 |
| **Mosque** | lha khang (*lha khang*) | ལྷ་ཁང | 清真寺 |
| – Grand Lhasa Mosque | lha khang chen (*lha khang chen mo*) | ལྷ་ཁང་ཆེན་མོ | 大清真寺 |
| – Chinese Khache Mosque | gya kha ché lha khang (*rgya kha che lha khang*) | རྒྱ་ཁ་ཆེ་ལྷ་ཁང | " " |
| – Small Lhasa Mosque | lha khang chung (*lha khang chung*) | ལྷ་ཁང་ཆུང | 小清真寺 |
| – Rapsel Alley Mosque | rap sel lha khang (*rab gsal lha khang*) | རབ་གསལ་ལྷ་ཁང | 绕赛巷清真寺 |
| – Far-Reaching Arrows | gyang da khang (*rgyang mda' khang*) | རྒྱང་མདའ་ཁང | 强达康清真寺 |
| – Dokdé Mosque | dok dé lha khang (*dog sde lha khang*) | དོག་སྡེ་ལྷ་ཁང | 朵底清真寺 |
| **Nangkor** | nang kor (*nang skor*) | ནང་སྐོར | 囊廓 |
| **Nangma (Tibetan music)** | nangma (*nang ma*) | ནང་མ | 囊玛 |
| **Nomad** | drok pa (*'brog pa*) | འབྲོག་པ | 游牧民 |
| **Norbulingka** | nörbulingkha (*nor bu gling kha*) | ནོར་བུ་གླིང་ཁ | 罗布林卡 |
| **Omen** | té ngen (*ltas ngan*) | ལྟས་ངན | 兆头 |

| ENGLISH | TRANSLITERATION<br>THL (*Wylie*) | TIBETAN | CHINESE |
| --- | --- | --- | --- |
| Outsider (non-Tibetan) | chi pa (*phyi pa*) | ཕྱི་པ་ | 外人 |
| Potala | potala (*po ta la*) | པོ་ཏ་ལ་ | 布达拉 |
| Ragyaba | rak gyap pa (*rags rgyab pa*) | རགས་རྒྱབ་པ་ | 热加巴（负尸人） |
| Saga Dawa | sa ga dawa dü chen (*sa ga zla ba dus chen*) | ས་ག་ཟླ་བ་དུས་ཆེན་ | 萨噶达瓦 |
| Tibetan (person) | böpa (*bod pa*) | བོད་པ་ | 藏民/藏族 |
| Tsidrung Lingka | tsé drung ling ka (*rtse drung gling ka*) | རྩེ་དྲུང་གླིང་ཀ | |
| Wapaling | wapaling (*wa pa gling*) | ཝ་པ་གླིང་ | 河坝林 |
| Singba Khache | sing pa kha ché (*sing pa kha che*) | སིང་པ་ཁ་ཆེ | 司巴/森巴 卡契 |

PLACE-NAMES

| ENGLISH | TRANSLITERATION<br>THL (*Wylie*) | TIBETAN | CHINESE |
| --- | --- | --- | --- |
| Amdo | Amdo (*a mdo*) | ཨ་མདོ་ | 安多 |
| Amdo (person) | Amdowa (*a mdo ba*) | ཨ་མདོ་བ་ | 安多人 |
| Baltistan | Belti yül (*bal ti yul*) | བལ་ཏི་ཡུལ་ | 巴勒提斯坦 |
| Batang | Batang (*'ba' thang*) | འབའ་ཐང་ | 巴塘 |

**PLACE-NAMES**

| ENGLISH | TRANSLITERATION THL (*Wylie*) | TIBETAN | CHINESE |
|---|---|---|---|
| Chakzam (Luding) | Chakzam (*lcags zam*) | ལྕགས་ཟམ་ | 泸定 |
| Chamdo | Chamdo (*chab mdo*) | ཆབ་མདོ་ | 昌都 |
| Chöl kha sum (3 regions) | Chöl kha sum (*chol kha gsum*) | ཆོལ་ཁ་གསུམ་ | 却喀松（藏地三区） |
| Darjeeling | Dörjeling (*rdo rje gling*) | རྡོ་རྗེ་གླིང་ | 大吉岭 |
| Dartsedo (Dartsendo) | Dartsedo (*dar rtse mdo*) | དར་རྩེ་མདོ་ | 康定/打箭炉 |
| Derge | Dégé (*sde dge*) | སྡེ་དགེ་ | 德格 |
| Déchen (Deqin) | Déchen (*bde chen*) | བདེ་ཆེན་ | 德勤 |
| Dokde | Dokdé (*dog sde*) | དོག་སྡེ་ | 夺底 |
| Drigung | Drigung (*'bri gung*) | འབྲི་གུང་ | 直贡 |
| Gyantse | Gyantsé (*rgyal rtse*) | རྒྱལ་རྩེ་ | 江孜 |
| Jyekundo | Kyégudo (*skye dgu mdo*) | སྐྱེ་དགུ་མདོ་ | 玉树 |
| Kalimpong | Kabuk (*ka sbug*) | ཀ་སྦུག་ | 噶伦堡 |
| Kashmir | Khaché yül (*kha che yul*) | ཁ་ཆེ་ཡུལ་ | 克什米尔 |
| Kham | Kham (*khams*) | ཁམས་ | 康（区） |

**PLACE-NAMES**

| ENGLISH | TRANSLITERATION THL (*Wylie*) | TIBETAN | CHINESE |
|---|---|---|---|
| Kuti (Nalam)* | Nyalam (*gnya' lam*) | གཉའ་ལམ་ | 聂拉木 |
| Ladakh | Ladak (*la dwags*) | ལ་དྭགས་ | 拉达克 |
| Lhasa | Lhasa (*lha sa*) | ལྷ་ས་ | 拉萨 |
| Lhatse | Lhatsé (*lha rtse*) | ལྷ་རྩེ་ | 拉孜 |
| Longju | Lungjuk (*lung mjug*) | ལུང་མཇུག | 郎久 |
| Shigatse | Shigatsé (*gzhis ka rtse*) | གཞིས་ཀ་རྩེ་ | 日喀则 |
| Siling/Xining | Ziling (*zi ling*) | ཟི་ལིང་ | 西宁 |
| Tau (Daofu) | Tau (*rta'u*) | རྟའུ | 道府 |
| Tsetang | Tsetang (*rtsed thang*) | རྩེད་ཐང་ | 泽当 |
| Ü-Tsang | Ü-Tsang (*dbus gtsang*) | དབུས་གཙང་ | 卫藏 （地区） |

# NOTES

Frequently cited sources have been identified by the following abbreviations.

FBIS       Foreign Broadcast Information Service
FO/DO      Foreign Office Records, Kew, U.K.
IKMEWA     Indian Tibetan Muslim Evacuees Welfare Association
IMEA       Ministry of External Affairs
IOR        India Office Records, British Library, London
NAI        Foreign and Political Department Proceedings, Indian National Archives
SDDX       *Shisanshi Dalai yang shoji he shisishi Dalai zhuanshi zuochuang dang'an xu-*
           *anbian* (Selected Files Relating to the Memorial Ceremony on the Demise
           of the 13th Dalai Lama and the Reincarnation and Installation of the 14th
           Dalai Lama)
SWJN       *Selected Works of Jawaharlal Nehru*
TOHAP      Tibetan Oral History Archive Project, digital archive, www.loc.gov/
           collections/tibetan-oral-history-project/about-this-collection/

## 1. BOUNDARIES OF BELONGING

1. Tibetans referred to the British team simply as Dékyi lingka (Tib. *bde skyid gling pa*),
after the name of the house in which the British Mission was located.

2. Frederick S. Chapman, "Lhasa Mission, 1936: Diary of Events," pt. VIII, p. 2 (MS
22/03/2006, Pitt Rivers Museum, Oxford), cited in "Lhasa United Football Team," *Tibet
Album,* December 5, 2006, Pitt Rivers Museum, http://tibet.prm.ox.ac.uk/photo_1998.131.385.
html. See also Alex McKay, "Kicking the Buddha's Head: India, Tibet and Footballing
Colonialism," in *Soccer in South Asia: Empire, Nation, Diaspora,* ed. Paul Dimeo and
James Mills (New York: Routledge, 2013), 89–104; Frederick S. Chapman, *Lhasa: Holy City*
(London: Chatto & Windus, 1938), 269.

3. Jigme Taring ['phreng Ring, 'jig Med Sum Rten Dbang Po Rnam Rgyal], H0203, Tibetan Oral History Archive Project (hereafter cited as TOHAP).

4. TOHAP HO203 Jigme Taring; TOHAP H0215 Shakabpa Wangchug Denden; Archibald T. Steele, "In the Kingdom of the Dalai Lama, Part V: The Priest King and His Councillors," *Chicago Daily News,* cited in Foreign Office Records (hereafter cited as FO) 371 46122 (1945).

5. Note that the Ladakhi Muslims on the Lhasa United team wore fezzes, which were an essential marker of Muslim identity in British India. See Dilip M. Menon, *Cultural History of Modern India* (New Delhi: Social Science Press, 2006), 115.

6. Peter Bishop, *The Myth of Shangri-La: Tibet, Travel Writing, and the Western Creation of Sacred Landscape* (Berkeley: University of California Press, 1989).

7. For a good overview of foreigners in central Tibet, see Hugh Richardson, "Foreigners in Tibet," in *High Peaks, Pure Earth: Collected Writings on Tibetan History and Culture,* ed. Michael Aris (London: Serindia Publications, 1998), 409–19. See also R. A. Stein, *Tibetan Civilization* (Stanford, CA: Stanford University Press, 1972), 84; George Bogle, "Political and Ethnographical Notes on Tibet and Other Parts of Asia," in *Bhutan and Tibet: The Travels of George Bogle and Alexander Hamilton, 1774–1777,* ed. Alistair Lamb (Hertingfordbury, U.K.: Roxford Books, 2002), 157, 287. For an insightful examination of how this terminology in Chinese *followed* that of Tibetan, see Matthew W. Mosca, *From Frontier Policy to Foreign Policy: The Question of India and the Transformation of Geopolitics in Qing China* (Stanford, CA: Stanford University Press, 2013), 131–35.

8. Évariste R. Huc, *Souvenirs d'un voyage dans la Tartarie et le Thibet pendant les années 1844, 1845 et 1846* (Pekin: Imprimerie des Lazaristes, 1924), 2:235.

9. See also Clements R. Markham, George Bogle, and Thomas Manning, *Narratives of the Mission of George Bogle to Tibet: And of the Journey of Thomas Manning to Lhasa.* (London: Trübner and Co., 1879), cxii.

10. Enseng Ho, "Inter-Asian Concepts for Mobile Societies," *Journal of Asian Studies* 76.4 (November 2017): 908.

11. Ibid., 922. For examples of transregional studies, see Nile Green, *Bombay Islam: The Religious Economy of the West Indian Ocean, 1840–1915* (Cambridge: Cambridge University Press, 2013); Eric Tagliacozzo, *Secret Trades, Porous Borders: Smuggling and States along a Southeast Asian Frontier, 1865–1915* (New Haven, CT: Yale University Press, 2009); Enseng Ho, *The Graves of Tarim: Genealogy and Mobility across the Indian Ocean* (Berkeley: University of California Press, 2006); Rian Thum, *The Sacred Routes of Uyghur History* (Cambridge, MA: Harvard University Press, 2014).

12. Two anonymous reviewers were instrumental in helping me see the forest through the trees and framing so eloquently the significance of this study.

13. David N. Gellner, *Monk, Householder, and Tantric Priest: Newar Buddhism and Its Hierarchy of Ritual* (Cambridge: Cambridge University Press, 1992); Sherry B. Ortner, *High Religion: A Cultural and Political History of Sherpa Buddhism* (Princeton, NJ: Princeton University Press, 1989); José Ignacio Cabezón, *Tibetan Ritual* (Oxford: Oxford University Press, 2010).

14. Geoffrey Samuel, *Civilized Shamans: Buddhism in Tibetan Societies* (Washington, DC: Smithsonian Institution Press, 1993), 39.

15. Marc Gaborieau and Ghulām Muḥammad, *Récit d'un voyageur musulman au Tibet* (Paris: Klincksieck, 1973); Anna Akasoy, Charles Burnett, and Ronit Yoeli-Tlalim,

eds., *Islam and Tibet: Interactions along the Musk Routes* (Farnham, U.K.: Ashgate, 2010); Bianca Horlemann, "Tibetans and Muslims in Northwest China: Economic and Political Aspects of a Complex Historical Relationship," *Asian Highlands Perspectives* 21 (2012): 141–86; A. M. Fischer, "The Muslim Cook, the Tibetan Client, His Lama, and Their Boycott: Modern Religious Discourses of Anti-Muslim Economic Activism in Amdo," in *Conflict and Social Order in Tibet and Inner Asia,* ed. Fernanda Pirie and Toni Huber (Leiden: Brill, 2008), 159–92; Abū Bakr Amīruddīn Tibbatī Nadvī and Parmananda Sharma, trans., *Tibet and Tibetan Muslims* (Dharamsala: Library of Tibetan Works and Archives, 2004).

16. Christopher Beckwith, "The Location and Population of Tibet According to Early Islamic Sources," *Acta Orientalia Academiae* 43 (1989): 163–70; Levon Khatchikian, "The Ledger of the Merchant Hovhannes Joughayetsi," in *Merchant Networks in the Early Modern World,* ed. Sanjay Subrahmanyam (Aldershot: Variorum, 1996), 124–58.

17. Leonard Zwilling, ed., *"More than the Promised Land": Letters and Relations from Tibet by the Jesuit Missionary António de Andrade (1580–1634),* trans. Michael J. Sweet (Boston: Institute of Jesuit Sources, Boston College, 2017), 24–30.

18. Sum pa mkhan po ye shes dpal 'byor (Sumpa Khenpo Yeshe Paljor), *Chos 'byung dpag bsam ljon bzang* [The Wish-Fulfilling Tree: A History of Buddhism], (Lanzhou: Kan su'u mi rigs dpe skrun khang, 1992), 232; José Ignacio Cabezón, "Islam in the Tibetan Cultural Sphere," in *Islam in Tibet,* ed. Gray Henry, Abdul Wahid Radhu, Marco Pallis, and Jane Casewit (Louisville, KY: Fons vitae, 1997), 19; Fengpei Wu and Songyun, *Xizang zhi—Weizang tongzhi* [Combined edition of Gazetteer of Tibet—General History of Ü-Tsang Tibet] (Lhasa: Xizang renmin chubanshe, [1721] 1982), 32; John Newman, "Islam in the Kālacakra Tantra," *Journal of the International Association of Buddhist Studies* 21.2 (1998): 316.

19. Mollica Dastider, *Understanding Nepal: Muslims in a Plural Society* (New Delhi: Har-Anand Publications, 2007), 90.

20. Ma Jianye, "Xizang lasa de huimin," *Huijiao Qingnian Yuebao* 32 (1947): 8–9. There is some debate over the actual roots of the term *khache*. Most simply suggest the term is derived from the Tibetan word for Kashmiri (*khaché*) or Kashmir (*khachul*), which existed long before the arrival of the Tibetan Muslims (e.g., a chief export of Kashmir was saffron, referring to it as "Kashmiri saffron" [*khaché 'kyé*]. Sarat Chandra Das, *Journey to Lhasa and Central Tibet* (New Delhi: Mañjusri Publishing House, [1902] 1970), 126; Abdul Wahid Radhu, *Islam in Tibet: Tibetan Caravans* (Louisville, KY: Fons vitae, 1997), 161. Some scholars suggest that the term is derived from the Ladakhi term for Kashmiri Muslims, *khachur,* sometimes Romanized *khachad*. Ataullah Siddiqui, "Muslims of Tibet," *Tibet Journal* 14.4 (1991): 76; Abū Bakr and Sharma, *Tibet and Tibetan Muslims,* 51. Gaborieau posits that the term is derived from Persian *khwâja,* see Marc Gaborieau, "Powers and Authority of Sufis among the Kashmiri Muslims in Tibet," *Tibet Journal* 20.3 (1995): 21. For an excellent overview of Ladkahi Muslims, see John Bray, "Readings on Islam in Ladakh: Local, Regional and International Perspectives," *Himalaya: Journal of the Association for Nepal and Himalayan Studies* 32.1 (2012): 13–21.

21. Graham Sandberg, *Tibet and the Tibetans* (London: Society for Promoting Christian Knowledge, 1906), 174; Chapman, *Lhasa, The Holy City,* 96; L. Austine Waddell, *Lhasa and Its Mysteries with a Record of the Expedition of 1903 to 1904* (London: Methuen & Co., 1905), 346; Wu and Songyun, *Xizang zhi—Weizang tongzhi,* 329; Ma Jianye, "Xizang Lasa de Huimin."

22. India Ministry of External Affairs (hereafter cited as IMEA), *Notes, Memoranda and Letters Exchanged and Agreements Signed between the Governments of India and China: White Paper* (New Delhi: Ministry of External Affairs, 1960), I:85, II:72, III:123.

23. Emily Yeh, "Living Together in Lhasa: Ethnic Relations, Coercive Amity and Subaltern Cosmopolitanism," in *The Other Global City*, ed. Shail Mayaram (New York: Routledge, 2009), 54–85; Charles Ramble, "Whither, Indeed, the Tsampa Eaters," *Himāl* 6.5 (1993): 21–25; Robert B. Ekvall, "The Tibetan Self-Image," *Pacific Affairs* 33.4 (1960): 375–82; Tenzin Dorjee and Howard Giles, "Cultural Identity in Tibetan Diasporas," *Journal of Multilingual and Multicultural Development* 26.2 (2005): 138–57; Dawa Norbu, "'Otherness' and the Modern Tibetan Identity," *Himāl* 5.3 (May–June 1992): 10–11.

24. For the figure 30,000 as Lhasa's pre-1959 population, see Melvyn C. Goldstein, *A History of Modern Tibet: The Calm Before the Storm, 1951–1955* (Berkeley: University of California Press, 2007), 20; Prem Nath Kaul, *Frontier Callings* (Delhi: Vikkas Publishing House, 1976), 103. In 1972, Nepali consul-general Dor Bohador Bista estimated Lhasa's population at just over 20,000. See Dor Bahadur Bista, *Report from Lhasa* (Kathmandu: Sajha Prakashan), 38. Precise estimates of Lhasa's Muslim population are difficult to come by and often confused by the ambiguity of the term "Hui" (Muslim Chinese), which is selectively applied both in the Republican and PRC periods to refer to *all* Muslims, including recent immigrants from the Chinese interior and other areas. In 1959 and 1960, the years for which we have the most precise estimates, Lhasa was, conservatively, home to 3,000 permanent Muslim residents (see *Times of India*, October 1, 1960, 7; "Corban Observed," June 19, 1959, Foreign Broadcast Information Service (hereafter cited as FBIS), China Regional Affairs, FRB-59–122). Marshall Broomhall's estimate from 1910 and that of one Tibetan Muslim in 1946 that Lhasa was home to over 1,000 Muslim households is certainly a gross exaggeration. See Yiwu, "Xizang Huimin" [Tibet's Hui], *Yuehua* 16.4–6 (1946): 12; Marshall Broomhall, *Islam in China: A Neglected Problem* (London: Morgan & Scott, 1910), 206; Thomas W. Arnold, *Preaching of Islam: A History of the Propagation of the Muslim Faith* (London: Constable & Co., 1913), 296. More cautious estimates suggested over 350 families in Lhasa, 150 in Shigatse, and another 20 in Tsetang. See Gaborieau and Muḥammad, *Récit d'un voyageur musulman au Tibet*, 30; Prince Peter of Greece, "The Moslems of Central Tibet," *Asian Affairs* 39.3–4 (1951): 234; Michael Henss, *The Cultural Monuments of Tibet: The Central Regions*, 2 vols. (New York: Prestel, 2014), I:31.

25. Gaborieau and Muḥammad, *Récit d'un voyageur musulman au Tibet*, 20.

26. Interview, Aman Malik, "Tibetan Muslim Community in Srinagar Witness Exhibition on 50 Years of Tibetans in Exile," Central Tibetan Administration, August 26, 2009, http://tibet.net/2009/08/26/tibetan-muslim-community-in-srinagar-witness-exhibition-on-50-years-of-tibetans-in-exile/ [accessed July 22, 2014].

27. José Ignacio Cabezón, "Islam on the Roof of the World," *Saudi Aramco World* 49.1 (1998): 19.

28. Luce Boulnois, *Poudre d'or et monnaies d'argent au Tibet (principalement au XVIIIe siècle)* (Paris: Editions du Centre national de la recherche scientifique, 1983), 154.

29. The text in Tibetan goes under a number of names, typically glossed as *Khache Phalu's Advice on the Art of Living* but more literally translated *Khache Phalu's Advice on the Law of Worldly Actions and Consequences*. For the most up-to-date overview and translation, see Nicolas Bommarito, "The Khache Phalu: A Translation and Interpretation," *Revue d'Etudes tibétaines* 39 (April 2016): 60–132. See also *Kha che pha lu'i 'jig rten las 'bras rtsi*

*lugs kyi bslab bya bzhugs so* (New Delhi, 1968), which is based on an uncorrected wood-block in Lhasa in 1936. For a corrected but slightly different version, see *Kha che pha lu'i 'jig rten las 'bras rtsi lugs kyi bslab bya bzhugs so* (New Delhi: Shes rig dpar khang, 2000). For an English translation, see Dawa Norbu, trans., *Khache Phalu's Advice on the Art of Living* (Dharamsala: Library of Tibetan Works and Archives, 1987).

30. Akhil Gupta, "The Song of the Nonaligned World: Transnational and the Reinscription of Space in Late Capitalism," *Cultural Anthropology* 7.1 (1992): 64.

31. "Note given by the Ministry of External Affairs, New Delhi, to the embassy of China in India," June 30, 1960, IMEA, IV, 63.

32. *New York Times,* August 12, 1959, 2.

33. Henss, *The Cultural Monuments of Tibet,* 1:44. The traditional Lingkor passed south past the Grand Mosque, where it would turn west, though today it passes in front of the Small Mosque.

34. "Letter #2 from Lhasa Khache to Kalimpong," Tibetan Muslim Refugee Association, n.d., 1959, 3.

35. "Monthly Report for the Month of August," Foreign and Political Department Proceedings, Indian National Archives (hereafter cited as NAI), September 2, 1960, 8.

36. "Note given by the Ministry of Foreign Affairs, Peking to the Embassy of India in China," September 23, 1960, IMEA, IV, 74.

37. Itty Abraham, "Bandung and State Formation in Post-Colonial Asia," in *Bandung Revisited: The Legacy of the 1955 Asian-African Conference for International Order,* ed. See Seng Tan and Amitav Acharya (Singapore: National University of Singapore Press, 2008), 51. For further discussion of this topic, see Michael R. Godley, "The Sojourners: Returned Overseas Chinese in the People's Republic of China," *Pacific Affairs* 62.3 (1989): 330–52.

38. Anna Lowenhaupt Tsing, "*Adat*/Indigenous: Indigeneity in Motion," in *Words in Motion: Toward a Global Lexicon* (Durham, NC: Duke University Press, 2009), 40.

39. Carole McGranahan, *Arrested Histories: Tibet, the CIA, and Memories of a Forgotten War* (Durham, NC: Duke University Press, 2010), 25.

40. A sampling of these would include these accounts from the eighteenth, nineteenth, and twentieth centuries: Heinrich Harrer, *Seven Years in Tibet* (New York: Dutton, 1954); Évariste Régis Huc and H. d' Ardenne de Tizac, *Souvenirs d'un voyage dans la Tartarie, le Thibet et la Chine* (Paris: Plon-Nourrit et cie, 1925); Ippolito Desideri, Michael J. Sweet, and Leonard Zwilling, *Mission to Tibet: the Extraordinary Eighteenth-century Account of Father Ippolito Desideri, S.J.* (Boston: Wisdom Publications, 2010).

41. Fang Jianchang, "Xizang Huizu yu qingzhensi yanjiu de ruogan wenti" [An Examination of the Number of Tibetan Hui and Mosques], *Huizu Yanjiu* 2 (1992): 27–30; Wu and Songyun, *Xizang zhi—Weizang tongzhi;* Jiao Yingqi, *Xizang zhi* [Gazetteer of Tibet] (Taipei: Wenhai chubanshe, [1741] 1966).


## 2. CONFRONTING THE UNEXPECTED

1. Xu Guangqiu, "The Issue of US Air Support for China during the Second World War, 1942–45," *Journal of Contemporary History* 36.3 (2001): 466–67. The Ledo Road would only be completed a month after Crozier and McCallum's flight, but even then the tonnage carried overland was a fraction of that airlifted. At the end of the war, in July 1945, 71,000 tons were flown over the Hump, compared to only 6,000 tons using the Ledo Road.

2. "5 U.S. Fliers Land on Lost Horizon," *New York Times,* January 19, 1944, 3.

3. McCallum estimated that his descent was less than 500 feet. See William B. Sinclair and Robert E. Crozier, *Jump to the Land of God: The Adventures of a United States Air Force Crew in Tibet* (Caldwell, ID: Caxton Printers, 1965), 27.

4. "5 U.S. Fliers Land on Lost Horizon," *New York Times,* January 19, 1944, 3.

5. H. J. McCallum, *Tibet: One Second to Live: A Pilot's Story* (Emlenton, PA: Staab Typographic, 1995), 53.

6. In the telling of Sinclair and Crozier, the air crew does not meet the Tibetan Muslim, Sanaullah, until they reach Tsetang. Sinclair and Crozier, *Jump to the Land of God,* 56.

7. In a letter dated March 8, 1707, Giuseppe da Ascoli wrote that they were mistaken for Kashmiri and adopted Kashmiri-style clothing when traveling. Luciano Petech, *I missionari italiani nel Tibet e nel Nepal,* vol. 2, pt. I (Rome: Libreria dello Stato, 1952), 24, 26.

8. Marc Gaborieau, "The Discovery of the Muslims of Tibet by the First Portuguese Missionaries," in Akasoy, Burnett, and Yoeli-Tlalim, *Islam and Tibet,* 257; Marc Gaborieau, "La découverte des musulmans du Tibet par les premiers missionnaires portugais," in *Vasco Da Gama e a India: Conferência Internacional: Paris, 11–13 maio, 1998* (Lisbon: Fundação Calouste Gulbenkian, 1999), 41–45.

9. Ghulām Muḥammad estimated the "permanent population of the city to be roughly twenty-five thousand residents," which is remarkably in line with estimates for mid-twentieth-century Lhasa. Gaborieau and Muḥammad, *Récit d'un voyageur musulman au Tibet,* 79; Goldstein, *The Calm Before the Storm,* 244; Kaul, *Frontier Callings,* 103.

10. Michael Henss, *The Cultural Monuments of Tibet: The Central Regions,* 2 vols. (New York: Prestel, 2014), 1:38. Henss writes correctly that the Outer Circular Road that encircles Lhasa is an "invisible town wall."

11. Knud Larsen and Amund Sinding-Larsen, *The Lhasa Atlas: Traditional Tibetan Architecture and Townscape* (Boston: Shambhala, 2001), 10–15, 77–79. Huc, *Souvenirs d'un voyage dans la Tartarie et le Thibet, pendant les années 1844, 1845 et 1846,* 386–87.

12. The exact number of mosques is often said to be five, which is technically correct given that the Khache Lingka Lhakhang (Tib. *Gling ka lha khang*) strictly speaking has two mosques, but for the sake of simplicity I speak of four in the course of this study, since there are four locations where mosques were erected. Wu Junkui, "Ka-shi-mi-er musilin linka, libaitang yu mudi," in *Lasa wen wu zhi* (Lhasa: Xizang zizhiqu wenwuguan liwei yuanhui, 1985), 88–89; Ciduo, "Lasa Huimin," *Xizang wenxue* 1 (1992): 115; Henss, *The Cultural Monuments of Tibet,* 1:31.

13. Brian Houghton Hodgson, "Route from Cathmandu in Nepal to Tazedo, on the Chinese Frontier with Some Occasional Allusions to the Manners and Customs of the Bhotiahs, by Amir a Cashmiro-Bhotiah by Birth, and by Vocation an Interpreter to the Traders on the Route Described," *Asiatic Researches* 17 (1832): 530.

14. Ghulām Muḥammad commented that after the second mosque was built the original, smaller mosque was used when only "twenty or thirty people were present for the recitations of the prayers." Gaborieau and Muḥammad, *Récit d'un voyageur musulman au Tibet,* 125; Zhu Xiu, "Lasa Jianwen Lu" [Heard and Seen in Lhasa], *Kaifa Xibei* 2.1 (1934): 44; Xue Wenbo, "Lasa de Huizu" [Lhasa Muslims], *Gansu Minzu Yanjiu* 2 (1986): 72.

15. Wu Junkui, in the *Lasa Wenwu zhi,* gives 1716 as the date, with no citation; see Xizang Zizhiqu Wenwu Guanli Weiyuan huibian, *Lasa Wenwu zhi* [A Survey of Cultural Relics in Lhasa]

(n.p., 1985), 56. The Chinese scholar Fang Jiancheng also notes that inside the Wanshou Temple a plaque dated 1794 states, "The Wanshou Temple in Zhashicheng [in northern Lhasa] was originally a mosque for Chinese Muslims [*neidi Huimin qingzhensi*], but because of a fracas [*naoshi*], in 1761, [the two Chinese ambans] razed it to the ground and replaced it with a Wanshou." Quoted in Fang Jianchang, "Xizang Huizu yu qingzhensi yanjiu de ruogan wenti," 28. For dating, see Cidan Dunzhu (Tsiden Tundrup), "Xizang qingzhensi kaolüe," *Xizang Daxue Xuebao (shehui kexue ban)* 29.3 (2014): 96–102; Triloki Nath Sharma, "The Predicament of Lhasa Muslims in Tibet," *Journal of the Institute of Muslim Minority Affairs* 10.1 (1989): 22; Desideri,Sweet, and Zwilling, *Mission to Tibet,* 265.

16. Xizang Zizhiqu Wenwu Guanli Weiyuan Huibian, *Lasa wenwu zhi,* 54.

17. Weise Zerenduoji [Tsering Woeser], "*Santiao laojie ganshou xinjiu Lasa*" [Encountering Old and New Lhasa through Three Old Streets], http://tibet.woeser.com/?p=19552 (accessed July 8, 2016); Tshe rdor, "Lha sa'i kha che" [Lhasa Khache], *Bod kyi rtsom rig sgyu rtsal* [Tibetan Art and Literature] 4 (1992): 113. See Gaborieau and Muḥammad, *Récit d'un voyageur musulman au Tibet,* 27–28, 129; Diana Altner, 2010. "Do All the Muslims of Tibet Belong to the Hui Nationality?," in Akasoy, Burnett, and Yoeli-Tlalim, *Islam and Tibet,* 350; Foreign Department, External A, Pros. January 1885, Nos. 96–98/98–2; Ma Jianye, "Xizang Lasa de Huimin," 12; Ma Yingfu, "Musilin, de qizhi piaoyang zai lasa," *Qingzhen Bao* 32 (1947): 8–9; Foreign Department, External A, Pros. January 1885, nos. 96–98, 98, Bourne, Resident Consular Officer, Ch'ung Ch'ing, West China, dated October 13, 1885; Xue Wenbo, "Lasa de Huizu," 72.

18. Some local people today refer to the Dokdé Mosque as "East of Hillside" Mosque (Tib. *ge ge shar*). Yang Xiaochun, "The Festival of Fast-Breaking Eid al-Fitr in the Great Mosque of Lhasa: Some Observations," *Études mongoles et sibériennes, centrasiatiques et tibétaines* 47 (December 2016), http://emscat.revues.org/2867 (accessed March 27, 2017); Altner, "Do All the Muslims of Tibet Belong to the Hui Nationality?," 350. Xue Wenbo offers an animated firsthand account of walking from Lhasa to the cemetery; see Xue Wenbo, *Xueling Chongze,* vol. 2 (Lanzhou: Xindaxiao yingchang chubanshe, 1999), 238.

19. Desideri, Sweet, and Zwilling, *Mission to Tibet,* 265.

20. Cidan Dunzhu, "Xizang qingzhensi kaolüe," 99; Xizang Zizhiqu Wenwu Guanli Weiyuan Huibian, *Lasa wenwu zhi,* 88.

21. In 2000, the traditional Tibetan-style mosque was torn down and replaced by a much larger Middle Eastern version. See Larsen and Sinding-Larsen, *The Lhasa Atlas,* 89; Gombozhab T. Tsybikov, *A Buddhist Pilgrim at the Shrines of Tibet* (Leiden: Brill, 2017), 86. See also Xizang Zizhiqu Wenwu Guanli Weiyuan huibian, *Lasa Wenwu zhi,* 55; Zhou Chuanbin, "Shijie wujishang de Yisilan wenhua" [Islamic Culture on the Roof of the World], *Xibei Minzu Yanjiu* 4 (2002): 149; Corneille Jest, "Kha-che and Gya-Kha-che, Muslim Communities in Lhasa (1990)," *Tibet Journal* 20.3 (1995): 10; Gombojab Tsybikov and Xianjun Wang. *Fojiao Xiangke zai Shengdi Xizang* [A Buddhist Pilgrim in Sacred Tibet] (Lhasa: Xizang ren min chu ban she, 1991), 109; Zhou Zhuanbin and Chen Bo, "Yisilan jiao zhuanru Xizang kao" [A Survey of Islam's Entry into Tibet], *Qinghai minzu yanjiu (shehui kexue ban)* 11.2 (2000): 107.

22. An exact number is difficult to assign, but it is certainly not 300 Khache as early as 1800 as some have asserted citing Samuel Turner, *An Account of an Embassy to the Court of the Teshoo Lama, in Tibet: Containing a Narrative of a Journey through Bootan, and Part of*

*Tibet* (London: Printed by W. Bulmer, 1800), 330–31. Turner indicated that there were "no less than three hundred Hindoos, Goseins, and Sunniasses." But such a statement allows us to safely assert that Muslims were in fact already present in Shigatse by 1800. By the 1950s, Prince Peter of Greece suggests 150 households in 1950; see his "The Moslems of Central Tibet," 234. See also Hodgson, "Route from Cathmandu in Nepal to Tazedo," 525. Like Lhasa, Shigatse Tibetan Muslims divided themselves by their ancestral ties to China and India, a distinction that both groups maintained into the modern era. Feng Yan, "Zoujin Xueyu Gaoyuan de musilin," *Huizu Wenxue* 1 (2014): 55.

23. Cidan Dunzhu, "Xizang qingzhensi kaolüe," 98.

24. Frederick M. Bailey, *No Passport to Tibet* (London: Hart-Davis, 1957), 183; Radhu, *Islam in Tibet,* 154; Sarat C. Das and William W. Rockhill, *Journey to Lhasa and Central Tibet* (New Delhi: Mañjuśrī Pub. House, 1970), 228–30. In 1960, the Indian consul reported eight families in Tsetang and nine families in Shigatse. NAI, "Reports from Lhasa," External Affairs, 366 6/35/R&I/60 (especially May and September). It is possible he was referring only to those "Barkor Khache" petitioning to be allowed to return to India.

25. For general references, see Hodgson, "Route from Cathmandu in Nepal to Tazedo," 517; Hughes Didier, *Les Portugais au Tibet: Les premières relations jésuites (1624–1635)* (Paris, 1996), 53; Gaborieau and Muḥammad, *Récit d'un voyageur musulman au Tibet,* 20, 65–67; Prince Peter of Greece, "The Moslems of Central Tibet," 234. Cidan Dunzhu, "Xizang qingzhensi kaolüe," 96–102. Gaborieau also includes Tri-Sambar, a town that he suggests is near Lhasa; other accounts indicate is close to the Sikkim border.

26. Richardson, *High Peaks, Pure Earth,* 1–2; Gillian Tan, "An Ethnography of Life and Changes among Tibetan Nomads of Minyag Dora Karmo, Ganzi Tibetan Autonomous Prefecture, Sichuan Province," Études *mongoles et sibériennes, centrasiatiques et tibétaines* 43–44 (2013), http://emscat.revues.org/2111 (accessed June 19, 2016).

27. Ü-Tsang is one of the three traditional provinces of Tibet formed by the merging of two earlier power centers of Ü (eastern area, including Lhasa) and Tsang (western area, including Gyantse and Shigatse).

28. Stein, *Tibetan Civilization,* 109. For the biases, connotations, and regionalisms embedded in the Anglophone term "Tibetan," see also Ekvall, "The Tibetan Self-Image"; Melvyn Goldstein and Matthew Kapstein, eds., *Buddhism in Contemporary Tibet: Religious Revival and Cultural Identity* (Berkeley: University of California Press, 1998); Samuel, *Civilized Shamans;* Tsering Shakya, *Dragon in the Land of Snow: A History of Modern Tibet since 1947* (New York: Columbia University Press, 1999); Tina Harris, *Geographical Diversions: Tibetan Trade, Global Transactions* (Athens: University of Georgia Press, 2013); Jinba Tenzin, *In the Land of the Eastern Queendom: The Politics of Gender and Ethnicity on the Sino-Tibetan Border* (Seattle: University of Washington Press, 2014).

29. Ekvall, "The Tibetan Self-Image," 377.

30. See Toni Huber, *The Holy Land Reborn: Pilgrimage & the Tibetan Reinvention of Buddhist India* (Chicago: University of Chicago Press, 2008); George Dreyfus, "Proto-Nationalism in Tibet," in *Tibetan Studies: Proceedings of the 6th Seminar of the International Association for Tibetan Studies, Fagernes,* ed. Per Kværne (Oslo: Institute for Comparative Research in Human Culture, 1994).

31. Sara Schneiderman, "Barbarians at the Border and Civilising Projects: Analysing Ethnic and National Identities in the Tibetan Context," in *Tibetan Borderlands,* ed. Paul

Christiaan Klieger (Leiden: Brill, 2006), 9–34. The concept that a Tibetan could be non-Buddhist on the surface seems somewhat preposterous, but it is indicative that the few scholars who venture such a claim tend to use the Tibetan Muslims as their example (as Shneiderman does in the above article, p. 17). Ramble, "Whither, Indeed, the Tsampa Eaters," and Ekvall, "The Tibetan Self-Image," both cite Tibetan Muslims to prove that non-Buddhists (*phyi-pa*) can be Tibetan. For a more politicized call for an ethnic (non-Buddhist) identity, see Dawa Norbu, "'Otherness' and the Modern Tibetan Identity."

32. Françoise Pommaret, "The Mon-pa Revisited: In Search of Mon," in *Sacred Spaces and Powerful Places in Tibetan Culture,* ed. Toni Huber (Dharamsala: Library of Tibetan Works and Archives, 1999), 53. See also William M. Coleman's introduction in "Making the State on the Sino-Tibetan Frontier: Chinese Expansion and Local Power in Batang, 1842–1939" (PhD diss., Columbia University, 2014), 1–32; Brigitte Steinmann, "National Hegemonies, Local Allegiances: Historiography and Ethnography of a Buddhist Kingdom," *European Bulletin of Himalayan Research* 25–26 (Autumn 2003–Spring 2004): 145–67.

33. Tsering Shakya, "Whither the Tsampa Eater," 9. For a deeper and more extended discussion of the term "indigenous" as related to Tibet, see Emily Yeh's perceptive analysis, "Tibetan Indigeneity: Translations, Resemblances, and Uptake," in *Indigenous Experience Today,* ed. Marisol de la Cadena and Orin Starn (Oxford: Berg, 2007), 69–98. The Russian explorer Tsybikov makes a similar comment in "Lhasa and Central Tibet."

34. Yeh, "Tibetan Indigeneity," 69.

35. Eric J. Hobsbawm and Terence O. Ranger, *The Invention of Tradition* (Cambridge: Cambridge University Press, 1983).

36. Max Weber, *Economy and Society,* trans. Ephraim Fischof (Berkeley: University of California Press, 1978), 389.

37. Gerald Roche, "The Tibetanization of Henan's Mongols: Ethnicity and Assimilation on the Sino-Tibetan Frontier," *Asian Ethnicity* 17.1 (2015): 129.

38. Dru Gladney, "Relational Alterity: Constructing Dungan (Hui), Uygur, and Kazakh Identities across China, Central Asia, and Turkey," *History and Anthropology* 9.4 (1996): 445–77.

39. Fredrik Barth, "Enduring and Emerging Issues in the Analysis of Ethnicity," in *The Anthropology of Ethnicity: Beyond "Ethnic Groups and Boundaries,"* ed. Hans Vermeulen and Cora Govers (Amsterdam: Het Sphinhuis, 1994), 11–32.

40. For a wonderfully written and accessible view into this period and the role Muslims played, see Luce Boulnois, "Gold, Wool and Musk: Trade in Lhasa in the Seventeenth Century," in *Lhasa in the Seventeenth Century: The Capital of the Dalai Lamas,* ed. Françoise Pommaret (Leiden: Brill, 2003), 133–56.

41. Prince Peter of Greece, "Moslems of Central Tibet," 238.

42. The exact numbers of men and boys invited typically change depending on the speaker. Discrepancies between Emily Yeh (seventeen boys and thirty men) and José Cabezón ("fourteen elders and thirty youth") are reflective of my interviews, in which the totals never exceeded fifty. See Yeh, "Living Together in Lhasa," 61; and José Ignacio Cabezón, "Islam in the Tibetan Cultural Sphere," in Radhu, *Islam in Tibet,* 17.

43. In 1933, in testimony to British officials, Ghulam Muḥammad swore that "Kingoo Napa the former ruler of Tibet had called the Muslims from Kashmir and had given them a written paper giving every religious freedom." FO_371_17051 (57), Letter from Special

Gharas Officer (Leh) to British Joint Commissioner (Ladakh), dated June 12, 1933. He also notes that the certificate was destroyed in 1913 as a result of the Chinese-Tibetan violence in Lhasa.

44.  Khatchikian, "The Ledger of the Merchant Hovhannes Joughayetsi," 160.

45.  Bogle, "Political and Ethnographical Notes on Tibet and Other Parts of Asia," 287.

46.  Songjun and Huang Peiqiao, *Xizhao Tulüe/Xizang Tukao* (Lhasa: Xizang renmin chubanshe, 1982), 223.

47.  Ma Shaoyun and Sheng Meixi, eds., *Weizang tuzhi* [Illustrated Atlas of Western Tibet] (Taipei: Wenhai chubanshe, [1792] 1970), xiajuan:7a.

48.  While there seems to be consensus that Faizullah was a contemporary of the Seventh Panchen Lama, other scholars (such as Abdul Wahid Radhu) suggest that he served the Third, Fourth, Fifth, or Sixth Panchen Lama; see Tashi Tsering, "The Advice of the Tibetan Muslim 'Phalu': A Preliminary Discussion of a Popular Buddhist/Islamic Literary Treatise," *Tibetan Review* 23.2 (February 1988): 12.

49.  Johan van Manen, "Khacche Phalu: A Tibetan Moralist," in *Sir Asutosh Mookerjee Silver Jubilee Volumes,* vol. 3 (Calcutta: Calcutta University, 1925), 147.

50.  Khache Phalu, *Khache Phalu's Advice on the Art of Living,* trans. Dawa Norbu (Dharamsala: Library of Tibetan Works and Archives, 1987), 18.

51.  Tshe-dbang rnam-rgyal, "Khache Pha lu'l bslab bya dngos grub chu mig ces bya bar dbye zhib kyl lta tshul rags tsam gleng ba" (A Brief Analytical Discussion on Khache Phalu's Advice Called Fountain of Obtainment), *Bod kyi rtsom rig sgyu rtsal* 8.4 (1981): 36–37. For further discussion on authorship and content, see also Mun pa thar, "Kha che pha lu'i bslab bya dngos sgrub chu mig ces bya ba'i sgyu rtsal rang bzhin skor che long tsam brjod pa (Elaborate Discussion on the Artful Nature of Khache Phalu's Advice Called Fountain of Obtainment)," *Bod ljongs sgyu rtsal zhib 'jug* 3:1 (1989): 45–55; Hor khang Bsod nams dpal 'bar, "Kha che pha lu'i 'jig rten las 'bras rtsi lugs kyi bslab bya'i nang don la dpyad pa" (On the Author of the Kha che pha lu and Its Contents), *Bod ljongs sgyu rtsal zhib 'jug* 2 (1993): 108–19.

52.  Tshe-dbang rnam-rgyal, "Khache Pha lu'l bslab bya dngos grub chu mig ces bya bar dbye zhib kyl lta tshul rags tsam gleng ba," iv.

53.  Ramble, "Whither, Indeed, the Tsampa Eaters," 22.

54.  "His Holiness the Dalai Lama Meets with the Tibetan Community in Los Angeles," http://tibet.net/2014/02/28/his-holiness-the-dalai-lama-meets-with-the-tibetan-community-in-la/ (accessed June 20, 2014). See also Rohit Singh, "Reimagining Tibet through the Lens of Tibetan Muslim History and Identity." *Oxford Handbooks Online,* Oxford University Press, 2015.

55.  Yeh, "Living Together in Lhasa," 62.

56.  Bogle, "A Memorandum on the Trade of Tibet," 156.

57.  NAI, Foreign Department, October 1, 1879, Political A, No. 134 No. 22, p. 2, dated June 30, 1879; Marc Gaborieau, "Les marchands musulmans *kashmírí* au Tibet, au Népal et en Inde du Nord," in *Marchands et hommes d'affaires asiatiques dans l'Océan Indien et la Mer de Chine, 13e–20e siècles,* ed. Denys Lombard and Jean Aubin (Paris: Éditions de l'EHESS, 1988), 195–98; Matthew W. Mosca, "Kashmiri Merchants and Qing Intelligence Networks in the Himalayas: The Ahmed Ali Case of 1830," in *Asia Inside Out: Connected Places* (Cambridge, MA: Harvard University Press, 2015), 221.

58.  For a detailed description of the Kashmiris' role in Kathmandu and across the trans-Himalaya region, see Marc Gaborieau, *Minorités musulmanes dans le Royaume Hindou du*

*Népal* (Nanterre: Laboratoire d'ethnologie, 1977), 31–54; Alfiani Fadzakir, "Muslims of Kathmandu: A Study of Religious Identity in a Hindu Kingdom" (PhD diss., Brunel University, 2001), 28–29.

59. John Powers and David Templeman, *Historical Dictionary of Tibet* (Metuchen, NJ: Scarecrow Press, 2012), 570; Melvyn C. Goldstein, *The New Tibetan-English Dictionary of Modern Tibetan* (Berkeley: University of California Press, 2001), 93.

60. While an exact date is difficult to identify with any precision, there are several hints that allow us with considerable confidence to suggest that both communities were in place by 1700. First, the Italian missionary Ippolito Desideri noted that the local Wapaling Khache "once had a burial near Lhasa; this was destroyed and they were ordered to make a new one further away from the town." Given that he resided in Lhasa in 1716–21, it seems reasonable that the cemetery was not newly constructed and that a cemetery had existed for this population previously, suggesting a residential population prior to 1700. Second, the Hui scholar Xue Wenbo while living in Lhasa in 1952 visited the cemetery and noted several tombstones (Ch. *beijie*). The earliest remaining headstone he discovered was dated "Qianlong 49" (1785), which confirms Desideri's account even if during his visit he did not document early to mid-eighteenth-century burials. The specific use of the Chinese prefix *gya-* is harder to pinpoint, but it is almost certainly predominantly a twentieth-century phenomenon.

61. For the best overview in English of this community and its relationship with the other ethnic groups in Lhasa, see Yeh, "Living Together in Lhasa"; Ma Jianye, "Xizang Lasa de Huimin," 5:13b–16b; Yiwu, "Xizang Huimin," 12.

62. Altner, "Do All the Muslims of Tibet Belong to the Hui Nationality?," 348–49; Gaborieau and Muḥammad, *Récit d'un voyageur Musulman au Tibet*, 25–27; Prince Peter of Greece, "The Moslems of Central Tibet," 237; Tshe rdor, "Lha sa'i kha che"; Yang Fangcan, *Sichuan tongzhi* [Gazetteer of Sichuan] (Taipei: Huawen shuju. [1816] 1967), 194:33b.

63. 'Brug lha, "bar skor khrom ra'i byung 'phel skor rags tsam bshad pa," *krung go'i bod kyi shes rig*, 60 (2002): 51–52.

64. Ciduo, "Lasa Huimin," 115; Bao Meng, *Xizang zoushu* [Memorials on Tibet] (Taibei: Guangwen Shuju, [1852] 1978), 1:30b–1:31a.

65. Tsha rong dbyangs can sgrol dkar, *Sde dpon mi drag gi sras mo gzhon nu ma zhig gis sge'u khung nas mthong ba'i bod kyi rgyal sa lha sa'i snang tshul mdor bsdus*, 154–55.

66. Xue Wenbo, *Xueling Chongze*, 2:292.

67. See Radhu, *Islam in Tibet*.

68. Janet Rizvi, "Leh to Yarkand: Travelling the Trans-Karakoram Trade Route," in *Recent Research on Ladakh 7. Proceedings of the 7th Colloquium of the International Association for Ladakh Studies, Bonn/St.Augustin, 12–15 June 1995*, ed. T. Dodin and H. Räther (Ulm: Universität Ulm, 1997), 379.

69. Rnam rgyal rgya mtsho (Namgyal Gyatso). *Bod rje chos rgyal gyi gdun rgyud sde dpon lha-rgya-ri'i gdun rabs rin chen phren ba* [The Precious Garland: A History of the Descendents of the Tibetan King Lha-rgyari-sde dpon] (New Delhi: Dpal 'byor dpar skrun khan, 1999) 41–42.

70. IOR/L/PS/11/31 P3777/1912 (October 1912); Ding Weizhi, Le Ge, and Xisheng Jin, eds., *Zhongguo guoqing congshu: Baixianshi jingji shehui diaocha* (Beijing: Zhongguo dabaike quanshu chubanshe, 1995), 84; Xu Guangzhi, Dawa, and Jun Zhao, *Yapian zhanzheng qianhou Xizang bainian lishi (1793–1893)* (Beijing: Minzu chubanshe, 2011), 130–32.

71. Frederick Chapman notes as much in his classic work: "some of them are descendants of the Dogra force that unsuccessfully attacked western Tibet a hundred years ago." Chapman, *Lhasa: The Holy City*, 96. Some sources mistakenly suggest the term came from the surname "Singh," though there is very little evidence to support such a claim. Rather both the Chinese and Tibetan sources glossed Dogra as "Sikh" (Tib. *sing pa*; Ch. *senba*) See also Abdul Ghani Sheikh, "Tibetan Muslims," *Tibet Journal* 16.4 (1991): 87; Xu Guangzhi, Dawa, and Jun Zhao, *Yapian zhanzheng qian-hou Xizang bainian lishi (1793–1893)*, 136.

72. Derek Waller neatly distilled the otherwise extremely complex historical lead-up to Zorawar Singh's fateful Tibetan campaign. See his *The Pundits: British Exploration of Tibet and Central Asia* (Lexington: University Press of Kentucky, 1990), 101. Matthew Mosca offers a broader perspective in *From Frontier Policy to Foreign Policy*, 262–64. See also Xu Guangzhi, Dawa, and Jun Zhao, *Yapian zhanzheng qian-hou Xizang bainian lishi (1793–1893)*, 137–56.

73. Bao Meng, *Xizang Zoushu*, 1:30b–1:31a. The term "Chantou Hui," literally, "turbaned Muslims," refers to non-Muslim Chinese or "Turkic" Muslims of Central Asia. Both *chantou* and *Huichan*, according to Xue Wenbo, remained in use in Chinese to describe the Barkor Khache. See Bao Meng, *Xizang zoushu*; F. R. Moreaes, *The Revolt in Tibet* (New York: Macmillan, 1960); Wenqing, Zhen Jia, and Baoyun, eds., *Chouban yiwu shimo* [The Complete Record on Managing Foreign Affairs] (Taibei: Guofeng chubanshe, [1930] 1963), 75:24a. It should also be noted that article 4 of the Treaty of Thapathali (1856) included the return of all "Sikh" prisoners of war.

74. For a good translation of both the Nepalese and Tibetan versions of this treaty, see Michael C. Walt van Pragg, *The Status of Tibet: History, Rights, and Prospects in International Law* (Boulder, CO: Westview Press, 1987), 292–96.

75. Ding Weizhi, Le Ge, and Xisheng Jin, *Zhongguo guoqing congshu*, 84.

76. Huang Louzhai, "Lhasa Muslim Ethnic and Group Identity" (Master's thesis, Central University of Nationalities, 2007), 23; Ataullah Siddiqui, "Muslims of Tibet," *Tibet Journal* 16.4 (1991): 74.

77. "Ghārib" is an Urdu term meaning "poor" that has Arabic roots.

78. Ragyapa should be distinguished from the slightly higher class of token (Tib. *rtogs ldan*) or corpse cutters. See Margaret Gouin, *Tibetan Rituals of Death: Buddhist Funerary Practices* (London: Routledge, 2010), 65; Rinchen Dolma Taring, *Daughter of Tibet* (London: Murray, 1970), 9; Jamyang Norbu, "The Lhasa Ripper," in *Trails of the Tibetan Tradition*, ed. Roberto Vitali (Dharamshala: Amnye Machen Institute, 2014), 233–50.

79. Intriguingly, *rags rgyab pa* literally translates as "those who live behind the bank." It is so similar in tone to the original meaning of *Wapaling* ("near the dyke") that one wonders if there is an early connection.

80. See Gaborieau and Muḥammad, *Récit d'un voyageur musulman au Tibet*, 134.

81. Tsha rong dbyangs can sgrol dkar, *Sde dpon mi drag gi sras mo gzhon nu ma zhig gis sge'u khung nas mthong ba'i bod kyi rgyal sa lha sa'i snang tshul mdor bsdus*, 103.

82. Gaborieau and Muḥammad, *Récit d'un voyageur musulman au Tibet*, 27.

83. Zhu Xiu, "Lasa Jianwen Lu," 57.

84. Yiwu, "Xizang Huimin," 12. The author also elucidates that the Wapaling community was made up primarily of Hui from Shaanxi, Sichuan, and Yunnan.

85. Ma Yingfu, "Musilin de Qizhi Piaoyang zai Lasa [The Muslim banner flying over Lhasa]," *Qingzhen Bao* 32 (1947): 8–9. See also Ma Jianye, "Xizang Lasa de Huimin [Muslims of Lhasa Tibet]," 12.

86. Zhongguo Dier Lishi Dang'anguan Zhongguo Zangxue Yanjiu Zhongxin, eds. *Huang Musong, Wu Zhongxin, Zhao Shouyu, Dai Zhuanxian fengshi banli zangshi baogao shu* [Huang Musong, Wu Zhongxin, Zhao Shouyu, Dai Zhuanxian: Reports of Envoys Sent to Handle Tibetan Affairs] (Beijing: Zhongguo Zangxue chubanshe, 1993), 29.

87. Xue Wenbo, "Lasa de Huizu," 70.

88. Ding Weizhi, Le Ge, and Xisheng Jin, *Zhongguo guoqing congshu,* 84.

89. "Corban Observed," June 19, 1959, Foreign Broadcast Information Service, China Regional Affairs, FRB-59–122.

90. The oral interviews of Prince Peter suggest 150 families in Shigatse and another 20 in Tsetang. The Indian consul mentions families in both cities being given permission to leave Tibet in 1960. See Prince Peter of Greece, "The Moslems of Central Tibet," 234; NAI, "Reports from Lhasa," External Affairs, 366 6/35/R&I/60 (esp. May and September).

91. Kaul, *Frontier Callings,* 107; Abū Bakr Amīruddīn Tibbatī Nadvī, *Tibet and Tibetan Muslims,* 50; Sharma, "The Predicament of the Lhasa Muslims in Tibet," 26.

92. "Detailed List of the Indian National Muslims of Kashmir Origin," TMRAA, 1960, 1–24. This list did not include children already in Indian schools at the time of the incident or the sixty plus Khache who had left on Hajj in 1959. See "Tibetans on Hajj Pilgrimage," *Times of India,* May 25, 1959, 3.

93. In 1964, a *People's Daily* article cited 800 Muslims in Lhasa celebrating Eid al-Adha at the mosque, all of whom would likely have been men. "Beijing Lasa Musilin Huan Dukai Bangjie," *Renmin Ribao,* February 17, 1964, 2; see also "Moslem Bairam Festival," February 18, 1964, Foreign Broadcast Information Service, FBIS-FRB-64–034. Many English-language articles either give the misimpression that only the Barkor Khache are "Tibetan Muslim" and thus after 1960 only Hui Muslim Chinese remained or tend to underestimate the actual number.

94. For an example of this, see Lasa shi Difangzhi, *Lasa shizhi,* 2:1275.

95. Ding Weizhi, Le Ge, and Xisheng Jin, eds., *Zhongguo guoqing congshu,* 84; Lasa shi Difangzhi, *Lasa shizhi,* 2:1275. Ma Rong indicates that "according to registration records, there were 1,195 Hui people officially registered in the TAR in 1964," a number that increased to 1,529 in 1985. One possibility for the discrepancy could be that the Khache registered as Tibetan in 1964. See Ma Rong, *Population and Society in Contemporary Tibet* (Hong Kong: Hong Kong University Press, 2010), 103.

96. For an excellent overview of the role of Ambans in Tibet (especially in the early twentieth century), see Daphon David Ho, "The Men Who Would Not Be Amban and the One Who Would," *Modern China* 34 (2008), esp. 212–15.

97. The right to have an envoy was granted by the Treaty of Thapathali (1856). Petech, *Aristocracy and Government in Tibet,* 6.

98. NAI, F&P Secret/External, May 1917, Nos. 4–11, also indicates Sikkimese could be tried by any Tibetan magistrate except at trade marts and on trade routes, where they were under the jurisdiction of British Trade Agents. Bryan J. Cuevas, *The Hidden History of the Tibetan Book of the Dead* (New York: Oxford University Press, 2003), 267n3, states that the "title of *lo-phyag* refers to the custom in Bhutan of dispatching a regular diplomatic representative to the Tibetan government in Lhasa as a mission of tribute," likely begun in 1730 and lasting until 1950. Thierry Mathou warns that "the traditional Tibet-Bhutan relationship should not be interpreted in terms of a superior/inferior syndrome, supposedly involving some form of Bhutanese vassalage to Tibet." See Thierry Mathou, "Bhutan-China

Relations: Towards a New Step in Himalayan Politics," in *The Spider and the Piglet: Proceedings of the First International Seminar on Bhutan Studies*, ed. Karma Ura and Sonam Kinga (Thimphu: Centre for Bhutan Studies, 2004), 388–411.

99. Sikkim, unlike the other Himalayan states, did not have a representative or agent in Lhasa. Foreign and Political Department, Secret-External, May 1917, Nos. 4–11, No. 8—dated Gangtok, the 21st (received 26th) December 1916.

100. Alex McKay, *Tibet and the British Raj: The Frontier Cadre, 1904–1947* (Richmond, Surrey: Curzon, 1997), 67.

101. Huc, *Souvenirs d'un voyage dans la Tartarie et le Thibet*, 395.

102. Yang Fangcan, *Sichuan Tongzhi*, 194:33b.

103. Ibid. Ü and Tsang form the two central provinces of Tibet. Ü is centered in Lhasa, Tsang in Shigatse. In Qing sources the terms "Nearer Tibet" and "Further Tibet" typically are deployed to refer to the Ü (Tib. *dbus*) and Tsang (Tib. *gtsang*) areas, respectively. See Mosca, "Kashmiri Merchants and Qing Intelligence Networks in the Himalayas, 240n5.

104. Sandberg, *Tibet and the Tibetans*, 174.

105. Foreign and Political Department, Secret-External, May 1917, Nos. 4–11; No. 8—dated Gangtok, the 21st (received 26th) December 1916 (Confidential).

106. Gaborieau and Muḥammad, *Récit d'un voyageur musulman au Tibet*, 26.

107. Rebecca Redwood French, *The Golden Yoke: The Legal Cosmology of Buddhist Tibet* (Ithaca, NY: Cornell University Press, 1995), 166.

108. Again, a key problem in such documents is the vocabulary employed. Typically such a representative was simply listed as the "Mohammadan leader" with no further indication of his status. See IOR Lhasa Mission Diaries, 315-X1 (October 1939); IOR/L/PS/12/4202 (2)Coll 36/30 2867—10th March 1946.

109. See Gaborieau and Muḥammad, *Récit d'un voyageur musulman au Tibet*, 26–27.

110. Xue Wenbo, *Xueling Chongze*, 2:295.

111. Prince Peter of Greece, "Moslems of Central Tibet," 234–35.

112. Tibetan Oral History Project (TOHP), Interview H0201 with Könchok Samden [Tib. *dkon mchog bsam gtan*], (India, June 1982), http://lcweb4.loc.gov/natlib/tohap/tei/H0201/seg02/text/0001.pdf (accessed April 11, 2015).

113. Chen Bo, "Lasa Musilin junti diaocha," *Xibei minzu yanjiu*, 1, 2000: 89. He also notes that according to oral histories the committee, in the past, used to have a designated leader with a single assistant and three committee members, and that the Small Mosque has an 11-member committee today.

114. Abū Bakr Amīruddīn Tibbatī Nadvī and Sharma, *Tibet and Tibetan Muslims*.

115. Gaborieau and Muḥammad, *Récit d'un voyageur musulman au Tibet*, 135.

116. Abū Bakr Amīruddīn Tibbatī Nadvī and Sharma, *Tibet and Tibetan Muslims*, 54. See also NAI, Foreign Department, Pro. No 284, 1904, which, quoting the Russian traveler Gombojab Tsibikov, are "under the jurisdiction of their own officials, whose position resembles that of Consuls or Chargés d'Affaires."

117. Mahood Butt, "Dalai Lama and the Muslims of Tibet," Office of Tibet (New York), February 19, 2005; Jamyang Norbu, "Reply to Ian Buruma, 'The Muslims of Tibet,'" *New York Review of Books*, October 4, 2001.

118. Fischer, "The Muslim Cook, the Tibetan Client, His Lama and Their Boycott."

## 3. HOW HALF-TIBETANS MADE TIBET WHOLE

1. Far fewer records exist discussing the culture and political implications of the Kokos: L. Austine Waddell, *Lhasa and Its Mysteries with a Record of the Expedition of 1903 to 1904* (London: Methuen & Company, 1905), 344–46; Broomhall, *Islam in China*, 344; NAI, "Chinese Primary School in Lhasa," External Affairs, August 28, 1937, No. 559-X (Secret); IOR/L/PS/12/4201 Coll 36/30/6472; FO 371–53613 "Gyantse News Report," November 29, 1946.

2. FO 371/35754 (1943).

3. For an account of the police being held, see FO 371/35754 (1942). Chang Jui-te indicates that "the Tibetan administration negotiated for the policemen's release for five months without success." See Chang Jui-te, "An Imperial Envoy: Shen Zonglian in Tibet, 1943–1946," in *Negotiating China's Destiny in World War II*, ed. Hans Van de Ven, Diana Lary, and Stephen R. MacKinnon (Stanford, CA: Stanford University Press, 2015), 54.

4. Warren W. Smith, *China's Tibet? Autonomy or Assimilation* (Lanham, MD: Rowman & Littlefield, 2008), 7. See also Anne-Marie Blondeau, Katia Buffetrille, and Wei Jing, *Authenticating Tibet: Answers to China's 100 Questions* (Berkeley: University of California Press, 2008), 13.

5. Fabienne Jagou, "From Lifanyuan to the Mongolian and Tibetan Affairs Commission," in *Managing Frontiers in Qing China: The Lifanyuan and Libu Revisited*, ed. Dittmar Schorkowitz and Ning Chia (Leiden: Brill, 2017), 313–14. Jagou also makes the significant point that the Qing's relationship with each of the three Tibetan provinces differed, with an Amban in charge of administration in Amdo, native chieftains (Ch. *tusi*) in Kham, and an Amban in Ü-Tstang, whose role was as a supervisor there to advise.

6. Clemens W. L. Metternich, *Mémoires, documents et écrits divers laissés par le Prince de Metternich, Chancelier de Cour et d'état: Pub. Par son fils le Prince Richard de Metternich, classés et réunis par M.a. de Klinkowström* (Paris: E. Plon, Nourrit et cie, 1881).

7. Melvyn C. Goldstein, "On Modern Tibetan History: Moving Beyond Stereotypes," in *Tibet and Her Neighbours: A History*, ed. Alex McKay (London: Hansjörg Mayer, 2003), 218.

8. Matthew Kapstein, *Buddhism between Tibet and China* (Boston: Wisdom Publications, 2009), 21–22; John Powers, *Introduction to Tibetan Buddhism* (Ithaca, NY: Snow Lion Publications, 1995), 145.

9. FO 371/10233 (1924).

10. Wolfgang Bertsch, "A Survey of Tibetan Paper Currency," *Bulletin of Tibetology*, n.s., 3 (1996): 3–5.

11. Sulmaan W. Khan, *Muslim, Trader, Nomad, Spy: China's Cold War and the People of the Tibetan Borderlands* (Chapel Hill: University of North Carolina Press, 2015), 2–6.

12. Some degree of their prominence and acceptance can be seen in the fact that Waddell quickly identifies and separates them from the Nepalese and Chinese in his categorization of the peoples of Lhasa. See Waddell, *Lhasa and Its Mysteries*, 214, 344, 346, 359.

13. For the best examination of this group, see Tirtha P. Mishra, "Nepalese in Tibet: A Case Study of Nepalese Half-Breeds (1856–1956)," *Contributions to Nepalese Studies* 30.1 (2003): 1–18. Documents referring to *Khatsara* (N. Kha char) in twentieth-century Tibet are numerous. For examples, see NAI, Political Department, No. 49(2)-X Secret, 1923; NAI, Foreign and Political Department, External, No. 215-X, 1930. I have encountered a single reference to a "Nepali-Mohammedan," though this appears to have been a Muslim

from Nepal rather than a Muslim Khachara. See FO 371/53616 (1946). Lewis, Tuladhar, and Tuladhar point out that the "Tibetan wife is called a *sem*, a derogatory Newari term expressing high caste disdain for Tibetans as dirty and low in status." See Todd T. Lewis, Subarna M. Tuladhar, and Labh R. Tuladhar, *Popular Buddhist Texts from Nepal: Narratives and Rituals of Newar Buddhism* (Albany: State University of New York Press, 2000), 84.

14. TOHAP HO203 Jigme Taring.

15. In oral interviews, many Tibetans, particularly those in Kham and Amdo, stated that the derogatory connotation is much diminished today and perhaps is something closer to the more neutral Hawaiian term "hapa."

16. Half-Tibetans were common across Tibet, but they are prominent only in the historical record in the twentieth century. Waddell in 1903 was told by the Nepalese consul that there were "2,000 Chinese and Kokos"; see Waddell, *Lhasa and Its Mysteries,* 346. Mishra estimates "approximately 1000 *Khacharas*" in the 1920s. See Mishra, "Nepalese in Tibet," *Nepalese Studies* 30.1 (2003): 4–5; FO 371/3689 (1919); FO 371/8014 (1921); FO 371/6608 (1921); FO 371/18107, 159–67 (1934).

17. Dor Bahadur Bista, "Nepalis in Tibet," Contributions to Nepalese Studies 8.1 (1980): 9; Prem Uprety, "Treaties between Nepal and Her Neighbors: A Historical Perspective," *Tribhuvan University Journal* 19.1 (1996) 16. Mishra, "Nepalese in Tibet," 1–2; NAI, Foreign and Political Department, Secret-External, May 1917, Nos. 4–11 (internally dated December 21, 1916); NAI, Foreign and Political Department, No. 49(2)-X Secret, 1923 (dated July 23, 1924); Giuseppe Tucci and Wim Swaan, *Tibet, Land of Snows* (New York: Stein and Day, 1967), 100. For some indication of this influence, see Patricia A. Berger, *Empire of Emptiness: Buddhist Art and Political Authority in Qing China* (Honolulu: University of Hawaii Press, 2003), 24–35.

18. Sanjay Upadhya, *Nepal and the Geo-Strategic Rivalry between China and India* (London: Routledge, 2012), 54–57; Prem R. Uprety, *Nepal-Tibet Relations, 1850–1930: Years of Hopes, Challenges, and Frustrations* (Kathmandu: Puga Nara, 1980), 71–73, 135–38.

19. Waddell, *Lhasa and Its Mysteries,* 214.

20. Treaty of Thapathali, 1856. Original treaty in Tibetan and Nepalese: http://web.prm.ox.ac.uk/tibet/photo_1998.285.330.1.html.

21. Outbreaks of violence occurred no fewer than half a dozen times between 1856 and 1950. One of the earliest accounts (1884) is described in Gaborieau and Muḥammad, *Récit d'un voyageur musulman au Tibet,* 139. See also NAI, Foreign Department, July 1884, Secret-E, No. 65; and for a later incident, NAI, Foreign Department, Secret-E, December 1910, Nos. 439–661.

22. Tirtha P. Mishra, "A Critical Assessment of the Nepal-Tibet Treaty 1856," in McKay, *Tibet and Her Neighbours,* 141–44; Uprety, *Nepal-Tibet Relations,* 136.

23. NAI, Foreign and Political Department, Secret—External, Proceedings, June 1921, Nos. 45–283; *Tibetan Affairs Newsletter,* No. 10, dated Lhasa, April 22, 1921 (received May 5).

24. FO 371/10233, Translation of a letter from the Prime Minister of Tibet to Major F. M. Bailey, dated September 18, 1923.

25. NAI, Foreign and Political Department, No. 49(2)-X Secret, 1923; Nepal-Tibet Affairs: Visit of Major F. M. Baily, Political Officer, Sikkim to Lhasa, Complaint from Tibetan Government regarding Nepalese half-breeds in Tibet.

26. Mishra, "Nepalese in Tibet."

27. Ann Frenchette suggests such tensions remain even today in Nepal, quoting one Tibetan: "Khatsaras take advantage of the Tibetan community. They claim they are Tibetan to get an education and then they claim they are Nepali to get work. . . . Khatsaras are not really Tibetan." See Ann Frechette, *Tibetans in Nepal: The Dynamics of International Assistance among a Community in Exile* (New York: Berghahn Books, 2002), 128.

28. Even the Newari Nepalese merchants who returned to Nepal had to pay for a *patiya*, or certificate of purification, and undertake a purification ritual in order to "readmitted" into their caste. For a description, see Chitta D. Hridaya and Kesar Lall, *Mimmanahpau: Letter from a Lhasa Merchant to His Wife* (New Delhi: Robin Books, 2002), 66–67.

29. Jamyang Norbu, "The Lhasa Ripper," in Vitali, *Trails of the Tibetan Tradition*, 235–36.

30. FO 371/13960, Extract from Confidential demi-official letter from Sardar Bhadur S. W. Laden La, Superintendent of Police, Darjeeling, dated October 7, 1929.

31. FO 371/13959, Telegram from W. P. Rosemeyer to to Political Office Sikkim, dated September 26, 1929.

32. Uprety, *Nepal-Tibet Relations, 1850–1930*, 132.

33. For a brief account, see Melvin C. Goldstein, *A History of Modern Tibet, 1913–1951: The Demise of the Lamaist State* (Berkeley: University of California Press, 1989), 163.

34. FO 371/13960, Extract from Confidential demi-official letter from Sardar Bhadur S. W. Laden La, Superintendent of Police, Darjeeling, dated October 7, 1929.

35. FO 371/13959, Memorandum from the Prime Minister of Nepal handed to the British Envoy, dated September 25, 1929.

36. FO 371/13959, Note dated September 8, handed to the British Envoy, Nepal, by Nepalese Officer on September 30, 1929.

37. FO 371/13959, dated September 8, 1929.

38. A complex figure, Lungshar is also described by Goldstein as a "forward thinking individual"; see Goldstein, *A History of Modern Tibet, 1913–1951*, 98. For an insightful critique, see Jamyang Norbu, "Black Annals: Goldstein and the Negation of Tibetan History," *Phalyul*, www.phayul.com/news/article.aspx?id=22113 (accessed April 15, 2015).

39. Uprety, *Nepal-Tibet Relations, 1850–1930*, 131–35.

40. Ibid.; Hsaio-ting Lin, *Tibet and Nationalist China's Frontier: Intrigues and Ethnopolitics, 1928–49* (Vancouver: University of British Columbia Press, 2006), 57.

41. Although Uprety's research has turned up documents supporting Nepal's claims of his citizenship, none of these seem to have been brought up at the time. See FO 371/13959, Telegram dated October 18, 1929.

42. FO 371/14702, dated February 7, 1930.

43. FO 371/14702, dated March 7, 1930.

44. For a succinct overview, see Hugh Richardson's account in Richardson, *High Peaks, Pure Earth*, 566–68.

45. For the clearest explanation of this, see NAI, Foreign and Political Department, No. 49(2)-X Secret, dated July 23, 1924; Upadhya, *Nepal and the Geo-Strategic Rivalry*, 54–57; Uprety, *Nepal-Tibet Relations, 1850–1930*, 71–73, 135–38.

46. For example, the Russian traveler Tsybikoff notes, incorrectly, that Nepalese "avoid marriage with Tibetans" but that the Khache "on the contrary, always marry Tibetans." "Lhasa and Central Tibet," *Annual Report of the Smithsonian Institution*, Washington, DC: Government Printing Office, 1903), 731; NAI, Foreign Department, External A, Pros.

January 1885, Nos. 96–98/98–2. See also Tsybikov, *A Buddhist Pilgrim at the Shrines of Tibet*, 85.

47. Ma Jianye, "Xizang Lasa de Huimin," 12.

48. Prince Peter of Greece, "The Moslems of Central Tibet," 237. His article, largely based on interviews with Tibetan Muslims in Kalimpong, likely adopted this exaggerated tone, as many ethnic groups do, seeking to emphasize their identity as distinct from their Tibetan Buddhist compatriots.

49. Gaborieau and Muhammad, *Récit d'un voyageur musulman au Tibet*, 22–23. Other accounts even suggest Khache daughters were required to pay an annual tax; see, e.g., Corneille Jest, "Kha-che and Gya-Kha-che: Muslim Communities in Lhasa (1990)," *Tibet Journal* 20.3 (1995): 9.

50. Ding Weizhi, Le Ge, and Xisheng Jin, *Zhongguo guoqing congshu*,85.

51. Lamb, *Bhutan and Tibet*, 287.

52. The single counter-evidence I have seen is the claim by some that there is archival evidence that contends, spuriously in my view, that in 1947 the Kashag forbid intermarriage between Tibetans and Muslims. For examples of intermarriage and assertions that a Chinese journalist made in 1947 that "Khache only married Tibetans," see Chen Bo, 2000. "Lasa musulin qunti diaocha" [Investigation of Lhasa Muslims], *Xibei minzu yanjiu* 1 (2000): 91; Ma Jianye, "Xizang Lasa de Huimin," 12.

53. FO 371/17051 (1933), dated June 12, 1933.

54. See FO 371/17051 (1933), dated June 12, 1933. Ghulam Muhammad tellingly ends his letter with the request, "We will be grateful if you [the British] will get the news published in the Indian newspapers in order to get us released from such tyrannous acts of the Tibetans."

55. Melvyn C. Goldstein, Dawei Sherap, and William R. Siebenschuh, *A Tibetan Revolutionary: The Political Life and Times of Bapa Phüntso Wangye* (Berkeley: University of California Press, 2006), 120.

56. The overwhelming majority of observers do not specify that it is Tibetan women who marry Khache, or vice versa; rather the comments suggest that Khaches of both sexes married Tibetans. Radhu, *Islam in Tibet*, 160. See also Tsybikov and Xianjun Wang, "Lhasa and Central Tibet," 731; Xue Wenbo, *Xueling Chongze*, 2:291.

57. Chen Bo, "A Multicultural Interpretation of an Ethnic Muslim Minority: The Case of the Hui Tibetans in Lhasa." *Journal of Muslim Minority Affairs* 23.1 (2003): 48. The Tibetan rate of interethnic exogamy is among the lowest, which suggests again that Tibetans treated Khaches as Tibetan.

58. Khan, *Muslim, Trader, Nomad, Spy*, 98–99.

59. Jest, "Kha-che and Gya-Kha-che," 9. See also Ram Rahul, "Kashmiri Muslims in Tibet," *International Studies* 3.2 (1961): 181, where he asserts, "In any case, the majority of [the Khaches] were born in Tibet but were always regarded by the Chinese and Tibetans as subjects of the Maharaja of Kashmir." The same assertion is made in his monograph, *The Government and Politics of Tibet* (Delhi: Vikas Publications, 1969), 97. As for Wapaling Khaches being "sojourners" (thus not permanent residents), see James Downs, *Lhassa of Tibet* (New Haven, CT: Human Relations Area Files, 1972), 20.

60. It is difficult to categorize Liu Manqing. She considered herself, when speaking in Chinese, to be a Han Chinese whose mother was ethnically Tibetan and whose father was Han but who practiced Islam. It is almost certain that her father, though of Chinese

ancestry, was a Wapaling Khache himself, fluent in Tibetan and raised in Lhasa. In the *Tibetan Mirror* newspaper, published in Kalimpong, which published a two-page interview with her, she was referred to as the "rgya mo lcam," or the Chinese lady. See Mthar phyin (Tharchin), ed., "Rgya nag gi pho nya?" [Envoy of China?]. *Yul phyogs so so'i gsar 'gyur me long (Tibetan Mirror)* 5.1 (June 27, 1930): 2–3.

61. Liu Manqing went by several names. As hinted at in chapter 2, many Khaches had both Tibetan and Chinese names. In Liu Manqing's case, it appears that some of her names reflect the influence of the Kham dialect. She had two additional Chinese names: Liu Manqing also went by the Chinese name Yongjin (Ch. 雍金) because it more closely approximated how her Tibetan name was pronounced in the Kham dialect. Finally, Dai Jitao, a prominent intellectual of the Nationalist period, gave Liu the name De Meixi (Ch. 德美西). See Ding Xiaowen, *Minguo zangdi "nü qinchai" liu manqing zhuan* (Nanchang: Ershi yishiji chubanshe, 2013); Fabienne Jagou, "Liu Manqing: A Sino-Tibetan Adventurer and the Origin of a New Sino-Tibetan Dialogue in the 1930s," *Revue d'Etudes tibétaines,* no. 17 (October 2009): 8. I am indebted also to Dr. Yudru Tsomu's insights on Liu Manqing.

62. There are conflicting accounts of Liu Manqing's early childhood and the ethnic makeup of her parents. It seems most likely to me that her father was Wapaling Khache since he was clearly Muslim and born in Lhasa. Liu Manqing offers very few clues in her own account: Liu Manqing, *Kang-Zang Yao Zheng* [A Mission to Xikang and Tibet] (Shanghai: Shangwu yinshuguan, 1933). See also Liu Manqing. "Xizang youji" [Travels to Tibet], *Shishi yuebao* 3.3 (1930): 204–5; Liu Liangmo, "Liu Manqing nüshi ziji de hua" [Miss Liu Manqing in Her Own Words], *Nüsheng* 1.2 (1932): 5–6.

63. Liu Liangmo. "Liu Manqing nüshi ziji de hua," 5.

64. Ibid., 6.

65. Huang Jingwan, Introduction to Liu Manqing, *Kang-Zang yaozheng.* For an overview of Liu Manqing's Hui identity, see Zhou Chuanbin, "Liu Manqing—Minquo shiqi de Xizang Huizu nüjie," *Xibei dier minzu xueyuan xuebao* 3 (2000): 60–64; Jagou, "A Sino-Tibetan Adventurer."

66. C. Y. W. Meng, "Miss Liu's Mission to Tibet," *China Weekly Review,* September 6, 1930, 22.

67. See "Tibet Changing Under New Order, Nanking's Envoy Says on Return: Social, Religious, and Political Conditions in Region Are Traced by Wang Wei-sung; General Huang Remains to Pave Way for Lama," *China Press,* November 24, 1934, 9.

68. In 1919, a delegation from Gansu representing the central government's interest spent five months in Lhasa. In 1930, Kongcho Chungnay / Könchok Jungné (Tib. *Dkon mchog 'byung gnas*), a Tibetan from the Yonghegong Temple in Beijing, with connections to the Nationalist government, traveled to Lhasa as well. For the 1919 visit, see Huang Yusheng, *Xizang difang yu zhongyang zhengfu guanxi shi* [Relations between Tibet's Local Government and China's Central Government] (Lhasa: Xizang renmin chubanshe, 1995), 226; on the 1930 mission, see FO 371/14702, dated February 5, 1930.

69. One press report, reflecting other reports, stated, "It has been 20 years since a special envoy was sent by the Chinese government to Lhassa." See "Tibet Changing under New Order."

70. For one such example, see "Tibetan Troops Reported Massing against Szechuan: Dalai Lama Dispatches 5 More Battalions; Liu Asks for Aid," *China Press,* May 18, 1932, 6.

71. As Tuttle has remarked, "This term is variously translated as 'Republic of Five Races' or 'Five Races Harmoniously Joined.' See Gray Tuttle, *Tibetan Buddhists in the Making of Modern China* (New York: Columbia University Press, 2005), 31. Other translations abound, including "five peoples republicanism." James A. Millward, *Eurasian Crossroads: A History of Xinjiang* (New York: Columbia University Press, 2007), 167.

72. Tuttle, *Tibetan Buddhists in the Making of Modern China*, 31.

73. For a detailed and insightful description of the *wuzu gonghe*, see James Leibold, *Reconfiguring Chinese Nationalism: How the Qing Frontier and Its Indigenes Became Chinese* (New York: Palgrave Macmillan, 2007), 37–41.

74. As Xiong Shili argued in his 1939 lectures demonstrating Chinese consanguinity among Han, Manchus, Mongols, Tibetans, and Hui. See Leibold, *Reconfiguring Chinese Nationalism*, 160.

75. Lin, *Tibet and Nationalist China's Frontier*, 73–74.

76. His full title was Special Commissioner to the great Priest, protector of the State, Propagator of Culture, Spacious in Benevolence, Perfect in Immaculate Intelligence, the Dalai Lama" (Ch. *zhiji huguo honghua puci yuanjue dashi dalai lama*). SDDX, 3 and 15, for the appointment of Huang Musong. See also Goldstein, *A History of Modern Tibet, 1913–1951*, 213n1, citing FO371/18105. See also FO 0371/1344.

77. Lin, *Tibet and Nationalist China's Frontier*, 73–74.

78. *Jiang Zhongzheng Zongtong Dang'an: Tejiao Wendian/Lingxiu Shigong/Jiji Zhibian* [President Chiang Kai-shek Collection: Specially Submitted Archives/Politics/Tibetan Issues]: "Chiang to Huang," October 10, 1934, vol. 3, no. 23040431, cited in Lin, *Tibet and Nationalist China's Frontier*, 78–79.

79. SDDX, 53–56; FO 371/18107, 158–60 (1934).

80. FO 371/18107, dated August 27, 1934.

81. "Chinese Politics: Mission to Tibet Disappoints—Reaction to Gen. Huang's Efforts in Lhasa: Friction on Border Feared," *North China Herald*, September 26, 1934, 450.

82. Tieh-tseng Li, *Tibet, Today and Yesterday* (New York: Bookman Associates, 1960), 168.

83. SDDX, 89; Goldstein, *A History of Modern Tibet, 1913–1951*, 233–34.

84. SDDX, 104.

85. Li, *Tibet, Today and Yesterday*, 168–72. It appears that a constellation of factors were behind Huang's swift exit. Citing the Nepalese consul, British reports also indicate that an effort to host a picnic on October 10, 1934, went badly when "Chinese officials and soldiers, with the exception of Huang himself, got very drunk and began to quarrel violently among themselves." FO 371/18107, 158–60 (1934); SDDX, 107–9.

86. See, e.g., the two most comprehensive accounts of Huang's visit: Goldstein, *A History of Modern Tibet, 1913–1951*, 224–51; Lin, *Tibet and Nationalist China's Frontier*, 71–85.

87. "Nanking to Station Resident at Lhassa," *Chinese Weekly Review*, December 15, 1934, 81.

88. "Tibet Pledges Aid to Nanking Regime," *New York Times*, February 10, 1935.

89. *North China Herald*, January 16, 1935, 9; Xiraonima [Sherab Nyima], *Jindai Zangshi Yanjiu* [Studies on Modern Tibetan Affairs] (Lhasa: Xizang ren min chu ban she, 2000), 371–72. As Goldstein notes, in 1939 "the office remained open but was being run by a low-status wireless operator and not until the arrival of Wu Zhongxin in 1940 did the Chinese government try to upgrade the office and the Chinese presence in Tibet." This was

no different from the British Mission. Goldstein states, "From the Tibetan point of view, neither the British Mission nor the Chinese Mission in Lhasa had any legal status; they were allowed to remain only to avoid giving offence." Goldstein, *A History of Modern Tibet, 1913–1951*, 329.

90. FO 371/20964 (1938). Upon his visit to Lhasa in 1936, Basil Gould remarked that earlier reports of Jiang's position and importance were "gravely inaccurate" and that his "influence is by no means inconsiderable."

91. Goldstein , *A History of Modern Tibet, 1913–1951*, 245.

92. FO 371/19254 (1935). Williamson would die in November.

93. FO 371/19254 (1935).

94. FO 371/19254 (1935).

95. NAI, No. 559-X (Secret) Confidential letter, D.O. No. 3(6)-L/37/2, dated Lhasa, August 28, 1937.

96. The English opened schools twice, and both were closed within a year by what Hugh Richardson labeled "conservative prejudice." See NAI, Ministry of External Affairs, North East Frontier Branch, Annual Report of the Indian Mission in Lhasa in Tibet during 1947, 8(23)-NEF/48; FO 371/19254, Copy of Letter from Political Officer in Sikkim to Foreign Secretary the Government of India, May 28, 1935. Huang Musong gives the impression that a "Han-Hui School" with 80 students existed when he arrived. This was the Grand Mosque school. See Huang Musong, *Huang Musong xiansheng yizhu: Xinjiang gaishu Xizang riji* [The Posthumous Work of Huang Musong: Xinjiang and Tibet]. (Taibei: Bianzhe kanyinben, 1964), 146.

97. NAI, "Chinese Primary School in Lhasa, "External Affairs, 1937, No. 559-X (Secret); Aiming Zhou, *Tibetan Education* (Beijing: China Intercontinental Press, 2004), 28.

98. Zhongguo Dier Lishi Dang'anguan Zhongguo Zangxue Yanjiu Zhongxin, eds., *Huang Musong, Wu Zhongxin, Zhao Shouyu, Dai Zhuanxian fengshi banli zangshi baogao shu* [Huang Musong, Wu Zhongxin, Zhao Shouyu, Dai Zhuanxian: Reports of envoys Sent to Handle Tibetan Affairs] (Beijing: Zhongguo Zangxue chubanshe, 1993), 254.

99. NAI, "Mr Richardson's Report on Tibetan Affairs," External Affairs, No. 315(2)-X. As Maggie Clinton's study makes clear, the fascist reading of the "black shirts" is likely not an exaggeration. See Maggie Clinton, *Revolutionary Nativism: Fascism and Culture in China, 1925–1937* (Durham, NC: Duke University Press, 2017).

100. The estimate of 300 to 400 is suspect on numerous levels. First, it is well documented that the number of soldiers sent to Lhasa was roughly 2,000. Then given the high casualty rate the actual number who stayed behind in Lhasa likely never exceeded 300 individuals, let alone "households." It bears repeating yet again, the Thirteenth Dalai Lama expressly indicated to all Chinese who remained in Tibet that they would be considered Tibetan subjects. Zhongguo Dier Lishi Dang'anguan Zhongguo Zangxue Yanjiu Zhongxin, *Huang Musong, Wu Zhongxin, Zhao Shouyu, Dai Zhuanxian fengshi banli zangshi baogao shu,* 29. See also FO 535/13, "Rev. J. R. Muir to Consul-General Wilkinson," enclosure 3 in no. 90 [April 19, 1910], 87; and Ho, "The Men Who Would Not Be Amban and the One Who Would," 210.

101. Zhongguo Dier Lishi Dang'anguan Zhongguo Zangxue Yanjiu Zhongxin, *Huang Musong, Wu Zhongxin, Zhao Shouyu, Dai Zhuanxian fengshi banli zangshi baogao shu,* 72.

102. Ibid., 29.

103. Huang Musong, "Shizang Jicheng."17:234–35.

104. One Chinese staffer notes in his autobiography that as soon as the Thirteenth Dalai Lama returned "peace reigned in Lhasa" and that "the Chinese, however, had become subjects of the Tibetan government." See Peter Richardus and Alex McKay, *Tibetan Lives: Three Himalayan Autobiographies* (Richmond, Surrey: Curzon, 1998), 175.

105. Lin, *Tibet and Nationalist China's Frontier,* 84. See also Maria Carrai, "Learning Western Techniques of Empire: Republican China and the New Legal Framework for Managing Tibet," *Journal of International Law* 30 (2017): 801–26.

106. Chris Vasantkumar, "What Is This 'Chinese' in Overseas Chinese? Sojourn Work and the Place of China's Minority Nationalities in Extraterritorial Chinese-ness," *Journal of Asian Studies* 71.2 (2012): 428.

107. Zhongguo Dier Lishi Dang'anguan Zhongguo Zangxue Yanjiu Zhongxin, *Huang Musong, Wu Zhongxin, Zhao Shouyu, Dai Zhuanxian fengshi banli zangshi baogao shu,* 108.

108. For a succinct discussion of corvée labor in Tibetan society, see Goldstein, *The Calm Before the Storm,* 10–13.

109. Hsu S. Kwang, "Arrival in Tibet of Nepalese Troops," *Weekly News,* no. 751, 1930, 1038.

110. FO 371/31700, Lhasa Letter, August 30,1942. For a slightly different emphasis on this telling, see Goldstein, *History of Modern Tibet, 1913–1951,* 383; and Lin, *Tibet and Nationalist China's Frontier,* 148.

111. FO371/31700, July 27 (1942).

112. FO371/31700 July 27 (1942).

113. For further details on Gorship Office, see Goldstein, *History of Modern Tibet, 1913–1951,* 382; see also FO 371/13959, Note Handed to British Envoy by Prime Minister of Nepal (1929); and FO 371/10233, Translation of a letter from the Prime Minister of Tibet to Major F. M. Bailey, dated September 18, 1923, which described it as follows: "The Tibetan Government, however, . . . with a view to maintain good relations between the two States and also to dispose of disputes, appointed a special officer called 'kor shib' i.e. 'Officer to enquire into the affairs of the Nepalese subjects.'" In Tibetan, this office is Phyi Rgyal Las Khungs; see Goldstein, *History of Modern Tibet, 1913–1951,* 381. While the creation of a "foreign office" only formally occurred in 1942, the Tibetan government had special bureaus to deal with foreign affairs and specific foreign countries (e.g., Nepal). See Goldstein, *A History of Modern Tibet, 1913–1951,* 386; Walt, *The Status of Tibet,* 72–74.

114. FO371/31700. Lhasa Letter, August 30, 1942.

115. NAI, Ministry of External Affairs, North East Frontier Branch, "Annual Report of the Indian Mission in Lhasa in Tibet during 1947," 8(23)-NEF/48; Lin, *Tibet and Nationalist China's Frontier,* 242n55.

116. FO 371/31700, Lhasa Letter for the week ending August 24 (1942).

117. For an overview of this event, see Lin, *Tibet and Nationalist China's Frontier,* 148; Zhang Ruide, "'Qinchai' Shiming: Shen Zonglian zai Lasa (1943–1946)" [A "Royal" Mission: Shen Zonglian in Tibet, 1943–1946], *Zhongyan Yanjiuyuan: jindaishi yanjiusuo jikan* 67 (2010): 59–96.

118. FO 371/35754 (1943)

119. IOR L/PS/12/4182, cited in Goldstein, *History of Modern Tibet, 1913–1951,* 384n35.

120.  FO371/31700, Weekly Lhasa Letter dated November 1 from Frank Ludlow.

121.  IOR/L/PS/12/4201; FO 371/31700 (1944); FO 371/46121 (1945); W. D. Shakabpa and Derek F. Maher, *One Hundred Thousand Moons: An Advanced Political History of Tibet* (Leiden: Brill, 2010), 893 (the authors mistakenly romanized Kong Qingxiang's name as "Gong Jingzong"). See also Lin, *Tibet and Nationalist China's Frontier*, 148.

122.  FO 371/31700, Lhasa Letter for the week ending August 24 (1942).

123.  See Zhang Ruide, "'Qinchai' Shiming," 64.

124.  For a list of the officials appointed by Shen, see Zhang Ruide, "'Qinchai' Shiming," 66–67.

125.  See Chang Jui-te, "An Imperial Envoy: Shen Zonglian in Tibet, 1943–1946," in Van de Ven, Lary, and MacKinnon, *Negotiating China's Destiny in World War II*, 59.

126.  FO 371/46190 (1945).

127.  Xu Baiyong, "Guomin zhengfu shiqi de guli Lasa xiaoxue jiqi chuanban," *Xizang Yanjiu* 1 (2008): 2–3.

128.  Xu Baiyong and Sa Renna, "Guomin zhengfu shiqi de guoli Lasa xiaoxue ji qi chuangban zhi yiyi" [An Introduction to the Founding of the Lhasa Elementary School in the Nationalist Period], *Xizang Yanjiu* 1 (2008): 1–2; Zhongguo Dier Lishi Dang'anguan Zhongguo Zangxue Yanjiu Zhongxin, *Huang Musong, Wu Zhongxin, Zhao Shouyu, Dai Zhuanxian Feng Shi Ban Li Zang Shi Bao Gao Shu*, 29, 254. As is typical with Chinese sources, Xu does not distinguish between half-Chinese and Chinese, Khache, and Hui or half-Tibetan and Tibetan. British reports explicitly note the participation of "half cast Chinese Mohammedans (locally known as Wo-pa-lings)." See FO 371/46190 (1945).

129.  Shen's success can be seen by the fact that the Chinese-run school by Wu's successor, Zhang Weibai (also referred to as Tang Fe-tang in British documents), only attracted twenty half-Chinese children. See NAI, Mr. Richardson's Report on Tibetan Affairs, External Affairs, 1939, No. 315(2)-X.

130.  FO 371/46123 55 (1945).

131.  FO 436/16518 (1945), cited in Lin, *Tibet and Nationalist China's Frontier*, 242n49.

132.  They do not all appear to be permanent Chinese residents but likely included Chinese merchants, half-Chinese, and perhaps even Wapaling Khaches. IOR L/PS/12/4202 (2)Coll 36/30, 5240, August 26, 1945.

133.  FO 371/46123 (1945).

134.  FO 371/46123 (1945).

135.  Goldstein, *A History of Modern Tibet, 1913–1951,* 716. See also FO 371/84458 (November 2, 1950)

136.  Yiwu, "Xizang Huimin," 12. Yiwu remarks that "three years earlier five [Khache] students studied in Mecca."

137.  Xue Wenbo notes that the Khache going to India "didn't need passports." See Xue Wenbo, *Xueling Chongze*, 2:293.

138.  Goldstein, *A History of Modern Tibet, 1913–1951,* 322–23.

139.  See NAI, Lhasa Mission Diaries, 315-X1 (1939); NAI, Telegram R., No. 2132, dated November 20, 1939

140.  See *Records of the Hajj: A Documentary History of the Pilgrimage to Mecca*, vol. 7 (London: Archive Editions, 1993), 26, 111, 124.

141. NAI, Ministry of External Affairs, Northeast Frontier Branch, Monthly Reports on Indian Mission (Lhasa) for 1949, 8(16)-NEF 1949.

142. This is not to say there were not difficulties. The trade mission mentioned above immediately ran into difficulties when the American State Department balked at accepting their "passport." See Goldstein, *History of Modern Tibet, 1913–1951*, 578.

## 4. HIMALAYAN ASIA

1. General Zhang Jingwu arrived in Lhasa with an advance party on August 9, 1951, followed by the Dalai Lama's return to Lhasa on August 17, and General Wang Qimei's arrival with the first troops (600) in early September. On October 26, 1951, a regiment of the 18th PLA Corps marched into the Tibetan capital under the command of the senior commander of the PLA, Zhang Guohua. This is often considered the official date for the "liberation" of Tibet. See Goldstein, *The Calm Before the Storm*, 206–8.

2. Goldstein, *A History of Modern Tibet, 1913–1951*, 543.

3. Elliot Sperling, "Tibet and China: The Interpretation of History Since 1950," *China Perspectives* 3.79 (2009): 25–37; Goldstein, *The Calm before the Storm*; Melvyn C. Goldstein, *A History of Modern Tibet: The Storm Clouds Descend, 1955–57* (Berkeley: University of California Press, 2014).

4. The subtitle of the second volume of Goldstein's magisterial series on modern Tibetan history, *Calm before the Storm*, is the biggest indication of how mainstream such a perspective has become.

5. Up through the 1930s Chinese copper coins from Sichuan were prominent in Kham and Amdo while Indian money was more common in central Tibet. Chinese silver dollars, however, tended to be accepted across Tibet through the 1950s. FO 371-19253-87(2). Regarding the Bank of China and the exchange rate, Annual Report from Tibet, NAI 3(19) R&I/53, 8.

6. Xue Wenbo, *Xueling chongze*, 1:176.

7. Typically, such histories are limited to facets of Tibet's relevance to the Cold War. See John K. Knaus, *Orphans of the Cold War: America and the Tibetan Struggle for Survival* (New York: Public Affairs, 1999); Mikel Dunham, *Buddha's Warriors: The Story of the CIA-Backed Tibetan Freedom Fighters, the Chinese Invasion, and the Ultimate Fall of Tibet* (New York: J. P. Tarcher, 2004); Kenneth J. Conboy and James Morrison, *The CIA's Secret War in Tibet* (Lawrence: University Press of Kansas, 2002). An excellent work that successfully blends a deeply Tibetan perspective with the issues of the Cold War is Carole McGranahan's *Arrested Histories*.

8. "Zhongguo renmin yiding yao jiefang Tibet" [The People's Republic of China Will Definitely Liberate Tibet], *Renmin Ribao*, September 7, 1949, 2.

9. Xue Wenbo, *Xueling chongze*, 2: 261; see also Xue Wenbo, *Xueling chongze*, 1:168.

10. Reports on Tibet, External Affairs, R&I, 1956, "Report for the month ending April 15, 1955," S. No. 45 55/ R&I/56.

11. Wlodzimierz Cieciura, "Ethnicity or Religion? Republican-Era Chinese Debates on Islam and Muslims," in *Islamic Thought in China: Sino-Muslim Intellectual Evolution from the 17th to the 21st Century*, ed. Jonathan N. Lipman (Edinburgh: Edinburgh University Press, 2016), 129.

12. Yufeng Mao, "A Muslim Vision for the Chinese Nation: Chinese Pilgrimage Missions to Mecca during World War II," *Journal of Asian Studies* 70.2 (2011): 382.

13. Xue Wenbo, *Xueling chongze,* 1:461.

14. Ibid., 168.

15. Xue Wenbo, *Xueling chongze,* 2:293.

16. Ibid., 292.

17. Ibid., 168.

18. Gyalo Thondup and Anne F. Thurston, *The Noodle Maker of Kalimpong: The Untold Story of My Struggle for Tibet* (New York: Perseus Books Group, 2015), 134; James C. Scott, *The Art of Not Being Governed: An Anarchist History of Upland Southeast Asia* (New Haven, CT: Yale University Press, 2009), 46–47.

19. NAI, "Annual Report for 1951 from Indian Mission," Lhasa, External Affairs, R&I, S. No. 36 3/19/ R&I/52.

20. Goldstein, *History of Modern Tibet, Volume 2: The Calm Before the Storm.*

21. Translation from Dawa Norbu, "When the Chinese Came to Tibet," *Worldview,* 1978, 24. A more literal translation would be "the Chinese Communists as grateful parents, they shower *dayang* down on us like rain."

22. Xue Wenbo, *Xueling chongze,* 1:176.

23. FO 371/120985 (1956).

24. Xue Wenbo, *Xueling chongze,* 1:176.

25. Chen Zonglie, "Ershi shiji wu-liu niandai: Cong guizu fudi dao baixing zuofang [The Fifties and Sixties: From the Mansions of Aristocrats to the Workshops of Common People]," *Xizang lüyou* 94.10 (2009): 20.

26. FO 371/120985, October 17, 1956.

27. NAI, Annual Report of the Indian Trade Agency, Yatung, for the Year 1957, "Trade and Economics," File No. 3(19) R&I/57.

28. Radhu, *Islam in Tibet,* 248–49.

29. The exact number is difficult to determine. The *Tibet Daily (Xizang Ribao)* gives the number 41, but it is not clear from where the number is derived. *Xizang Ribao,* December 27, 1957. For the number of Barkor Khaches for 1946, see Yiwu. "Xizang Huimin," 4.

30. *Zhongghuo yisilanjiao jianzhi* [An Overview of Islam in China] (Beijing: Zongjiao wenhua chubanshe, 2011), 574, 583–84, 590.

31. The Chinese response likely refers to the fact that during the Bandung Conference in 1955, Zhou Enlai spoke with the Saudi prime minister, who gave permission for future Chinese Muslims to make the pilgrimage. NAI, "Reports on Tibet," External Affairs, 1956, S. No. 45, 55/R&I/56.(Note Muslims traveling to Mekka for the 1957 Hajj had to leave in 1956). See also Chiara Betta, Caifeng Lan, and Cheng Fang, *The Other Middle Kingdom: A Brief History of Muslims in China* (Indianapolis: University of Indianapolis Press, 2004), 13. The first group to attempt the Hajj in 1953 had traveled to Pakistan, where they were refused visas by Saudi officials. See Yitzhak Shichor, *East Wind over Arabia: Origins and Implications of the Sino-Saudi Missile Deal* (Berkeley: Institute of East Asian Studies [and] Center for Chinese Studies, University of California, 1989), 3.

32. Yusuf Naik, "Memories of my Father, Abdul Ghani, in Tibet," *Tibet Journal* 20.3 (1995): 31–32. See also Chen Bo, "Lasa musulin qunti diaocha," 88n1.

33. Xue Wenbo, *Xueling chongze,* 2:295.

34. Ibid.

35. Suo Qiong, "Fofa shengdi de yisilan wenming," *Xizang minsu* 4 (2002): 60.

36. Tubten Khétsun [Thus bstan mkhas btsun], *dka' sdug 'og gi byung ba brjod pa* (Dharamsala: shes rig dpar khang, 1998), 297.

37. Dawa Norbu, *Tibet: The Road Ahead* (London: Rider, 1997), 121.

38. Dundul Namgyal Tsarong and Trinlay Chödron, *In The Service of His Country: The Biography of Dasang Damdul Tsarong, Commander General of Tibet* (Ithaca, NY: Snow Lion Publications, 2000), 199; Xue Wenbo, "Lasa de huizu [Lhasa Muslims]," 70.

39. Xue Wenbo, *Xueling chongze,* 1:173. There is some confusion in the sources regarding the exact nature of the schools. In his description, Xue Wenbo describes two schools: a Tibetan school and a Hui school. It appears from all other sources that this must have been the Chinese school.

40. For an especially detailed and multifaceted defense of this perspective, see Xue Wenbo, *Xueling chongze,* 2:293–95.

41. NAI, Annual Report from Tibet (Lhasa)—1952, Ministry of External Affairs, R&I Branch, File No. 3(19) R&I/53, "General Report on the Indian Consulate General, Lhasa, Tibet."

42. Mathou, "Bhutan-China Relations"; Karma Ura and Sonam Kinga, *The Spider and the Piglet,* 392.

43. See Article 2 in the Convention between Great Britain and China relating to Sikkim and Tibet (1890). The article goes on to state that "neither the Ruler of the State nor any of its officers shall have official relations, formal or informal, with any other country." Charles U. Aitchison, *A Collection of Treaties, Engagements and Sanads Relating to India and Neighbouring Countries.* (Calcutta: Government of India Central Publication Branch, 1929); see also FO 371/112196 for "India's North-East Frontier Policy," May 19, 1954, which demonstrates British efforts to trace the potential merits of China's territorial "tributary" claims.

44. See D. S. Khan, "Nepal's Relations with British India," *Regional Studies* 5.3 (1987): 56–85. On the role of the Rana rule and their relations with the British, see Pramode Shamshere Rana, *A Chronicle of Rana Rule* (Kathmandu: R. Rana, 1999).

45. Jawaharlal Nehru, "Policy regarding China and Tibet (18 November 1950)," in *Selected Works of Jawaharlal Nehru,* 2nd ser., ed. S. Gopal, vol. 15, pt. II (1984): 343.

46. NAI, Annual Report from Tibet (Lhasa)—1952, Ministry of External Affairs, R&I Branch, File No. 3(19) R&I/53.

47. NAI, "Annual Report from Tibet (Lhasa), Ministry of External Affairs, 3(19) R&I/53 (1952). The report indicates that "the annual payment of Rs. 10,000 by Tibet to Nepal under the 1856 Treaty was made without any objection from the Chinese.

48. *The Statesman* (India), March 15, 1952, 7.

49. "Sovereignty of Tibet: Nepalese Treaty Still Stands," *Times of India,* April 7, 1954, 9.

50. Leo E. Rose, *Nepal: Strategy for Survival* (Berkeley: University of California Press, 1971), 204.

51. SWJN, vol 25, 461fn5. There appears to be confusion to this day about when the last payment was made. Some assert the last of these payments appears to have been made the previous year, on March 7, 1952. But press reports suggest that the last payment was made in 1953.

52. "Nepal Asked to Contact China: Ties with Tibet," *Times of India,* May 14, 1954, 1.

53. "Nepali Rebels in Tibet," *Times of India,* February 10, 1952, 3; "Nepalese Rebel Said to Plan New Attack," *New York Times,* May 9, 1952, 2; FBIS, FRB 52–167 (August 25, 1952).

54. Hong Kong Radio broadcasts May 5, 22, 1950, quoted in Shen-yu Dai, "Peking, Kathmandu and Delhi," *China Quarterly* 16 (1963): 87.

55. George N. Patterson, *God's Fool* (Garden City, NY: Doubleday, 1957), 235.

56. George Patterson, "The Five Fingers of China," *Indian Review* (February 1965): 57.

57. Such rumors were commonplace,, with one report indicating that some Tibetans in Tawang (in NEFA) were telling locals that the "region's occupation would be 'as [a] morning walk' for the PLA and that Bhutan would soon have to choose between Indian and China." NAI, External 7(1)P/52 "Fortnightly review of Sino-Tibetan intelligence, late December 1951," quoted in Bérénice Guyot-Réchard, *Shadow States: India, China and the Himalayas, 1910–1962* (Cambridge: Cambridge University Press, 2017), 204. For a recent example, see Ashok Kapur, *India and the South Asian Strategic Triangle* (London: Routledge, 2011), 92–93; and Geeta Kochhar and Pramod Jaiswal, *Unique Asian Triangle: India-China-Nepal* (New Delhi: G. B. Books, 2016).

58. In Anglophone literature, even brief analyses of Kunwar Inderjit Singh are limited to works on Nepal. Some works that have given extended analysis are Upadhya, *Nepal and the Geo-Strategic Rivalry between China and India,* 71–76; Margaret W. Fisher and Joan V. Bondurant, *Indian Views of Sino-Indian Relations* (Berkeley, CA: Institute of International Studies, 1956), 152–62.

59. DO133/36, April 2, 1952. Kathmandu Dispatch No. 5 offers a fairly clear government account of how the uprising unfolded.

60. Bhuwan L. Joshi and Leo E. Rose, *Democratic Innovations in Nepal: A Case Study of Political Acculturation* (Berkeley: University of California Press, 1966), 100–101; Werner Levi, "Nepal's New Era," *Far Eastern Survey* 28.10 (1959): 150–56; Ernesto Rech, "Il Nepal e la Repubblica Popolare Cinese," *Cina,* 3 (1957): 108–9. Later Zhou Enlai would indicate that Singh arrived with "thirty-seven persons armed with nineteen rifles and 500 bullets." See SWJN, 27, 19.

61. For discussion of distance, trade, and expense per kilometer, see "Imported goods from China Arrive in Kyirong," *Kathmandu Post,* May 19, 2016.

62. "Replace Indian Ambassador," *Times of India,* February 22, 1952, 6.

63. "Dr. K. I. Singh in Tibet," *Himalayan Times,* March 9, 1952, 3.

64. Margaret C. Godley, "The Communist Menace on India's Northern Frontier," *Truth,* April 2, 1954.

65. "Dr. K. I. Singh Halted," *Himalayan Times,* April 5, 1952, 5; a similar assertion appeared in "Dr. K. I. Singh Reported Inclusion in Liberation Army," *Times of India,* April 27, 1952.

66. Red-Inspired Gang Seizes Vital Town in Western Nepal: Escaped Rebel Leads Movement?," *Times of India,* July 17, 1953, 5.

67. DO133/36 May 20, 1952. General Bijaya later recanted this view, but the Nepalese government instead argued that he might "turn that direction" and be used to establish a puppet government in a "liberated area" in Nepal.

68. Peter Aufschnaiter, *Peter Aufschnaiter's Eight Years in Tibet* (Bangkok: Orchid Press, 2002), 196. Aufschnaiter's itinerary accords with most accounts and "is regarded as the

shortest route to Lhasa." See Y. P. Pant, "Nepal-China Trade Relations," *Economic Weekly,* April 14, 1962, 621. See also DO133/36 February 7, 1952.

69. DO133/36 April 4, 1952. The British seemed to be under the impression that he had not been apprehended by the Chinese forces and suggest that Singh and his group were slowly moving towards Lhasa without opposition.

70. Shibbanlal Saksena, "Dr. K. I. Singh," *National Herald* (Lucknow) November 18, 1955, 4; DO133/36, February 7, 1952.

71. Fisher and Bondurant, *Indian Views of Sino-Indian Relations,* 160–61.

72. DO133/37 June 13, 1952.

73. DO133/37 June 13, 1952.

74. DO133/37 June 13, 1952.

75. DO133/38 September 15, 1952.

76. DO133/37 May 7, 1952. See also *The Statesman,* June 11, 1952; the Nepalese representative in Lhasa indicated that Singh had left no later than August 15, 1952. DO133/38 September 15, 1952.

77. Hua Xuan, "60 nianqian Zhong-Ni jiaowang miwen," *Zhongwen Xinwen Zhoukan,* September 30, 2014, 81.

78. Ibid., 81–22.

79. In many instances it is insinuated that Singh gave speeches or worked with the Chinese on fomenting an uprising in Nepal. Aside from blind assertions and purely anecdotal evidence, I have found little foundation for such accusations. A similar conclusion was reached by British officials: FO 371/112196 February 19, 1954. For examples of Singh playing a more active role, see "Dr. Singh for Nepal: Peking Gesture Welcomed, *Times of India,* August 1955, 11; "Behind the Tibet Uprising," *Pakistan Horizon* 12.2 (1959): 163–64.

80. "Dr. K. I. Singh to Stay in Politics," *Times of India,* September 18, 1955, 9; see also "Dr. Singh's Return to Nepal: Not to Preach Communism," *Times of India,* September 15, 1955, 5.

81. In Chinese, I have found only two sentences in a single three-paragraph article that openly and formally acknowledged Singh's stay in China around the time he became prime minister. See Shi Ming, "Kong-ying-Xin'ge," *Shijie Zhishi* 16 (1957): 18.

82. "Sovereignty of Tibet: Nepalese Treaty Still Stands," *Times of India,* April 7, 1954, 9.

83. Nehru, speech given in Kathmandu on June 16, 1951. Quoted in Sam Cowan, "The Indian Checkposts, Lipu Lekh, and Kalapani," *The Record,* December 15, 2015. See also FO 37/112196, February 19, 1954. For similar sentiments, see his speech: Nehru, Speech in Indian Parliament, December 6, 1950.

84. United Nations, "No. 4307—Agreement Between the Republic of India and the People's Republic of China on Trade and Intercourse between Tibet Region of China and India (April 29, 1954)," in *Treaty Series: Treaties and International Agreements Registered or Filed and Recorded with the Secretariat of the United Nations,* vol. 299, 1958, 70.

85. Parliamentary Debate, May 18, 1954.

86. Hua Xuan, "60 nianqian Zhong-Ni jiaowang miwen," 82.

87. SWJN, vol. 25, 460. The fact that this visit, the cessation of the annual tributes, and the need for a new relationship with Tibet were all tied together in the public mind is evident in the press at the time. See "Nepal to Consult India: Relations with Tibet," *Times of India,* April 30, 1954, 1.

88. SWJN, vol. 27, 17.

89. SWJN, vol. 27, 83.

90. Nehru, "Policy regarding China and Tibet (18 November 1950)," 346; see also Dibyesh Anand, "Strategic Hypocrisy: The British Imperial Scripting of Tibet's Geopolitical Identity." *Journal of Asian Studies* 68.1 (2009): 245–46.

91. George M. T. Kahin, *The Asian-African Conference, Bandung, Indonesia, April 1955* (Ithaca, NY: Cornell University Press, 1956), 50.

92. Chen Jian, "China and the Bandung Conference," in *Bandung Revisited: The Legacy of the 1955 Asian-African Conference for International Order,* ed. See Seng Tan and Amitav Acharya (Singapore: National University of Singapore Press, 2008), 132–59; Wang Gungwu, "The Question of the 'Oversea Chinese,'" *Journal of Southeast Asian Affairs* (1976): 101–10; Yufeng Mao, "When Zhou Enlai Met Gamal Abdel Nasser," in *Bandung 1955: Little Histories,* ed. Antonia Finnane and Derke McDougall (Caulfield: Monash University Press, 2010), 89–108.

93. Abraham Itty, "Bandung and State Formation in Post-Colonial Asia," in See Seng Tan and Acharya, *Bandung Revisited,* 57.

94. SWJN, vol. 27, 18.

95. David Mozingo, "The Sino-Indonesian Dual Nationality Treaty," *Asian Survey* 1.10 (1961): 25.

96. Philip A. Kuhn, *Chinese among Others: Emigration in Modern Times* (Lanham, MD: Rowman & Littlefield, 2008), 330.

97. "Dr. Singh for Nepal: Peking Gesture Welcomed," *Times of India,* August 24, 1955.

98. "Robin Hood of the Himalayas," *Time* 70.6 (August 5, 1957): 22.

99. Girilal Jain, *India Meets China in Nepal* (New York: Asia Publishing House, 1959), 112. Singh remained in politics, ultimately serving for a record-setting four-month term as prime minister. See Rose, *Nepal: Strategy for Survival,* 216–17.

100. A. S. Bhasin, *Documents on Nepal's Relations with India and China, 1949–66* (Bombay: Academic Books, 1970), 254. See also "Nepal Surrenders Concessions in Tibet," *New York Times,* September 25, 1956. The agreement followed to a considerable degree that of India's Sino-Indian Trade and Intercourse Agreement signed two years earlier. It is interesting to note the agreement was officially binding in three languages: Chinese, Nepali and English.

101. Bhasin, *Documents on Nepal's Relations with India and China,* 254.

102. Many Western accounts treat the introduction as one of many "modern" inventions introduced by Westerners, though clearly individuals like Heinrich Harrer and Frank Ludlow did promote their popularity (and the actual making of home movies). For Tsarong Dasang Dadul and Charles Bell, see FO 371/20222, September 14, 1936. See also Peter H. Hansen, "Tibetan Horizon: Tibet and the Cinema in the Early 20th Century," in *Imagining Tibet: Perceptions, Projections and Fantasies,* ed. Thierry Dodin and Heinz Rather (Boston:Wisdom Publications, 2001), 96.

103. Harrer, *Seven Years in Tibet,* 271–78; Richard Starks and Miriam Murcutt, *Lost in Tibet: The Untold Story of Five American Airmen, a Doomed Plane, and the Will to Survive* (Guilford, CT: Lyons Press, 2012), 125–27).

104. Abdul Aziz had strong familial ties with Ladakh but had been born in Lhasa and never returned to Ladakh. For the sake of consistency I refer to him as a Barkor Khache based on the fact that he did not have and did not claim Indian citizenship on the basis of his

Ladakhi heritage until after 1959. Abdul Wahid Radhu described Abdul Aziz as "more Tibetan than Ladakhi" and indicated he "was born in Lhasa where he had spent his childhood and youth . . . through his grandmother he had Chinese blood and his manner reflected his close contact with the Tibetan nobility" See Radhu, *Islam in Tibet,* 79, 95 (quote). Charles Bell, who deserves credit for mentioning Tsarong's early adoption of film, inexplicably claims that Tibetans "have no cinemas." Charles Bell, *Portrait of the Dalai Lama* (London: Collins, 1946).

105. The two brothers were more commonly known as the "Tsakhur brothers," a common Tibetan practice of referring to individuals by the name of their residence. Radhu, *Islam in Tibet,* 157. For comments about cinema in Tibet, see NAI, Reports on Tibet, External Affairs, R&I, 1956, S. No. 45 55/ R&I/56, Office of the Consul General of India, Lhasa, Tibet, "Report for the period ending 15 October, 1955;" S. No. 20 55/ R&I/55; NAI, Reports on Tibet, External Affairs, R&I, 1956, S. No. 45 55/ R&I/56, Office of the Consul General of India, Lhasa, Tibet, "Report for the period ending 15 April, 1956" (see also following report, "September 1956").

106. NAI, Reports on Tibet, External Affairs, R&I, 1955, S. No. 20 55/ R&I/55.

107. NAI, Reports on Tibet, External Affairs, R&I, 1955, S. No. 20 55/ R&I/56.

108. NAI, Reports on Tibet, External Affairs, R&I, 1955, S. No. 20 55/ R&I/56.

109. NAI, "Report for the Month of June, 1958," External Affairs, 6(35) R&I/58.

110. NAI, "Report for the Month of December, 1958," External Affairs, 6(35) R&I/58.

111. NAI, "Report for the Month of December, 1958," External Affairs, 6(35) R&I/58.

112. NAI, "Reports from Lhasa for the Month of January, 1959," External Affairs, S. No. 231 6(35) R&I/59.

113. NAI, "Reports from Lhasa, External Affairs, R&I, 1959, S. No. 231, 6/35/R&I/59.

114. NAI, "Reports on Tibet, Month of May," External Affairs, R&I, 1955, S. No. 45 55/ R&I/56.

115. NAI, "Reports on Tibet, Month of May," External Affairs, R&I, 1955, S. No. 45 55/ R&I/56.

116. NAI, "Reports on Tibet, Month of September," External Affairs, R&I, 1955, S. No. 45, 55/ R&I/56.

117. NAI, "Annual Report of the Indian Trade Agency, Yatung for the Year 1957."

118. Melvyn. *A History of Modern Tibet: The Storm Clouds Descend,* 41.

119. The use of Tibetan currency extended across Tibet, including those areas claimed by India. India sought to alter local border groups' preference for Tibetan currency by setting up incentives to use Indian money. Yet this was overtaken by their greater worries of Chinese currency, and by 1957 "people found in possession of PRC dollars upon returning from Tibet were fined." See Guyot-Réchard, *Shadow States,* 211.

120. NAI, "Annual Reports from Lhasa for 1956," 3(19) R&I/57.

121. NAI, "Reports (other than annual) from Tibet," Report for the Month of November 1958, 6(35) R&I/58.

122. NAI, "Reports (other than annual) from Tibet," Report for the Month of November 1958, 6(35) R&I/58.

123. NAI, "Reports from Lhasa," External Affairs," S. No. 231, 6/35R&I/59.

124. NAI, "Reports from Lhasa," External Affairs," S. No. 231, 6/35R&I/59.

125. NAI, "Annual Reports for 1958 from Lhasa," S. No. 209, 3(19) R&I/59.

## 5. THE TIBETAN MUSLIM INCIDENT OF 1960

1. Mao had been making menacing comments since the summer of 1958 about preparing for possible full-scale rebellion. See "Mao Zedong's Remarks on the CCP Central Committee's Instruction on Mobilizing 2,000 Youth to Enter Tibet for Participating in Production" (January 22, 1959), in Mao Zedong, *Mao Zedong xizang gongzuo wenxuan* [A Selection of Mao Zedong's Writings on Tibet] (Beijing: Zhongyang wenxian chubanshe, 2001), 164. Also see Mao Zedong, *Jianguo yilai Mao Zedong wengao* [Mao Zedong's Manuscripts since the Founding of the People's Republic] (Beijing: Zhongyang wenxian, 1987), 8:46.

2. Chen Jian, "The Tibetan Rebellion of 1959 and China's Changing Relations with India and the Soviet Union," *Journal of Cold War Studies* 8.3 (2006): 54.

3. The situation in Tibet and ethnically Tibetan areas like Amdo (Qinghai) and Kham (Sichuan) had been deteriorating for some time. See Dawa Norbu, "1959 Tibetan Rebellion: An Interpretation," *China Quarterly* 77 (1979): 84–85.

4. S. H. Steinberg, *The Statesman's Year Book: Statistical and Historical Annual of the States of the World for the Year 1957* (London: Macmillan, 1957), 1435.

5. NAI, R&I, 1959, S. No. 231 External Affairs, 6/35/ R&I/59, Reports from Lhasa, January Monthly Report, February 4, 1959.

6. NAI, R&I, 1959, S. No. 231 External Affairs, 6/35/ R&I/59, Reports from Lhasa, January Monthly Report, February 4, 1959.

7. "Motion Re: Situation Arising out of Recent Events in Tibet" Statement, May 4, 1959, *Rajya Sabha Debates*, vol. 25 (New Delhi: Council of States Secretariat, 1959), cols. 1671–8430.

8. NAI, R&I, 1959, S. No. 231 External Affairs, 6/35/ R&I/59, Reports from Lhasa, March, April, and May Monthly Report, June 1, 1959, 5.

9. Goldstein, *A History of Modern Tibet: The Storm Clouds Descend,* 9; Tubten Khétsun and Matthew Akester, *Memories of Life in Lhasa under Chinese Rule* (New York: Columbia University Press, 2008), 22–23; McGranahan, *Arrested Histories,* 105.

10. Shakya, *Dragon in the Land of Snow,* 192–93. See also Weise Zerenduoji [Tsering Woeser], *Sha Jie: Sishi nian de jiyi jinqu, jingtouxia de xizang wenge* [Forbidden Memory: Tibet during the Cultural Revolution] (Taibei: Dakuai wenhua chuban, 2006), 123.

11. Shampho would survive, only to die several years later as a result of injuries suffered in a criticism session during the Cultural Revolution. See 'Ju-chen Thub-bstan-rnam-rgyal (Juchen Thupten Namgyal), *Dpal ldan bka blon khri zur 'ju-chen thub-bstan-rnam-rgyal mchog gi sku tshe'i lo rgyus dang 'brel ba'i nye rabs bod kyi byung ba brjod pa'i gtam tshogs srid pa'i me long zhes bya ba* [The Mirror of Life: The Autobiography of Former Senior Kalon Juchen Thupten Namgyal, and Related Happenings Pertaining to Tibetan Affairs]. (Chauntra, India, 2014), 245; NAI, R&I, 1959, S. No. 231, External Affairs, 6/35/ R&I/59, Reports from Lhasa, March, April, and May Monthly Report, June 1, 1959, 4.

12. 'Ju-chen, Thub-bstan-rnam-rgyal, *Dpal Ldan Bka Blon Khri Zur 'ju-Chen Thub-Bstan-Rnam-Rgyal Mchog Gi Sku Tshe'i Lo Rgyus Dang 'brel Ba'i Nye Rabs Bod Kyi Byung Ba Brjod Pa'i Gtam Tshogs Srid Pa'i Me Long Zhes Bya Ba,* 5:245.

13. Shakya, *Dragon in the Land of Snow,* 192.

14. NAI, R&I, 1959, S. No. 231, External Affairs, 6/35/ R&I/59, Reports from Lhasa, March, April, and May Monthly Report, June 1, 1959, 4. See also Parshotam Mehra, *From*

*Conflict to Conciliation: Tibetan Polity Revisited. A Brief Historical Conspectus of the Dalai Lama–Panchen Lama Standoff, ca. 1904–1989* (Wiesbaden: Harrassowitz, 2004), 134.

15. "Xizang panguo jituan biran miewang Xizang renmin qiantu guangming canlan Jiefang jun yi xunsu pingding lasa panluan Zai sengsu gejie aiguo renmin xiezhu xia Zheng chengsheng qianjin saodang xizang qita difang de panfei" [The traitorous Tibetan clique is certain to be exterminated; the future of Tibet's people is bright and glorious; PLA swiftly pacifies Lhasa's armed rebellion, and with help from clergy and lay patriots mopped up Tibetan traitorous elements in other areas], *Renmin ribao*, March 29, 1959, 1; See also Nai-min Ling, "Xinhua News Agency," in *Tibet, 1950–1967* (Hong Kong: Union Research Institute, 1968), 351.

16. NAI R&I, 1959, S. No. 231 External Affairs, 6/35/ R&I/59, Reports from Lhasa, March, April, and May Monthly Report, June 1, 1959, 15.

17. "Nepalese Consulate Damaged," *Himalayan Times*, April 19, 1959, 4; "Propaganda Drive in Tibet," *Hindustan Times*, April 6, 1959, 1.

18. *Renmin ribao*, March 29, 1959, 1 (for an English translation, see *Tibet: 1950–1967*, 348–54). Li Jianglin suggests that 63 PLA soldiers were killed, compared to 545 Tibetans, and that 4,815 were wounded and taken prisoner. Jianglin Li, *Tibet in Agony: Lhasa 1959*, trans. Susan Wilf (Cambridge, MA: Harvard University Press, 2016).

19. "Speakers Denounce Rebels," FBIS (Foreign Broadcast Information Service), April 16, 1959: FRB-59-074; Zhang Chunxiu, "Lasa de Qingzhensi he musilin mudi" [Mosques and Muslim Cemeteries of Lhasa], *Zhongguo Musilin* 1 (2002): 28; "Xizang renmin yongyuan zhongyu zuguo, Lasa liang wan ren kongqian da shiwei, Zai budalagong qian renmen fenfen kongsu panfei de taotian zuixing [The Tibetan people are forever loyal to the homeland, an unprecedented twenty-thousand people hold rally in Lhasa, In front of the Potala Palace people one after the other denounce the rebels' monstrous crimes], *Renmin ribao*, April 16, 1959, 1–2.

20. One source, with only the loosest reasoning, attempts to invert this by suggesting that since the Muslims fought *against* the Chinese, the PLA burned the mosque to the ground. W. Y. Tsao, *Free China Review* 10 (1960): 19.

21. Tubten Khétsun and Matthew Akester, *Memories of Life in Lhasa under Chinese Rule*, 150.

22. *Renmin ribao*, March 31, 1959, 1. It is worth noting Wang's support did not go unrewarded. Less than a year later, his demonstration of unfaltering Party loyalty led to his promotion from primary school vice principal to the post of vice-mayor of Lhasa.

23. "Huanhu zhengfu wei xizang renmin chuhai; Qingzhu xizang renmin zouxiang xinsheng, Xizang renmin relie yonghu taoping panni" [Hail the government for removing the Tibetan people from harm's way, Celebrate the Tibetan people's moving towards a new life; The Tibetan people fervently endorse the suppression of the rebels], *Renmin ribao*, April 2, 1959, 1.

24. *Renmin ribao*, April 16, 1959, 1.

25. "Miejue renxing lingren fazhi, Xizang panfei waxin sharen zui'e taotian" [Inhuman! Deplorable! Tibetan rebels heinously murder by ripping out hearts] April 26, 1959, 4; "Xizang panfei de 'weijiao jun'—yiguan qinshou he pizhe jiasha de chailang" [Tibetan rebels "Protect Religion Army"—Animals decked out in dress cloths; Wolves wearing monk's robes], May 5, 1959, 2.

26. Tsarong and Chödron Trinlay. *In the Service of His Country*, 146–47.

27. "The Revolution in Tibet and Nehru's Philosophy," *Renmin ribao,* May 6, 1959.

28. "Xizang de geming he Nihelu de zhexue," *Renmin ribao,* May 6, 1959, 1. For an English version, see "The Revolution in Tibet and Nehru's Philosophy," in *Concerning the Question of Tibet* (Beijing: Foreign Languages Press, 1959), 39–276.

29. "The Revolution in Tibet and Nehru's Philosophy," *Renmin ribao,* May 6, 1959, 1.

30. Ibid.

31. While Chinese newspapers consistently referred to all Khache as "Hui," most of the community had registered, if they registered, as Tibetan in their household registration (*hukou*) and later, when introduced, in the identity cards (*shenfenzheng*). In Lhasa, Hui (Tib. *hürik*) was reserved for Muslim Chinese. The implications of this are significant given that a Tibetan Muslim registering as Hui was far more common in the eastern Tibetan areas of Kham and Amdo, which fell outside of the territory that would eventually form the Tibetan Autonomous Region. I can find no record of any usage of the term "Zang-Hui" for the Lhasa community prior to the 1980s.

32. Tubten Khétsun and Akester, *Memories of Life in Lhasa under Chinese Rule,* 150.

33. IMEA X, October 14, 1963, 88.

34. IKMEWA 1959, n.d. [April 1959?], Letter #1 to Kalimpong, 3.

35. IKMEWA, n.d. [November 1959?], Letter #2 to Kalimpong.

36. NAI R&I, 1959, S. No. 231 External Affairs, 6/35/ R&I/59, Reports from Lhasa, June, July, and August Monthly Report, 4, 1959, 5.

37. NAI, R&I, 1959, S. No. 231 External Affairs, 6/35/ R&I/59, Reports from Lhasa, September Monthly Report, October 4, 1959, 5.

38. "Trouble Tibet," Oral Answers to Questions, April 20, 1959, in *Rajya Sabha Debates,* cols. 1671–8430.

39. Naik, "Memories of my Father, Abdul Ghani, in Tibet," 33.

40. NAI, "Reports (other than annual) from Tibet, Report for the Month of November," 6(35) R&I/58; IMEA I, May 13, 1959, 84.

41. NAI, 6(35) R&I/58, "Reports (other than annual) from Tibet, Report for the Month of November, 1958," December 1, 1958.

42. IMEA I, May 13, 1959, 84–85.

43. IMEA I, July 8, 1959, 86.

44. NAI, R&I, 1959, S. No. 231, External Affairs, 6/35/ R&I/59, Reports from Lhasa, Month of March, April and May, 1959, dated June 1, 1959.

45. NAI, R&I, 1959, S. No. 231 External Affairs, 6/35/ R&I/59, Reports from Lhasa, June, July, and August Monthly Report, September 4, 1959, 5. The Chinese offer a slightly different account, suggesting that "only after talks between Mr. Chhibber and the 'headman' of these Kachis in April of this year, did such things happen that that 'headman' taking advantage of a prayer meeting announced to all Kachis that they all must fill revised 'applications' for registration as citizens of India which were distributed by the Consulate-General of India." See IMEA I, July 17, 1959, 90.

46. IMEA II, "Note given by the Ministry of External Affairs, New Delhi, to the Embassy of China in India," September 24, 1959, 90–91. See also IMEA I, May 13, 1959 85.

47. IMEA I, "Letter from the Director of the Foreign Bureau in Tibet to the Consul-General of India in Lhasa, July 17, 1959, 89.

48. Yang Gongsu, *Cangsang jiushi nian: yige waijiao teshi di huiyi* (Haike: Hainan chubanshe, 1999), 207.

49. NAI R&I, 1959, S. No. 231 External Affairs, 6/35/ R&I/59, Reports from Lhasa, March, April, and May Monthly Report, June 1, 1959, 16. See also "Some Nepalese in Custody in Tibet," *Himalayan Times,* June 21, 1959, 1; "Sherpas Held in Lhasa," *Hindustan Times,* June 19, 1959, 5.

50. NAI R&I, 1959, S. No. 231 External Affairs, 6/35/ R&I/59, Reports from Lhasa, June, July, and August Monthly Report, September 4, 1959, 5.

51. "Identity Cards for All in Lhasa," *Hindustan Times,* April 18, 1959, 1.

52. "500 Tibetan Women Force Way into Indian Consulate," *Times of India,* May 19, 1959, 1.

53. Himalayan Times 1959-08—Trade with Tibet Severely Hit (August 9 1959), SWJN, 51:435.

54. NAI, "Annual report from Lhasa, Gyantse and Yatung 1959," Ministry of External Affairs, Secret, 3(19)R&I/60: 9.

55. "Silver Reacts to Chinese Move to Declare Indian Currency Illegal," *Times of India,* August 7, 1959.

56. IMEA II, August 14, 1959, 72.

57. IMEA I, May 13, 1959, 84–85.

58. IKMEWA 1959, n.d. [April 1959?], Letter #1 to Kalimpong, 1–4. The translation is Fazaillah Chisti's.

59. SWJN, vol .52, 176. Lok Sabha, Oral Answers to Questions, September 7, 1959.

60. SWJN, vol. 52, 177. Lok Sabha, Oral Answers to Questions, September 7, 1959.

61. The hajj is traditionally taken from the eighth to twelfth day of the last month of the Islamic calendar, which in 1959 would correspond to June 15–19.

62. Madhavan K. Palat, ed., *Selected Works of Jawaharlal Nehru, 1 May–30 June, 1959* (vol. 49), 2nd ser. (New Delhi: Jawaharlal Nehru Memorial Fund, 2014), 581; "Tibetan Pilgrims Stranded," *Hindustan Times,* May 28, 1959, 9; "Tibetan Muslims Not Allowed on Haj," *Times of India,* August 12, 1959.

63. Madhavan K. Palat, ed., *Selected Works of Jawaharlal Nehru, 1–31 July, 1959,* (vol. 50), 2nd ser. (New Delhi: Jawaharlal Nehru Memorial Fund, 2014), July 18, 1959,. 207–8.

64. IKMEWA 1959, n.d. [April 1959?], Letter #1 to Kalimpong, 1; emphasis in original. The translation is Fazaillah Chisti's.

65. IKMEWA 1959, n.d. [April 1959?], Letter #1 to Kalimpong, 4.

66. IKMEWA 1959, n.d. [November 1959?], Letter #2 to Kalimpong Khache, 4.

67. IKMEWA, "Letter to Secretary Home Passport Department," May 23, 1955. Faizulah Chisti served in numerous clubs and on the chamber of commerce. Amanullah Chisti, interview, March 26, 2010.

68. It is unclear on exactly what date Faizullah Chisti and the Kalimpong delegation met with Nehru. According to one report they left for Delhi in August, while a question asked of Nehru in the Rajya Sabha in February 1960 refers to "six Ladakhi Muslims from Kalimpong" who approached the Government for the 121 Ladakhi Muslim families now staying in Lhasa" which he replied in the affirmative. See "Indian Merchants to Meet Mr. Nehru," *Himalayan Times,* August 23, 1959, 4; "Repatriation of Ladakhi Muslims from Lhasa," Written Answers to Questions, February 24, 1959, in *Rajya Sabha Debates* (New Delhi: Council of States Secretariat, 1959), cols. 1671–72.

69. Newspaper editors seemed to pick up the story particularly between August 6 and 23, 1959. Several examples: "Traders Harrassed in Many Parts of Tibet," *Times of India,* August 6, 1959, 1; "No Registration as Indian Citizens: China's Ban on our Nationals in Tibet," *Times of*

*India,* August 12, 1959, 1; "Concerns over Safety of Indians in Tibet," *Hindustan Times,* August 12, 1959, 1; "Nehru Says China Flouts Tibet Pact," August 7, 1959, 1; "New Delhi Says Reds Detain Five in Tibet," *New York Times,* August 12, 1959, 2.

70. IMEA I, 84–5; 89–90; IKMEWA n.d. [November 1959?], Letter #2 to Kalimpong; Plea on Kashmiri Muslims in Tibet Rejected by China," *Times of India,* February 27, 1960, 1.

71. Kahin, *The Asian-African Conference, Bandung, Indonesia, April 1955,* 50.

72. David P. Mozingo, *Chinese Policy toward Indonesia, 1949–1967* (Ithaca, NY: Cornell University Press, 2007), 168–75.

73. J. A. C. Mackie, "Anti-Chinese Outbreaks in Indonesia, 1959–1968," in *The Chinese in Indonesia* (Honolulu: University Press of Hawaii, 1976), 92.

74. FBIS (Foreign Broadcast Information Service), "CPR Interference in Indonesia Scored," December 30, 1959: FRB-59–254.

75. Thomas S. Mullaney, *Coming to Terms with the Nation: Ethnic Classification in Modern China* (Berkeley: University of California Press, 2011).

76. Vasantkumar, "What Is This 'Chinese' in Overseas Chinese?," 441.

77. SWJN, vol. 51, "In the Rajya Sabha: Indian Traders in Tibet," August 13, 1959, 449. See also *Parliamentary Debates: Rajya Sabha Official Report,* vol. 26, nos. 1–13, cols. 451–57 (New Delhi: Rajya Sabha Secretariat, 1959).

78. IMEA II, "Note given by Ministry of External Affairs, New Delhi, to the Embassy of China in India, September 24, 1959, 90–91.

79. IMEA II, "Note given by Ministry of External Affairs, New Delhi, to the Embassy of China in India," September 24, 1959, 89.

80. IMEA III, "Note given by Ministry of Foreign Affairs of China to the Embassy of India in China," December 31, 1959, 123.

81. IMEA III, "Note given by Ministry of Foreign Affairs of China to the Embassy of India in China," December 31, 1959, 124.

82. NAI, "Annual Report of the Indian Trade Agent Gyantse (Tibet) for the year 1959," Annual Report from Lhasa, Gyantse and Yatung, Ministry of External Affairs, Secret, 3(19) R&I/60: 17.

83. NAI, "Annual report from Lhasa, Gyantse and Yatung 1959," Ministry of External Affairs, Secret, 3(19) R&I/60: 16.

84. "Note given by the Ministry of External Affairs, New Delhi, to the Embassy of China, India," vol. 2, October 29, 1959, 121.

85. "Note given by the Ministry of External Affairs, New Delhi, to the Embassy of China, India," vol. 2, October 29, 1959, 121.

86. IKMEWA 1959, n.d. [November 1959?], Letter #2 to Kalimpong, 1–2. The translation is Fazaillah Chisti's.

87. NAI,"Monthly Report for the month of September, 1959 (dated 7 October, 1959)," Reports from Lhasa, External Affairs, R&I, 1959, S. No. 231 6/35/ R&I/59, p. 5.

88. NAI,"Monthly Report for the month of October and November, 1959, (dated 7 December, 1959)," Reports from Lhasa, External Affairs, R&I, 1959, S. No. 231 6/35/ R&I/59, p. 9.

89. "Monthly Report for the month of December, 1959," Reports from Lhasa, External Affairs, R&I, 1959, S. No. 231 6/35/ R&I/59, January 6, 1960: 8.

90. NAI, "Monthly Report for the Month of June, July and August," dated September 4, 1959, "Reports from Lhasa, External Affairs, S. No. 231 6/35/R&I/59.

91. NAI, "Monthly Report for the Month of June, July and August," dated September 4, 1959, Reports from Lhasa, External Affairs, S. No. 231 6/35/R&I/59.

92. Bista, *Report from Lhasa,* 142. This is a conservative estimate since Bista noted over 500 Nepali and Khatsara who remained in Lhasa in 1974, with 1,000 leaving in 1960; this roughly aligns with Charles Bell's estimate in 1921 that roughly 300 Nepali and 800 Khatsara lived in central Tibet. See NAI, Foreign and Political Department, Secret—External, Proceedings, June 1921, Nos. 271: "Newsletter," No. 10, dated Lhasa, April 22, 1921.

93. NAI, "Monthly Report for the month of October and November, 1959 (dated 7 December, 1959)," Reports from Lhasa, External Affairs, R&I, 1959, S. No. 231 6/35/R&I/59, p. 11.

94. NAI, "Monthly Report for the month of October and November, 1959 (dated 7 December, 1959)," Reports from Lhasa, External Affairs, R&I, 1959, S. No. 231 6/35/R&I/59, p. 11

95. Bista, "Nepalis in Tibet," 10; NAI, "Monthly Report for the month of October and November, 1959 (dated December 7, 1959)," Reports from Lhasa, External Affairs, R&I, 1959, S. No. 231 6/35/ R&I/59, p. 10.

96. For Chinese understanding of this, see Yang Gongsu, *Cangsang jiushi nian,* 206–7. For the Nepalese perspective, see Fadzakir, "Muslims of Kathmandu," 147–48.

97. Quoting TASS statement issued on September 12, 1959. CIA Sino-Indian Border Dispute (1963).

98. Vladislav M. Zubok, "The Khrushchev-Mao Conversations, 31 July-3 August 1958 and 2 October 1959," *Cold War International History Project Bulletin,* no. 12–13 (2001): 266.

99. Ibid.

100. Ibid.

101. "Note given by the Ministry of External Affairs, New Delhi, to the Embassy of China, India," vol. 4, April 25, 1960, 102.

102. "Monthly Report for the Month of April, 1960," Reports from Lhasa, External Affairs, R&I, 1960, S. No. 366 6/35/ R&I/60, May 4, 1960, 5.

103. IMEI, Vol 3&4, 56.

104. IMEI, Vol 3&4, 56.

105. IMEI, IV, "Note given by Ministry of External Affairs, New Delhi, to the Embassy of China in India," April 13, 1960, 57.

106. IMEA IV, "Note given by Ministry of External Affairs, New Delhi, to the Embassy of China in India," April 13, 1960, 57.

107. IMEA IV, "Note given by Ministry of External Affairs, New Delhi, to the Embassy of China in India," April 1,3 1960, 58.

108. IMEA IV, "Note given by Ministry of External Affairs, New Delhi, to the Embassy of China in India," April 13, 1960, 59.

109. IKMEWA. April 20, 1960. The following week the Indian government confirmed with Faizullah Chisti that all Khaches residing in Kalimpong "of Indian origin" are eligible for registration as Indian citizens.

110. IMEA, "Note given by the Ministry of External Affairs, New Delhi, to the Embassy of China, India," vol. 4, April 25, 1960, 102.

111. NAI, "Monthly Report for the Month of May, 1960," *Reports from Lhasa, External Affairs,* R&I, 1960, S. No. 366 6/35/ R&I/60, June 7, 1960, 5.

112. NAI, "Monthly Report for the Month of May, 1960," *Reports from Lhasa, External Affairs,* R&I, 1960, S. No. 366 6/35/ R&I/60, June 7, 1960, 5.

113. IMEA, "Note given by the Ministry of External Affairs, New Delhi, to the Embassy of China in India," June 30, 1960, 63.

114. IMEA, "Note given by the Ministry of External Affairs, New Delhi, to the Embassy of China in India," June 30, 1960, 64. The Indian Government in its note says as much informing the Chinese that the "meeting at the Lhasa Athletic stadium on June 20 were calculated to victimize certain leading Ladakhi Muslims and to intimidate the rest of the community."

115. IMEA IV, "Note given by the Ministry of External Affairs, New Delhi, to the Embassy of China in India," July 14, 1960, 67.

116. IMEA IV, "Note given by the Ministry of External Affairs, New Delhi, to the Embassy of China in India," July 14, 1960, 67; see also NAI, "Monthly Report for the Month of July, 1960," Reports from Lhasa, External Affairs, R&I, 1960, S. No. 366 6/35/ R&I/60, August 6, 1960, 5.

117. IMEA IV, "Note given by the Ministry of External Affairs, New Delhi, to the Embassy of China in India," July 14, 1960, 67; see also NAI, "Monthly Report for the Month of July, 1960," Reports from Lhasa, External Affairs, R&I, 1960, S. No. 366 6/35/ R&I/60, August 6, 1960, 5.

118. "Red Terror in Tibet: Nepalese Muslims' Experience." *Times of India,* August 6, 1960, 1.

119. NAI, "Monthly Report for the Month of July, 1960," Reports from Lhasa, External Affairs, R&I, 1960, S. No. 366 6/35/ R&I/60, dated August 6, 1960, 5.

120. "Lasa jihui qingzhu pandeng shijie zuigaofeng," *Renmin ribao,* May 29, 1960, 2. Kaul (along with the Nepali consul) is reported to have attended.

121. "Lasa shenghui huanyin shoupi guilai dengshan dui yuan," *Renmin ribao,* June 9, 1960, 3. The *Himalayan Times,* displaying the desire to twist all of China's deeds to nefarious ends at the time, (mis)translated the slogan as "The conquest of Mount Everest by the Chinese team [is] the beginning of the Communist attempt to conquer the world." "Chinese Propaganda in Lhasa," *Himalayan Times,* June 26, 1960, 9; Kaul, *Frontier Callings,* 107.

122. *Tibetan Daily,* May 14, 1960. Quoted in NAI, Monthly Report for the Month of May, 1960, dated June 7, 1960.

123. NAI, Monthly Report for the Month of July, 1960, Reports from Lhasa, External Affairs, R&I, 1960, S. No. 366 6/35/ R&I/60, dated August 6, 1960; "Monthly Report for the Month of October, 1960," Reports from Lhasa, External Affairs, R&I, 1960, S. No. 366 6/35/ R&I/60, dated November 4, 1960.

124. NAI, Monthly Report for the Month of May, Reports from Lhasa, External Affairs, R&I, 1960, S. No. 366 6/35/ R&I/60, 1960, dated June 7, 1960.

125. "Mess Halls for Lhasa," *Hindustan Times,* July 29, 1960, 7. "Lasa gebumen guanfan kaizhan jixu geming yundong," *Renmin ribao,* July 29, 1960, 3; Kaul, *Frontier Callings,* 109. The campaigns in Tibet occurred on a slightly different chronology than in China proper. But in 1959 and through much of 1960 collectivization and communization with an effort for Tibet to "catch up" were implemented. In the autumn of 1960, it was suddenly decided to postpone such reforms for four years.

126. "Tibetans Abroad Urged to Return," *Hindustan Times,* June 20, 1960, 1.

127. NAI, "Monthly Report for the Month of August, 1960," Reports from Lhasa, External Affairs, R&I, 1960, S. No. 366 6/35/ R&I/60, dated September 2, 1960, 7.

128. NAI, "Monthly Report for the Month of August, 1960," Reports from Lhasa, External Affairs, R&I, 1960, S. No. 366 6/35/ R&I/60, dated September 2, 1960, 8.

129. IMEA, "Note given by the Ministry of Foreign Affairs, Peking, to the Embassy of India in China," September 23, 1960, 73.

130. IMEA, "Note given by the Ministry of Foreign Affairs, Peking, to the Embassy of India in China," September 23, 1960, 73.

131. IMEA, "Note given by the Ministry of Foreign Affairs, Peking, to the Embassy of India in China," September 23, 1960, 74.

132. "Monthly Political Report for the Month of January, 1961," Reports (other than annual) from Lhasa (Tibet), External Affairs, R&I, 1961, S. No. 89 6/35/ R&I/61,
dated February 6, 1961, 11.

133. NAI, "Monthly Report for the Month of September, 1960," Reports from Lhasa, External Affairs, R&I, 1960, S. No. 366 6/35/ R&I/60, dated October 4, 1960, 7.

134. NAI, "Monthly Report for the Month of September, 1960," Reports from Lhasa, External Affairs, R&I, 1960, S. No. 366 6/35/ R&I/60, dated October 4, 1960, 2.

135. Archive of the Foreign Ministry of the People's Republic of China, 118–01046–01, Telegram from Tibetan Foreign Affairs Office to Foreign Ministry, December 22, 1960, 3.

136. NAI, "Monthly Report for the Month of October, 1960," Reports from Lhasa, External Affairs, R&I, 1960, S. No. 366 6/35/ R&I/60, dated November 4, 1960, 5.

137. Archive of the Foreign Ministry of the People's Republic of China, 118–01046–01, Telegram from Tibetan Foreign Affairs Office to Foreign Ministry, December 22, 1960, 3; emphasis in original. Quoted and translated in Khan, *Muslim, Trader, Nomad, Spy*, 103.

138. NAI, "Monthly Report for the Month of September, 1960" *Reports from Lhasa*, External Affairs, R&I, 1960, S. No. 366 6/35/ R&I/60, dated October 4, 1960, 7. Faizullah Chisti registered eight families (42 individuals) from Tsetang. See IKWMA, "Detail List of the Indian National Muslims of Kashmiri Origin, 1960," 20 (internally numbered).

139. NAI, "Monthly Report for the Month of October, 1960," Reports from Lhasa, External Affairs, R&I, 1960, S. No. 366 6/35/ R&I/60, dated November 4, 1960, 8.

140. NAI, "Tibetan Refugees for Sikkim," *Times of India*, October 1, 1960, 7; Chen Bo, "A Multicultural Interpretation of an Ethnic Muslim Minority: The Case of the Hui Tibetans in Lhasa," *Journal of Muslim Minority Affairs* (2003): 56.

141. NAI, "Monthly Report for the Month of October, 1960," Reports from Lhasa, External Affairs, R&I, 1960, S. No. 366 6/35/ R&I/60, dated November 4, 1960, 8.

142. NAI, "Monthly Report for the Month of October, 1960," Reports from Lhasa, External Affairs, R&I, 1960, S. No. 366 6/35/ R&I/60, dated November 4, 1960, 5.

143. NAI, "Monthly Report for the Month of August, 1960," Reports from Lhasa, External Affairs, R&I, 1960, S. No. 366 6/35/ R&I/60: dated September 2, 1960, 10.

144. NAI, "Monthly Report for the Month of September, 1960," Reports from Lhasa, External Affairs, R&I, 1960, S. No. 366 6/35/ R&I/60, dated October 4, 1960, 7.

145. NAI, "Annual Political Report for the Year 1960 of the Consulate General of India, Tibet, Lhasa," Annual Report from Lhasa and Gyantse, Ministry of External Affairs. Secret, 3(19) R&I/60, dated March 22, 1961, 3.

146. Bista, *Report from Lhasa*, 142.

147. NAI, "Indian Trade Agency Annual Report, Yatung, Tibet for the Year 1959," Annual Report from Lhasa, Gyantse and Yatung, Ministry of External Affairs, Secret, 3(19) R&I/60, dated June 20, 1960.

148. NAI, "Annual Political Report for the Year 1960 of the Consulate General of India, Tibet, Lhasa," Annual Report from Lhasa and Gyantse, Ministry of External Affairs, Secret, 3(19) R&I/60, dated March 22, 1961, 3.

149. Chen Bo through oral interviews, examination of official papers and his own estimates comes to a similar number. See Chen Bo, "Muslim Minority—The Case of the Hui Tibetans in Lhasa," 56.

150. Kaul, *Frontier Callings,* 107.

151. NAI, "Annual Political Report for the Year 1960 of the Consulate General of India, Tibet, Lhasa," Annual Report from Lhasa and Gyantse, Ministry of External Affairs, Secret, 3(19) R&I/60, dated March 22, 1961, 10–11.

152. IMEA, "Note given by the Ministry of Foreign Affairs, Peking, to the Embassy of India in China," September 23, 1960, 74.

153. NAI. "Monthly Report for the Month of October, 1960," Reports from Lhasa, External Affairs, R&I, 1960, S. No. 366 6/35/ R&I/60, dated November 4, 1960, 10. In December, Haji Abdul Kadir Malik and Haji Habibullah Naik, both seriously ill, were released but too unwell to travel. Families of Barkor Khache were as late as July 1961 still being granted permission (and transportation) to leave China. See NAI, "Monthly Report for the Month of July, 1961," Reports (other than annual) from Lhasa (Tibet), External Affairs, R&I, 1961, S. No. 89 6/35/ R&I/61, dated August 2, 1961, 4.

154. NAI, "Monthly Political Report for the Month of March, 1961," Reports (other than annual) from Lhasa (Tibet). External Affairs, R&I, 1961, S. No. 89 6/35/ R&I/61,
dated April 4, 1961, 7.

155. NAI, "Monthly Political Report for the Month of March, 1961," Reports (other than annual) from Lhasa (Tibet), External Affairs, R&I, 1961, S. No. 89 6/35/ R&I/61,
dated April 4, 1961, 7.

156. "5 Indian Muslims Held in Tibet," *Times of India,* February 18, 1964, 5; Naik, "Memories of my Father, Abdul Ghani, in Tibet," 35. Naik, though the oldest of the group, emerged seventeen years later mentally strong but physically exhausted. He died soon after his release. Later documents would include Abdul Ahat, who was the son of the consulate cook.

157. NAI, "Monthly Report for the Month of October, 1960," Reports from Lhasa, External Affairs, R&I, 1960, S. No. 366 6/35/ R&I/60, dated November 4, 1960, 5.

158. Weise Zerenduoji [Tsering Woeser], *Sha Jie,* 133.

159. NAI, "Annual Reports from Lhasa and Gyantse," December 4, 1961. Weise Zerenduoji [Tsering Woeser], *Sha Jie,* 133. Batt would go on to take low-level municipal offices in Lhasa, while his son, Abdul Halim, a nine-year-old boy in 1960, returned to study with two Hui imams and would later serve as imam.

160. Chen Bo, "A Multicultural Interpretation of an Ethnic Muslim Minority," 56.

161. NAI, "Monthly Political Report for the Month of February, 1961," Reports (other than annual) from Lhasa (Tibet), External Affairs, R&I, 1961, S. No. 89 6/35/ R&I/61, dated March 6, 1961, 7.

162. NAI, "Monthly Political Report for the Month of February, 1961," Reports (other than annual) from Lhasa (Tibet), External Affairs, R&I, 1961, S. No. 89 6/35/ R&I/61. dated March 6, 1961, 7.

163. The remaining Wabaling Khache community in 1961 is generally estimated to be roughly 800 to 1,000 individuals. See "Beijing Lasa musilin huandu kaizhaijie," *Renmin ribao,* February 17, 1964, 2; Chen Bo, "Lasa musulin qunti diaocha," 91; Khan, *Muslim, Trader, Nomad, Spy,* 101.

164. NAI, "Monthly Political Report for the Month of January, 1961," Reports (other than annual) from Lhasa (Tibet), External Affairs, R&I, 1961, S. No. 89 6/35/ R&I/61, dated February 6, 1961, 7.

165. Khan, *Muslim, Trader, Nomad, Spy,* 102.

166. NAI, "Monthly Political Report for the Month of September," Reports (other than annual) from Lhasa (Tibet), External Affairs, R&I, 1961, S. No. 89 6/35/ R&I/61, dated October 4, 1961. See also Catriona Bass, *Inside the Treasure House: A Time in Tibet* London: Gollancz, 1990), 72–73.

167. "Monthly Political Report for the Month of November," Reports (other than annual) from Lhasa (Tibet), External Affairs, R&I, 1961, S. No. 89 6/35/ R&I/61, dated December 4, 1961, 2. See Chen Bo, "Muslim Minority—The Case of the Hui Tibetans in Lhasa," 56.

168. "Monthly Political Report for the Month of December," Reports (other than annual) from Lhasa (Tibet), External Affairs, R&I, 1961, S. No. 89 6/35/ R&I/61, dated January 4, 1962, 2.

169. Archive of the Foreign Ministry of the People's Republic of China, 118–01046–01, Telegram from Tibetan Foreign Affairs Office to Foreign Ministry, December 22, 1960, 3. Quoted in Khan, *Muslim, Trader, Nomad, Spy,* 101.

170. "Monthly Political Report for the Month of December," Reports (other than annual) from Lhasa (Tibet), External Affairs, R&I, 1961, S. No. 89 6/35/ R&I/61, dated January 4, 1962, 2.

171. Chen Bo, "Lasa musulin qunti diaocha," 91; Tubten Khétsun and Akester, *Memories of Life in Lhasa under Chinese Rule,* 150–51; Abū Bakr Amīruddīn Tibbatī Nadvī and Sharma, *Tibet and Tibetan Muslims,* 85. Chen Bo concludes that if one includes all people whose participation would later have them labeled traitors to the state (Ch. *panguo jituan*) over 56 individuals were negatively affected. Tubten Khétsun suggests that several of those who were imprisoned were executed in 1970 during the "One Smash and Three Antis" campaign.

172. Tubten Khétsun and Akester, *Memories of Life in Lhasa under Chinese Rule,* 151.

173. Bass, *Inside the Treasure House: A Time in Tibet,* 72–73.

## 6. PRISONERS OF SHANGRI-LA

1. Bstan-'dzin-rgya-mtsho, *Freedom in Exile: The Autobiography of the Dalai Lama* (New York: HarperCollins, 1990), 139–41.

2. As is often the case with such iconic events, the Dalai Lama's journey is often described as one undertaken by a small band of ill-equipped monks. But in his autobiography, although stating that he arrived at the Indian border with "eighty travelers," he also indicated an escort of some 400, with the escape party itself "approaching one hundred people." See Bstan-'dzin-rgya-mtsho, *Freedom in Exile,* 140–44.

3. SWJN, 48: 507.

4. "Report of Speech, New Delhi, 9 April 1959," SWJN, 48: 447.

5. "To Amrit Kaur: Tibetan Refugees," April 11, 1959, SWJN, 48: 451.

6. SWJN, 48: 225.

7. "China Policy," May 9, 1959, SWJN 49: 571–72.

8. Fiona McConnell, *Rehearsing the State: The Political Practices of the Tibetan Government-in-Exile* (Malden, MA: Blackwell, 2016), 54.

9. A.V. Arakeri, *Tibetans in India: The Uprooted People and Their Cultural Transplantation* (New Delhi: Reliance Pub. House, 1998), 34.

10. Bstan-'dzin-rgya-mtsho, *Freedom in Exile*, 151.

11. Ibid.

12. Ibid.

13. Pia A. Oberoi, *Exile and Belonging: Refugees and State Policy in South Asia* (New Delhi: Oxford University Press, 2006), 100.

14. "Tibet's Stateless Nationals III: Tibetan Refugees in India," www.tibetjustice.org/wp-content/uploads/2016/09/TJCIndiaReport2016.pdf, 36.

15. Arakeri, *Tibetans in India*, 34.

16. IKMWA, "Letter to Superintendent of Police, Darjeeling," undated [October 1960]. The letter indicates that Indian border guards will cause delays by opening and inspecting all the luggage.

17. "Tibetans Told to Quit Border Area: 4000 Tibetan Refugees in Darjeeling," *Himalayan Times*, November 6, 1960, 3.

18. IKMWA, "Memorial on Behalf of Indian Kashmiri and Ladakhi Muslims," November 11, 1960.

19. Tina Harris, *Geographical Diversions: Tibetan Trade, Global Transactions* (Athens: University of Georgia Press, 2013), 11.

20. In the early 1950s it was less than 20,000. Likely the semipermanent population in 1960 nearly doubled this number. Kalimpong today is just shy of 50,000 permanent residents. See *India, Census of India 1951: West Bengal (Darjeeling)* (Allahabad: Superintendent, Census Operations, Uttar Pradesh, 1954), i.

21. George Patterson, making light of the fact, notes that the State Oracle (Tib. *chod je*) sold his regalia used in the possession rituals to Prince Peter of Greece. See George Patterson, "Kalimpong: 'The Nest of Spies,'" *Twentieth Century*, June 1958, 527.

22. IKMWA, "Undernoted Poor Widows Destitute Members," n.d. The list enumerates thirty-eight heads of household, totaling 175 individuals.

23. IMEA, "Note given by the Ministry of External Affairs, New Delhi to the Embassy of China in India," October 30, 1963, 92.

24. "4090 Tibetans in Kalimpong," *Himalayan Times*, December 11, 1960, 1.

25. George Woodcock, "Tibetan Refugees in a Decade of Exile," *Pacific Affairs* 43.3 (1970): 415.

26. Ibid., 416. Numerous Tibetan refugees mention the accusations that Chinese spies are among them. See Interview with Wangmo (Interview #67), Tibet Oral History Project, www.tibetoralhistory.org/interviews.html. Even today there are incidents of spying on Tibetan refugees; see "Man Suspected of Spying on Tibetans in Sweden on behalf of China," March 1, 2017, www.thelocal.se/20170301/man-suspected-of-spying-on-tibetans-in-sweden-on-behalf-of-china.

27. "Neither Chance nor Chinese," *Thought* 12.17 (April 23, 1960): 1–2.

28. Patterson, "Kalimpong: 'The Nest of Spies,'" 523.

29. SWJN, 48: 223; Tsering Shakya, in his history of Tibet, notes that Mao also referred to Kalimpong as a place where "they specialize in sabotaging Tibet." Shakya, *Dragon in the Land of Snow*, 158–59.

30. Patterson, "Kalimpong: 'The Nest of Spies,'" 523.

31. SWJN, 49: 550.

32. IMEA, Enclosure to the Government of India, December 20, 1960, 107–8; IMEA, "Note given by the Ministry of External Affairs, New Delhi, to Embassy of China in India," May 23 1962. The local press also highlighted these issues: "Tibetans Told to Quit Border Area: 4000 Tibetan Refugees in Darjeeling," *Himalayan Times*, November 6, 1960, 3; "4090 Tibetans in Kalimpong," *Himalayan Times*, December 11, 1960, 1. See IMEA, "Note given by the Embassy of China in India to the Ministry of External Affairs," February 2, 1961, 111.

33. IKMWA, Dalai Lama Letter to Faizullah Chisti, November 19, 1960, 1. It is instructive to compare the Dalai Lama's change in tone from his May 7, 1959, letter to Nehru, which demanded that "the entire Chinese military force should be withdrawn from Tibet and not a single soldier be left behind." See "Dalai Lama to Nehru, 7 May 1959," SWJN 49: 664.

34. IKMWA, "Letter to First Secretary to the Political Officer in Sikkim," December 18, 1960.

35. IKWMA, "Registered Letter No. 8(3)-NGO/59," February 4, 1961.

36. IKWMA, "Letter to the Dalai Lama," undated [included as enclosure December 18, 1960].

37. IKWMA, "Letter to the Dalai Lama," undated [included as enclosure December 18, 1960].

38. IKWMA, "Letter to the Dalai Lama," undated [included as enclosure December 18, 1960].

39. McGranahan, *Arrested Histories*, 16–17.

40. IKMWA, "List of Kashmiri Traders of Indian Origin with no R.C.s under Form 'B,'" April 4, 1960.

41. IKMWA, "Letter to Consul General for India," February 8, 1961.

42. IKMWA, "Extract from the Resolution of a General Meeting of the Members of Indian Muslims of Kashmiri-Ladakahi origin," November 19, 1960, 1.

43. IKMWA, "List of Indian Muslims Repatriated From Tibet." The list includes names, ages, and occupations.

44. Chisti in correspondence often uses the approximate figures of 800 leaving for Kashmir and 300 remaining in the two hill towns of Darjeeling and Kalimpong. But in a detailed list, the number of Khaches living in Darjeeling District is nearly 400 individuals, with 150 of those in Kalimpong and 250 in Darjeeling. A 1963 letter cites 600 Khaches living in Srinagar, confirming something closer to a 600/400 split. See IKMWA, "Letter to Secretary of the Government of India, [August] 1964; IKMWA, "List of Indian Muslims Repatriated from Tibet Now Residing in Darjeeling District," [1963]; IKMWA, "Letter to M. J. Desai, Ministry of External Affairs," July 15, 1963.

45. IKMWA, "Letter regarding the Dispatch and Rehabilitation of Kashmiri Muslim Evacuees of Indian Nationals," February 2, 1961.

46. IKMWA, "Annexure A," 1961; IKMWA "Letter to Subdivisional Officer, Kalimpong," March 16, 1961.

47. IKMWA, "Letter to Subdivisional Officer, Kalimpong," July 26, 1961; IKMWA, "Letter to Assistant Traffic Superintendent, Siliguri" July 10, 1961; IKMWA, Telegram to Deputy Commissioner Srinagar," August 10, 1961; "Evacuees from Tibet Leave for Srinagar," *Himalayan Times,* July 9, 1961.

48. IKMWA, "Letter to M. J. Desai, Secretary, Ministry of External Affairs," June 28, 1962.

49. IKMWA, "Letter to Faizullah Chisti from P. N. Kaul E.IV/2(123)62," July 7, 1962.

50. IKMWA, "Letter to Deputy Comissioner Darjeeling," February 13, 1963.

51. IKMWA, "Letter to Faizullah Chisti from P. N. Kaul E.IV/2(123)162," August 19, 1963.

52. IKMWA, "Letter to Secretary of the Government of India, [August] 1964. Date confirmed, Interview, Kalimpong, June 4, 2015.

53. IKMWA, "Letter to Political Officer in Sikkim," December 5, 1960; IKMWA, "Letter to Consul General for India in Lhasa," February 2, 1961.

54. IKMWA, "Letter to Political Officer in Sikkim," January 27, 1962.

55. IKMWA, "Letter to S. Sinha, Director Ministry of External Affairs," n.d.

56. IKMWA, "Draft List of Items by Box," January 27, 1962; IKMWA, "Letter to Political Officer in Sikkim," January 27, 1962. The boxes were sent earlier, but because they were delivered without labels or lists, they were unsure how to distribute the items because he had sent the list under separate cover to Assia Bibib Zariff, a Khache widow, to avoid difficulty with the local authorities.

57. IMEA, VIII, "Note given by the Ministry of External Affairs, New Delhi, to the Embassy of China in India," January 1, 1963:

58. IMEA X, "Note given by the Ministry of Foreign Affairs, Peking, to the Embassy of India in China," December 6, 1963, 93.

59. IMEA X, "Note given by the Ministry of External Affairs, New Delhi, to the Embassy of China in India," October 14, 1963, 88.

60. IMEA X, "Note given by the Ministry of External Affairs, New Delhi, to the Embassy of China in India," January 18, 1964, 98–99.

61. IKMWA, "Appeal to Mr. M. C. Chagla, Minister-in-Charge, Foreign Affairs," June 5, 1967.

62. IKMWA, "Letter to Faizullah Chisti from S. P. Chakroborty, No. C411/1/67-TB," July 13, 1967.

63. "List of Indian Muslims Repatriated from TIbet Now Residing in Darjeeling District," [1963].

64. For exact numbers, see IKMWA, "Letter to Prime Minister for Jamou & Kashmir," April 4, 1961; also IKMWA, "Letter to Subdivisional Officer, Kalimpong," March 16, 1961; IKMWA "Letter to Subdivisional Officer, Kalimpong," July 26, 1961. See also Adfar Rashid Shah, "Exploring Ethnicities: A Socio-Cultural Profile of Tibetan Community in Indian Kashmir," *Tibet Journal* 37.3 (2012): 50. See Dawa Norbu, *Red Star over Tibet* (London: Collins, 1974), 147.

65. For a more detailed explanation of this process, see Tremblay, "Kashmir's Secessionist Movement Resurfaces: Ethnic Identity, Community Competition, and the State," *Asian Survey* 49.6 (2009): 926–97; S. P. Sathe, "Article 370: Constitutional Obligations and Compulsions," *Economic and Political Weekly* 25.17 (1990), 932–33.

66. IKMWA, "Letter to Criminal Investigation Department from P. N. Kaul," March 28, 1962; IKMWA, "Telegram to Jawaharlal Nehru," June 18, 1963; IKMWA, "Letter to Secretary, Ministry of Home Affairs," July 15, 1963.

67. IKMWA, "Letter from D.N. Kaul Superintendent of Police, Srinagar," March 28, 1962.

68. Ji Kaiyun, "Zhongdong huaqiao huaren ruogan wenti yanjiu" [Studies on the question of the number of Overseas Chinese in the Middle East], *Zhongdong Wenti Yanjiu* 1 (2015): 141; Justin Jacobs, "Exile Island: Xinjiang Refugees and the 'One China' Policy in Nationalist Taiwan, 1949–1971," *Journal of Cold War Studies* 18.1 (Winter 2016): 192. For many, Kashmir was simply a way station on the way to Turkey or the Middle East, but a considerable number remained in Srinagar.

69. IKMWA, "Letter to Jawaharlal Nehru," June 18, 1963.

70. IKMWA, "Letter to Secretary to the Government of India, Ministry of Home Affairs," July 15, 1963.

71. IKMWA, "Letter to Secretary to the Government of India, Ministry of Home Affairs," July 15, 1963.

72. Masood Butt, "Muslim Tibetan," *Tibetan Bulletin,* January–February 1994, 9; Shah, "Exploring Ethnicities," 50.

73. Monisa Qadri, "Tibetans of Kashmir," originally published in *Rising Kashmir,* January 19, 2013. Revised version: http://igsss.org/blog/tibetans-of-kashmir.

74. Tsarong and Chödron Trinlay, *In the Service of His Country,* 147. These seem likely to be the Siling (Qinghai) Khache mentioned also in the ROC records.

75. Waijiaobu dang'an guan, Zhongyang yanjiuyuan (Taiwan) [Archives of the Ministry of Foreign Affairs, Academia Sinica (Taiwan)], 11-WAA-00382, November 1961, cited in Hyeju Jeong, "A Song of the Red Sea: Communities and Networks of Chinese Muslims in the Hijaz," *Dirasat,* no. 12 (2006): 21. For a firsthand account, see also Bai Yimin, *Maiji zhi you* (Lanzhou: Gansu minzu chubanshe, 2005), 99–102.

76. Ma Bufang was recalled for forcefully marrying his cousin's daughter (often referred to as his "niece"), but he remained in Saudi Arabia until his death in 1975. Yin Ling, "Ma Bufang dang Shate 'Dashi'" [Ma Bufang Serving as Ambassador to Saudi Arabia], *Longmenzhen* 4 (2008): 4–6.

77. Jacobs, "Exile Island," 199.

78. *Foreign Relations of the United States,* vol. 19, Document 370, "Telegram from the Department of State to the embassy in the Republic of China," April 2, 1959, 2473–74.

79. *Foreign Relations of the United States,* vol. 19, Document 370, "Memorandum From the Assistant Secretary of State for Far Eastern Affairs (Parsons) to Secretary of State Herter," October 14, 1959, 2473–74.

80. Oral Interview, Kathmandu, April 4, 2010. Other Khaches suggest that upon arrival in Saudi Arabia visa complications resulted in imprisonment and a return to India. See Fadzakir, "The Muslims of Kathmandu," 50–51.

81. Maulana Abu Ala Maududi, originally from Hyderbad and vociferously anticolonial and pro-Pakistan Islamic state, had close ties to the Saudi royal family and in 1961 had proposed the establishment of an Islamic university in Medina.

82. IKMWA, "Draft Petition to Repatriate to Saudi Arabia," 1969.

83. IKMWA, "Draft Petition to Repatriate to Saudi Arabia," 1969.

84. Chisti's list includes heads of households and individual members of the family totaling over 600 individuals. IKMWA, "List of Khache Petitioning to Migrate to Saudi Arabia" 1969.

85. IKMWA, "Letter to His Majesty the King of Saudi Arabia," n.d. [1969].

86. IKMWA, "Letter to His Majesty the King of Saudi Arabia," n.d. [1969].

87. Carole McGranahan, "Refusal and the Gift of Citizenship," *Cultural Anthropology* 31.3 (2016): 334–41.

88. Ibid., 340.

89. Ibid.

90. Official estimates suggest that by June 1959 over 20,000 Tibetan refugees had arrived in India and eventually that number was in excess of 80,000. Dagmar Bernstorff and Hubertus Welck, *Exile as Challenge: The Tibetan Diaspora* (Hyderabad, India: Orient Longman, 2003), 133.

91. Ibid., 139.

92. Jessica Falcone and Tsering Wangchuk, "'We're Not Home': Tibetan Refugees in India in the Twenty-First Century," *India Review* 7.3 (2008): 167.

93. Woodcock, "Tibetan Refugees in a Decade of Exile," 414.

94. Lobsang Sangay, "Tibet: An Exile's Journey," *Journal of Democracy* 14.3 (2003): 122.

95. Masood Butt became head of the Department of Information and International Relations; Yusef Naik, head of the Department of Health; and Tahir Shamo, head of the Africa and Middle East Office. See Dorjee and Giles, "Cultural Identity in Tibetan Diasporas," 140; Bernstorff and Welck, *Exile as Challenge,* 125; Government of Tibet in Exile, "Tibetan Muslim Conference," November 13, 1995, Dharamsala, India, for an archived version, www.tibet.ca/cms/en/library/wtn/archive/old?y = 1995&m = 11&p = 14_1.

96. Trine Brox, "Constructing a Tibetan Demos in Exile," *Citizenship Studies* 16.(3–4 (2005): 461.

97. In more recent decades, the rejection of the Green Book (and the voluntary tax that accompanies it) has been used by some Tibetans to disassociate themselves from the CTA. For a discussion of this, see Falcone and Tsering Wangchuk, "'We're Not Home,'" 174; See also "Indian Citizenship: A Dilemma for Tibetans," *Contact: A Free Monthly Publication for Tibetan Issues and Community Information,* September 18, 2013, www.contactmagazine.net/articles/indian-citizenship-dilemma-tibetans/.

98. McConnell, *Rehearsing the State,* 136.

99. Brox, "Constructing a Tibetan Demos in Exile," 464; Andrew Heywood, *Politics* (New York: Palgrave, 2002), 69.

100. IKWMA, "Letter to the Dalai Lama," n.d. [1961].

101. "Tibetan Muslim Refugees in Kashmir," *Tibetan Review,* May 1976, 16.

102. Ibid.

103. Dhundup, "Tibetan Muslims Facing Crisis of Identity," *Tibetan Review,* September 1978, 9.

104. Masood Butt, "Muslims of Tibet," *Tibetan Bulletin* (1994): 9.

105. "Tibetans to Become More Active," *Tibetan Review,* December 1995, 9–10.

106. "Sojourn in Kashmir and a Visit to the Tibetan Muslim Community," http://b.buddharocks.org/2012/07/sojourn-in-kashmir-and-visit-to-tibetan_17.html; "The Dalai

Lama Welcomes Tibetan Muslims to Join CTA," Wednesday, July 18, 2012, www.phayul.com/news/article.aspx?id=31759.

107. "Dismantling the Kalachakra Sand Mandala, Visiting Educational Projects and a Lunch Hosted by the Muslim Co-ordination Committee, Leh," www.dalailama.com/news/2014/dismantling-the-kalachakra-sand-mandala-visiting-educational-projects-and-a-lunch-hosted-by-the-muslim-co-ordination-committee-leh

108. Muzaffar Raina, "Dalai Lama Thrills a Corner of Kashmir," *Telegraph India,* July 12, 2012, www.telegraphindia.com/1120715/jsp/nation/story_15730816.jsp.

109. Hakeem Irfan, "No Kashmiri Tibetan Muslims at Dharamshala conference" *Economic Times,* April 28, 2016, http://economictimes.indiatimes.com/news/politics-and-nation/no-kashmiri-tibetan-muslims-at-dharamshala-conference/articleshow/52017585.cms.

110. Fadzakir, "The Muslims of Kathmandu," 52.

111. Tawseef Yousef, Tawheed Yousef, and Shamim Ahmad Shah, "A Micro-level Study on Residential Houses of Tibetan Community in Srinagar," *European Academic Research* 1.5 (2013): 777.

112. "Uyghur, Tibetan Muslims Were Granted Citizenship Rights," *Early Times,* October 17, 2016, www.earlytimes.in/m/newsdet.aspx?q=187254; "Why Modi Government Should Grant J&K Citizenship Rights To Hindu and Sikh Refugees," *Swarajya.* See also https://swarajyamag.com/politics/why-modi-government-should-grant-jandk-citizenship-rights-to-hindu-and-sikh-refugees.

113. "Tibetan Refugees in Srinagar Vote for 'Identity,'" December 15, 2014, http://m.greaterkashmir.com/news/kashmir/tibetan-refugees-in-srinagar-vote-for-identity/182369.html.

114. "Indo-Tibetans of Kashmir," July 23, 2012, www.tibetsun.com/features/2012/07/23/indo-tibetans-of-kashmir.

115. "Reclaiming Their Kashmir Identity: A Story of Indo-Tibetans," *Kashmir Newz,* September 22, 2006, www.kashmirnewz.com/n00039.html.

116. "Indo-Tibetans of Kashmir," July 23, 2012, www.tibetsun.com/features/2012/07/23/indo-tibetans-of-kashmir.

117. *State Bank of India v. Zaffar Ullah Nehru,* Civil Appeal Nos. 12237–12238 (2016): 52–53.

118. *State Bank of India v. Zaffar Ullah Nehru,* Civil Appeal Nos. 12237–12238 (2016): 14.

119. "Tibet's Stateless Nationals III: Tibetan Refugees in India," http://www.tibetjustice.org/wp-content/uploads/2016/09/TJCIndiaReport2016.pdf,107.

120. "Tibetans in India Get Voting Rights after 55 Years," February 13, 2014, www.tibetsun.com/news/2014/02/13/tibetans-in-india-get-voting-rights-after-55-years. Many both inside and outside the Tibetan refugee community have suggested that the rejection of Tibetan applications for Indian citizenship was done at the request of the CTA, since if "all Tibetans in exile in India succeeded in securing Indian citizenship, then the government in exile would not have a constituency to govern." Falcone and Tsering Wangchuk, "'We're Not Home,'" 69.

121. Tenzin Pelkyi, "Tibet in Limbo: An Exile's Account of Citizenship in a World of Nation-States," January 6, 2016, http://thediplomat.com/2016/01/tibet-in-limbo-an-exiles-account-of-citizenship-in-a-world-of-nation-states/.

122. "Anand Bodhi, 25-Yr-Old First Tibetan to Be Indian Citizen," *Times of India,* http://timesofindia.indiatimes.com/india/25-yr-old-first-Tibetan-to-be-Indian-citizen/articleshow/7323090.cms.

123. For an excellent synopsis of India's citizenship laws, see Niraja Gopal Jayal, "Citizenship," in *The Oxford Handbook of the Indian Constitution,* ed. Sujit Choudhry, Madhav Khosla, and Pratap B. Mehta, 2016: 171–79.

124. Paragraph 28, quoted in *Phuntsok Wangyal vs. Ministry of External Affairs; Lobsang Wangyal vs. Union of India; Tenzin Dhonden vs. Union of India,* W.P.(C). 3539/2016, 4275/2016, and 7983/2016.

125. Deepak Parvatiyar, "Tibetans: From Refugees to Voters," December 23, 2014, www.elections.in/blog/tibetans-from-refugees-to-voters/.

126. *Phuntsok Wangyal vs. Ministry of External Affairs; Lobsang Wangyal vs. Union of India; Tenzin Dhonden vs. Union of India,* W.P.(C). 3539/2016, 4275/2016, and 7983/2016.

127. "Tibetans-in-Exile Divided over Right to Vote," January 19, 2015, www.dailypioneer.com/sports/tibetans-in-exile-divided-over-right-to-vote.html.

128. In both the 2005 and 2008 surveys, more than 25 percent of Hui indicated they intended to stay five years or more. See Tanzen Lhundup and Ma Rong, "Temporary Labor Migration in Three Cities, in the Tibet Autonomous Region," *China Tibetology* 2 (September 2011): 16.

129. Wikileaks, March 5, 2008, Chengdu Consulate.

130. Donald S. Lopez, *Prisoners of Shangri-La: Tibetan Buddhism and the West* (Chicago: University of Chicago Press, 1999).

131. Manjari C. Miller. *Wronged by Empire: Post-Imperial Ideology and Foreign Policy in India and China* (Stanford, CA: Stanford University Press, 2013), 81.

132. Gerald James Larson, "Partition: The 'Pulsing Heart that Grieved,'" *Journal of Asian Studies* 73.1 (2014): 5–8.

Abū Bakr Amīruddīn Tibbatī Nadvī and Parmananda Sharma, trans. *Tibet and Tibetan Muslims.* Dharamsala: Library of Tibetan Works and Archives, 2004.

Aitchison, Charles U. *A Collection of Treaties, Engagements and Sanads Relating to India and Neighbouring Countries.* Calcutta: Government of India Central Publication Branch, 1929.

Akasoy, Anna, Charles Burnett, and Ronit Yoeli-Tlalim, eds. *Islam and Tibet: Interactions along the Musk Routes.* Farnham, U.K.: Ashgate, 2010.

Altner, Diana. "Do All the Muslims of Tibet Belong to the Hui Nationality?" In *Islam and Tibet: Interactions along the Musk Routes,* ed. Anna Akasoy, Charles Burnett, and Ronit Yoeli-Tlalim. Farnham, U.K.: Ashgate, 2011, 339–52.

Anand, Dibyesh. "Strategic Hypocrisy: The British Imperial Scripting of Tibet's Geopolitical Identity." *Journal of Asian Studies* 68.1 (2009): 227–52.

Anon. "Dismantling the Kalachakra Sand Mandala, Visiting Educational Projects and a Lunch Hosted by the Muslim Co-ordination Committee, Leh," June 16, 2014. www.dalailama.com/news/2014/dismantling-the-kalachakra-sand-mandala-visiting-educational-projects-and-a-lunch-hosted-by-the-muslim-co-ordination-committee-leh.

Arakeri, A. V. *Tibetans in India: The Uprooted People and Their Cultural Transplantation.* New Delhi: Reliance Pub. House, 1998.

Archive Editions, eds. *Records of the Hajj: A Documentary History of the Pilgrimage to Mecca.* Vols. 1–8. London: Archive Editions, 1993.

Arnold, Thomas W. *Preaching of Islam: A History of the Propagation of the Muslim Faith.* London: Constable & Company, 1913.

Aufschnaiter, Peter. *Peter Aufschnaiter's Eight Years in Tibet.* Bangkok: Orchid Press, 2002.

Bai Yimin. *Maiji zhi you* [Travels to Mecca]. Lanzhou: Gansu Minzu Chubanshe, 2005.

Bailey, Frederick M. *No Passport to Tibet.* London: Hart-Davis, 1957.

Barth, Fredrik. "Enduring and Emerging Issues in the Analysis of Ethnicity." In *The Anthropology of Ethnicity: Beyond "Ethnic Groups and Boundaries,"* ed. Hans Vermeulen and Cora Govers. Amsterdam: Het Sphinhuis, 1994, 11–32.

Bass, Catriona. *Inside the Treasure House: A Time in Tibet.* London: Gollancz, 1990.

Beckwith, Christopher. "The Location and Population of Tibet According to Early Islamic Sources." *Acta Orientalia Academiae* 43 (1989): 163–70.

Bell, Charles A. *The People of Tibet.* Oxford: Clarendon Press, 1928.

———. *Portrait of the Dalai Lama.* London: Collins, 1946.

———. *The Religion of Tibet.* Oxford: Clarendon Press, 1931.

———. *Tibet, Past & Present.* Oxford: Clarendon Press, 1924.

Berger, Patricia A. *Empire of Emptiness: Buddhist Art and Political Authority in Qing China.* Honolulu: University of Hawaii Press, 2003.

Bertsch, Wolfgang. "A Survey of Tibetan Paper Currency." *Bulletin of Tibetology,* n.s., 3 (1996): 3–22.

Betta, Chiara, Caifeng Lan, and Cheng Fang. *The Other Middle Kingdom: A Brief History of Muslims in China.* Indianapolis: University of Indianapolis Press, 2004.

Bhasin, A.S. *Documents on Nepal's Relations with India and China, 1949–66.* Bombay: Academic Books, 1970.

Bishop, Peter. *The Myth of Shangri-La: Tibet, Travel Writing, and the Western Creation of Sacred Landscape.* Berkeley: University of California Press, 1989.

Bista, Dor Bahadur. "Nepalis in Tibet." *Contributions to Nepalese Studies* 8.1 (1980): 2–19.

———. *Report from Lhasa.* Kathmandu: Sajha Prakashan, 1979.

Blondeau, Anne-Marie, Katia Buffetrille, and Wei Jing. *Authenticating Tibet: Answers to China's 100 Questions.* Berkeley: University of California Press, 2008.

Bogle, George. "A Memorandum on the Trade of Tibet." In *Bhutan and Tibet: The Travels of George Bogle and Alexander Hamilton, 1774–1777,* ed. Alastair Lamb. Hertingfordbury: Roxford Books, 2002, 156–60.

Bommarito, Nicolas. "The Khache Phalu: A Translation and Interpretation." *Revue d'Etudes tibétaines* 39 (April 2016): 60–132.

Boulnois, Luce. "Gold, Wool and Musk: Trade in Lhasa in the Seventeenth Century." In *Lhasa in the Seventeenth Century: The Capital of the Dalai Lamas,* ed. Françoise Pommaret. Leiden: Brill, 2003, 133–56.

———. *Poudre d'or et monnaies d'argent au Tibet (principalement au XVIIIe siècle).* Paris: Editions du Centre national de la recherche scientifique, 1983.

Bray, John. "Readings on Islam in Ladakh: Local, Regional and International Perspectives." *Himalaya, Journal of the Association for Nepal and Himalayan Studies* 32.1 (2012): 13–21.

Broomhall, Marshall. *Islam in China: A Neglected Problem.* London: Morgan & Scott, 1910.

Brox, Trine. "Constructing a Tibetan Demos in Exile." *Citizenship Studies* 16.3–4 (2005): 451–67.

'Brug lha (Druk lha). "Bar skor khrom ra'i byung 'phel skor rags tsam bshad pa" [A Brief Discussion on Barkor Market's Origin and Development]. *Krung go'i bod kyi shes rig* 60 (2002): 41–56.

Bstan-,dzin-rgya-mtsho. *Freedom in Exile: The Autobiography of the Dalai Lama.* New York: HarperCollins, 1990.

Bue, Erberto F. Lo. "Scholars, Artists and Feasts." In *Lhasa in the Seventeenth Century: The Capital of the Dalai Lamas,* ed. Francoise Pommaret. Boston: Brill, 2003, 179–98.

Cabezón, José Ignacio. "Islam in the Tibetan Cultural Sphere." In *Islam in Tibet: [And] Tibetan Caravans,* ed. Abdul Wahid Radhu. Louisville, KY: Fons vitae, 1997, 15–34.

———. "Islam on the Roof of the World." *Saudi Aramco World* 49.1 (1998): 12–23.

———. *Tibetan Ritual.* Oxford: Oxford University Press, 2010.

Carrai, Maria. "Learning Western Techniques of Empire: Republican China and the New Legal Framework for Managing Tibet." *Journal of International Law* 30 (2017): 801–26.

Chang Jui-te. "An Imperial Envoy: Shen Zonglian in Tibet, 1943–1946." In *Negotiating China's Destiny in World War II,* ed. Hans Van de Ven, Diana Lary, and Stephen R. MacKinnon. Stanford, CA: Stanford University Press, 2015, 52–69.

Chapman, F. Spencer. *Lhasa, the Holy City.* London: Chatto & Windus, 1938.

Chen Bo. "Lasa musulin qunti diaocha" [Investigation of Lhasa Muslims]. *Xibei minzu yanjiu.* 1 (2000): 87–94.

———. "A Multicultural Interpretation of an Ethnic Muslim Minority: The Case of the Hui Tibetans in Lhasa." *Journal of Muslim Minority Affairs* 23.1 (2003): 41–61.

Chen Jian. "China and the Bandung Conference." In *Bandung Revisited: The Legacy of the 1955 Asian-African Conference for International Order,* ed. See Seng Tan and Amitav Acharya. Singapore: National University of Singapore Press, 2008, 132–59.

———. "The Tibetan Rebellion of 1959 and China's Changing Relations." *Journal of Cold War Studies* 8.3 (2006): 54–101.

Chen Zonglie. "Ershi shiji wu-liu niandai: Cong guizu fudi dao baixing zuofang [The Fifties and Sixties: From the Mansions of Aristocrats to the Workshops of Common People]." *Xizang lüyou* 94.10 (2009): 18–21.

———. *Mu ji xue yu shun jian: 20 shiji wu-liu shiniandai de Xizang* [Witnessing the Snow Land: The Sixties and Fifties in Tibet]. Beijing: Zhongguo Zangxue Chubanshe, 2005.

Cidan Dunzhu [Tsiden Tundrup]. "Lasa jieju musilin shiju yanjiu" [Survey of the Lhasa Muslim Community]. *Meili Zhongguo* 9 (2009): 160.

———. "Xizang qingzhensi kaolüe." *Xizang daxue xuebao (shehui kexue ban)* 29.3 (2014): 96–102.

———. "Xizang Shiju Musilin kaolüe." *Zhongguo Zangxue* 2 (2012): 104–9.

Ciduo. "Lasa Huimin." *Xizang wenxue* 1 (1992): 110–19.

Cieciura, Wlodzimierz. "Ethnicity or Religion? Republican-Era Chinese Debates on Islam and Muslims." In *Islamic Thought in China: Sino-Muslim Intellectual Evolution from the 17th to the 21st Century,* ed. Jonathan N. Lipman. Edinburgh: Edinburgh University Press, 2016, 107–46.

Clinton, Maggie. *Revolutionary Nativism: Fascism and Culture in China, 1925–1937.* Durham, NC: Duke University Press, 2017.

Coleman, William M. "Making the State on the Sino-Tibetan Frontier: Chinese Expansion and Local Power in Batang, 1842–1939." PhD diss., Columbia University, 2014.

Conboy, Kenneth J., and James Morrison. *The CIA's Secret War in Tibet.* Lawrence: University Press of Kansas, 2002.

Cooper, James. "Western and Japanese Visitors to Lhasa: 1900–1950." *Tibet Journal* 28.4 (2003): 91–94.

Cuevas, Bryan J. *The Hidden History of the Tibetan Book of the Dead.* New York: Oxford University Press, 2003.

Cutting, C. Suydam. "In Lhasa—The Forbidden." *Journal of the American Museum of Natural History* 37 (1936): 103–26.

Das, Sarat C., and William W. Rockhill. *Journey to Lhasa and Central Tibet*. New Delhi: Mañjuśrī Pub. House, 1970.

Dastider, Mollica. *Understanding Nepal: Muslims in a Plural Society*. New Delhi: Har-Anand Publications, 2007.

Dawa Norbu, trans. *Khache Phalu's Advice on the Art of Living*. Dharamsala: Library of Tibetan Works and Archives, 1987.

———. "'Otherness' and the Modern Tibetan Identity." *Himāl* 5.3 (May–June 1992): 10–11.

———. *Red Star over Tibet*. London: Collins, 1974.

———. *Tibet: The Road Ahead*. London: Rider, 1997.

———. "Tibet in Sino-Indian Relations: The Centrality of Marginality." *Asian Survey* 37.11 (1997): 1078–95.

———. "1959 Tibetan Rebellion: An Interpretation." *China Quarterly* 77 (1979): 74–93.

Desideri, Ippolito, Michael J. Sweet, and Leonard Zwilling. *Mission to Tibet: the Extraordinary Eighteenth-Century Account of Father Ippolito Desideri, S.J.* Boston: Wisdom Publications, 2010.

Dhompa, Tsering W. *Coming Home to Tibet: A Memoir of Love, Loss, and Belonging*. Boulder, CO: Shambhala, 2016.

Didier, Hughes. *Les Portugais au Tibet: Les premières relations jésuites (1624–1635)*. Paris, 1996.

Ding Weizhi, Le Ge, and Xisheng Jin, eds. *Zhongguo guoqing congshu: Baixianshi jingji shehui diaocha* [Analysis of Economic and Social Characteristics of 100 Counties and Cities in China]. Beijing: Zhongguo dabaike quanshu chubanshe, 1995.

Ding Xiaowen. *Minguo Zang Di "nü Qin Chai" Liu Manqing Zhuan* [Biography of Liu Manqing: A Republican-Era Female Envoy to Tibet]. Nanchang: Ershi yishiji chubanshe, 2013.

Dorjee, Tenzin, and Howard Giles. "Cultural Identity in Tibetan Diasporas." *Journal of Multilingual and Multicultural Development* 26.2 (2005): 138–57.

Downs, James. *Lhassa of Tibet*. New Haven, CT: Human Relations Area Files, 1972.

Dreyfus, George. "Proto-Nationalism in Tibet." In *Tibetan Studies: Proceedings of the 6th Seminar of the International Association for Tibetan Studies, Fagernes*, ed. Per Kværne. Oslo: Institute for Comparative Research in Human Culture, 1994, 205–18.

Dunham, Mikel. *Buddha's Warriors: The Story of the CIA-Backed Tibetan Freedom Fighters, the Chinese Invasion, and the Ultimate Fall of Tibet*. New York: J. P. Tarcher, 2004.

Dbyangs can sgrol dkar, Tsha rong. *Sde dpon mi drag gi sras mo gzhon nu ma zhig gis sge'u khung nas mthong ba'i bod kyi rgyal sa lha sa'i snang tshul mdor bsdus* [Autobiographical Reminiscences on the Social Life and Customs of Lhasa, Tibet and an Account of Her Life and Tsarong Family]. Ed. bkra shis tshe ring. Dharamsala: Amnye Machen Institute, 2006.

Ekvall, Robert B. "The Tibetan Self-Image." *Pacific Affairs* 33.4 (1960): 375–82.

Ernst, Carl W. *Eternal Garden: Mysticism, History, and Politics at a South Asian Sufi Center*. Albany: State University of New York Press, 1992.

Fadzakir, Alfiani. "Muslims of Kathmandu: A Study of Religious Identity in a Hindu Kingdom." PhD diss., Brunel University, 2001.

Fang Jianchang. "Xizang Huizu yu qingzhensi yanjiu de ruogan wenti" [An Examination of the Number of Tibetan Hui and Mosques]. *Huizu yanjiu* 2 (1992): 27–30.

Feng Yan. "Zoujin Xueyu Gaoyuan de musilin" [Muslims on the Snowy Plateau]. *Huizu wenxue* 1 (2014): 55.

Fischer, A. M. "The Muslim Cook, the Tibetan Client, His Lama, and Their Boycott: Modern Religious Discourses of Anti-Muslim Economic Activism in Amdo." In *Conflict and Social Order in Tibet and Inner Asia,* ed. Fernanda Pirie and Toni Huber. Leiden: Brill, 2008, 159–92.

Fisher, Margaret W., and Joan V. Bondurant. *Indian Views of Sino-Indian Relations.* Berkeley, CA: Institute of International Studies, 1956.

Foreign Broadcast Information Service (FBIS). "CPR Interference in Indonesia Scored." December 30, 1959. FRB-59–254.

———. "Corban Observed." June 19, 1959: FRB-59–122.

———. "Speakers Denounce Rebels." April 16, 1959. FRB-59–074.

Frechette, Ann. *Tibetans in Nepal: The Dynamics of International Assistance among a Community in Exile.* New York: Berghahn Books, 2002.

French, Rebecca Redwood. *The Golden Yoke: The Legal Cosmology of Buddhist Tibet.* Ithaca, NY: Cornell University Press, 2002.

Gaborieau, Marc. "La découverte des musulmans du Tibet par les premiers missionnaires portugais." In *Vasco da Gama e a India: Conferência Internacional: Paris, 11–13 Maio, 1998.* Lisbon: Fundação Calouste Gulbenkian, 1999, 41–45.

———. "The Discovery of the Muslims of Tibet by the First Portuguese Missionaries." In *Islam and Tibet: Interactions along the Musk Routes,* ed. Anna Akasoy, Charles Burnett, and Ronit Yoeli-Tlalim. Farnham, U.K.: Ashgate, 2010, 253–80.

———. "Powers and Authority of Sufis among the Kashmiri Muslims in Tibet." *Tibet Journal* 20.3 (1995):21–31.

———. "Les marchands musulmans *kashmírí* au Tibet, au Népal et en Inde du Nord." In *Marchands et hommes d'affaires asiatiques dans l'Océan Indien et la Mer de Chine, 13e-20e siècles,* ed. Denys Lombard and Jean Aubin. Paris: Éditions de l'EHESS, 1988, 195–98.

———. *Minorités musulmanes dans le Royaume Hindou du Népal.* Nanterre: Laboratoire d'ethnologie, 1977.

Gaborieau, Marc, and Ghulām Muh.ammad. *Récit d'un voyageur musulman au Tibet.* Paris: Klincksieck, 1973.

Gellner, David N. *Monk, Householder, and Tantric Priest: Newar Buddhism and Its Hierarchy of Ritual.* Cambridge: Cambridge University Press, 1992.

Giersch, C. Patterson. "Across Zomia with Merchants, Monks, and Musk: Process Geographies, Trade Networks, and the Inner-East–Southeast Asian Borderlands." *Journal of Global History* 5 (2010): 215–39.

———. "Afterword: Why Kham? Why Borderlands? Coordinating New Research Programs for Asia." *Cross-Currents: East Asian History and Culture Review* 19 (2016): 202–13.

Gladney, Dru. "Relational Alterity: Constructing Dungan (Hui), Uygur, and Kazakh Identities across China, Central Asia, and Turkey." *History and Anthropology* 9.4 (1996): 445–77.

Godley, Michael R. "The Sojourners: Returned Overseas Chinese in the People's Republic of China." *Pacific Affairs* 62.3 (1989): 330–52.

Goldstein, Melvyn, and Matthew Kapstein, eds. *Buddhism in Contemporary Tibet: Religious Revival and Cultural Identity.* Berkeley: University of California Press, 1998.

Goldstein, Melvyn C. *A History of Modern Tibet, 1913–1951: The Demise of the Lamaist State.* Berkeley: University of California Press, 1989.

———. *A History of Modern Tibet: The Calm Before the Storm, 1951–1955.* Berkeley: University of California Press, 2007.

———. *A History of Modern Tibet: The Storm Clouds Descend, 1955–57.* Berkeley: University of California Press, 2014.

———. "On Modern Tibetan History: Moving Beyond Stereotypes." In *Tibet and Her Neighbours: A History,* ed. Alex McKay. London: Hansjörg Mayer, 2003, 217–26.

———. *The New Tibetan-English Dictionary of Modern Tibetan.* Berkeley: University of California Press, 2001.

———. "The Revival of Monastic Life in Drepung Monastery." In *Buddhism in Contemporary Tibet: Religious Revival and Cultural Identity,* ed. Melvyn C. Goldstein and Matthew Kapstein. Berkeley: University of California Press, 1998.

Goldstein, Melvyn C., Dawei Sherap, and William R. Siebenschuh. *A Tibetan Revolutionary: The Political Life and Times of Bapa Phüntso Wangye.* Berkeley: University of California Press, 2004.

Gopal, Sarvepalli. *Jawaharlal Nehru: A Biography (Volume Three, 1956–1964).* Cambridge, MA: Harvard University Press, 1976.

Gouin, Margaret. *Tibetan Rituals of Death: Buddhist Funerary Practices.* London: Routledge, 2010.

Green, Nile. *Bombay Islam: The Religious Economy of the West Indian Ocean, 1840–1915.* Cambridge: Cambridge University Press, 2013.

———. "Forgotten Futures: Indian Muslims in the Trans-Islamic Turn to Japan." *Journal of Asian Studies* 72.3 (2013): 611–31.

Gros, Stéphane. "Tricks of the Trade: Debt and Imposed Sovereignty in Southernmost Kham in the Nineteenth to Twentieth Centuries." *Cross-Currents: East Asian History and Culture Review* 19 (2016): 148–73.

Gupta, Akhil. "The Song of the Nonaligned World: Transnational Identities and the Reinscription of Space in Late Capitalism." *Cultural Anthropology* 7.1 (1992): 63–79.

Guyot-Réchard, Bérénice. *Shadow States: India, China and the Himalayas, 1910–1962.* Cambridge: Cambridge University Press, 2017.

Halbfass, Wilhelm. *India and Europe: An Essay in Understanding.* Albany: State University of New York Press, 1988.

Hansen, Peter H. "Tibetan Horizon: Tibet and the Cinema in the Early 20th Century." In *Imagining Tibet: Perceptions, Projections and Fantasies,* ed. Thierry Dodin and Heinz Rather. Boston: Wisdom Publications, 2001, 91–110.

Harrer, Heinrich. *Seven Years in Tibet.* New York: Dutton, 1954.

Harris, Tina. *Geographical Diversions: Tibetan Trade, Global Transactions.* Athens: University of Georgia Press, 2013.

Henry, Gray, Abdul Wahid Radhu, Marco Pallis, and Jane Casewit, eds. *Islam in Tibet.* Louisville, KY: Fons vitae, 1997.

Henss, Michael. *The Cultural Monuments of Tibet: The Central Regions.* 2 vols. New York: Prestel, 2014.

Heywood, Andrew. *Politics.* New York: Palgrave, 2002.

Ho, Daphon David. "The Men Who Would Not Be Amban and the One Who Would: Four Frontline Officials and Qing Tibet Policy, 1905–1911." *Modern China* 34 (2008): 210–46.

Ho, Enseng. *The Graves of Tarim: Genealogy and Mobility across the Indian Ocean*. Berkeley: University of California Press, 2006.

Hobsbawm, Eric J., and Terence O. Ranger. *The Invention of Tradition*. Cambridge: Cambridge University Press, 1983.

Hodgson, Brian Houghton. "Route from Cathmandu in Nepal to Tazedo, on the Chinese Frontier with Some Occasional Allusions to the Manners and Customs of the Bhotiahs, by Amir a Cashmiro-Bhotiah by Birth, and by Vocation an Interpreter to the Traders on the Route Described." *Asiatic Researches* 17 (1832): 513–34.

Hor khang Bsod nams dpal 'bar. "Kha che pha lu'i 'jig rten las 'bras rtsi lugs kyi bslab bya'i nang don la dpyad pa" [Analyzing the Contents of Khache Phalu's Advice on Abiding by the Karma of Life). *Bod ljongs sgyu rtsal zhib 'jug.* 2 (1993): 108–19.

Horlemann, Bianca. 2012. "Tibetans and Muslims in Northwest China: Economic and Political Aspects of a Complex Historical Relationship." *Asian Highlands Perspectives* 21 (2012): 141–86.

Hostetler, Laura. "The Qing Court and Peoples of Central and Inner Asia: Representations of Tributary Relationships from the Huang Qing Zhigong tu." In *Managing Frontiers in Qing China: The Lifanyuan and Libu Revisited,* ed. Dittmar Schorkowitz and Ning Chia. Leiden: Brill, 2017, 192–223.

Hridaya, Chitta D., and Kesar Lall. *Mimmanahpau: Letter from a Lhasa Merchant to His Wife*. New Delhi: Robin Books, 2002.

Hua Xuan. "60 nianqian Zhong-Ni jiaowang miwen" [60-Year-Old Secret Sino-Nepalese Relations]. *Zhongwen xinwen zhoukan,* September 30, 2014.

Huang Luosai. "Lasa Zang-Hui zuqun rentong yanjiu" [Lhasa Zang-Hui ethnic identity]. Master's thesis, Central University of Nationalities, 2007.

Huang Musong. "Shizang Jicheng" [Record of an Envoy's Journey to Tibet]. In *Minguo cangshi shiliao huibian,* ed. Zhang Yuxin and Shuangzhi Zhang, vol. 17: 234–35. Beijing: Xueyuan chubanshe, 2005.

———. *Huang Musong xiansheng yizhu: Xinjiang gaishu Xizang riji* [The Posthumous Work of Huang Musong: Xinjiang and Tibet]. Taibei: Bianzhe kanyinben, 1964.

Huang Yusheng. *Xizang difang yu zhongyang zhengfu guanxi shi* [Relations between Tibet's Local Government and China's Central Government]. Lhasa: Xizang remin chubanshe, 1995.

Huber, Toni. *The Holy Land Reborn: Pilgrimage & the Tibetan Reinvention of Buddhist India*. Chicago: University of Chicago Press, 2008.

Huc, Évariste R. *Souvenirs d'un voyage dans la Tartarie et le Thibet pendant les années 1844, 1845 et 1846*. Vol. 2. Pekin: Imprimerie des Lazaristes, 1924.

Huc, Évariste Régis, and H. d' Ardenne de Tizac. *Souvenirs d'un voyage dans la Tartarie, le Thibet et la Chine*. Paris: Plon-Nourrit et cie, 1925.

Hutt, Michael. Review of *Muna Madan: A Play in the Jhyaure Folk Tradition* by Laxmi Prasad Devkota, Nirala Publications, New Delhi, 1995. *Contributions to Nepalese Studies* 21.2 (1994): 253–57.

India Ministry of External Affairs (IMEA). *Notes, Memoranda and Letters Exchanged and Agreements Signed between the Governments of India and China: White Paper*. Vols. 1–14. [New Delhi]: Ministry of External Affairs, 1959–68.

India Office Library and Records (IOR). [British intelligence on China in Tibet, 1903–1950]. Leiden: IDC, 2002.

Indian Tibetan Muslim Evacuees Welfare Association (IKMEWA). Fazulla Chisti Personal Papers, 1959–69.

Irfan, Hakeem. "No Kashmiri Tibetan Muslims at Dharamshala Conference." *Economic Times,* April 28, 2016, http://economictimes.indiatimes.com/news/politics-and-nation/no-kashmiri-tibetan-muslims-at-dharamshala-conference/articleshow/52017585.cms.

Itty, Abraham. "Bandung and State Formation in Post-Colonial Asia." *In Bandung Revisited: The Legacy of the 1955 Asian-African Conference for International Order,* ed. Seng Tan and Amitav Acharya. Singapore: National University of Singapore Press, 2008, 48–67.

Jacobs, Justin. "Exile Island: Xinjiang Refugees and the 'One China' Policy in Nationalist Taiwan, 1949–1971." *Journal of Cold War Studies* 18.1 (2016): 188–218.

Jagou, Fabienne. "From Lifanyuan to the Mongolian and Tibetan Affairs Commission." In *Managing Frontiers in Qing China: The Lifanyuan and Libu Revisited,* ed. Dittmar Schorkowitz and Ning Chia. Leiden: Brill, 2017, 312–35.

———. "Liu Manqing: A Sino-Tibetan Adventurer and the Origin of a New Sino-Tibetan Dialogue in the 1930s." *Revue d'etudes tibétaines,* no. 17 (October 2009): 5–20.

Jain, Girilal. *India Meets China in Nepal.* New York: Asia Publishing House, 1959.

Jamyang Norbu. "Black Annals: Goldstein and the Negation of Tibetan History." *Phalyul,* www.phayul.com/news/article.aspx?id=22113.

———. "The Lhasa Ripper." In *Trails of the Tibetan Tradition,* ed. Roberto Vitali. Dharamshala: Amnye Machen Institute, 2014, 233–50.

Jayal, Niraja Gopal. "Citizenship." In *The Oxford Handbook of the Indian Constitution,* ed. Sujit Choudhry, Madhav Khosla, and Pratap B. Mehta. Oxford: Oxford University Press, 2016, 163–79.

Jeong, Hyeju. "A Song of the Red Sea: Communities and Networks of Chinese Muslims in the Hijaz." *Dirasat,* no. 12 (2016).

Jest, Corneille. "Kha-che and Gya-Kha-che: Muslim Communities in Lhasa (1990)." *Tibet Journal* 20.3 (1995): 8–20.

Ji Kaiyun. "Zhongdong huiaqiao huaren ruogan wenti yanjiu" [Studies on the Question of the Number of Overseas Chinese in the Middle East]. *Zhongdong wenti yanjiu* 1 (2015): 139–73.

Jian Zhixiang. "Zhongguo zuji tonghun de fazhan qushi chutan—dui renkou pucha shuju de fenxi yu taolun" [The Recent Trend of the Ethnic Intermarriages in China: An Analysis of the Census Data]. *Shehuixue Yanjiu* (2016): 123–45.

Jiao Yingqi. *Xizang zhi* [Gazetteer of Tibet]. Taipei: Wenhai chubanshe, [1721] 1966.

Jiesite Ke'erneiye. "Kaqie he jia-kaqie—Lasa de musilin shequ (Khache and Chinese Khache – Lhasa's Muslim Quarter)" *Xizang minsu* 4 (1997): 11–12.

Jinba Tenzin. "Memory Politics at Work in a Gyalrong Revolt in the Early Twentieth Century." *Cross-Currents: East Asian History and Culture Review* 19 (2016): 174–201.

———. *In the Land of the Eastern Queendom: The Politics of Gender and Ethnicity on the Sino-Tibetan Border.* Seattle: University of Washington Press, 2014.

Joshi, Bhuwan L, and Leo E. Rose. *Democratic Innovations in Nepal: A Case Study of Political Acculturation.* Berkeley: University of California Press, 1966.

'Ju-chen, Thub-bstan-rnam-rgyal (Juchen Thupten Namgyal). *Dpal ldan bka blon khri zur 'juchen thub-bstan-rnam-rgyal mchog gi sku tshe'i lo rgyus dang, brel ba'i nye rabs bod kyi byung ba brjod pa'i gtam tshogs srid pa'i me long zhes bya ba* [The Mirror of Life: The

Autobiography of Former Senior Kalon Juchen Thupten Namgyal, and Related Happenings Pertaining to Tibetan Affairs]. 20 vols. Chauntra, India, 2014.

Kahin, George M. T. *The Asian-African Conference, Bandung, Indonesia, April 1955*. Ithaca, NY: Cornell University Press, 1956.

Kapstein, Matthew. *Buddhism between Tibet and China*. Boston: Wisdom Publications, 2009.

Kapur, Ashok. *India and the South Asian Strategic Triangle*. London: Routledge, 2011.

Kaul, Prem Nath. *Frontier Callings*. Delhi: Vikkas Publishing House, 1976.

Kennedy, Andrew Bingham. *The International Ambitions of Mao and Nehru: National Efficacy Beliefs and the Making of Foreign Policy*. New York: Cambridge University Press, 2012.

Kha che Pha lu. *Kha che pha lu'i 'jig rten las 'bras rtsi lugs kyi bslab bya bzhugs so* [Khache Phalu's Advice on the Art of Living]. New Delhi: n.p. 1968.

———. *Kha che pha lu'i 'jig rten las 'bras rtsi lugs kyi bslab bya bzhugs so* [Khache Phalu's Advice on the Art of Living]. New Delhi: shes rig dpar khang, 2000.

———. *Khache Phalu's Advice on the Art of Living*. Trans. Dawa Norbu. Dharamsala: Library of Tibetan Works and Archives, 1987.

Khan, D. S. "Nepal's Relations with British India." *Regional Studies* 5.3 (1987): 56–85.

Khan, Sulmaan W. *Muslim, Trader, Nomad, Spy: China's Cold War and the People of the Tibetan Borderlands*. Chapel Hill: University of North Carolina Press, 2015.

Khatchikian, Levon. "The Ledger of the Merchant Hovhannes Joughayetsi." In *Merchant Networks in the Early Modern World*, ed. Sanjay Subrahmanyam. Aldershot: Variorum, 1996, 124–58.

Knaus, John K. *Orphans of the Cold War: America and the Tibetan Struggle for Survival*. New York: Public Affairs, 1999.

Kochhar, Geeta, and Pramod Jaiswal. *Unique Asian Triangle: India-China-Nepal*. New Delhi: G. B. Books, 2016.

Kuhn, Philip A. *Chinese among Others: Emigration in Modern Times*. Lanham, MD: Rowman & Littlefield, 2008.

Lamb, Alastair, ed. *Bhutan and Tibet: The Travels of George Bogle and Alexander Hamilton, 1774–1777*. Hertingfordbury, U.K.: Roxford Books, 2002.

Larson, Gerald James. "Partition: The 'Pulsing Heart That Grieved.'" *Journal of Asian Studies* 73.1 (2014): 5–8.

Lee, Christopher J. "Between a Moment and an Era: The Origins and Afterlives of Bandung." In *Making a World after Empire: The Bandung Moment and Its Political Afterlives*, ed. Christopher J. Lee. Athens: Ohio University Press, 2010, 1–42.

Leibold, James. *Reconfiguring Chinese Nationalism: How the Qing Frontier and Its Indigenes Became Chinese*. New York: Palgrave Macmillan, 2007.

Levi, Werner. "Nepal's New Era." *Far Eastern Survey* 28.10 (1959): 150–56;

Lewis, Todd T. "Newar-Tibetan Trade and the Domestication of 'Sim.halasārthabāhu Avadāna.'" *History of Religions* 33.2 (1993): 135–60.

Lewis, Todd T., Subarna M. Tuladhar, and Labh R. Tuladhar. *Popular Buddhist Texts from Nepal: Narratives and Rituals of Newar Buddhism*. Albany: SUNY Press, 2000.

Li, Jianglin. *Tibet in Agony: Lhasa 1959*. Trans. Susan Wilf. Cambridge, MA: Harvard University Press, 2016.

Li, Tiezheng. *Tibet, Today and Yesterday.* New York: Bookman Associates, 1960.

Lin, Hsiao-ting. "The 1934 Chinese Mission to Tibet: A Re-examination." *Journal of the Royal Asiatic Society of Great Britain & Ireland* 12 (2002): 327–41.

———. *Tibet and Nationalist China's Frontier: Intrigues and Ethnopolitics, 1928–49.* Vancouver: University of British Columbia Press, 2006.

Ling, Nai-min. *Tibet, 1950–1967.* Hong Kong: Union Research Institute, 1968.

Liu Liangmo. 1932. "Liu Manqing nüshi ziji de hua" [Miss Liu Manqing in Her Own Words]. *Nüsheng* 1.2 (1932): 5–6.

Liu, Manqing. *Kang-Zang yaozheng* [A Mission to Xikang and Tibet]. Shanghai: Shangwu yinshuguan, 1933.

———. "Xizang youji" [Travels to Tibet]. *Shishi yuebao* 3.3 (1930): 204–5.

Liu, Xuecheng. *Sino-Indian Border Dispute and Sino-Indian Relations.* Lanham, MD: University Press of America, 1994.

Lopez, Donald S. *Prisoners of Shangri-La: Tibetan Buddhism and the West.* Chicago: University of Chicago Press, 1999.

Lopez, Donald S., and Jinpa Thupten. *Dispelling the Darkness: A Jesuit's Quest for the Soul of Tibet.* Cambridge, MA: Harvard University Press, 2017.

Ma Jianye. "Xizang Lasa de Huimin" [Muslims of Lhasa Tibet]. *Huijiao qingnian yuebao* 32 (1947): 12.

Ma Lining. "Jiekai Xizang Musilin shenmi de miansha." [Removing the Mysterious Veil of Islam in Tibet]. *Sichou zhi lu* 19 (2012): 5–14.

Ma, Rong. *Population and Society in Contemporary Tibet.* Hong Kong: Hong Kong University Press, 2010.

Ma Rongjiu. "Domestic Politics and India's Foreign Policy Making in the Sino-Indian Territorial Dispute (1959–1962)." *Journal of Asian Public Policy* 7.1 (2014): 102–13.

Ma Shaoyun and Sheng Meixi, eds. *Weizang tuzhi* [Illustrated Atlas of Western Tibet] Taipei: Wenhai chubanshe, [1792] 1970.

Ma Yingfu. "Musilin de qizhi piaoyang zai Lasa" [The Muslim Banner Flying over Lhasa]. *Qingzhen bao* 32 (1947): 8–9.

Mackie, J. A. C. "Anti-Chinese Outbreaks in Indonesia, 1959–1968." In *The Chinese in Indonesia: Five Essays,* ed. J. A. C. Mackie. Honolulu: University Press of Hawaii, 1976, 77–138.

Manen, Johan van. "Khacche Phalu: A Tibetan Moralist." In *Sir Asutosh Mookerjee Silver Jubilee Volumes,* vol. 3. Calcutta: Calcutta University, 1925, 147–85.

Mao, Yufeng. "When Zhou Enlai Met Gamal Abdel Nasser." In *Bandung 1955: Little Histories,* ed. Antonia Finnane and Derke McDougall. Caulfield, Australia: Monash University Press, 2010, 89–108.

———. 2011. "A Muslim Vision for the Chinese Nation: Chinese Pilgrimage Missions to Mecca during World War II." *Journal of Asian Studies* 70.2 (2011): 373–95.

Mao Zedong. *Mao Zedong xizang gongzuo wenxuan* [A Selection of Mao Zedong's Writings on Tibet]. Beijing: Zhongyang wenxian chubanshe, 2001.

Markham, Clements R., George Bogle, and Thomas Manning. *Narratives of the Mission of George Bogle to Tibet: And of the Journey of Thomas Manning to Lhasa.* London: Trübner and Co., 1879.

Mathou, Thierry. "Bhutan-China Relations: Towards a New Step in Himalayan Politics." In *The Spider and the Piglet: Proceedings of the First International Seminar on Bhutan*

*Studies,* ed. Karma Ura and Sonam Kinga. Thimphu: Centre for Bhutan Studies, 2004, 388–411.

McCallum, H. J. *Tibet: One Second to Live: A Pilot's Story.* Emlenton, PA: Staab Typographic, 1995.

McConnell, Fiona. *Rehearsing the State: The Political Practices of the Tibetan Government-in-Exile.* Malden, MA: Blackwell, 2016.

McGranahan, Carole. *Arrested Histories: Tibet, the CIA, and Memories of a Forgotten War.* Durham, NC: Duke University Press, 2010.

———. "Refusal and the Gift of Citizenship." Cultural Anthropology 31.3 (2016): 334–41.

McKay, Alex. *Tibet and Her Neighbours: A History.* London: Hansjörg Mayer, 2003.

———. *Tibet and the British Raj: The Frontier Cadre, 1904–1947.* Richmond, Surrey: Curzon, 1997.

———. "Kicking the Buddha's Head: India, Tibet and Footballing Colonialism." In *Soccer in South Asia: Empire, Nation, Diaspora,* ed. Paul Dimeo and James Mills. New York: Routledge, 2013, 89–104.

Mehra, Parshotam. *From Conflict to Conciliation: Tibetan Polity Revisited. A Brief Historical Conspectus of the Dalai Lama–Panchen Lama Standoff, ca. 1904–1989.* Wiesbaden: Harrassowitz, 2004.

Meng, Bao. *Xizang zoushu* [Memorials on Tibet]. Taibei: Guangwen shuju, [1852] 1978.

Meng, C. Y. W. "Miss Liu's Mission to Tibet." *China Weekly Review,* September 6, 1930, 22.

Menon, Dilip M. *Cultural History of Modern India.* New Delhi: Social Science Press, 2006.

Metternich, Clemens W. L. *Mémoires, Documents et écrits divers laissés par le Prince de Metternich, Chancelier de Cour et d'état: Pub. par son fils le Prince Richard de Metternich, classés et réunis par M.a. de Klinkowström.* Paris: E. Plon, Nourrit et cie, 1881.

Miller, Manjari C. *Wronged by Empire: Post-Imperial Ideology and Foreign Policy in India and China.* Stanford CA: Stanford University Press, 2013.

Millward, James A. *Eurasian Crossroads: A History of Xinjiang.* New York: Columbia University Press, 2007.

Ministry of External Affairs (MEA), Government of India. *Notes, Memoranda and Letters Exchanged and Agreements Signed between the Governments of India and China: White Paper.* Vols 1–14. [New Delhi], 1959–68.

Minorsky, Vladimir, V. V. Bartol'd, and Clifford Edmund Bosworth. *Hudūd al-'Ālam; "The Regions of the World"; a Persian Geography, 372 A.H.–982 A.D.* London: Luzac, 1970.

Mishra, Tirtha P. "A Critical Assessment of the Nepal-Tibet Treaty 1856." In *Tibet and Her Neighbours: A History,* ed. Alex McKay. London: Hansjörg Mayer, 2003, 137–46.

———. "Nepalese in Tibet: A Case Study of Nepalese Half-Breeds (1856–1956)." *Nepalese Studies* 30.1 (2003): 1–18.

Moreaes, F. R. *The Revolt in Tibet.* New York: Macmillan, 1960.

Mosca, Matthew W. *From Frontier Policy to Foreign Policy: The Question of India and the Transformation of Geopolitics in Qing China.* Stanford: Stanford University Press, 2013.

———. "Kashmiri Merchants and Qing Intelligence Networks in the Himalayas: The Ahmed Ali Case of 1830." In *Asia Inside Out: Connected Places,* ed. Eric Tagliacozzo, Helen F. Siu, Peter Perdue. Cambridge, MA: Harvard University Press, 2015, 219–42.

Mozingo, David P. *Chinese Policy toward Indonesia, 1949–1967.* Ithaca, NY: Cornell University Press, 2007.

———. "The Sino-Indonesian Dual Nationality Treaty." *Asian Survey* 1.10 (1961): 25–31.

Mthar phyin [Tharchin], ed. "Rgya nag gi pho nya?" [Envoy of China?]. *Yul phyogs so so'i gsar 'gyur me long* [Tibetan Mirror] 5.1 (June 27, 1930): 2–3.

Mullaney, Thomas S. *Coming to Terms with the Nation: Ethnic Classification in Modern China.* Berkeley: University of California Press, 2011.

Mun pa thar. "Kha che pha lu'i bslab bya dngos sgrub chu mig ces bya ba'i sgyu rtsal rang bzhin skor che long tsam brjod pa" [A Discussion on the Artful Nature of Khache Phalu's Advice on the Art of Living]. *Bod ljongs sgyu rtsal zhib 'jug* 2 (1989): 45–55.

Naik, Yusuf. "Memories of My Father, Abdul Ghani, in Tibet." *Tibet Journal* 20.3 (1995): 31–35.

Nehru, Jawaharlal. "Policy regarding China and Tibet (18 November 1950)." In *Selected Works of Jawaharlal Nehru,* ed. S. Gopal. New Delhi: Jawaharlal Nehru Memorial Fund, 2nd ser., vol. 4, pt. 2 (1984): 342–46.

Newman, John. "Islam in the Kālacakra." *Journal of the International Association of Buddhist Studies* 21.2 (1998): 311–72.

*New York Times.* "India's Traders Held by Chinese: New Delhi Says Reds Detain Five in Tibet and Prevent Hundreds from Returning." August 12, 1959, 2.

Oberoi, Pia A. *Exile and Belonging: Refugees and State Policy in South Asia.* New Delhi: Oxford University Press, 2006.

Ortner, Sherry B. *High Religion: A Cultural and Political History of Sherpa Buddhism.* Princeton, NJ: Princeton University Press, 1989.

Pant, Y. P. "Nepal-China Trade Relations." *Economic Weekly,* April 14, 1962, 621–24.

Patterson, George N. "The Five Fingers of China." *Indian Review* (February 1965): 57.

———. *God's Fool.* Garden City, NY: Doubleday, 1957.

———. "Kalimpong: 'The Nest of Spies.'" *Twentieth Century* (June 1958): 523–31.

Petech, Luciano. *I missionari italiani nel Tibet e nel Nepal.* Rome: Libreria dello Stato, 1952.

Pollock, Sheldon. "Rāmāyana and Political Imagination in India." *Journal of Asian Studies* 52.2 (1993): 261–97.

Pommaret, Françoise. "The Mon-pa Revisited: In Search of Mon." In *Sacred Spaces and Powerful Places in Tibetan Culture,* ed. Toni Huber. Dharamsala: Library of Tibetan Works and Archives, 1999, 52–73.

Powers, John. *Introduction to Tibetan Buddhism.* Ithaca, NY: Snow Lion Publications, 1995.

Powers, John, and David Templeman. *Historical Dictionary of Tibet.* Metuchen, NJ: Scarecrow Press, 2012.

Prince Peter of Greece. "The Moslems of Central Tibet." *Asian Affairs* 39.3–4 (1951): 232–40.

Radhu, Abdul Wahid. *Islam in Tibet: [And] Tibetan Caravans.* Louisville: Fons Vitae, 1997.

Rahul, Ram. *The Government and Politics of Tibet.* Delhi: Vikas Publications, 1969.

———. "The Government of Tibet." *International Studies* 4.2 (1962): 169–93.

———. "Kashmiri Muslims in Tibet." *International Studies* 3.2 (1961): 181–83.

Raina, Muzaffar. "Dalai Lama Thrills a Corner of Kashmir." *Telegraph India,* July 12, 2012. www.telegraphindia.com/1120715/jsp/nation/story_15730816.jsp [accessed March 2, 2017].

Rajesh, M. N. "A Case Study of Tibetan Muslims." In *Approaching Islam,* ed. R. L. Hangloo. New Delhi: Black and White, 2005, 203–14.

Ramble, Charles. "Whither, Indeed, the Tsampa Eaters." *Himāl* 6.5 (1993): 21–25.

Rech, Ernesto. "Il Nepal e la Repubblica popolare cinese." *Cina* 3 (1957): 108–9.

*Renmin Ribao.* "Huanhu zhengfu wei xizang renmin chuhai; Qingzhu xizang renmin zouxiang xinsheng, Xizang renmin relie yonghu taoping panni" [Hail the government for removing the Tibetan people from harm's way; Celebrate the Tibetan people's moving towards a new life; The Tibetan people fervently endorse the suppression of the rebels]. April 2, 1959, 1.

———. "Miejue renxing lingren fazhi, Xizang panfei waxin sharen zui'e taotian" [Inhuman! Deplorable! Tibetan Rebels Heinously Murder by Ripping Out Hearts]. April 26, 1959, 4.

———. "Xizang panfei de 'weijiao jun'—yiguan qinshou he pizhe jiasha de chailang" [Tibetan Rebels 'Protect Religion Army'—Animals Dressed in Nice Clothes; Wolves Wearing Monk's Robes]. May 5, 1959, 2.

———. "Xizang panguo jituan biran miewang Xizang renmin qiantu guangming canlan Jiefang jun yi xunsu pingding lasa panluan Zai sengsu gejie aiguo renmin xiezhu xia Zheng chengsheng qianjin saodang xizang qita difang de panfei" [The traitorous Tibetan clique is certain to be exterminated; The future of Tibet's people is bright and glorious; PLA swiftly pacifies Lhasa armed rebellion, and with help from clergy and lay patriots, mop up Tibetan traitorous elements in other areas]. March 29, 1959, 1.

———. "Xizang renmin yongyuan zhongyu zuguo, Lasa liang wan ren kongqian da shiwei, Zai budalagong qian renmen fenfen kongsu panfei de taotian zuixing" [The Tibetan People Are Forever Loyal to the Homeland; An Unprecedented Twenty-Thousand People Hold Rally in Lhasa in Front of the Potala Palace; People One After the Other Denounce the Rebels' Monstrous Crimes]. April 16, 1959, 1–2.

Richardson, Hugh. "Foreigners in Tibet." In *High Peaks, Pure Earth: Collected Writings on Tibetan History and Culture,* ed. Michael Aris, London: Serindia Publications, 1998, 409–19.

———. *High Peaks, Pure Earth: Collected Writings on Tibetan History and Culture.* Ed.. Michael Aris, London: Serindia Publications, 1998.

Richardus, Peter, and Alex McKay. *Tibetan Lives: Three Himalayan Autobiographies.* Richmond, Surrey: Curzon, 1998.

Rizvi, Janet. "Leh to Yarkand: Travelling the Trans-Karakoram Trade Route." In *Recent Research on Ladakh 7: Proceedings of the 7th Colloquium of the International Association for Ladakh Studies, Bonn/St. Augustin, 12–15 June 1995,* ed. T. Dodin and H. Räther. Ulm: Universität Ulm, 1997, 379–411.

Rnam rgyal rgya mtsho (Namgyal Gyatso). *Bod rje chos rgyal gyi gdun rgyud sde dpon lha-rgya-ri,i gdun rabs rin chen phren ba* [The Precious Garland: A History of the Descendants of the Tibetan King Lha-rgyari-sde dpon]. New Delhi: Dpal 'byor dpar skrun khañ, 1999.

Roche, Gerald. "The Tibetanization of Henan's Mongols: Ethnicity and Assimilation on the Sino-Tibetan Frontier." *Asian Ethnicity* 17.1 (2015): 128–49.

Roche, Gerald, and Hiroyuki Suzuki. "Mapping the Minority Languages of the Eastern Tibetosphere." *Studies in Asian Geolinguistics* 6 (2017): 28–42.

Roemer, Stephanie. *The Tibetan Government-in-Exile: Politics at Large.* London: Routledge, 2008.

Rose, Leo E. *Nepal: Strategy for Survival.* Berkeley: University of California Press, 1971.

Saksena, Shibbanlal. "Dr. K. I. Singh." *National Herald* (Lucknow), November 18, 1955, 4.

Samuel, Geoffrey. *Civilized Shamans: Buddhism in Tibetan Societies.* Washington, DC: Smithsonian Institution Press, 1993.

———. "Songs of Lhasa." *Ethnomusicology* 20.3 (1976): 407–49.

Sandberg, Graham. *Tibet and the Tibetans.* London: Society for Promoting Christian Knowledge, 1906.

Schwieger, Peter. *The Dalai Lama and the Emperor of China: A Political History of the Tibetan Institution of Reincarnation.* New York : Columbia University Press, 2015.

Scott, James C. *The Art of Not Being Governed: An Anarchist History of Upland Southeast Asia.* New Haven, CT: Yale University Press, 2009.

Shah, Adfar Rashid. "Exploring Ethnicities: A Socio-Cultural Profile of the Tibetan Community in Indian Kashmir." *Tibet Journal* 37.3 (2012): 47–70.

Shakabpa, W. D. *Tibet: A Political History.* New Haven, CT: Yale University Press, 1967.

Shakabpa, W. D., and Derek F. Maher. *One Hundred Thousand Moons: An Advanced Political History of Tibet.* Leiden: Brill, 2010.

Shakya, Tsering. *Dragon in the Land of Snow: A History of Modern Tibet since 1947.* New York: Columbia University Press, 1999.

———. "Whither the Tsampa Eater." *Himāl* 6.5 (1993): 8–11.

Sharma, Triloki Nath. "The Predicament of Lhasa Muslims in Tibet." *Journal of the Institute of Muslim Minority Affairs* 10.1 (1989): 21–27.

Sheikh, Abdul Ghani. "Tibetan Muslims." *Tibet Journal* 16.4 (1991): 86–89.

Shichor, Yitzhak. *East Wind over Arabia: Origins and Implications of the Sino-Saudi Missile Deal.* Berkeley: Institute of East Asian Studies [and] Center for Chinese Studies, University of California, 1989.

Shneiderman, Sara. "Barbarians at the Border and Civilising Projects: Analysing Ethnic and National Identities in the Tibetan Context." In *Tibetan Borderlands,* ed. Paul Christiaan Klieger. Leiden: Brill, 2006, 9–34.

Siddiqui, Ataullah. "Muslims of Tibet." *Tibet Journal* 14.4 (1991): 71–85.

Sinclair, William B., and Robert E. Crozier. *Jump to the Land of God: The Adventures of a United States Air Force Crew in Tibet.* Caldwell, ID: Caxton Printers, 1965.

Singh, Rohit. "Reimagining Tibet through the Lens of Tibetan Muslim History and Identity." *Oxford Handbooks Online,* Oxford University Press. www.oxfordhandbooks. com/view/10.1093/oxfordhb/9780199935420.001.0001/oxfordhb-9780199935420-e-7.

Smith, Warren W. *China's Tibet? Autonomy or Assimilation.* Lanham, MD: Rowman and Littlefield, 2008.

Song, Liming. 1997. "General Huang Musong's Mission to Lhasa and the Sino-Tibetan Negotiations in 1934." In *Proceedings of the 7th Seminar of the International Association for Tibetan Studies, Graz 1995,* vol. 2: 903–16, ed. Helmut Krassner and Ernst Steinkellner. Vienna: Verlag der Österreichischen Akademie der Wissenschaften.

Sperling, Elliot. "Tibet and China: The Interpretation of History since 1950." *China Perspectives* 3.79 (2009): 25–37.

Starks, Richard, and Miriam Murcutt. *Lost in Tibet: The Untold Story of Five American Airmen, a Doomed Plane, and the Will to Survive.* Guilford, CT: Lyons Press, 2012.

Stein, R. A. *Tibetan Civilization.* Stanford, CA: Stanford University Press, 1972.

Steinberg, S. H. *The Statesman's Year Book: Statistical and Historical Annual of the States of the World for the Year 1957.* London: Macmillan, 1957.

Steinmann, Brigitte. "National Hegemonies, Local Allegiances: Historiography and Ethnography of a Buddhist Kingdom." *European Bulletin of Himalayan Research* 25–26 (Autumn 2003–Spring 2004): 145–67.

Sum pa mkhan po ye shes dpal 'byor. *Chos 'byung dpag bsam ljon bzang* [The Wish-Fulfilling Tree: A History of Buddhism]. Lanzhou: Kan su'u mi rigs dpe skrun khang, 1992.

Suo Qiong. "Fofa shengdi de yisilan wenming" [Islamic Culture in a Buddhist Sacred Land]. *Xizang minsu* 4 (2002): 55–61.

Tagliacozzo, Eric. *Secret Trades, Porous Borders: Smuggling and States along a Southeast Asian Frontier, 1865–1915.* New Haven, CT: Yale University Press, 2009.

Tan, Gillian. "An Ethnography of Life and Changes among Tibetan Nomads of Minyag Dora Karmo, Ganzi Tibetan Autonomous Prefecture, Sichuan Province." *Études mongoles et sibériennes, centrasiatiques et tibétaines* 43–44 (2013). http://emscat.revues.org/2111.

Tan, See Seng, and Amitave Acharaya. Introduction to *Bandung Revisited: The Legacy of the 1955 Asian-African Conference for International Order,* ed. See Seng Tan and Amitave Acharaya. Singapore: National University of Singapore Press, 2008.

Tan Chee-Beng. "Reterritorialization of a Balinese Chinese Community in Quanzhou, Fujian." *Modern Asian Studies* 44.3 (2010): 547–66.

Taring, Rinchen D. *Daughter of Tibet.* London: Murray, 1970.

Thondup, Gyalo, and Anne F. Thurston. *The Noodle Maker of Kalimpong: The Untold Story of My Struggle for Tibet.* New York: Persus Books Group, 2015.

Thum, Rian. *The Sacred Routes of Uyghur History.* Cambridge, MA: Harvard University Press, 2014.

*Tibetan Review.* "Tibetan Refugees in Kashmir." May 15–17, 1976.

*Times of India.* "5 Indian Muslims Held in Tibet." February 18, 1964, 5.

———. "Five Indians Held in Custody by Chinese." September 8, 1959, 3.

———. "Kashmiri Muslim Families Return." November 16, 1960, 1.

———. "Plea on Kashmiri Muslims in Tibet Rejected by China." February 27, 1960, 1.

———. "Red Terror in Tibet: Nepalese Muslims' Experience." August 6, 1960, 1.

———. "Tibetan Refugees for Sikkim." October 1, 1960, 7.

Tontini, Roberta. *Muslim Sanzijing: Shifts and Continuities in the Definitions of Islam in China.* Leiden: Brill, 2016.

Tsarong, Dundul Namgyal, and Trinlay Chödron. *In The Service of His Country: The Biography of Dasang Damdul Tsarong, Commander General of Tibet.* Ithaca, NY: Snow Lion Publications, 2000.

Tsering, Topgyal. "Identity Insecurity and the Tibetan Resistance against China." *Pacific Affairs* 86.3 (2013): 515–38.

Tshe-dbang rnam-rgyal. "Khache Pha lu'i bslab bya dngos grub chu mig ces bya bar dbye zhib kyi lta tshul rags tsam gleng ba" [A Brief Analytical Discussion on the Khache Phalu's Advice on the Art of Living]. *Bod kyi rtsom rig sgyu rtsal* 8.4 (1981): 36–42.

Tshe rdor. "Lha sa'i kha che" [Lhasa Khache]. *Bod kyi rtsom rig sgyu rtsal.* 4 (1992): 112–28.

Tsing, Anna Lowenhaupt. "*Adat*/Indigenous: Indigeneity in Motion." *Words in Motion: Toward a Global Lexicon.* Durham, NC: Duke University Press, 2009.

Tsybikov, Gombozhab T. *A Buddhist Pilgrim at the Shrines of Tibet.* Leiden: Brill, 2017.

———. "Lhasa and Central Tibet." *Annual Report of the Board of Regents of the Smithsonian Institution, 1903.* Washington, DC: Smithsonian Institution, 1904, 727–46.

———. "Journey to Tibet." *Geographical Journal* 23.1 (1904): 92–97.

Tubten Khétsun [Thus bstan mkhas btsun]. *dka' sdug 'og gi byung ba brjod pa* [An account of Painful Events]. Dharamsala: shes rig dpar khang, 1998.

Tubten Khétsun, and Matthew Akester. *Memories of Life In Lhasa under Chinese Rule.* New York: Columbia University Press, 2008.

Tucci, Giuseppe, and Wim Swaan. *Tibet, Land of Snows.* New York: Stein and Day, 1967.

Turner, Samuel. *An Account of an Embassy to the Court of the Teshoo Lama, in Tibet: Containing a Narrative of a Journey through Bootan, and Part of Tibet.* London: Printed by W. Bulmer, 1800.

Tuttle, Gray. *Tibetan Buddhists in the Making of Modern China.* New York: Columbia University Press, 2005.

United Nations. "No. 4307—Agreement between the Republic of India and the People's Republic of China on Trade and Intercourse between Tibet Region of China and India, (April 29, 1954)." Treaty series: treaties and international agreements registered or filed and recorded with the Secretariat of the United Nations, vol. 299: 59–81.

Upadhya, Sanjay. *Nepal and the Geo-Strategic Rivalry between China and India.* London: Routledge, 2012.

Uprety, Prem R. *Nepal-Tibet Relations, 1850–1930: Years of Hopes, Challenges, and Frustrations.* Kathmandu: Puga Nara, 1980.

———. "Treaties between Nepal and Her Neighbors: A Historical Perspective." *Tribhuvan University Journal* 19.1 (1996): 15–24.

Ura, Karma, and Sonam Kinga, eds. *The Spider and the Piglet: Proceedings of the First International Seminar on Bhutan Studies.* Thimphu: Centre for Bhutan Studies, 2004.

Vasantkumar, Chris. 2012. "What Is This 'Chinese' in Overseas Chinese? Sojourn Work and the Place of China's Minority Nationalities in Extraterritorial Chinese-ness." *Journal of Asian Studies* 71.2 (2012): 423–46.

Vitali, Roberto, ed. *Trails of the Tibetan Tradition.* Dharamsala: Amnye Machen Institute, 2014.

Waddle, L. Austine. *Lhasa and Its Mysteries with a Record of the Expedition of 1903 to 1904.* London: Methuen & Co., 1905.

Waller, Derek M. *The Pundits: British Exploration of Tibet and Central Asia.* Lexington: University Press of Kentucky, 1990.

Walt van Pragg, Michael C. *The Status of Tibet: History, Rights, and Prospects in International Law.* Boulder, CO: Westview Press, 1987.

Wang Gungwu. "The Question of the 'Oversea Chinese.'" *Journal of Southeast Asian Affairs* (1976): 101–10.

Wang Shengmin. "You Lasa ji" [Travels to Lhasa: West to Tibet from Sichuan]. *Xuesheng,* 1917, 4.8 (1917): 189–90.

Weber, Max. *Economy and Society.* Trans. Ephraim Fischof. Berkeley: University of California Press, 1978.

Weise Zerenduoji [Tsering Woeser]. *Sha jie: Sishi nian de jiyi jinqu, jingtouxia de Xizang wenge* [Forbidden Memory: Tibet during the Cultural Revolution]. Taipei: Dakuai wenhua chuban, 2006.

———. "*Santiao laojie ganshou xinjiu Lasa*" [Encountering Old and New Lhasa through Three Old Streets]. http://tibet.woeser.com/?p=19552.

Wenqing, Zhen Jia, and Baoyun, eds. *Chouban yiwu shimo* [The Complete Record on Managing Foreign Affairs]. Taipei: Guofeng chubanshe, [1930] 1963.

Wu, Fengpei, and Songyun. *Xizang zhi - Weizang tongzhi* [Combined edition of Gazetteer of Tibet–General history of Ü-Tsang Tibet]. Lhasa: Xizang renmin chubanshe, [1721] 1982.

Wu Junkui. "Ka-shi-mi-er musilin linka, libaitang yu mudi [Kashmiri Muslim garden, mosque and cemetary]." In *Lasa wen wu zhi*. Lhasa: Xizang zizhiqu wenwuguan liwei yuanhui, 1985.

Xinhua News Agency. "Communiqué on the Revolt," March 28, 1959. In *Tibet, 1950–1967*, ed. Ling Nai-min. Hong Kong: Union Research Institute, 1968, 350.

*Xizang Ribao* [Tibet Daily]. "Untitled." December 27, 1957. In *Tibet, 1950–1967*, ed. Ling Nai-min. Hong Kong: Union Research Institute, 1968, 520.

Xizang Zizhiqu Wenwu Guanli Weiyuan huibian. *Lasa wenwu zhi* [A Survey of Cultural Relics in Lhasa]. n.p., 1985.

Xu Chengcang. *Lasa shi zhi* [Gazetteer of Lhasa City]. Beijing Shi: Zhongguo zang xue chubanshe, 2008.

Xu Baiyong and Sa Renna. "Guomin zhengfu shiqi de guoli Lasa xiaoxue ji qi chuangban zhi yiyi" [Primary School of Lhasa and the Significance of Its Foundation during the Republic of China]. *Xizang Yanjiu* 1 (2008): 1–9.

Xu Guangqiu. "The Issue of US Air Support for China during the Second World War, 1942–45." *Journal of Contemporary History* 36.3 (2001): 466–67.

Xu Guangzhi, Dawa, and Jun Zhao. *Yapian zhanzheng qian-hou Xizang bainian lishi (1793–1893)* [One Hundred Years of Tibetan History before and after the Opium War, 1793–1893]. Beijing: Minzu chubanshe, 2011.

Xue Wenbo. "Lasa de Huizu" [Lhasa's Hui]. *Gansu minzu yanjiu* 2 (1986): 68–76.

———. *Xueling Chongze*. Vol. 2. Lanzhou: Xindaxiao yingchang chubanshe, 1999.

Yang Gongsu. *Cangsang jiushi nian: yige waijiao teshi di huiyi*. Haike: Hainan chubanshe, 1999.

Yang Fangcan. *Sichuan tongzhi* [Gazetteer of Sichuan]. Taibei: Huawen Shuju, [1816] 1967.

Yang Xiaochun. "The Festival of Fast-Breaking Eid al-Fitr in the Great Mosque of Lhasa: Some Observations." *Études mongoles et sibériennes, centrasiatiques et tibétaines* 47 (December 2016). http://emscat.revues.org/2867.

Yang Xiaoqun. "Guonei guanyu Xizang shiju musilin yanjiu shuping" [Review of Domestic Studies of Indigenous Muslims]. *Minzu Yanjiu* 3 (2011): 127–35.

Yeh, Emily. "Living Together in Lhasa: Ethnic Relations, Coercive Amity and Subaltern Cosmopolitanism." In *The Other Global City*, ed. Shail Mayaram. New York: Routledge, 2009, 54–85.

———. "Tibetan Indigeneity: Translations, Resemblances, and Uptake." In *Indigenous Experience Today*, ed. Marisol de la Cadena and Orin Starn. Oxford: Berg, 2007, 69–98.

Yin Ling. "Ma Bufang dang Shate 'Dashi'" [Ma Bufang Serving as Ambassador to Saudi Arabia]. *Longmenzhen* 4 (2008): 4–6.

Yiwu. "Xizang Huimin" [Tibet's Hui]. *Yuehua* 16.4–6 (1946): 12.

Zarcone, Thierry, and V. V. Bartol'd. *Musulmans et soufis du Tibet*. Milan: Archè, 2005.

Zhang Chunxiu. "Lasa de Qingzhensi he musilin mudi" [Mosques and Muslim Cemeteries of Lhasa]. *Zhongguo Musilin* 1 (2002): 27–28.

Zhang Ruide. "'Qinchai' Shiming: Shen Zonglian zai Lasa (1943–1946)" [An "Imperial" Mission: Shen Zonglian in Tibet, 1943–1946]. *Zhongyan Yanjiuyuan: Jindaishi Yanjiusuo Jikan* 67 (2010): 59–96.

Zhongguo Dier Lishi Dang'anguan Zhongguo Zangxue Yanjiu Zhongxin, eds. *Huang Musong, Wu Zhongxin, Zhao Shouyu, Dai Zhuanxian fengshi banli zangshi baogao shu*

[Huang Musong, Wu Zhongxin, Zhao Shouyu, Dai Zhuanxian: Reports of Envoys Sent to Handle Tibetan Affairs]. Beijing: Zhongguo Zangxue chubanshe, 1993.

———. *Shisanshi Dalai yuanji zhiji he shisishi Dalai zhuanshi zuochuang dang'an xuanbian* [SDDX] [Selected Files Relating to the Memorial Ceremony on the Demise of the 13th Dalai Lama and the Reincarnation and Installation of the 14th Dalai Lama]. Beijing: Zhongguo zangxue chubanshe, 1990.

Zhou, Aiming. *Tibetan Education.* Beijing: China Intercontinental Press, 2004.

Zhou Chuanbin. "Liu Manqing—Minguo shiqi de Xizang Huizu nüjie" [Liu Manqing: A Republican-Era Tibetan Muslim Woman]. *Xibei dier minzu xueyuan xuebao* 3 (2000): 60–64.

———. "Shijie wujishang de Yisilan wenhua" [Islamic Culture on the Roof of the World]. *Xibei Minzu Yanjiu* 4 (2002): 146–59.

Zhu Xiu. "Lasa Jianwen Lu" [Heard and Seen in Lhasa]. *Kaifa Xibei* 2.1 (1934): 56.

Zubok, Vladislav M. "The Khrushchev-Mao Conversations, 31 July–3 August 1958 and 2 October 1959." *Cold War International History Project Bulletin,* no. 12–13 (2001): 266.

Zwilling, Leonard, ed. *"More Than the Promised Land": Letters and Relations from Tibet by the Jesuit Missionary António de Andrade (1580–1634).* Trans. Michael J. Sweet. Boston: Institute of Jesuit Sources, Boston College, 2017.

8, 93; Indian government and, 143–44; Indian government regard for, 134; Khache, revered by, 8, 131, 146–47; Khache in India and, 145; on Khaches' linguistic ability, 24; Kong Qingzong and, 58; Ma Bufang and, 63; Ma Bufang negotiations, 63; as mediator, 65; on Nehru, 125; Nepal and, 75, 80; PRC protest over India giving sanctuary to, 128; reincarnation search, 49; return to Lhasa (August 1951), 66, 186n1; Thupten Ninje as representative of, 142; on Tibetan Buddhist/Tibetan Muslim relations, 33; Tibetan independence goal, 91, 125

Darjeeling, India: benefits to Khache youth, 139; Khaches remaining in, 134, 136; Tibetan refugees and, 127–28; travel to, 63

Dartsedo (*Kangding*), 39

Dawa Norbu, 69, 72

Deo, Arvind, 121

Desai, Morarji, 103, 105fig.

Desideri, Ippolito, 17

Dokdé Mosque (*dog sde lha khang*), Lhasa, 17

Dolkar, Namgyal, 150

Drigung, 18

Dutt, Subimal, 103

education: Jiang Zhiyu's reforms, 52–53; in Kalimpong, India, 135; under occupation, 72; Shen Zonglian's reforms, 61; of Tibetan youth, 71, 126; travel to India for, 63

Egypt, 140

Ekvall, Robert B., 19

Faizullah, 22–23, 172n48

Five Principles of Peaceful Coexistence (*Panchsheel*), 80–82, 86, 125, 154

Foreign Affairs Bureau, 58–59, 98–100

Foreigner's Act and Rules, 138

Freedom Books, 145, 146

French, Rebecca Redwood, 31

Gaborieau, Marc, 16, 28, 31, 165n20, 170n25

Ganden Podrang, 7

Gangtok, 126

Gansu province, 29, 68, 140, 181n68

Gharib Khache, 27–28, 32, 174n77

Goldstein, Melvyn, 36, 65, 69, 89

Grand Mosque (*lha khang chen*), Lhasa, 16, 17, 22, 29, 52–53, 57, 120

Great Prayer Festival (*smon lam chen mo*), 7, 40, 41

Green Books (*lag deb ljang khu*), 145, 146

Gupta, Akhil, 8

Gushri Khan, 21

Gyalpo, Sherpa, 41–44, 57, 90

Gyalpo Affair of 1929, 41–44, 57, 90

Gyantse, 7, 18, 39, 111, 170n27

Habibullah, Haji, 114

hajj, 63, 71, 103, 140

Han Chinese, 29, 48, 56, 67–68

Harrer, Heinrich, 12, 15, 78, 86, 192n102

Harris, Tina, 127

Himalayan Asia: post-liberation period interactions, 73–76; Seventeen Point Agreement of 1951 and, 67–73; Singh's redefining of, 76–86; transregionalism of, 4–5, 8, 24, 36–37, 67–68

Ho, Enseng, 4–5

Hobsbawm, Eric J., 20

Hsiao-ting Ling, 49, 54–55

Huang Musong, 29, 37, 49, 49–57, 58, 183n96

Huc, Évariste R., 4, 30

Hui: Chinese identity and, 56; exile, indented length of, 209n128; Gansu Khache, 140; Grand Mosque (*lha khang chen*), Lhasa, 29; Grand Mosque presence of, 152fig.; Indian Hui population, 29; influx of, 29; Khache as, 73, 195n31; Muslim Chinese population, 28–29, 175n93; Muslims in Tibet as, 5, 6; PRC loyalty of, 67; in Saudi Arabia, 140; schools, 188n39; Sichuan, 28–29; Siling Khache, 27, 28–29, 39, 63, 206n74; term use, 6; Tibetanized Hui, 27; Tibetan use of, 195n31; Xue's perceptions of, 68–71; Yunnan, 28–29; Zang-Hui term, 21, 67–68, 151, 195n31. *See also* Qinghai Khaches; Siling Khache; Xue Wenbo

*Huizu* (pan-Muslim nationalism), 68

identity issues: overview, 1–4; arrested histories concept, 11–12; Chinese identity, 56; Dalai Lamas support, 7; defining Tibetan Muslims, 5–6; earliest Khache community, 7; external confusion over, 6, 20–21, 26, 39, 44–45, 102–3; Himalayan Asia and, 8; inter-Asian dimensions, 4, 8, 11–12, 102–3, 151; Kashmiri identity, 132–33; as Kashmiri Indians, 8–11; Kashmiri settlers, 6; Khache (term) use, 6; Khache integration, 8; Khache multilingualism, 7; pejorative term use, 6; refugee status as, 125–26; Tibetan as Buddhist assumption, 7; as Tibetan Chinese, 8–11; Tibetan identity loss, 142–43;